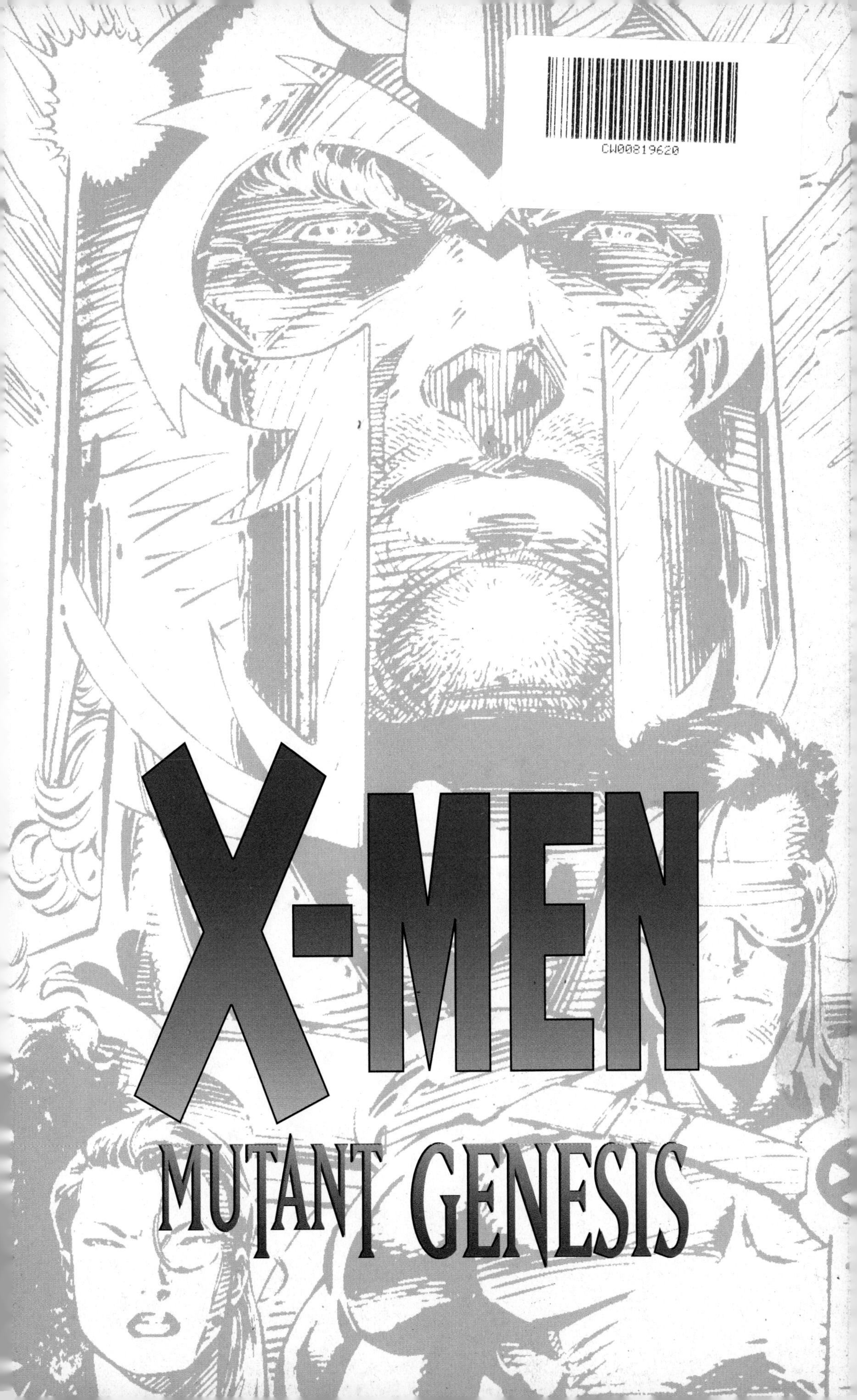
X-MEN
MUTANT GENESIS

[redacted]

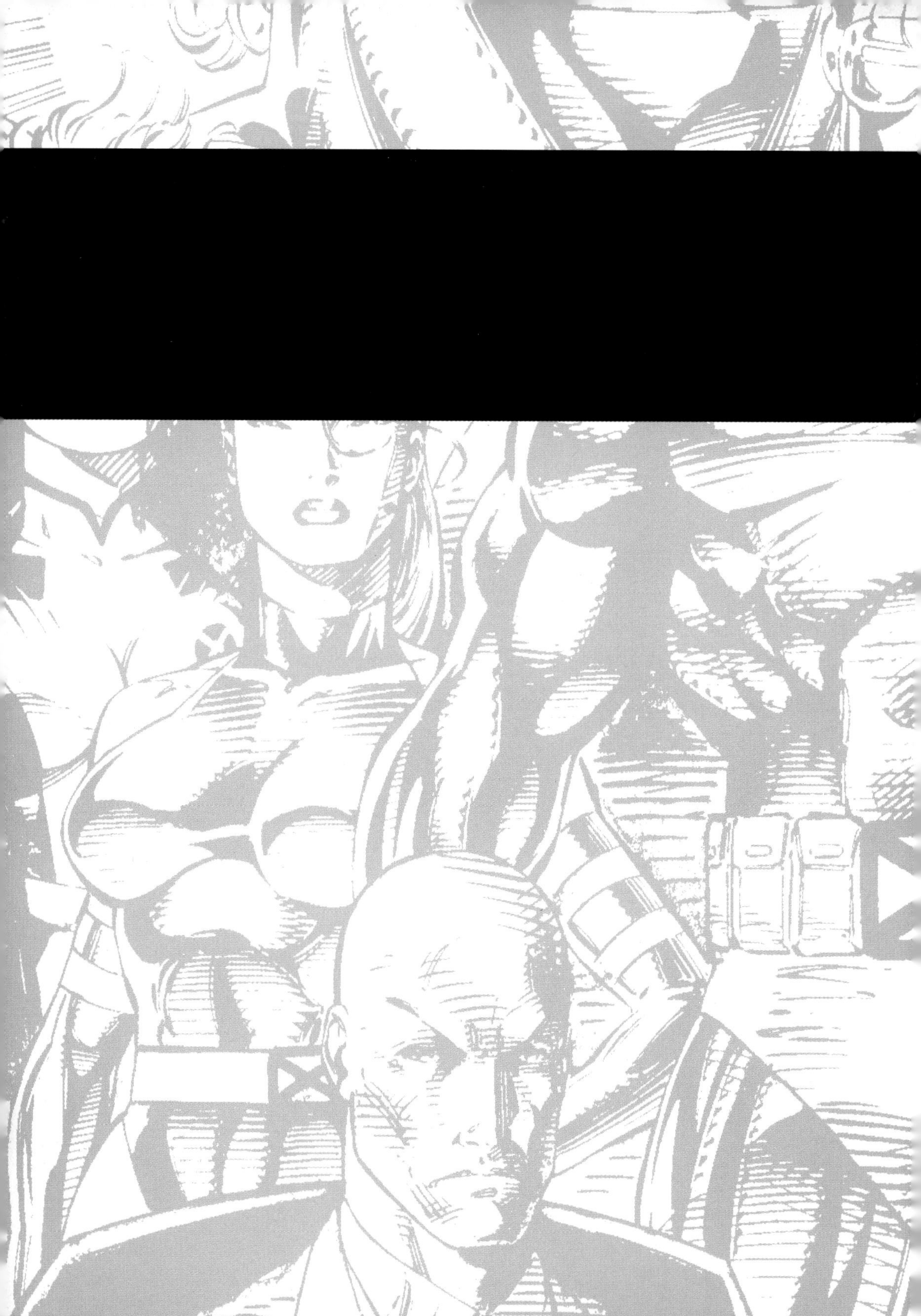

X-MEN LEGENDS VOL. 1: MUTANT GENESIS. Contains material originally published in magazine form as X-MEN (Vol. 2) #1-7. Third printing 2003. ISBN# 0-7851-0895-5. Published by MARVEL COMICS, a division of MARVEL ENTERTAINMENT GROUP, INC. OFFICE OF PUBLICATION: 10 East 40th Street, New York, NY 10016. Copyright © 1991, 1992 and 1995 Marvel Characters, Inc. All rights reserved. $17.95 per copy in the U.S. and $28.75 in Canada (GST #R127032852); Canadian Agreement #40668537. All characters featured in this issue and the distinctive names and likenesses thereof, and all related indicia are trademarks of Marvel Characters, Inc. No similarity between any of the names, characters, persons, and/or institutions in this magazine with those of any living or dead person or institution is intended, and any such similarity which may exist is purely coincidental. **Printed in Canada.** STAN LEE, Chairman Emeritus. For information regarding advertising in Marvel Comics or on Marvel.com, please contact Russell Brown, Executive Vice President, Consumer Products, Promotions and Media Sales at 212-576-8561 or rbrown@marvel.com

10 9 8 7 6 5 4 3

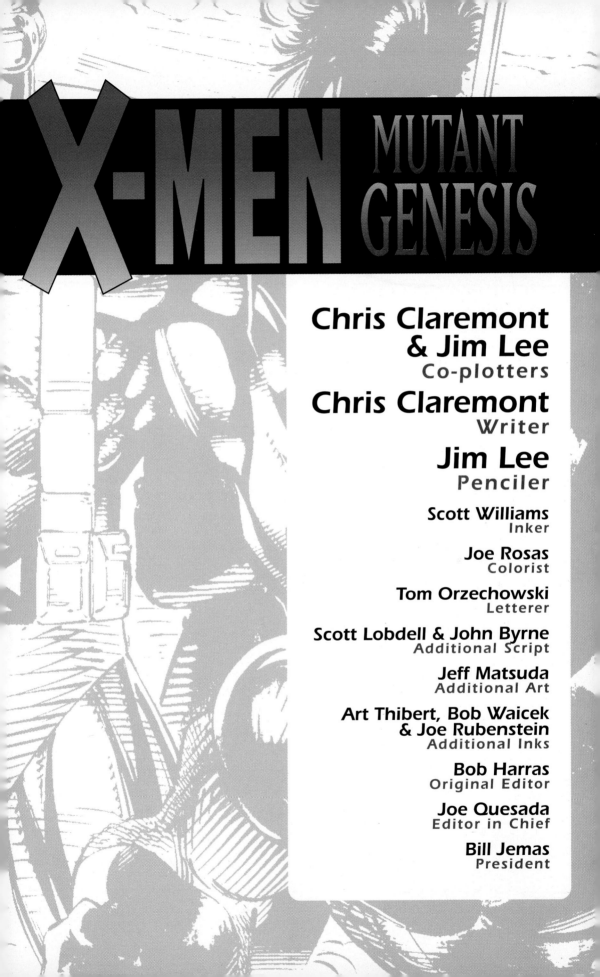

X-MEN MUTANT GENESIS

Chris Claremont & Jim Lee
Co-plotters

Chris Claremont
Writer

Jim Lee
Penciler

Scott Williams
Inker

Joe Rosas
Colorist

Tom Orzechowski
Letterer

Scott Lobdell & John Byrne
Additional Script

Jeff Matsuda
Additional Art

Art Thibert, Bob Waicek & Joe Rubenstein
Additional Inks

Bob Harras
Original Editor

Joe Quesada
Editor in Chief

Bill Jemas
President

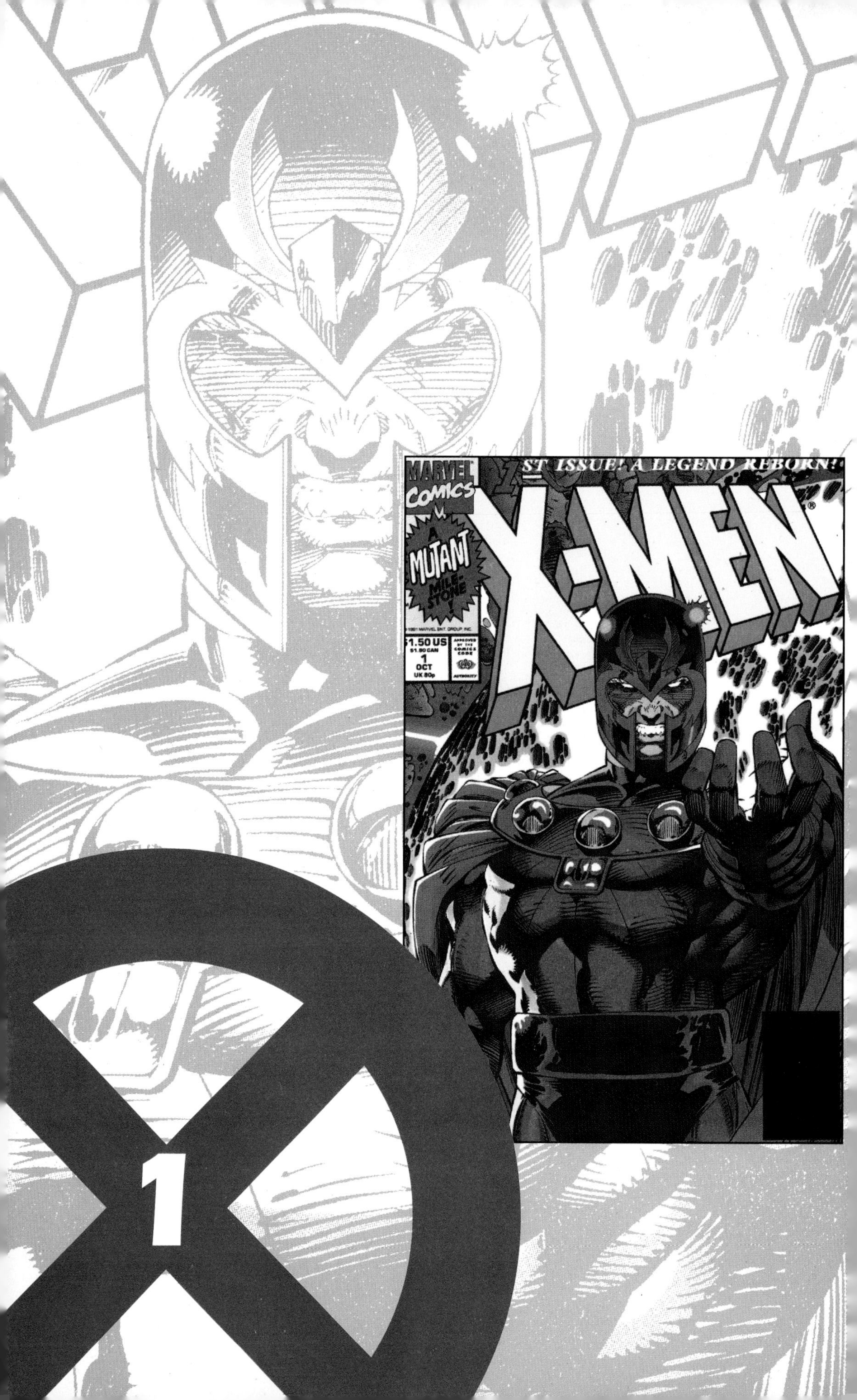
ST ISSUE! A LEGEND REBORN!
MARVEL COMICS
X-MEN
A MUTANT MILE-STONE!
$1.50 US
$1.90 CAN
1
OCT
UK 80p
APPROVED BY THE COMICS CODE AUTHORITY
1

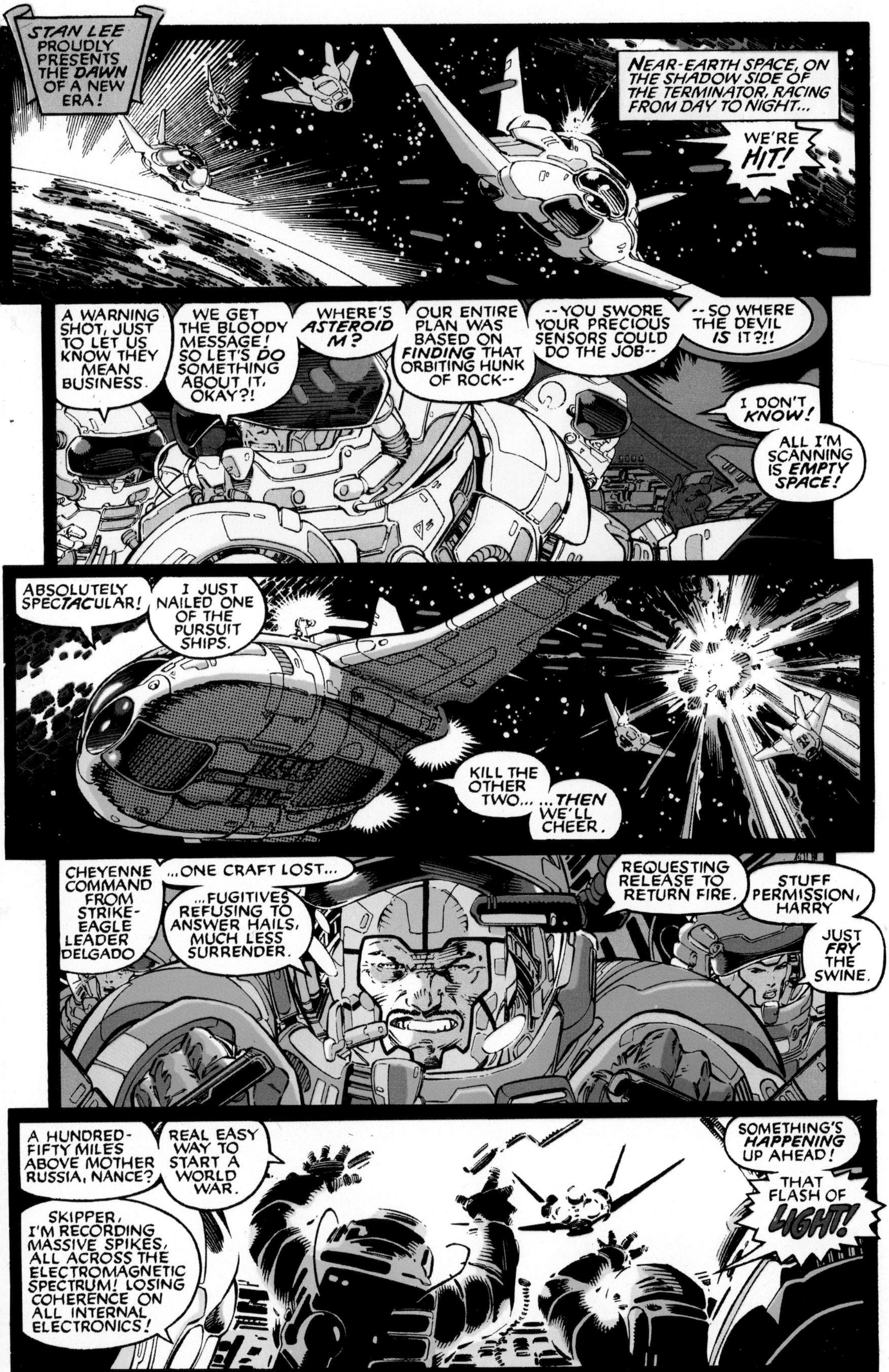
STAN LEE PROUDLY PRESENTS THE DAWN OF A NEW ERA!
NEAR-EARTH SPACE, ON THE SHADOW SIDE OF THE TERMINATOR, RACING FROM DAY TO NIGHT...
WE'RE HIT!
A WARNING SHOT, JUST TO LET US KNOW THEY MEAN BUSINESS.
WE GET THE BLOODY MESSAGE! SO LET'S DO SOMETHING ABOUT IT, OKAY?!
WHERE'S ASTEROID M?
OUR ENTIRE PLAN WAS BASED ON FINDING THAT ORBITING HUNK OF ROCK--
--YOU SWORE YOUR PRECIOUS SENSORS COULD DO THE JOB--
--SO WHERE THE DEVIL IS IT?!!
I DON'T KNOW!
ALL I'M SCANNING IS EMPTY SPACE!
ABSOLUTELY SPECTACULAR!
I JUST NAILED ONE OF THE PURSUIT SHIPS.
KILL THE OTHER TWO... ...THEN WE'LL CHEER.
CHEYENNE COMMAND FROM STRIKE-EAGLE LEADER DELGADO
...ONE CRAFT LOST...
...FUGITIVES REFUSING TO ANSWER HAILS, MUCH LESS SURRENDER.
REQUESTING RELEASE TO RETURN FIRE.
STUFF PERMISSION, HARRY
JUST FRY THE SWINE.
A HUNDRED-FIFTY MILES ABOVE MOTHER RUSSIA, NANCE?
REAL EASY WAY TO START A WORLD WAR.
SKIPPER, I'M RECORDING MASSIVE SPIKES, ALL ACROSS THE ELECTROMAGNETIC SPECTRUM! LOSING COHERENCE ON ALL INTERNAL ELECTRONICS!
SOMETHING'S HAPPENING UP AHEAD!
THAT FLASH OF LIGHT!

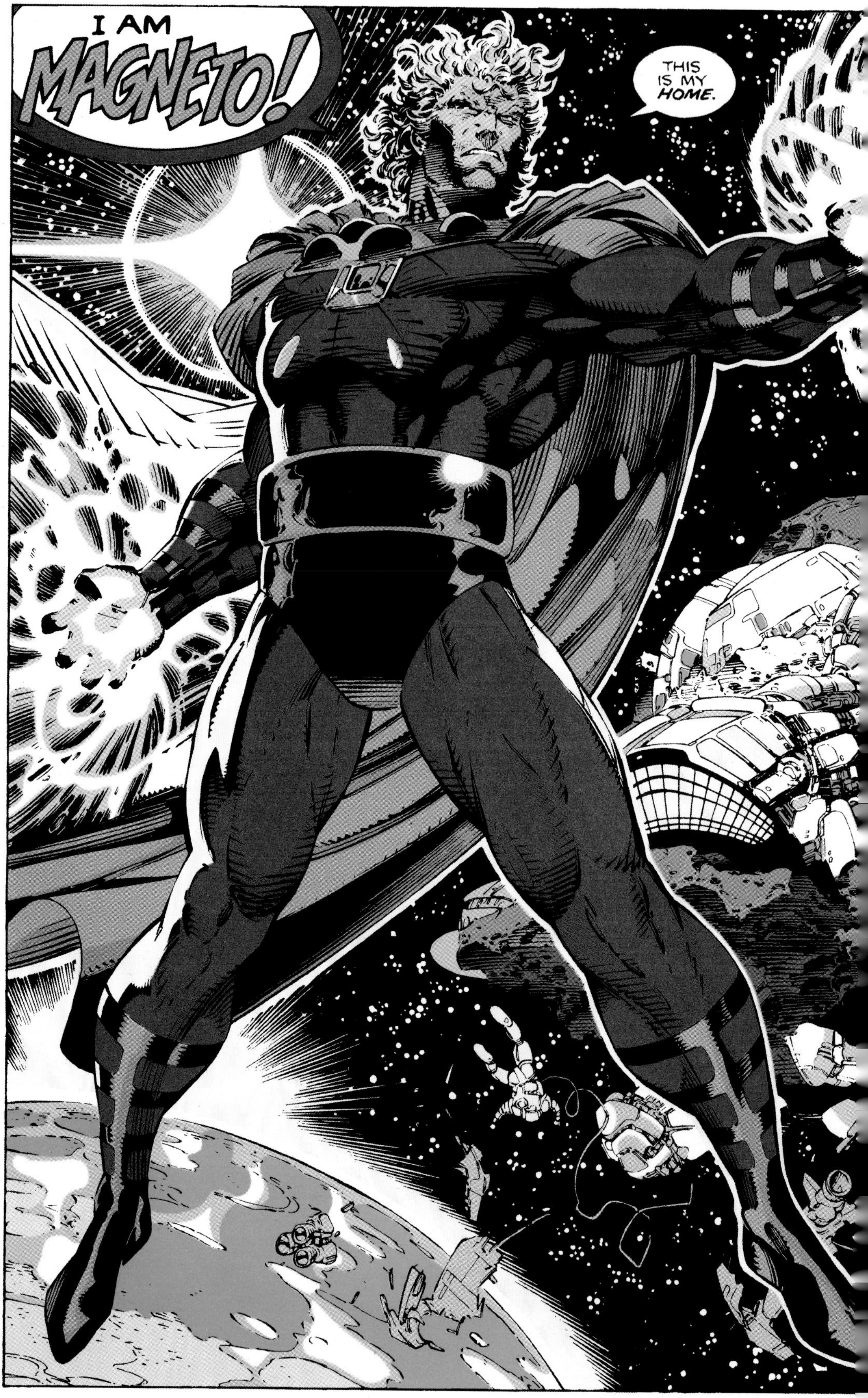
I AM MAGNETO!
THIS IS MY HOME.

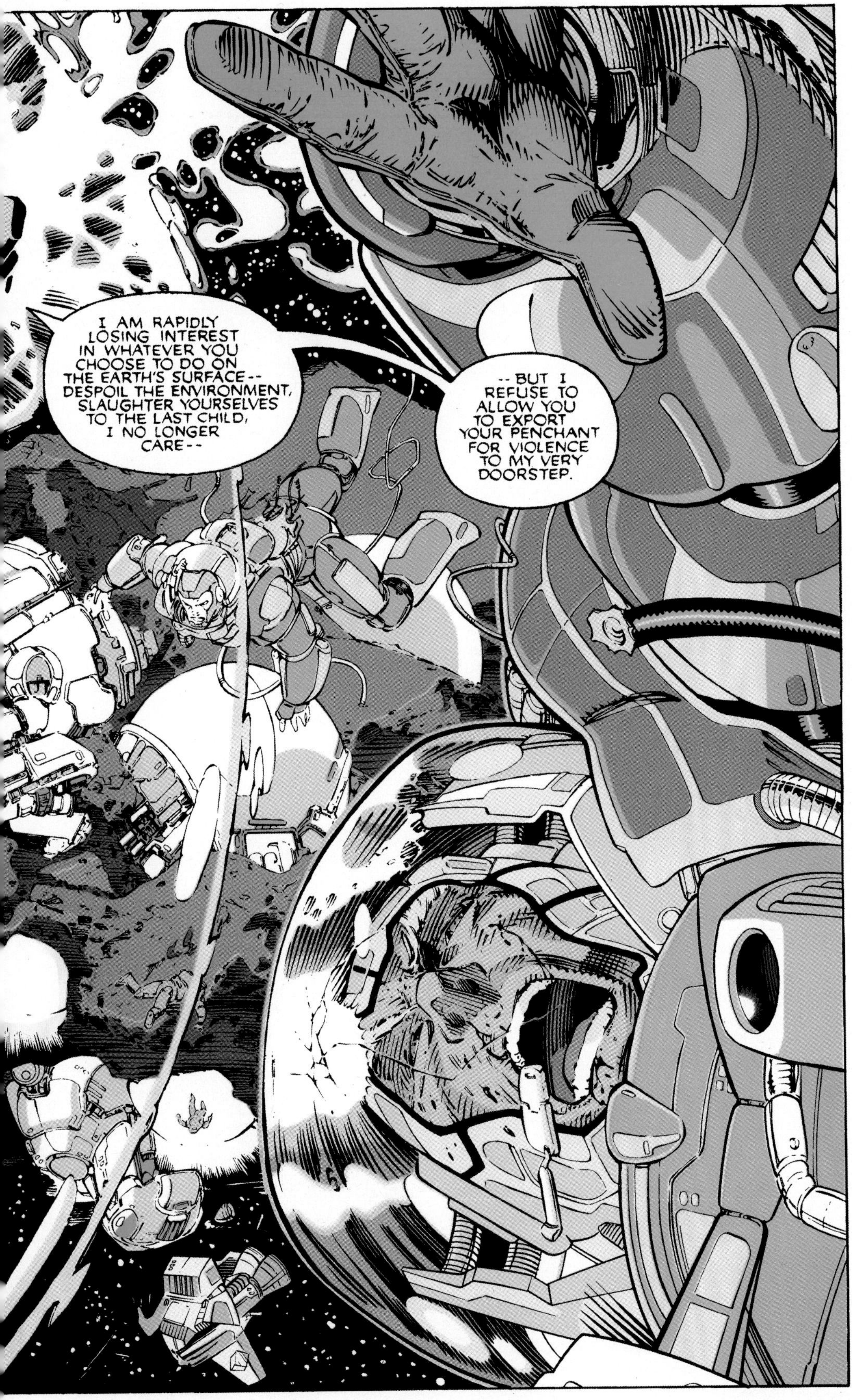
I AM RAPIDLY LOSING INTEREST IN WHATEVER YOU CHOOSE TO DO ON THE EARTH'S SURFACE--DESPOIL THE ENVIRONMENT, SLAUGHTER YOURSELVES TO THE LAST CHILD, I NO LONGER CARE--
--BUT I REFUSE TO ALLOW YOU TO EXPORT YOUR PENCHANT FOR VIOLENCE TO MY VERY DOORSTEP.

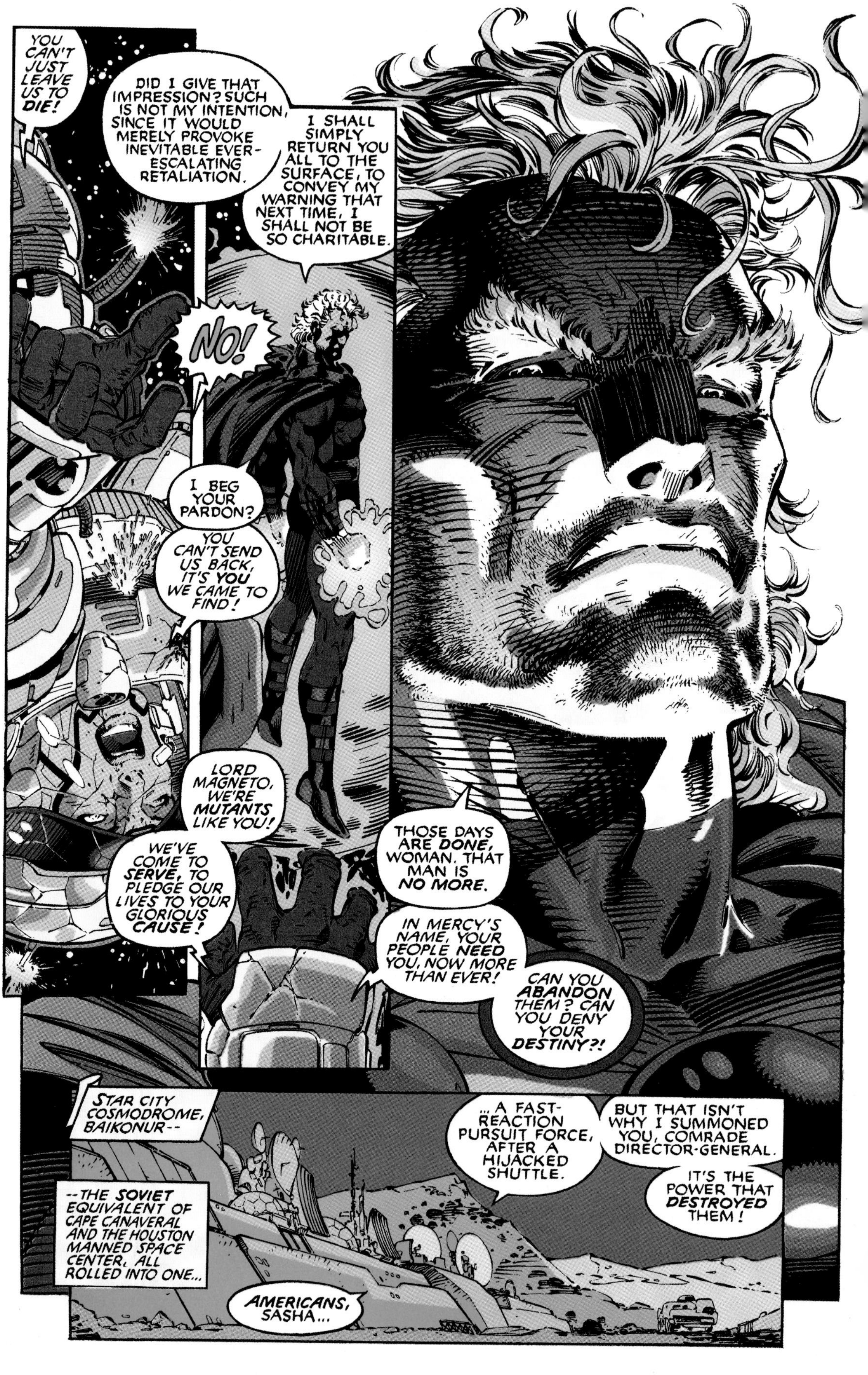
YOU CAN'T JUST LEAVE US TO DIE!
DID I GIVE THAT IMPRESSION? SUCH IS NOT MY INTENTION, SINCE IT WOULD MERELY PROVOKE INEVITABLE EVER-ESCALATING RETALIATION.
I SHALL SIMPLY RETURN YOU ALL TO THE SURFACE, TO CONVEY MY WARNING THAT NEXT TIME, I SHALL NOT BE SO CHARITABLE.
NO!
I BEG YOUR PARDON?
YOU CAN'T SEND US BACK, IT'S YOU WE CAME TO FIND!
LORD MAGNETO, WE'RE MUTANTS LIKE YOU!
WE'VE COME TO SERVE, TO PLEDGE OUR LIVES TO YOUR GLORIOUS CAUSE!
THOSE DAYS ARE DONE, WOMAN. THAT MAN IS NO MORE.
IN MERCY'S NAME, YOUR PEOPLE NEED YOU, NOW MORE THAN EVER!
CAN YOU ABANDON THEM? CAN YOU DENY YOUR DESTINY?!
STAR CITY COSMODROME, BAIKONUR--
--THE SOVIET EQUIVALENT OF CAPE CANAVERAL AND THE HOUSTON MANNED SPACE CENTER, ALL ROLLED INTO ONE...
AMERICANS, SASHA...
...A FAST-REACTION PURSUIT FORCE, AFTER A HIJACKED SHUTTLE.
BUT THAT ISN'T WHY I SUMMONED YOU, COMRADE DIRECTOR-GENERAL.
IT'S THE POWER THAT DESTROYED THEM!

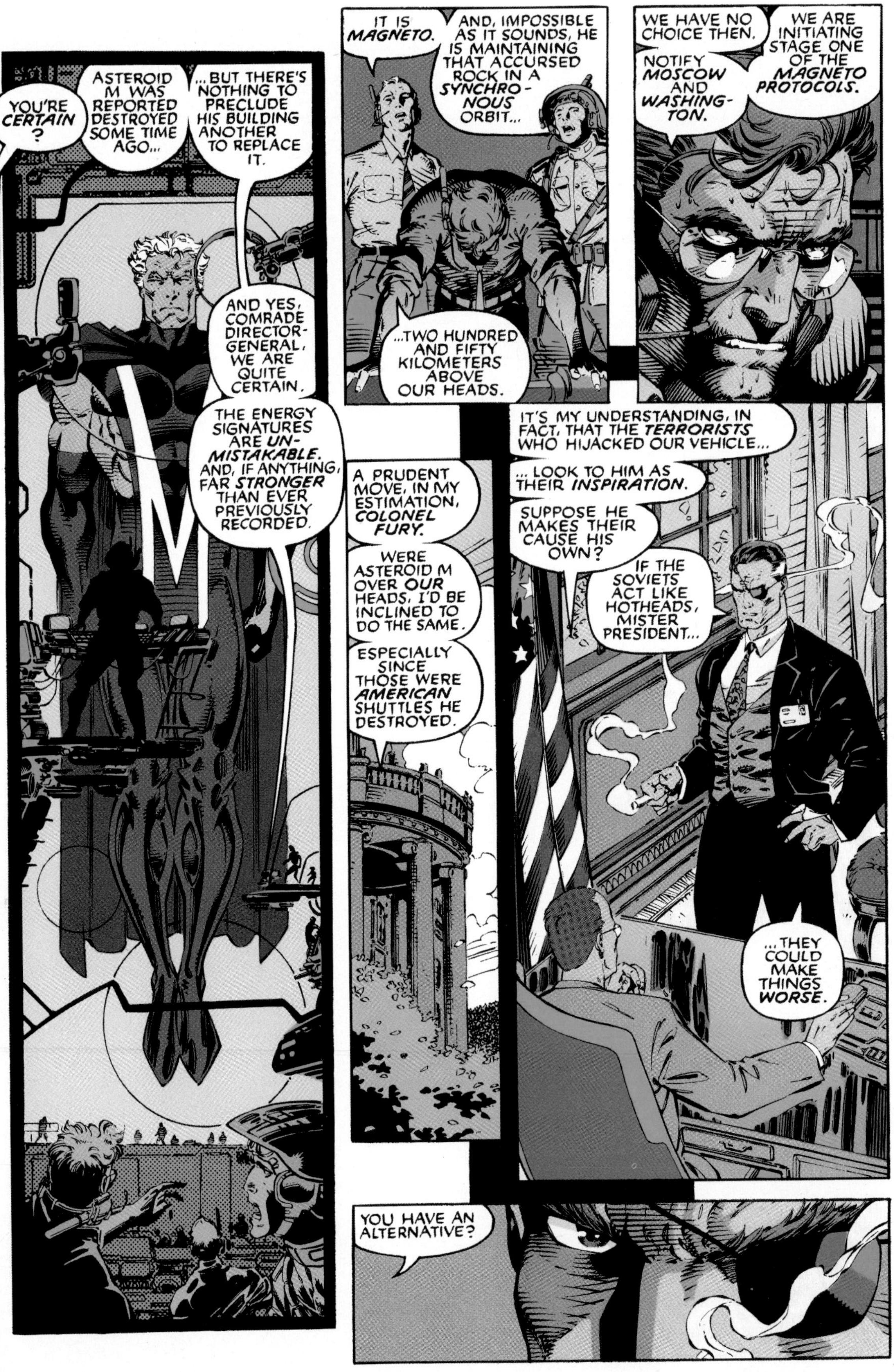
YOU'RE CERTAIN ?
ASTEROID M WAS REPORTED DESTROYED SOME TIME AGO...
...BUT THERE'S NOTHING TO PRECLUDE HIS BUILDING ANOTHER TO REPLACE IT.
AND YES, COMRADE DIRECTOR-GENERAL, WE ARE QUITE CERTAIN.
THE ENERGY SIGNATURES ARE UN-MISTAKABLE. AND, IF ANYTHING, FAR STRONGER THAN EVER PREVIOUSLY RECORDED.
IT IS MAGNETO.
AND, IMPOSSIBLE AS IT SOUNDS, HE IS MAINTAINING THAT ACCURSED ROCK IN A SYNCHRO-NOUS ORBIT...
...TWO HUNDRED AND FIFTY KILOMETERS ABOVE OUR HEADS.
WE HAVE NO CHOICE THEN.
NOTIFY MOSCOW AND WASHING-TON.
WE ARE INITIATING STAGE ONE OF THE MAGNETO PROTOCOLS.
A PRUDENT MOVE, IN MY ESTIMATION, COLONEL FURY.
WERE ASTEROID M OVER OUR HEADS, I'D BE INCLINED TO DO THE SAME.
ESPECIALLY SINCE THOSE WERE AMERICAN SHUTTLES HE DESTROYED.
IT'S MY UNDERSTANDING, IN FACT, THAT THE TERRORISTS WHO HIJACKED OUR VEHICLE...
...LOOK TO HIM AS THEIR INSPIRATION.
SUPPOSE HE MAKES THEIR CAUSE HIS OWN?
IF THE SOVIETS ACT LIKE HOTHEADS, MISTER PRESIDENT...
...THEY COULD MAKE THINGS WORSE.
YOU HAVE AN ALTERNATIVE?

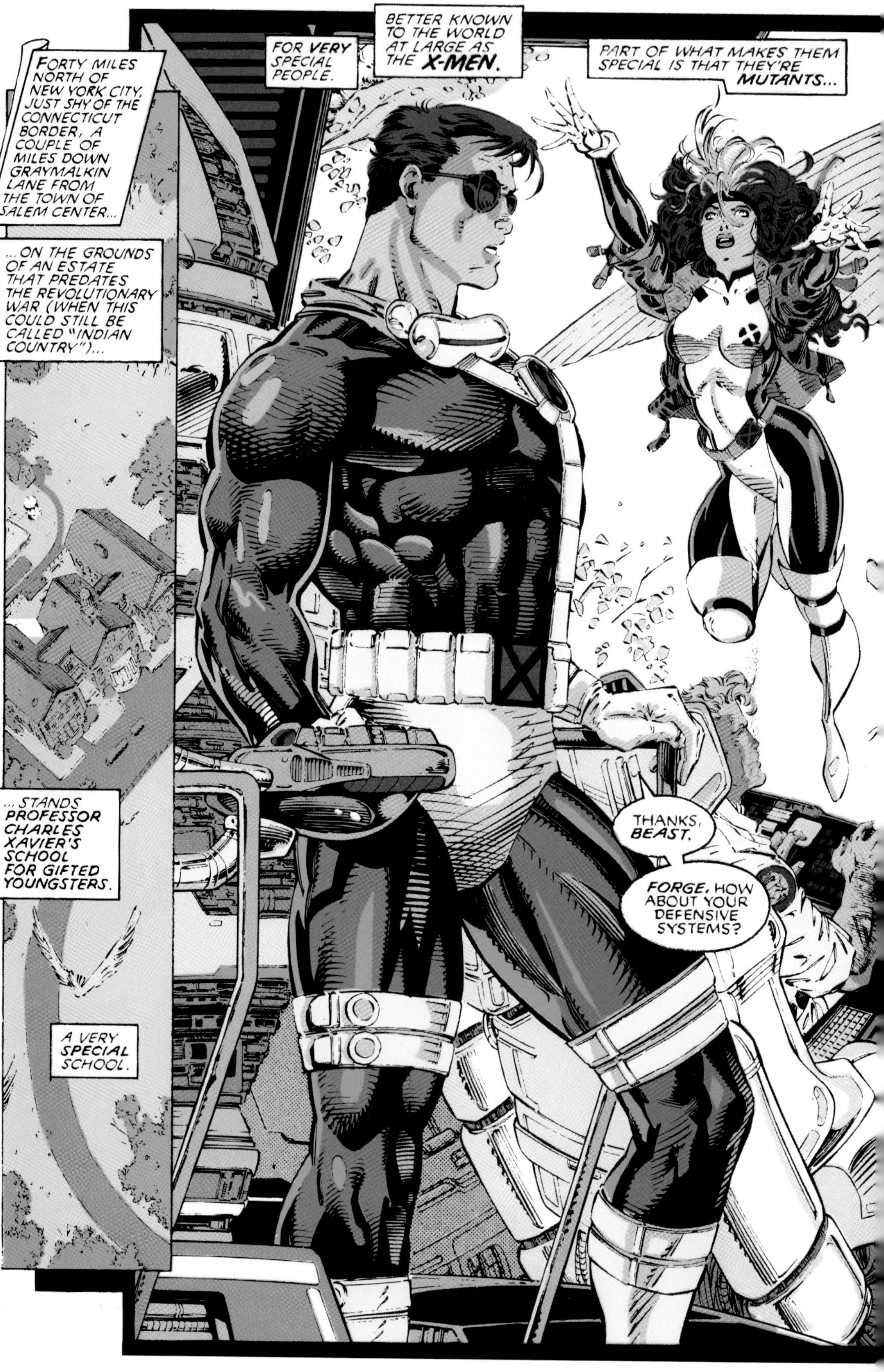
FORTY MILES NORTH OF NEW YORK CITY, JUST SHY OF THE CONNECTICUT BORDER, A COUPLE OF MILES DOWN GRAYMALKIN LANE FROM THE TOWN OF SALEM CENTER...
...ON THE GROUNDS OF AN ESTATE THAT PREDATES THE REVOLUTIONARY WAR (WHEN THIS COULD STILL BE CALLED "INDIAN COUNTRY")...
...STANDS PROFESSOR CHARLES XAVIER'S SCHOOL FOR GIFTED YOUNGSTERS.
A VERY SPECIAL SCHOOL.
FOR VERY SPECIAL PEOPLE.
BETTER KNOWN TO THE WORLD AT LARGE AS THE X-MEN.
PART OF WHAT MAKES THEM SPECIAL IS THAT THEY'RE MUTANTS...
THANKS, BEAST.
FORGE, HOW ABOUT YOUR DEFENSIVE SYSTEMS?

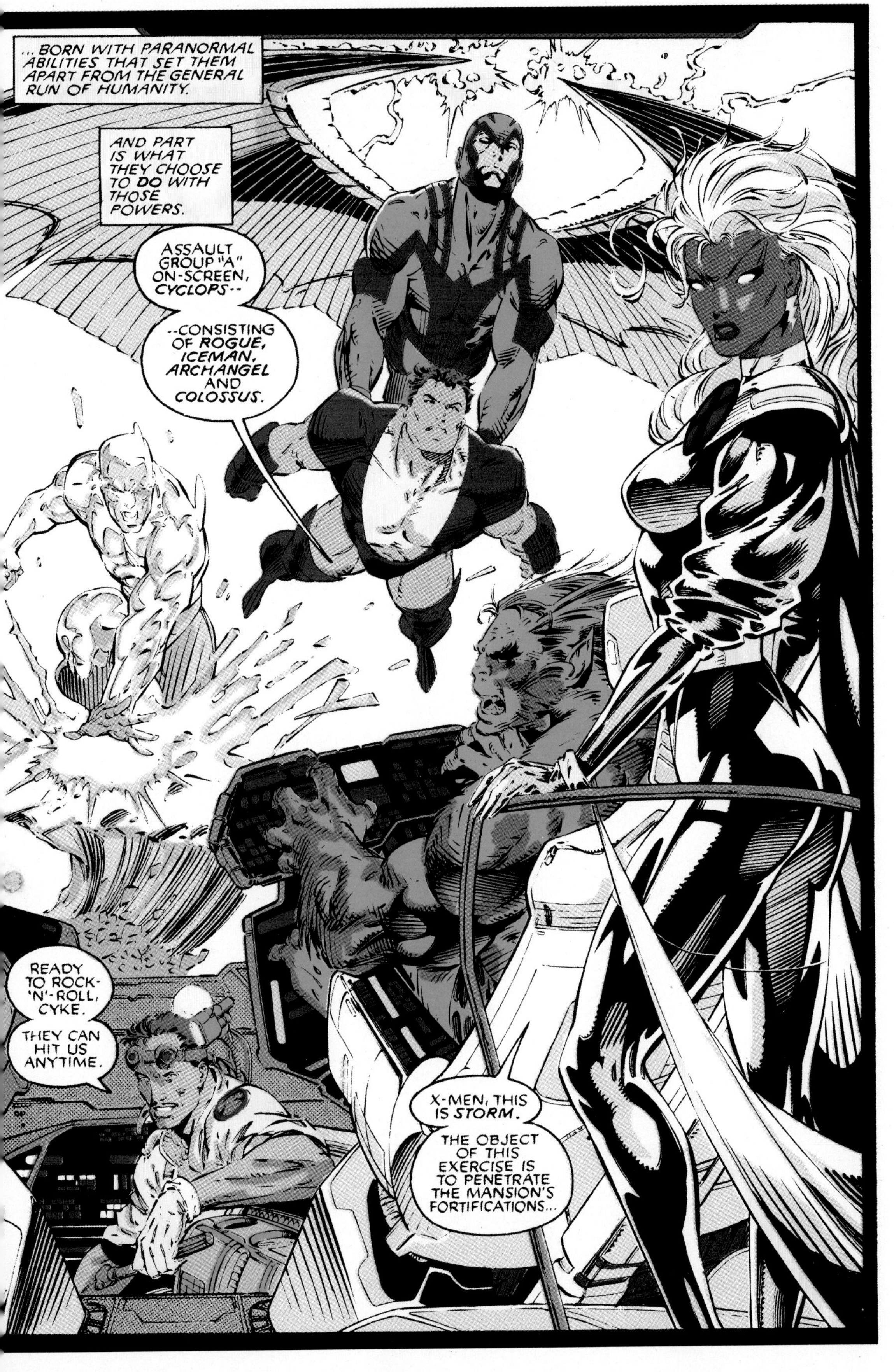
...BORN WITH PARANORMAL ABILITIES THAT SET THEM APART FROM THE GENERAL RUN OF HUMANITY.
AND PART IS WHAT THEY CHOOSE TO DO WITH THOSE POWERS.
ASSAULT GROUP "A" ON-SCREEN, CYCLOPS--
--CONSISTING OF ROGUE, ICEMAN, ARCHANGEL AND COLOSSUS.
READY TO ROCK-'N'-ROLL, CYKE.
THEY CAN HIT US ANYTIME.
X-MEN, THIS IS STORM.
THE OBJECT OF THIS EXERCISE IS TO PENETRATE THE MANSION'S FORTIFICATIONS...

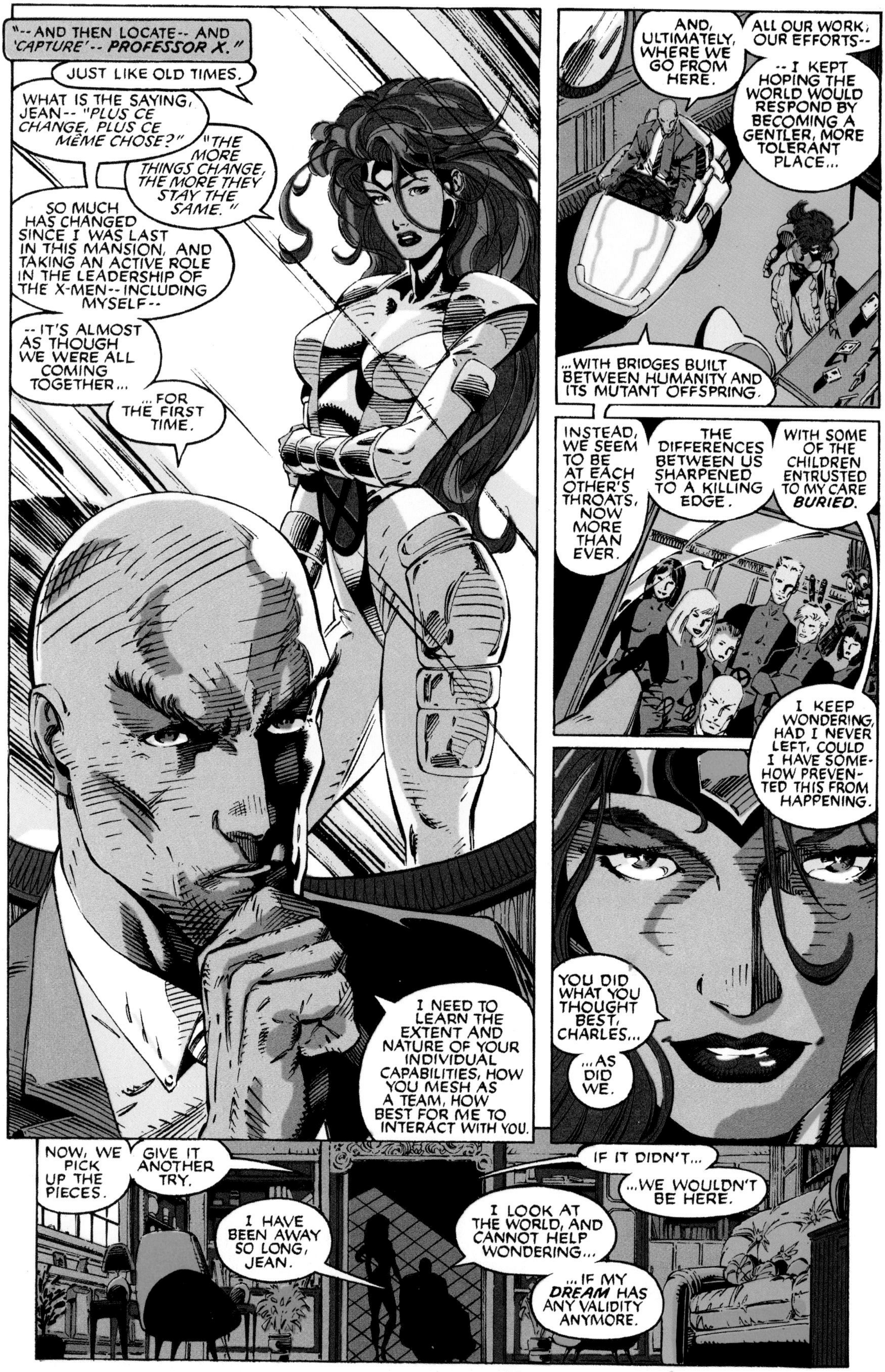
"-- AND THEN LOCATE-- AND 'CAPTURE' -- PROFESSOR X."
JUST LIKE OLD TIMES.
WHAT IS THE SAYING, JEAN-- "PLUS CE CHANGE, PLUS CE MÊME CHOSE?"
"THE MORE THINGS CHANGE, THE MORE THEY STAY THE SAME."
SO MUCH HAS CHANGED SINCE I WAS LAST IN THIS MANSION, AND TAKING AN ACTIVE ROLE IN THE LEADERSHIP OF THE X-MEN--INCLUDING MYSELF--
-- IT'S ALMOST AS THOUGH WE WERE ALL COMING TOGETHER...
...FOR THE FIRST TIME.
I NEED TO LEARN THE EXTENT AND NATURE OF YOUR INDIVIDUAL CAPABILITIES, HOW YOU MESH AS A TEAM, HOW BEST FOR ME TO INTERACT WITH YOU.
AND, ULTIMATELY, WHERE WE GO FROM HERE.
ALL OUR WORK, OUR EFFORTS--
-- I KEPT HOPING THE WORLD WOULD RESPOND BY BECOMING A GENTLER, MORE TOLERANT PLACE...
...WITH BRIDGES BUILT BETWEEN HUMANITY AND ITS MUTANT OFFSPRING.
INSTEAD, WE SEEM TO BE AT EACH OTHER'S THROATS, NOW MORE THAN EVER.
THE DIFFERENCES BETWEEN US SHARPENED TO A KILLING EDGE.
WITH SOME OF THE CHILDREN ENTRUSTED TO MY CARE BURIED.
I KEEP WONDERING, HAD I NEVER LEFT, COULD I HAVE SOMEHOW PREVENTED THIS FROM HAPPENING.
YOU DID WHAT YOU THOUGHT BEST, CHARLES...
...AS DID WE.
NOW, WE PICK UP THE PIECES.
GIVE IT ANOTHER TRY.
I HAVE BEEN AWAY SO LONG, JEAN.
IF IT DIDN'T...
...WE WOULDN'T BE HERE.
I LOOK AT THE WORLD, AND CANNOT HELP WONDERING...
...IF MY DREAM HAS ANY VALIDITY ANYMORE.

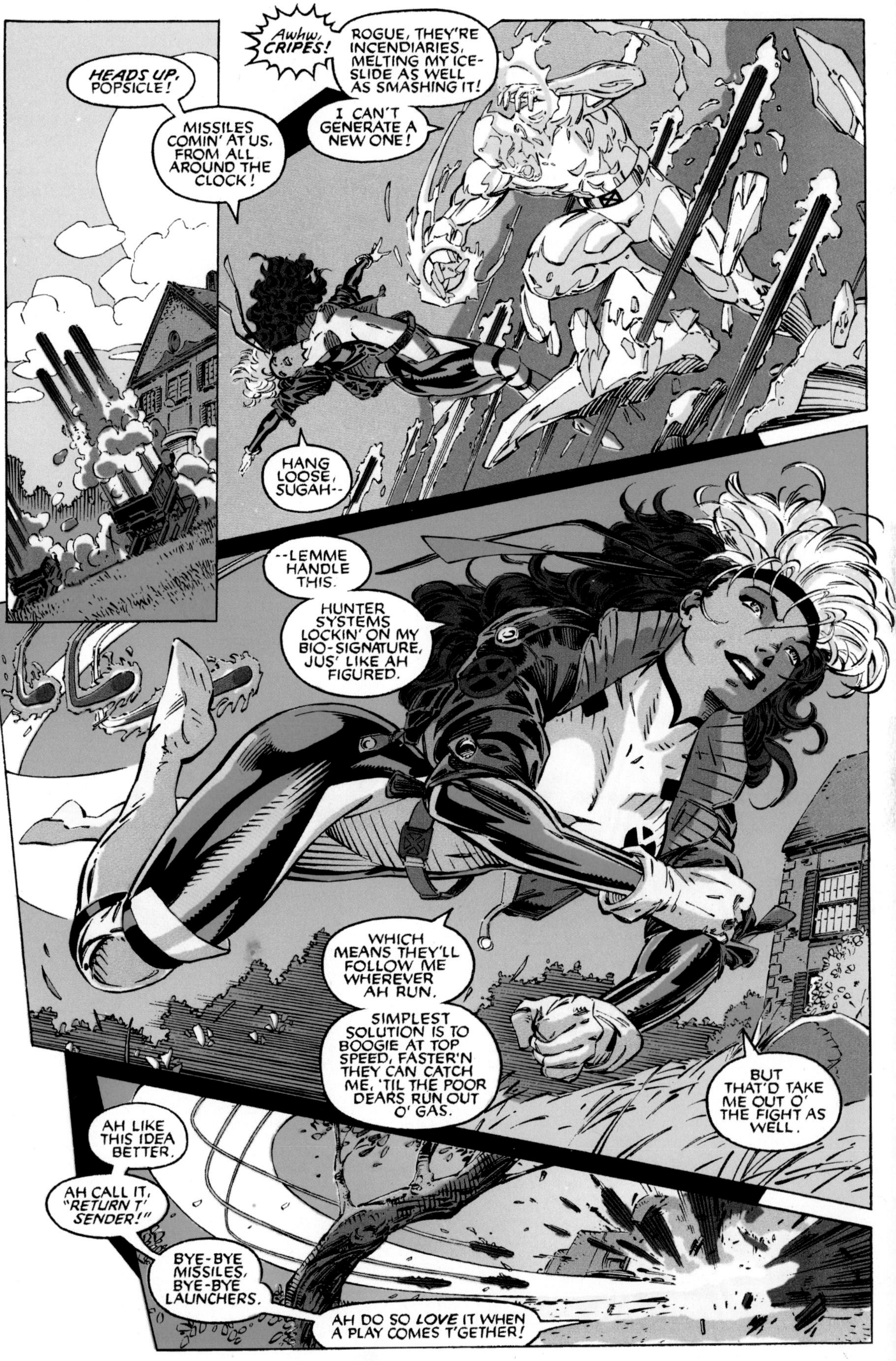
HEADS UP, POPSICLE!
MISSILES COMIN' AT US, FROM ALL AROUND THE CLOCK!
Awhw, CRIPES!
ROGUE, THEY'RE INCENDIARIES, MELTING MY ICE-SLIDE AS WELL AS SMASHING IT!
I CAN'T GENERATE A NEW ONE!
HANG LOOSE, SUGAH--
--LEMME HANDLE THIS.
HUNTER SYSTEMS LOCKIN' ON MY BIO-SIGNATURE, JUS' LIKE AH FIGURED.
WHICH MEANS THEY'LL FOLLOW ME WHEREVER AH RUN.
SIMPLEST SOLUTION IS TO BOOGIE AT TOP SPEED, FASTER'N THEY CAN CATCH ME, 'TIL THE POOR DEARS RUN OUT O' GAS.
BUT THAT'D TAKE ME OUT O' THE FIGHT AS WELL.
AH LIKE THIS IDEA BETTER.
AH CALL IT, "RETURN T' SENDER!"
BYE-BYE MISSILES, BYE-BYE LAUNCHERS.
AH DO SO LOVE IT WHEN A PLAY COMES T'GETHER!

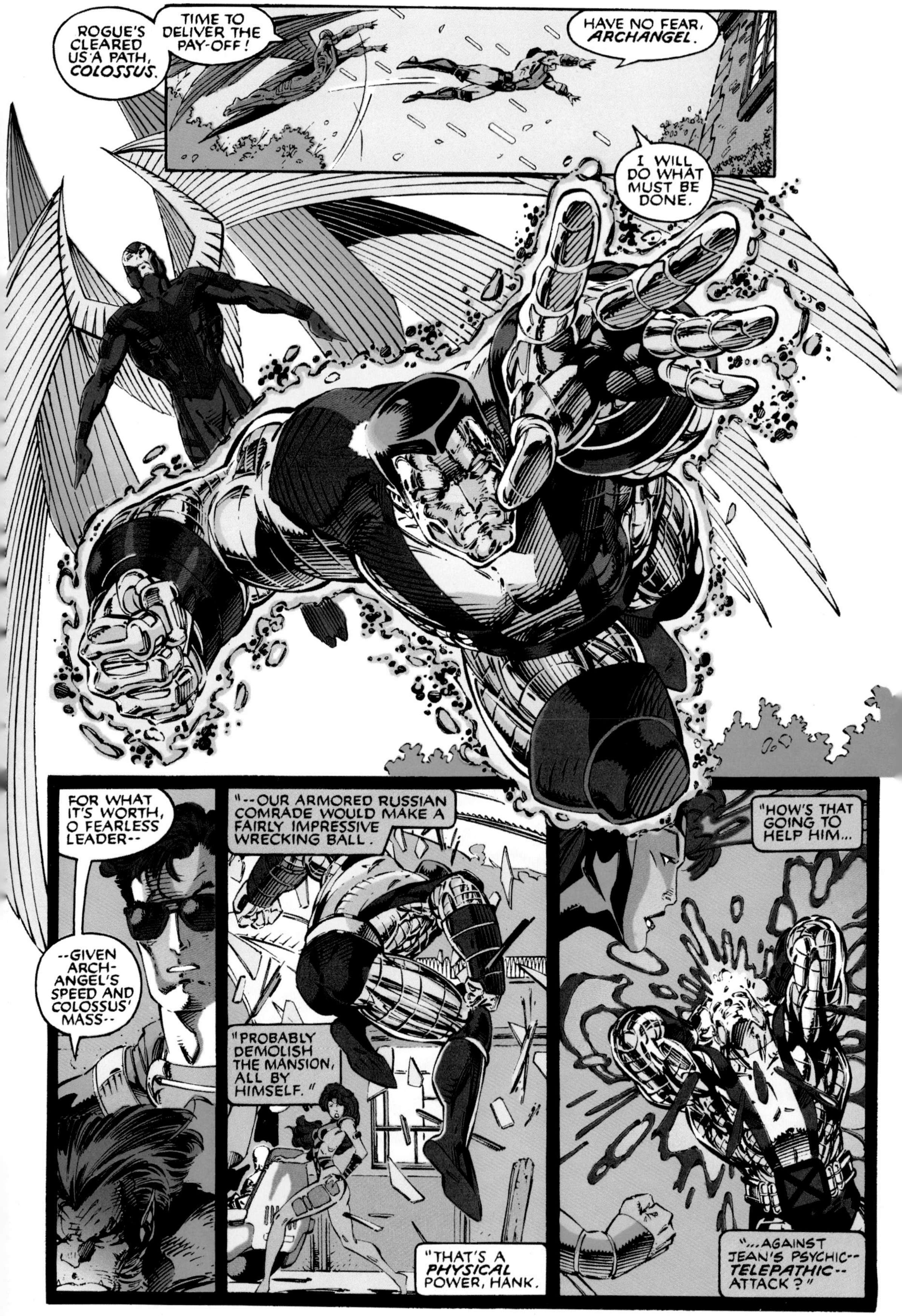
ROGUE'S CLEARED US A PATH, COLOSSUS.
TIME TO DELIVER THE PAY-OFF!
HAVE NO FEAR, ARCHANGEL.
I WILL DO WHAT MUST BE DONE.
FOR WHAT IT'S WORTH, O FEARLESS LEADER--
--GIVEN ARCH-ANGEL'S SPEED AND COLOSSUS' MASS--
"--OUR ARMORED RUSSIAN COMRADE WOULD MAKE A FAIRLY IMPRESSIVE WRECKING BALL.
"PROBABLY DEMOLISH THE MANSION, ALL BY HIMSELF."
"THAT'S A PHYSICAL POWER, HANK.
"HOW'S THAT GOING TO HELP HIM...
"...AGAINST JEAN'S PSYCHIC--TELEPATHIC--ATTACK?"

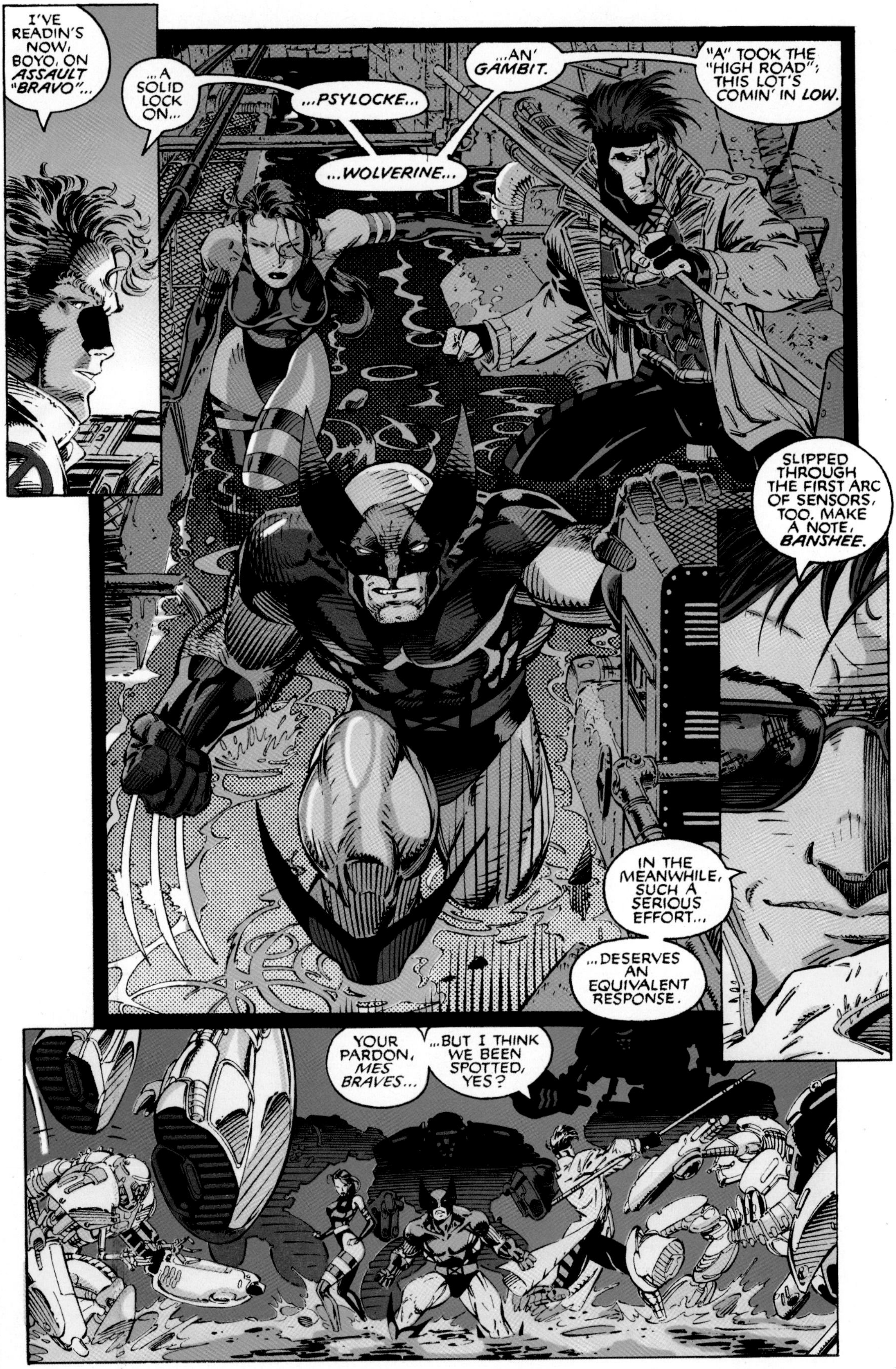

I'VE READIN'S NOW, BOYO, ON *ASSAULT "BRAVO"*...
...A SOLID LOCK ON...
...*PSYLOCKE*...
...*WOLVERINE*...
...AN' *GAMBIT.*
"A" TOOK THE "HIGH ROAD"; THIS LOT'S COMIN' IN *LOW.*
SLIPPED THROUGH THE FIRST ARC OF SENSORS, TOO. MAKE A NOTE, *BANSHEE.*
IN THE MEANWHILE, SUCH A SERIOUS EFFORT...
...DESERVES AN EQUIVALENT RESPONSE.
YOUR PARDON, *MES BRAVES*...
...BUT I THINK WE BEEN SPOTTED, YES?

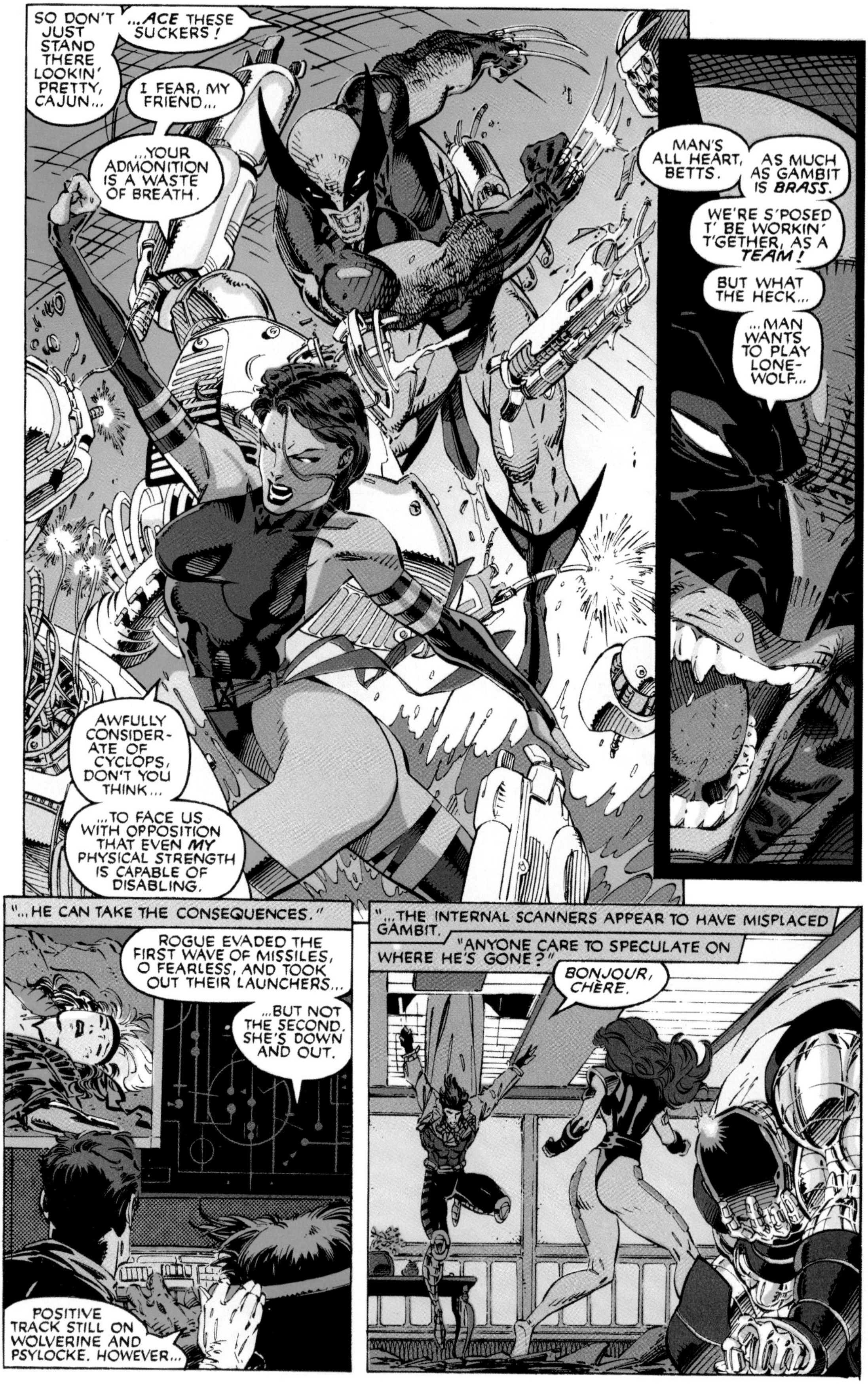
SO DON'T JUST STAND THERE LOOKIN' PRETTY, CAJUN...
...ACE THESE SUCKERS!
I FEAR, MY FRIEND...
...YOUR ADMONITION IS A WASTE OF BREATH.
MAN'S ALL HEART, BETTS.
AS MUCH AS GAMBIT IS BRASS.
WE'RE S'POSED T' BE WORKIN' T'GETHER, AS A TEAM!
BUT WHAT THE HECK...
...MAN WANTS TO PLAY LONE-WOLF...
AWFULLY CONSIDER-ATE OF CYCLOPS, DON'T YOU THINK...
...TO FACE US WITH OPPOSITION THAT EVEN MY PHYSICAL STRENGTH IS CAPABLE OF DISABLING.
"...HE CAN TAKE THE CONSEQUENCES."
ROGUE EVADED THE FIRST WAVE OF MISSILES, O FEARLESS, AND TOOK OUT THEIR LAUNCHERS...
...BUT NOT THE SECOND. SHE'S DOWN AND OUT.
POSITIVE TRACK STILL ON WOLVERINE AND PSYLOCKE. HOWEVER...
"...THE INTERNAL SCANNERS APPEAR TO HAVE MISPLACED GAMBIT.
"ANYONE CARE TO SPECULATE ON WHERE HE'S GONE?"
BONJOUR, CHÈRE.

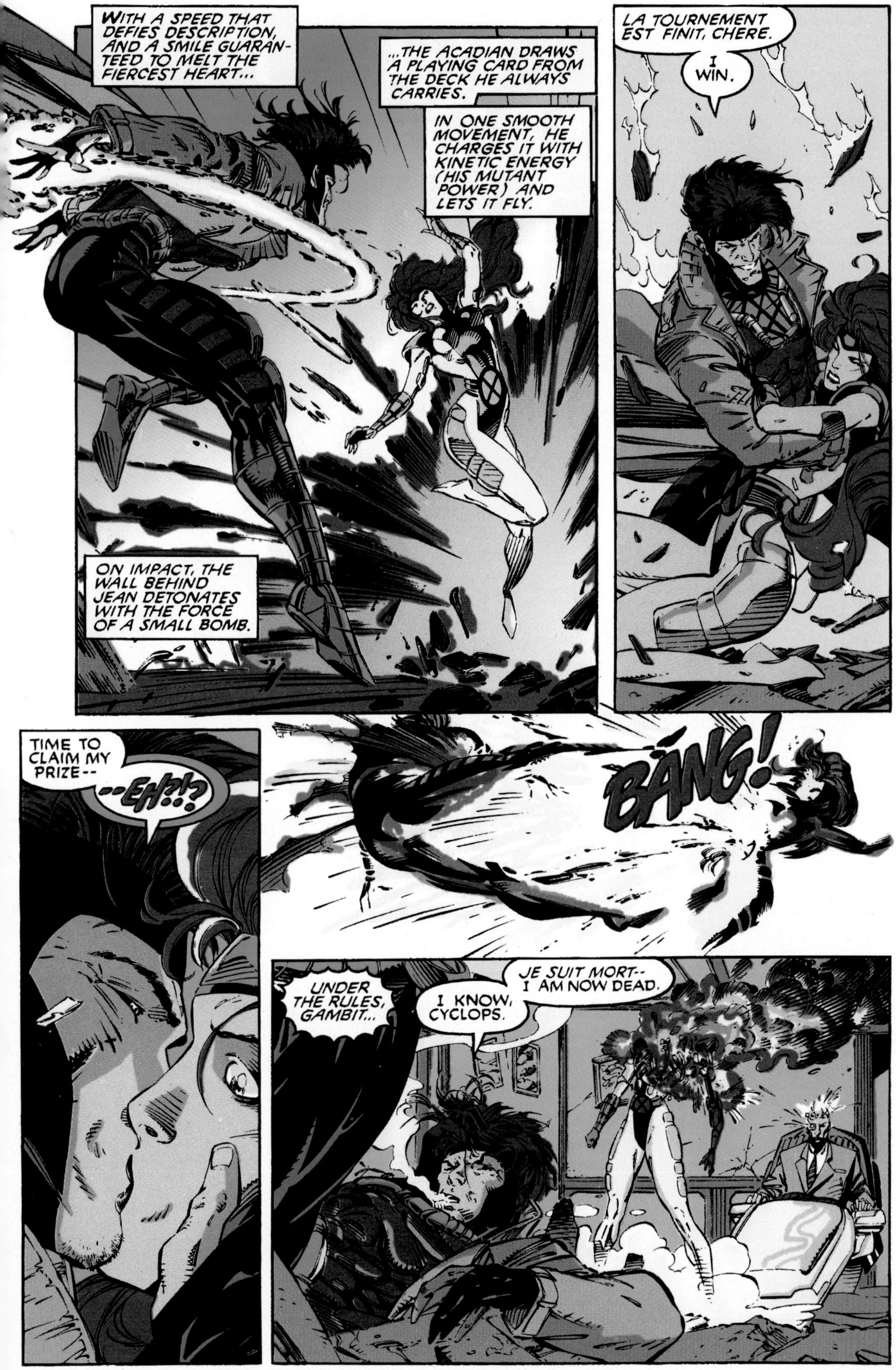
WITH A SPEED THAT DEFIES DESCRIPTION, AND A SMILE GUARANTEED TO MELT THE FIERCEST HEART...
...THE ACADIAN DRAWS A PLAYING CARD FROM THE DECK HE ALWAYS CARRIES.
IN ONE SMOOTH MOVEMENT, HE CHARGES IT WITH KINETIC ENERGY (HIS MUTANT POWER) AND LETS IT FLY.
ON IMPACT, THE WALL BEHIND JEAN DETONATES WITH THE FORCE OF A SMALL BOMB.
LA TOURNEMENT EST FINIT, CHERE.
I WIN.
TIME TO CLAIM MY PRIZE--
--EH?!?
BANG!
UNDER THE RULES, GAMBIT...
JE SUIT MORT-- I AM NOW DEAD.
I KNOW, CYCLOPS.

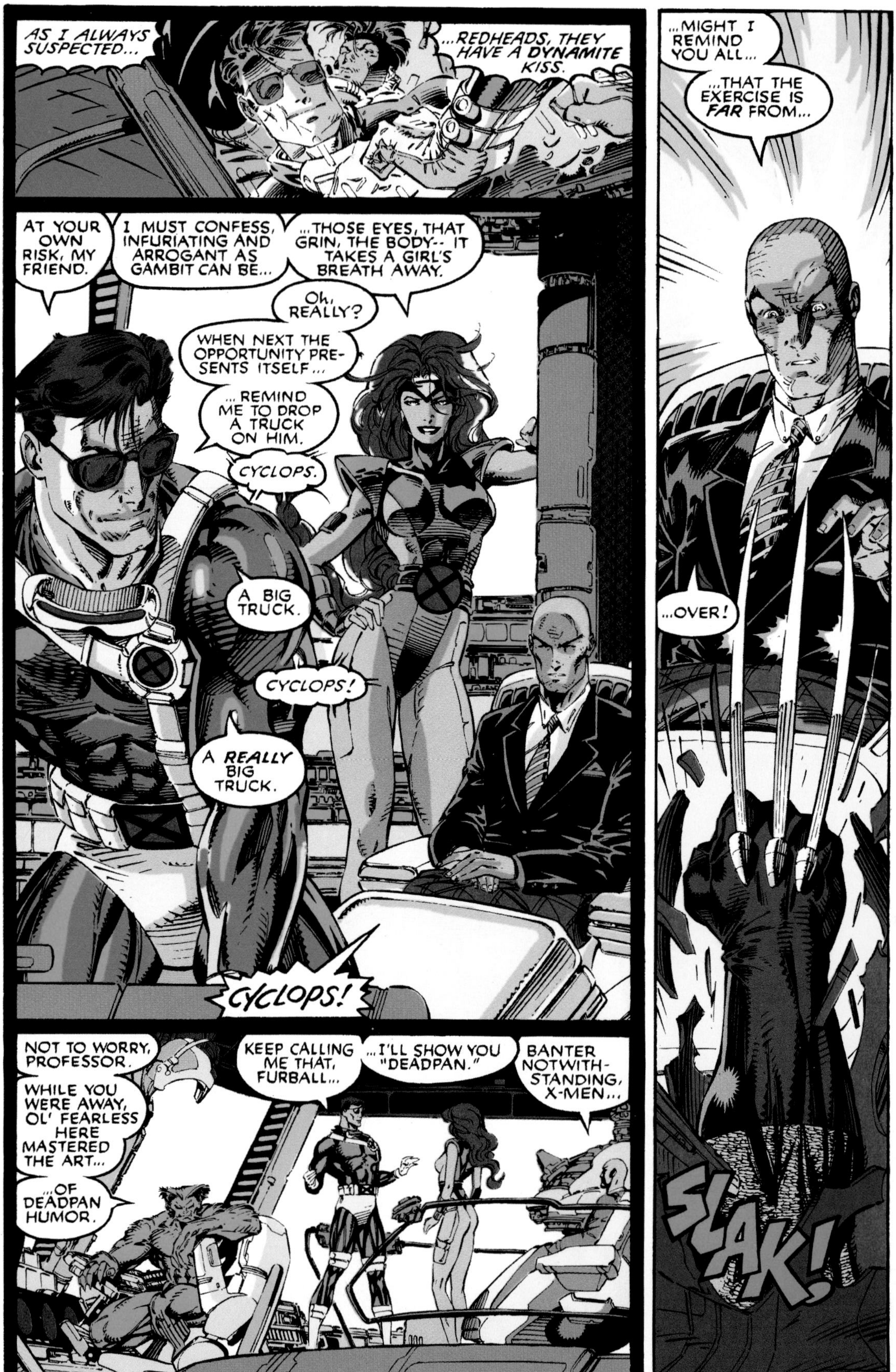
AS I ALWAYS SUSPECTED...
...REDHEADS, THEY HAVE A DYNAMITE KISS.
AT YOUR OWN RISK, MY FRIEND.
I MUST CONFESS, INFURIATING AND ARROGANT AS GAMBIT CAN BE...
...THOSE EYES, THAT GRIN, THE BODY-- IT TAKES A GIRL'S BREATH AWAY.
Oh, REALLY?
WHEN NEXT THE OPPORTUNITY PRESENTS ITSELF...
...REMIND ME TO DROP A TRUCK ON HIM.
CYCLOPS.
A BIG TRUCK.
CYCLOPS!
A REALLY BIG TRUCK.
CYCLOPS!
NOT TO WORRY, PROFESSOR.
WHILE YOU WERE AWAY, OL' FEARLESS HERE MASTERED THE ART...
...OF DEADPAN HUMOR.
KEEP CALLING ME THAT, FURBALL...
...I'LL SHOW YOU "DEADPAN."
BANTER NOTWITHSTANDING, X-MEN...
...MIGHT I REMIND YOU ALL...
...THAT THE EXERCISE IS FAR FROM...
...OVER!
SLAK!

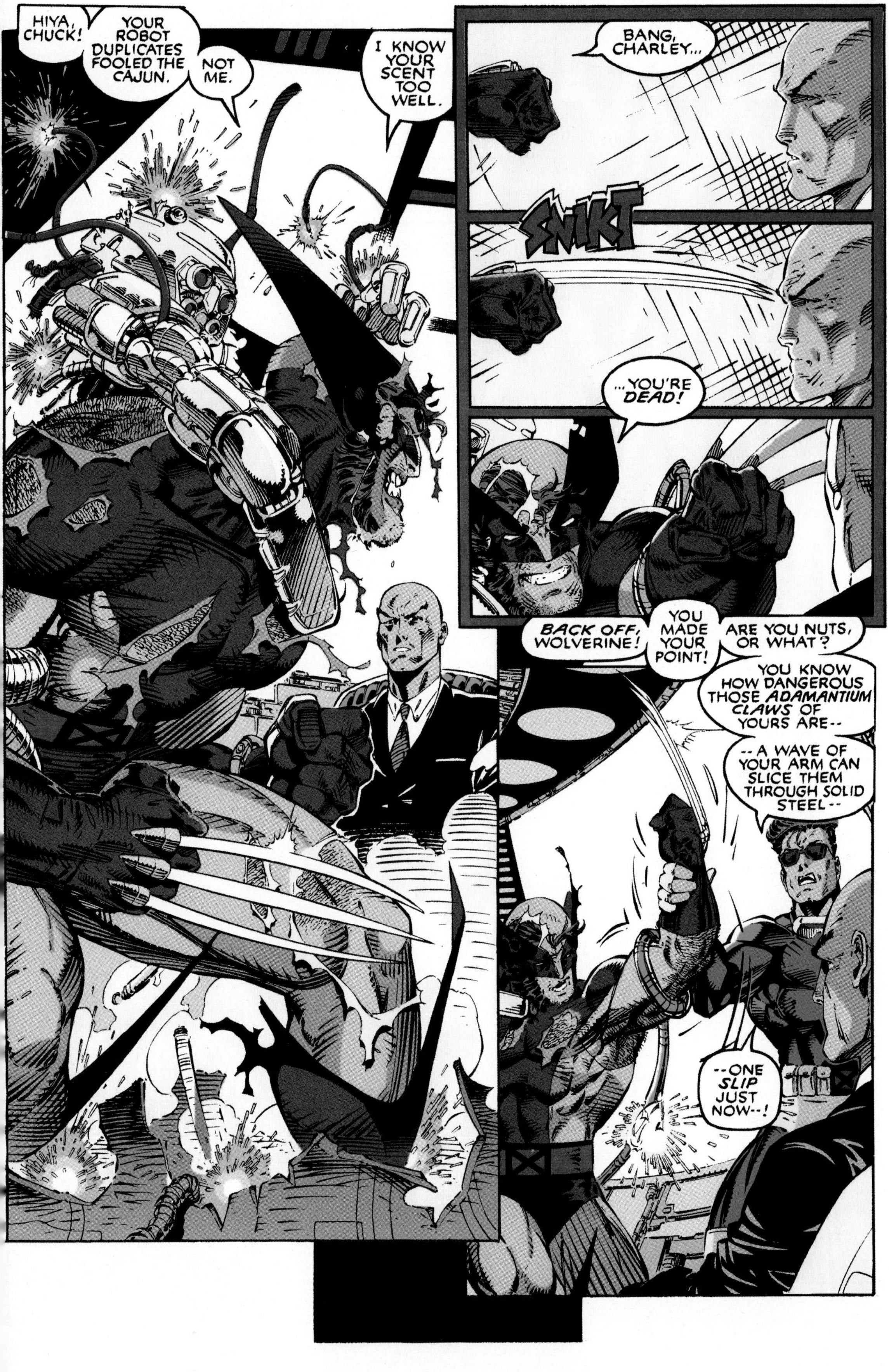
HIYA, CHUCK!
YOUR ROBOT DUPLICATES FOOLED THE CAJUN.
NOT ME.
I KNOW YOUR SCENT TOO WELL.
BANG, CHARLEY...
SNIKT
...YOU'RE DEAD!
BACK OFF, WOLVERINE!
YOU MADE YOUR POINT!
ARE YOU NUTS, OR WHAT?
YOU KNOW HOW DANGEROUS THOSE ADAMANTIUM CLAWS OF YOURS ARE--
--A WAVE OF YOUR ARM CAN SLICE THEM THROUGH SOLID STEEL--
--ONE SLIP JUST NOW--!

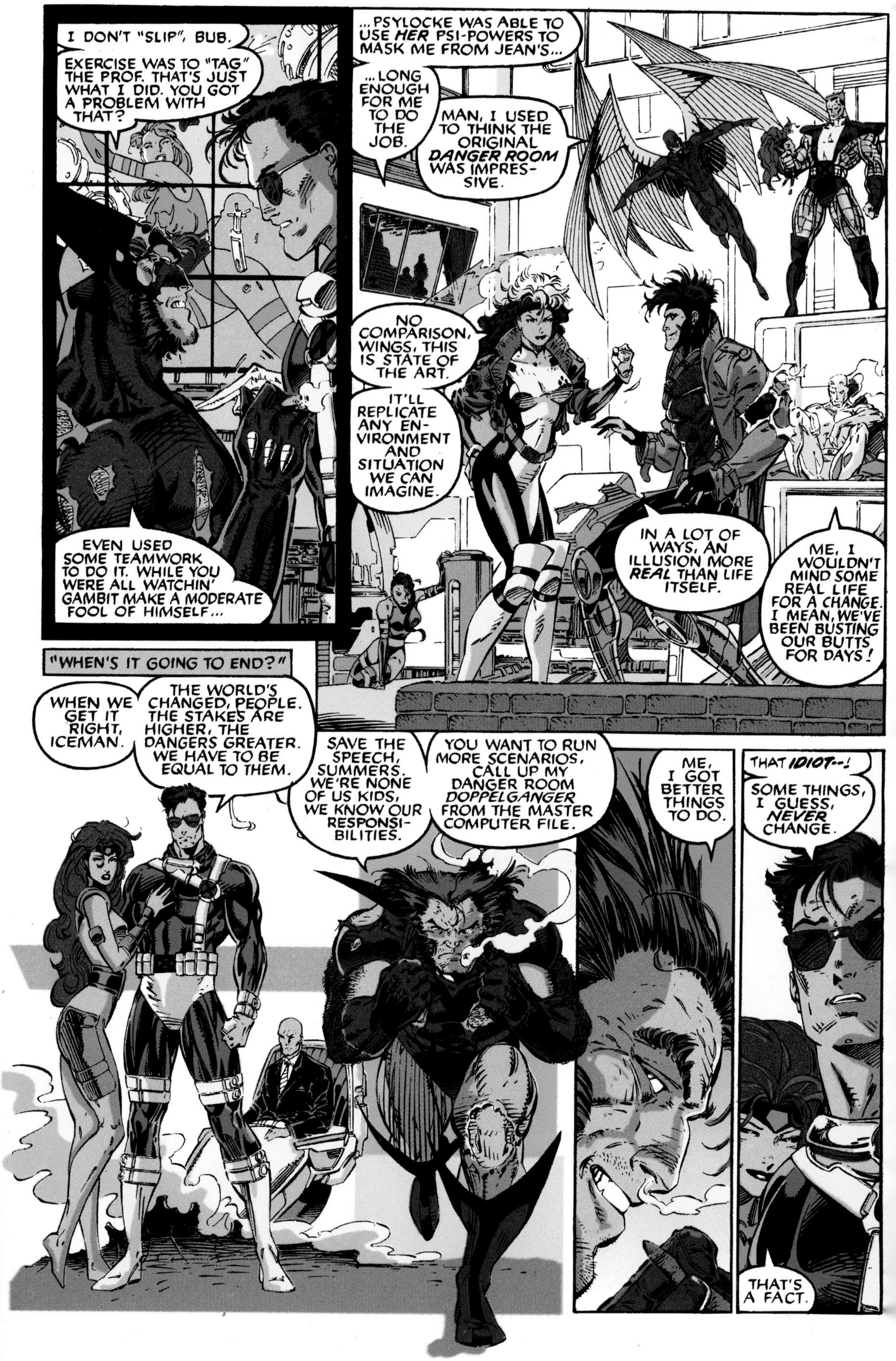

I DON'T "SLIP", BUB.
EXERCISE WAS TO "TAG" THE PROF. THAT'S JUST WHAT I DID. YOU GOT A PROBLEM WITH THAT?
EVEN USED SOME TEAMWORK TO DO IT. WHILE YOU WERE ALL WATCHIN' GAMBIT MAKE A MODERATE FOOL OF HIMSELF...
...PSYLOCKE WAS ABLE TO USE HER PSI-POWERS TO MASK ME FROM JEAN'S...
...LONG ENOUGH FOR ME TO DO THE JOB.
MAN, I USED TO THINK THE ORIGINAL DANGER ROOM WAS IMPRESSIVE.
NO COMPARISON, WINGS, THIS IS STATE OF THE ART.
IT'LL REPLICATE ANY ENVIRONMENT AND SITUATION WE CAN IMAGINE.
IN A LOT OF WAYS, AN ILLUSION MORE REAL THAN LIFE ITSELF.
ME, I WOULDN'T MIND SOME REAL LIFE FOR A CHANGE. I MEAN, WE'VE BEEN BUSTING OUR BUTTS FOR DAYS!
"WHEN'S IT GOING TO END?"
WHEN WE GET IT RIGHT, ICEMAN.
THE WORLD'S CHANGED, PEOPLE. THE STAKES ARE HIGHER, THE DANGERS GREATER. WE HAVE TO BE EQUAL TO THEM.
SAVE THE SPEECH, SUMMERS. WE'RE NONE OF US KIDS, WE KNOW OUR RESPONSIBILITIES.
YOU WANT TO RUN MORE SCENARIOS, CALL UP MY DANGER ROOM DOPPELGANGER FROM THE MASTER COMPUTER FILE.
ME, I GOT BETTER THINGS TO DO.
THAT IDIOT--!
SOME THINGS, I GUESS, NEVER CHANGE.
THAT'S A FACT.

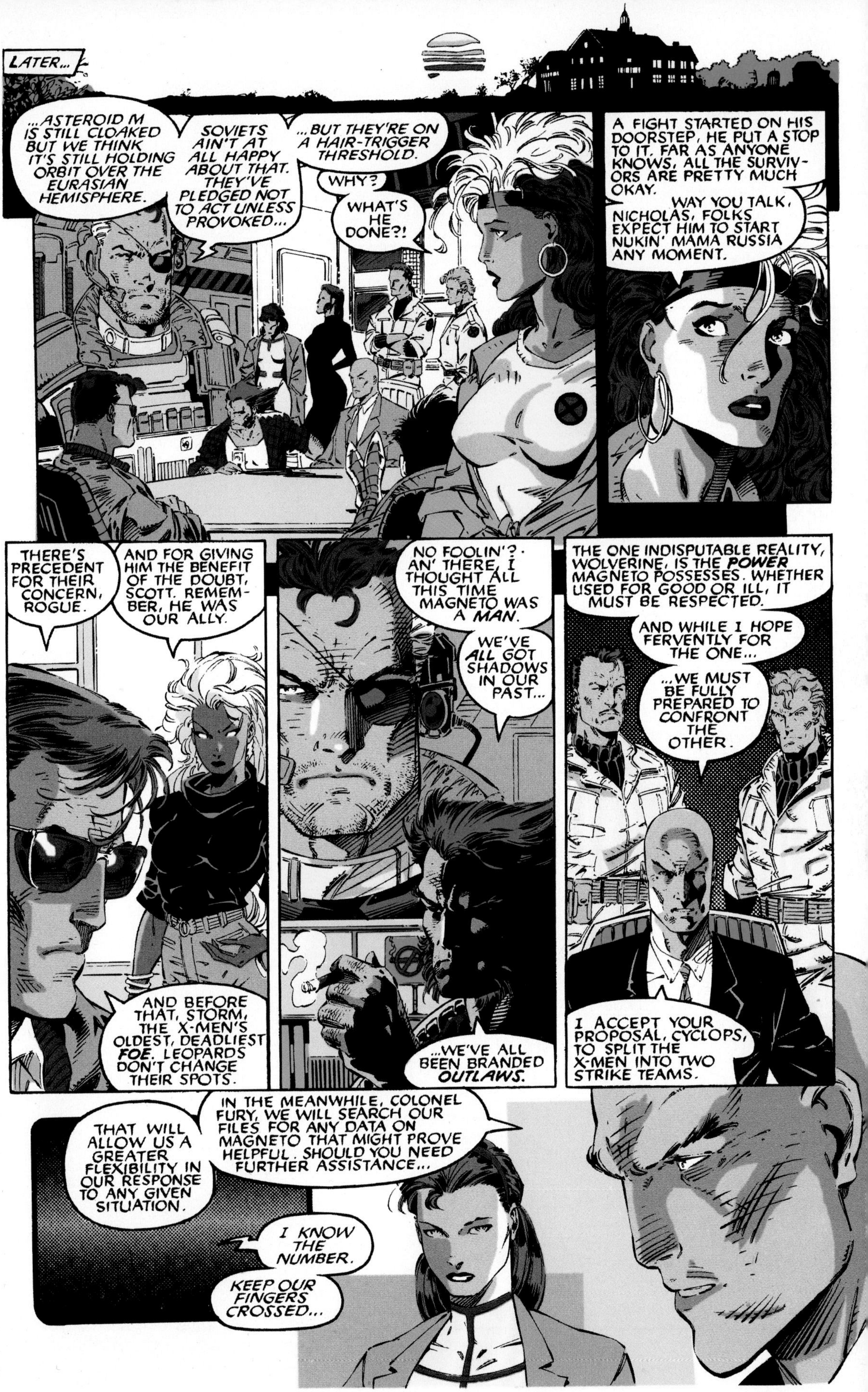
LATER...
...ASTEROID M IS STILL CLOAKED BUT WE THINK IT'S STILL HOLDING ORBIT OVER THE EURASIAN HEMISPHERE.
SOVIETS AIN'T AT ALL HAPPY ABOUT THAT. THEY'VE PLEDGED NOT TO ACT UNLESS PROVOKED...
...BUT THEY'RE ON A HAIR-TRIGGER THRESHOLD.
WHY?
WHAT'S HE DONE?!
A FIGHT STARTED ON HIS DOORSTEP, HE PUT A STOP TO IT. FAR AS ANYONE KNOWS, ALL THE SURVIVORS ARE PRETTY MUCH OKAY.
WAY YOU TALK, NICHOLAS, FOLKS EXPECT HIM TO START NUKIN' MAMA RUSSIA ANY MOMENT.
THERE'S PRECEDENT FOR THEIR CONCERN, ROGUE.
AND FOR GIVING HIM THE BENEFIT OF THE DOUBT, SCOTT. REMEMBER, HE WAS OUR ALLY.
AND BEFORE THAT, STORM, THE X-MEN'S OLDEST, DEADLIEST FOE. LEOPARDS DON'T CHANGE THEIR SPOTS.
NO FOOLIN'? AN' THERE, I THOUGHT ALL THIS TIME MAGNETO WAS A MAN.
WE'VE ALL GOT SHADOWS IN OUR PAST...
...WE'VE ALL BEEN BRANDED OUTLAWS.
THE ONE INDISPUTABLE REALITY, WOLVERINE, IS THE POWER MAGNETO POSSESSES. WHETHER USED FOR GOOD OR ILL, IT MUST BE RESPECTED.
AND WHILE I HOPE FERVENTLY FOR THE ONE...
...WE MUST BE FULLY PREPARED TO CONFRONT THE OTHER.
I ACCEPT YOUR PROPOSAL, CYCLOPS, TO SPLIT THE X-MEN INTO TWO STRIKE TEAMS.
THAT WILL ALLOW US A GREATER FLEXIBILITY IN OUR RESPONSE TO ANY GIVEN SITUATION.
IN THE MEANWHILE, COLONEL FURY, WE WILL SEARCH OUR FILES FOR ANY DATA ON MAGNETO THAT MIGHT PROVE HELPFUL. SHOULD YOU NEED FURTHER ASSISTANCE...
I KNOW THE NUMBER.
KEEP OUR FINGERS CROSSED...

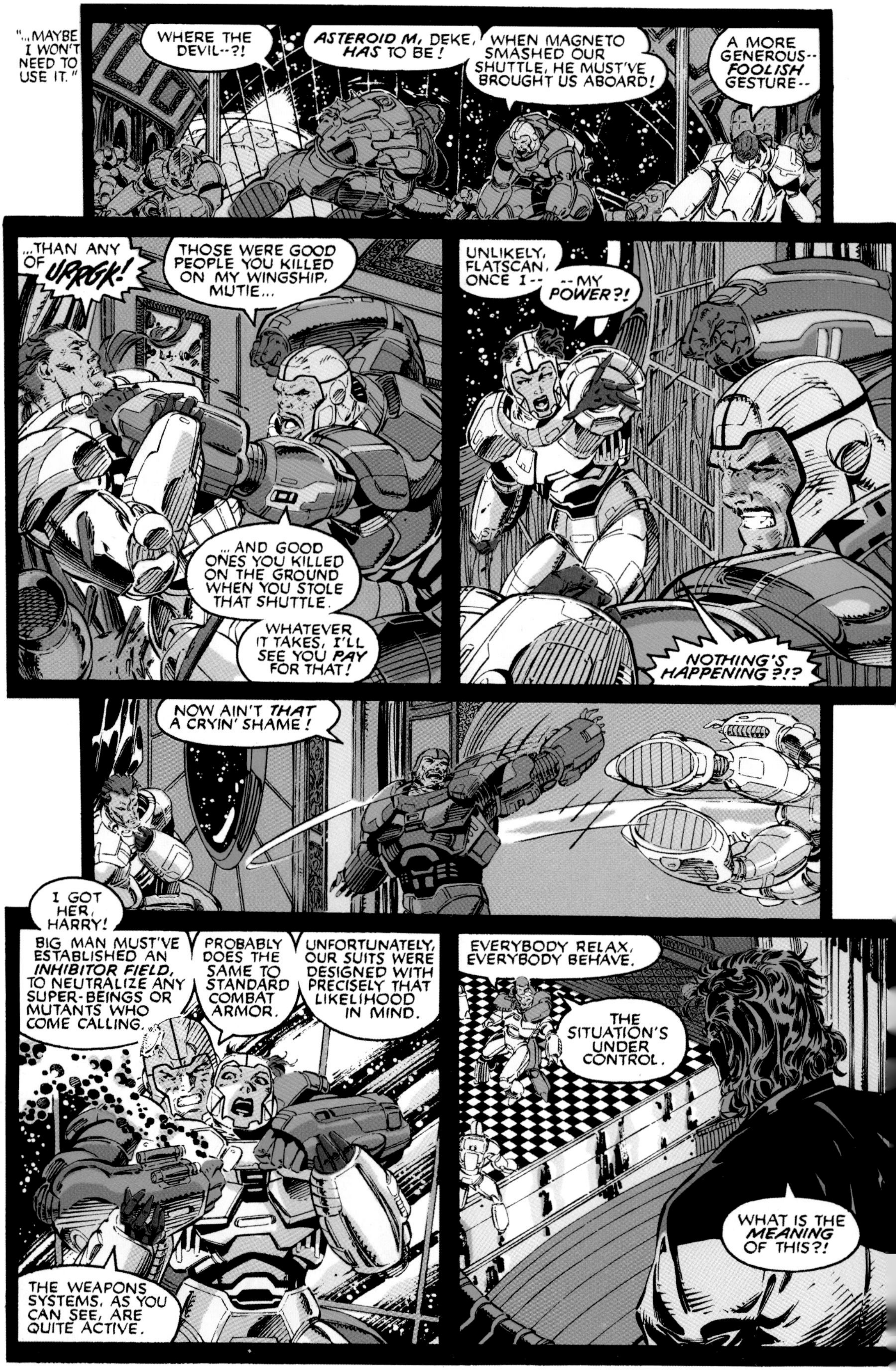
"...MAYBE I WON'T NEED TO USE IT."
WHERE THE DEVIL--?!
ASTEROID M, DEKE, HAS TO BE!
WHEN MAGNETO SMASHED OUR SHUTTLE, HE MUST'VE BROUGHT US ABOARD!
A MORE GENEROUS--FOOLISH GESTURE--
...THAN ANY OF URRGK!
THOSE WERE GOOD PEOPLE YOU KILLED ON MY WINGSHIP, MUTIE...
...AND GOOD ONES YOU KILLED ON THE GROUND WHEN YOU STOLE THAT SHUTTLE.
WHATEVER IT TAKES, I'LL SEE YOU PAY FOR THAT!
UNLIKELY, FLATSCAN, ONCE I--
--MY POWER?!
NOTHING'S HAPPENING?!?
NOW AIN'T THAT A CRYIN' SHAME!
I GOT HER, HARRY!
BIG MAN MUST'VE ESTABLISHED AN INHIBITOR FIELD, TO NEUTRALIZE ANY SUPER-BEINGS OR MUTANTS WHO COME CALLING.
PROBABLY DOES THE SAME TO STANDARD COMBAT ARMOR.
UNFORTUNATELY, OUR SUITS WERE DESIGNED WITH PRECISELY THAT LIKELIHOOD IN MIND.
THE WEAPONS SYSTEMS, AS YOU CAN SEE, ARE QUITE ACTIVE.
EVERYBODY RELAX, EVERYBODY BEHAVE.
THE SITUATION'S UNDER CONTROL.
WHAT IS THE MEANING OF THIS?!

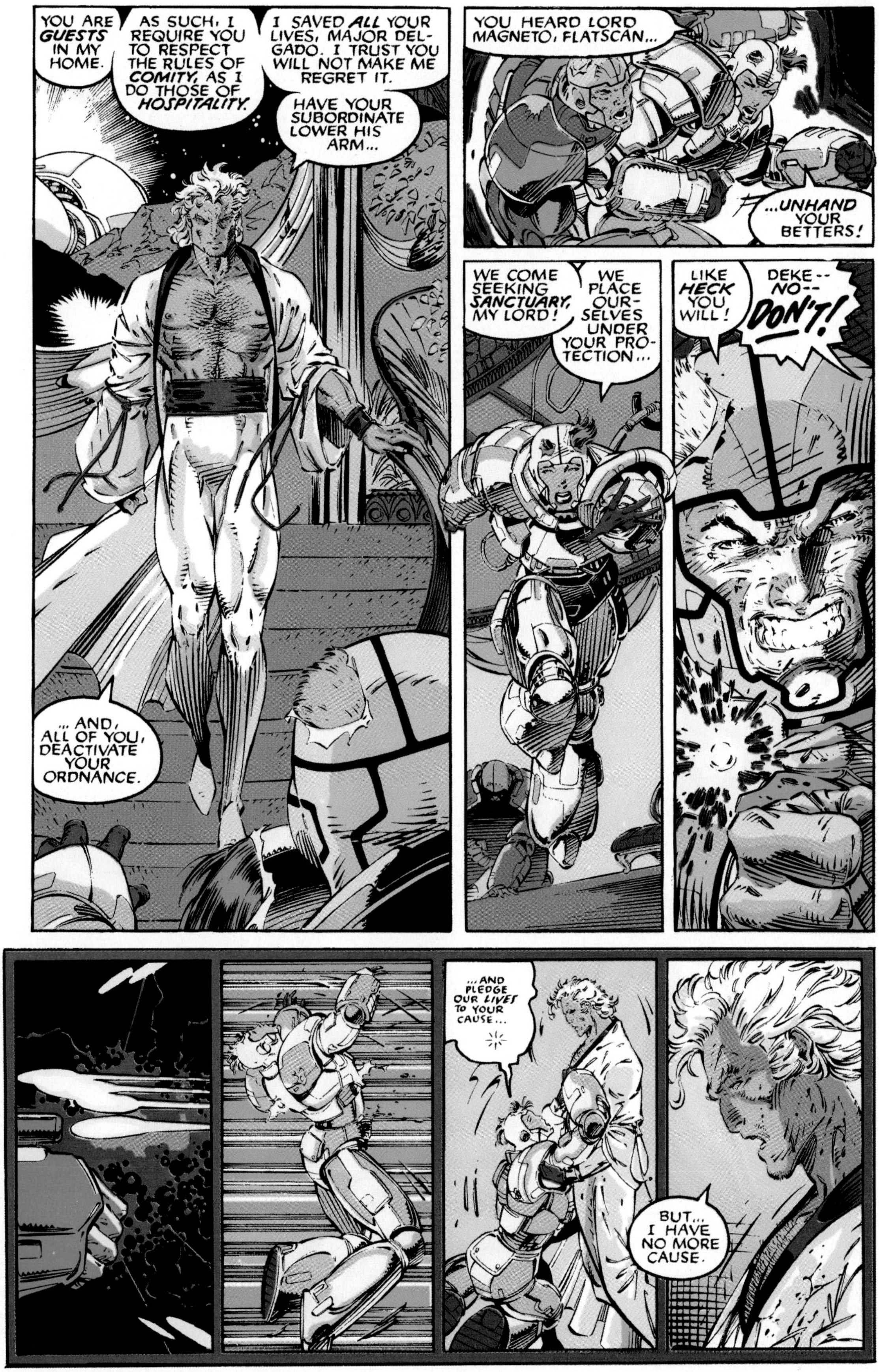
YOU ARE GUESTS IN MY HOME.
AS SUCH, I REQUIRE YOU TO RESPECT THE RULES OF COMITY, AS I DO THOSE OF HOSPITALITY.
I SAVED ALL YOUR LIVES, MAJOR DELGADO. I TRUST YOU WILL NOT MAKE ME REGRET IT.
HAVE YOUR SUBORDINATE LOWER HIS ARM...
... AND, ALL OF YOU, DEACTIVATE YOUR ORDNANCE.
YOU HEARD LORD MAGNETO, FLATSCAN...
...UNHAND YOUR BETTERS!
WE COME SEEKING SANCTUARY, MY LORD!
WE PLACE OURSELVES UNDER YOUR PROTECTION...
LIKE HECK YOU WILL!
DEKE-- NO-- DON'T!
...AND PLEDGE OUR LIVES TO YOUR CAUSE...
BUT... I HAVE NO MORE CAUSE.

I *WARNED* YOU! YOUR MECHANISMS ARE QUITE IMPRESSIVELY SHIELDED, THAT IS TRUE.

BUT I AM THE *MASTER OF MAGNETISM.*

I DRAW ON THE PRIMAL FORCES OF THE *EARTH* ITSELF.

IT IS CHILD'S-PLAY TO SUBVERT YOUR POWER SUIT'S ELECTRONICS...

M-MY ARM-- MY *GUN*--!

I CAN'T *STOP* IT!

HARRY-- NANCE-- *HELP* ME!

...AND BEND ITS SYSTEMRY TO *MY* WILL.

ARGH!

I'M SORRY, MAGNETO, THIS SHOULDN'T HAVE HAPPENED.

TOO LATE, FLATSCAN, FOR WEASELY WORDS TO SAVE YOU.

WE ARE OFFICERS OF THE LAW! WE HAVE EVERY RIGHT TO PURSUE AND APPREHEND THESE CRIMINALS.

OFFICERS, MAJOR, OF NO LAW I RECOGNIZE. AND THE RIGHTS YOU POSSESS HERE ARE THOSE...

...I CHOOSE TO GIVE YOU.

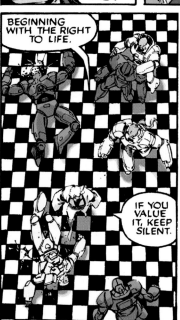

BEGINNING WITH THE RIGHT TO LIFE.

IF YOU *VALUE* IT, KEEP SILENT.

DREAD LORD, I AM *FABIAN CORTEZ.*

FORGIVE MY INTRUSION, I SHARE YOUR GRIEF, ANNEMARIE WAS A VALUED COMRADE...

...BUT YOU MUST KNOW THE GREAT POWERS BELOW WILL OF A CERTAINTY REACT TO WHAT HAS HAPPENED HERE.

THEY WILL DO SO TO THEIR REGRET.

LORD, *WE* KNOW YOUR STRENGTH IS A MATCH FOR ANY POWERS THEY MARSHAL AGAINST YOU, BUT ALL THEY WILL SEE IS A LONE MAN.

FOR DETERANCE TO BE CREDIBLE...

...IT MUST BE COUCHED IN TERMS THOSE FLATSCANS UNDERSTAND.

"FLATSCANS"?

THOSE GENETIC DEAD ENDS UNBLESSED WITH OUR MUTANT ABILITIES.

WHAT... "TERMS", CORTEZ, DO YOU SUGGEST?

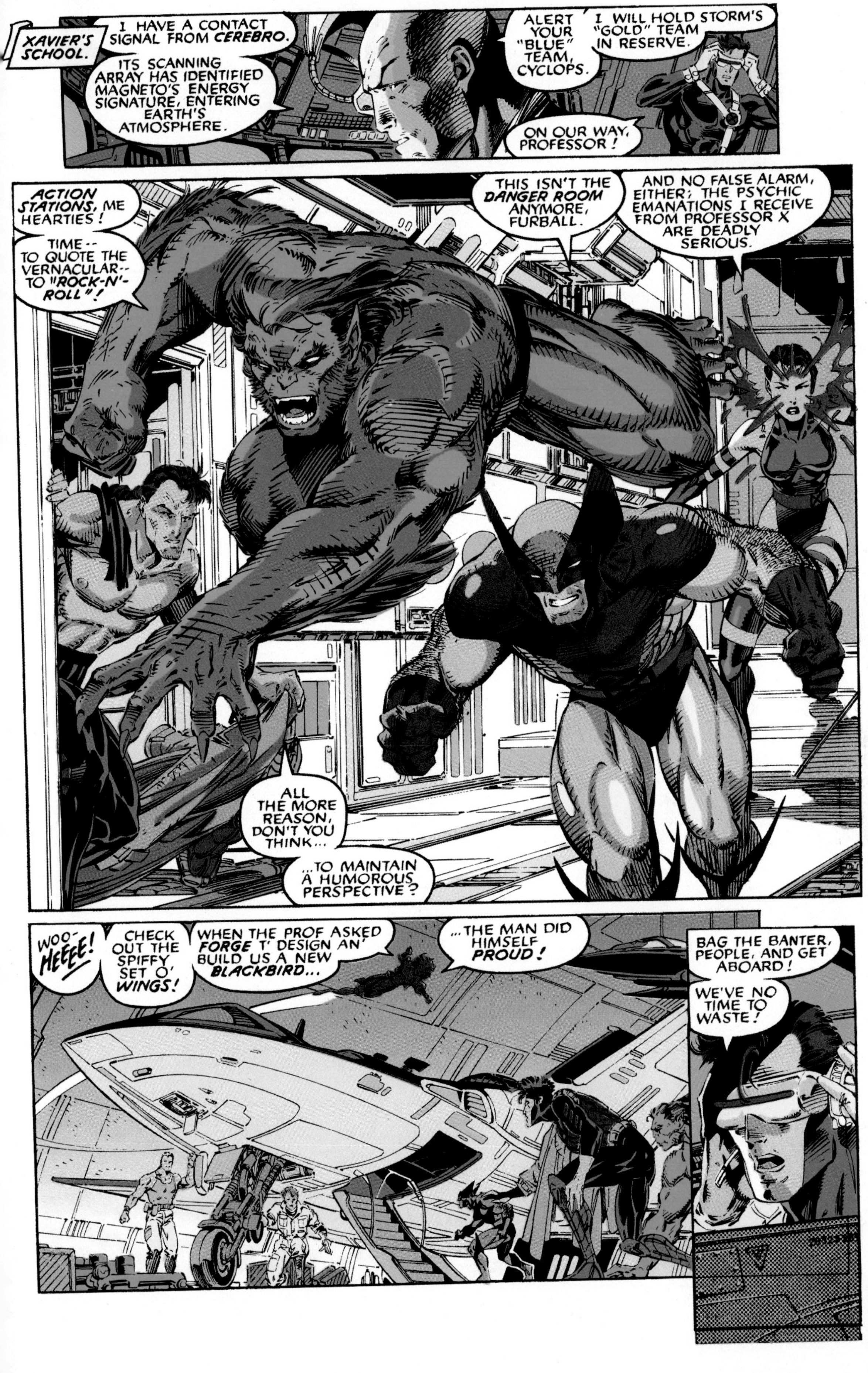
XAVIER'S SCHOOL.
I HAVE A CONTACT SIGNAL FROM CEREBRO.
ITS SCANNING ARRAY HAS IDENTIFIED MAGNETO'S ENERGY SIGNATURE, ENTERING EARTH'S ATMOSPHERE.
ALERT YOUR "BLUE" TEAM, CYCLOPS.
I WILL HOLD STORM'S "GOLD" TEAM IN RESERVE.
ON OUR WAY, PROFESSOR!
ACTION STATIONS, ME HEARTIES!
TIME-- TO QUOTE THE VERNACULAR-- TO "ROCK-N'-ROLL"!
THIS ISN'T THE DANGER ROOM ANYMORE, FURBALL.
AND NO FALSE ALARM, EITHER; THE PSYCHIC EMANATIONS I RECEIVE FROM PROFESSOR X ARE DEADLY SERIOUS.
ALL THE MORE REASON, DON'T YOU THINK...
...TO MAINTAIN A HUMOROUS PERSPECTIVE?
WOO-HEEEE!
CHECK OUT THE SPIFFY SET O' WINGS!
WHEN THE PROF ASKED FORGE T' DESIGN AN' BUILD US A NEW BLACKBIRD...
...THE MAN DID HIMSELF PROUD!
BAG THE BANTER, PEOPLE, AND GET ABOARD!
WE'VE NO TIME TO WASTE!

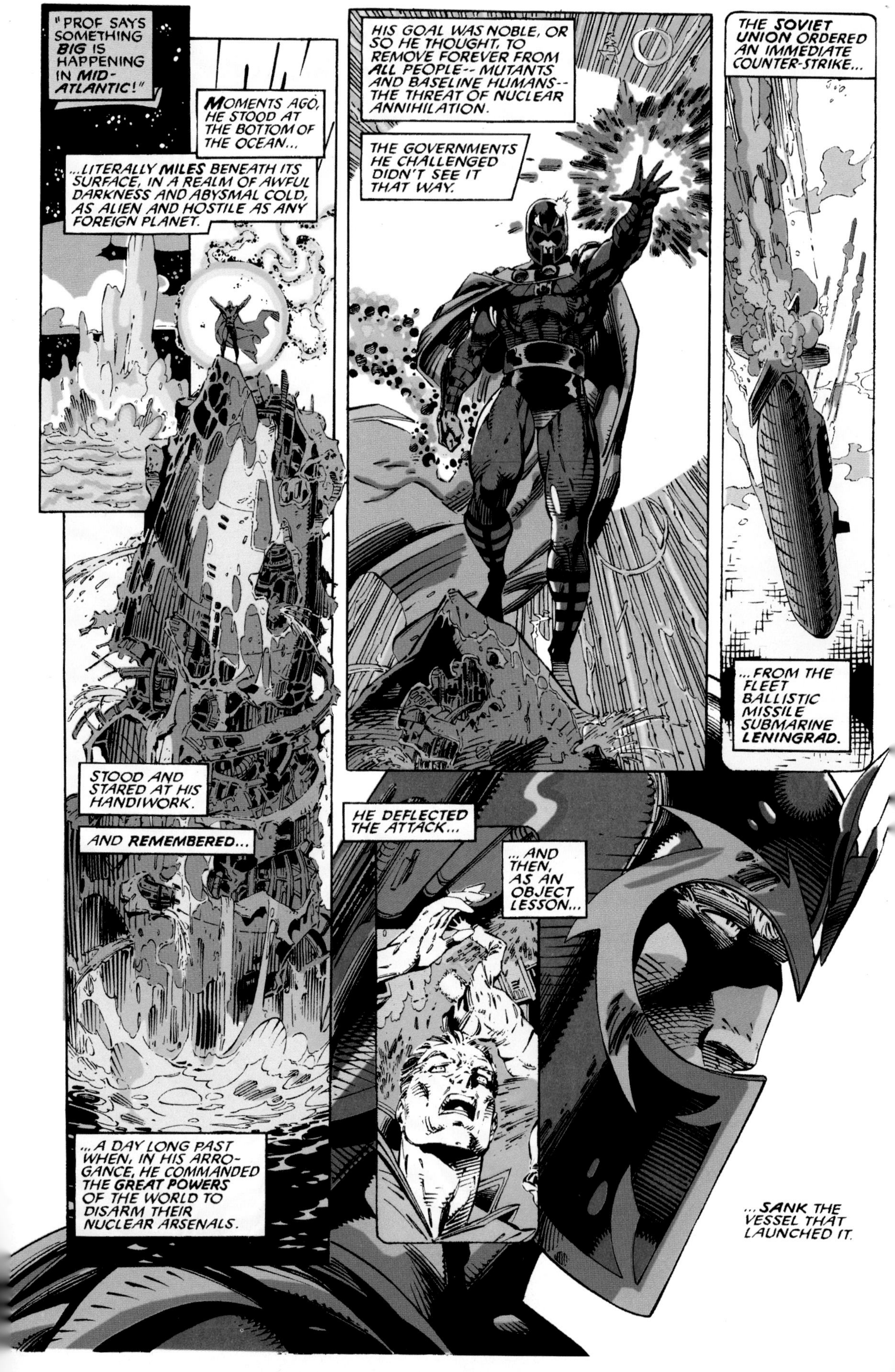
"PROF SAYS SOMETHING BIG IS HAPPENING IN MID-ATLANTIC!"
MOMENTS AGO, HE STOOD AT THE BOTTOM OF THE OCEAN...
...LITERALLY MILES BENEATH ITS SURFACE, IN A REALM OF AWFUL DARKNESS AND ABYSMAL COLD, AS ALIEN AND HOSTILE AS ANY FOREIGN PLANET.
HIS GOAL WAS NOBLE, OR SO HE THOUGHT, TO REMOVE FOREVER FROM ALL PEOPLE-- MUTANTS AND BASELINE HUMANS-- THE THREAT OF NUCLEAR ANNIHILATION.
THE GOVERNMENTS HE CHALLENGED DIDN'T SEE IT THAT WAY.
THE SOVIET UNION ORDERED AN IMMEDIATE COUNTER-STRIKE...
...FROM THE FLEET BALLISTIC MISSILE SUBMARINE LENINGRAD.
STOOD AND STARED AT HIS HANDIWORK.
AND REMEMBERED...
...A DAY LONG PAST WHEN, IN HIS ARROGANCE, HE COMMANDED THE GREAT POWERS OF THE WORLD TO DISARM THEIR NUCLEAR ARSENALS.
HE DEFLECTED THE ATTACK...
...AND THEN, AS AN OBJECT LESSON...
...SANK THE VESSEL THAT LAUNCHED IT.

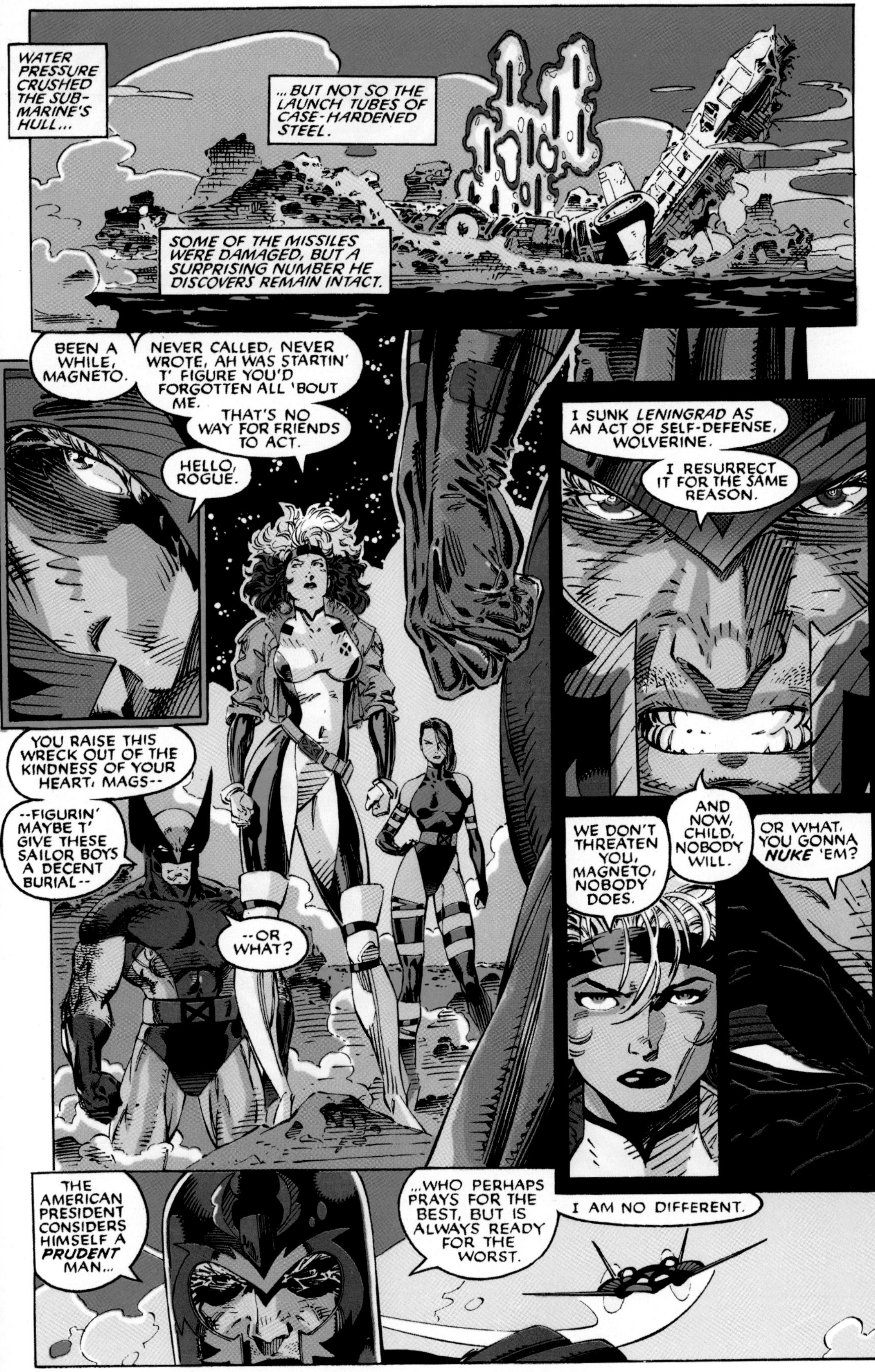

WATER PRESSURE CRUSHED THE SUB-MARINE'S HULL...
...BUT NOT SO THE LAUNCH TUBES OF CASE-HARDENED STEEL.
SOME OF THE MISSILES WERE DAMAGED, BUT A SURPRISING NUMBER HE DISCOVERS REMAIN INTACT.
BEEN A WHILE, MAGNETO.
NEVER CALLED, NEVER WROTE, AH WAS STARTIN' T' FIGURE YOU'D FORGOTTEN ALL 'BOUT ME.
THAT'S NO WAY FOR FRIENDS TO ACT.
HELLO, ROGUE.
I SUNK LENINGRAD AS AN ACT OF SELF-DEFENSE, WOLVERINE.
I RESURRECT IT FOR THE SAME REASON.
YOU RAISE THIS WRECK OUT OF THE KINDNESS OF YOUR HEART, MAGS--
--FIGURIN' MAYBE T' GIVE THESE SAILOR BOYS A DECENT BURIAL--
--OR WHAT?
WE DON'T THREATEN YOU, MAGNETO. NOBODY DOES.
AND NOW, CHILD, NOBODY WILL.
OR WHAT, YOU GONNA NUKE 'EM?
THE AMERICAN PRESIDENT CONSIDERS HIMSELF A PRUDENT MAN...
...WHO PERHAPS PRAYS FOR THE BEST, BUT IS ALWAYS READY FOR THE WORST.
I AM NO DIFFERENT.

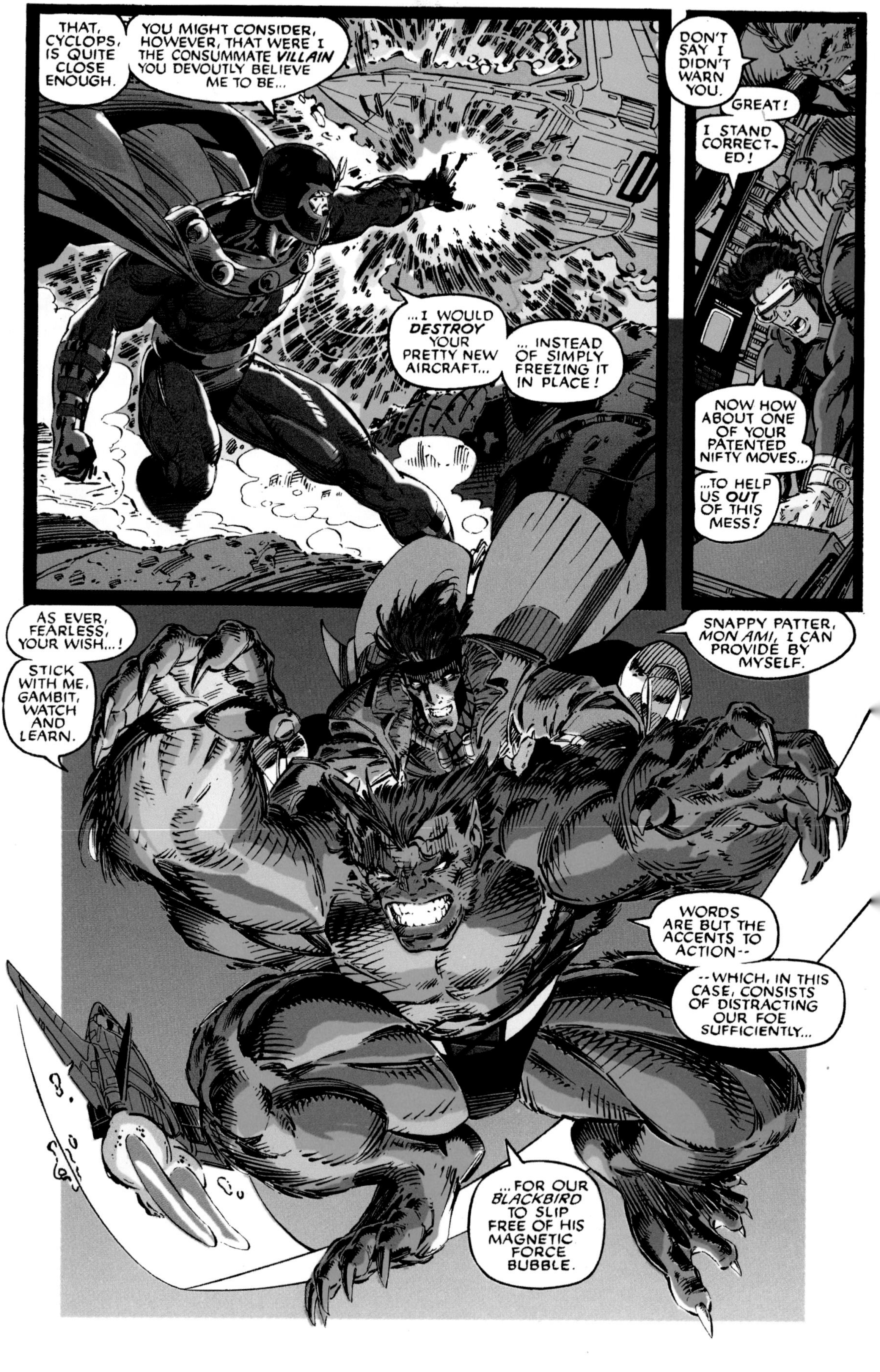
THAT, CYCLOPS, IS QUITE CLOSE ENOUGH.
YOU MIGHT CONSIDER, HOWEVER, THAT WERE I THE CONSUMMATE VILLAIN YOU DEVOUTLY BELIEVE ME TO BE...
...I WOULD DESTROY YOUR PRETTY NEW AIRCRAFT...
... INSTEAD OF SIMPLY FREEZING IT IN PLACE!
DON'T SAY I DIDN'T WARN YOU.
GREAT!
I STAND CORRECT-ED!
NOW HOW ABOUT ONE OF YOUR PATENTED NIFTY MOVES...
...TO HELP US OUT OF THIS MESS!
AS EVER, FEARLESS, YOUR WISH...!
STICK WITH ME, GAMBIT, WATCH AND LEARN.
SNAPPY PATTER, MON AMI, I CAN PROVIDE BY MYSELF.
WORDS ARE BUT THE ACCENTS TO ACTION--
--WHICH, IN THIS CASE, CONSISTS OF DISTRACTING OUR FOE SUFFICIENTLY...
...FOR OUR BLACKBIRD TO SLIP FREE OF HIS MAGNETIC FORCE BUBBLE.

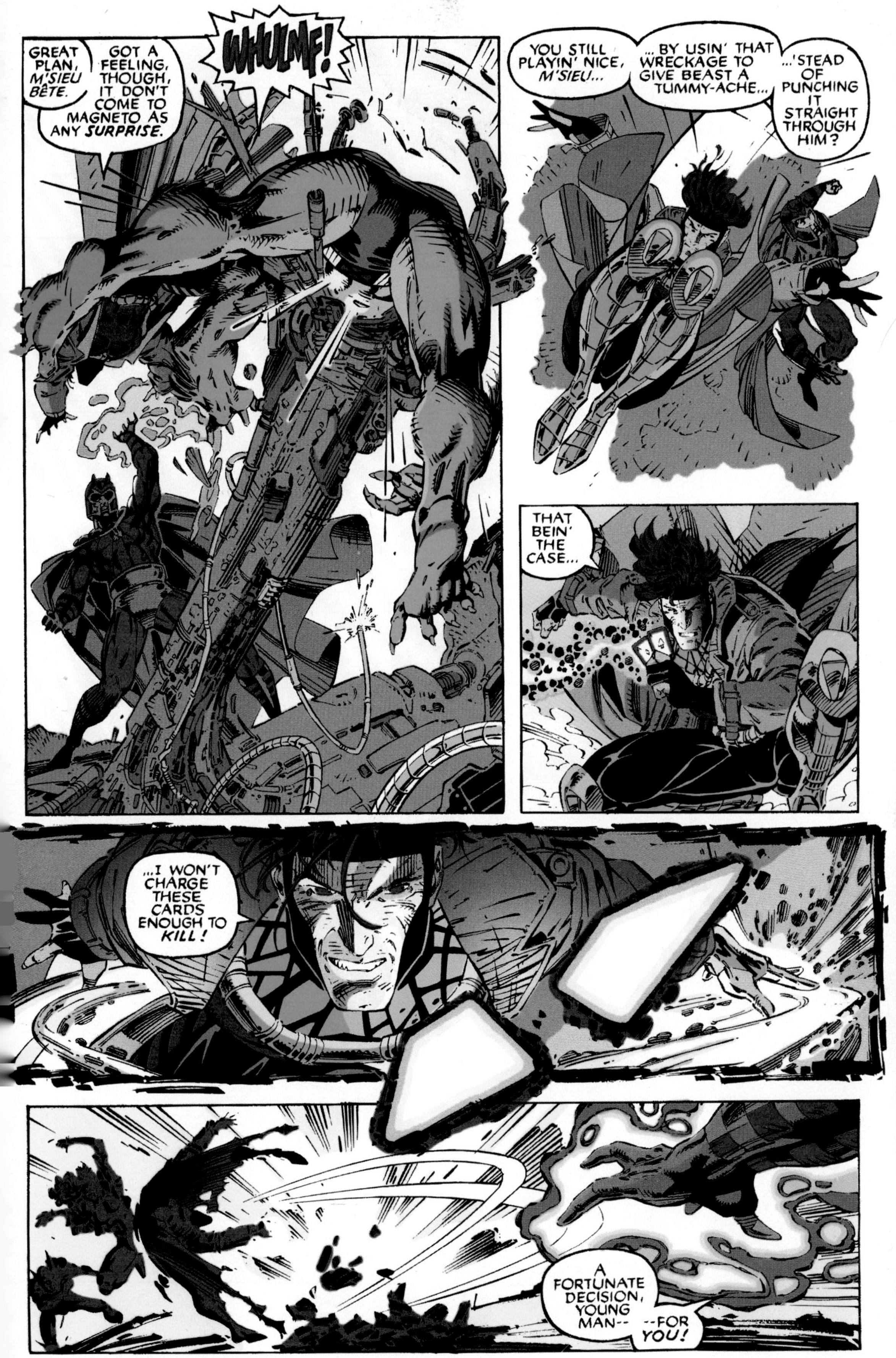
GREAT PLAN, M'SIEU BÊTE.
GOT A FEELING, THOUGH, IT DON'T COME TO MAGNETO AS ANY SURPRISE.
WHULMF!
YOU STILL PLAYIN' NICE, M'SIEU...
... BY USIN' THAT WRECKAGE TO GIVE BEAST A TUMMY-ACHE...
...'STEAD OF PUNCHING IT STRAIGHT THROUGH HIM?
THAT BEIN' THE CASE...
...I WON'T CHARGE THESE CARDS ENOUGH TO KILL!
A FORTUNATE DECISION, YOUNG MAN--
--FOR YOU!

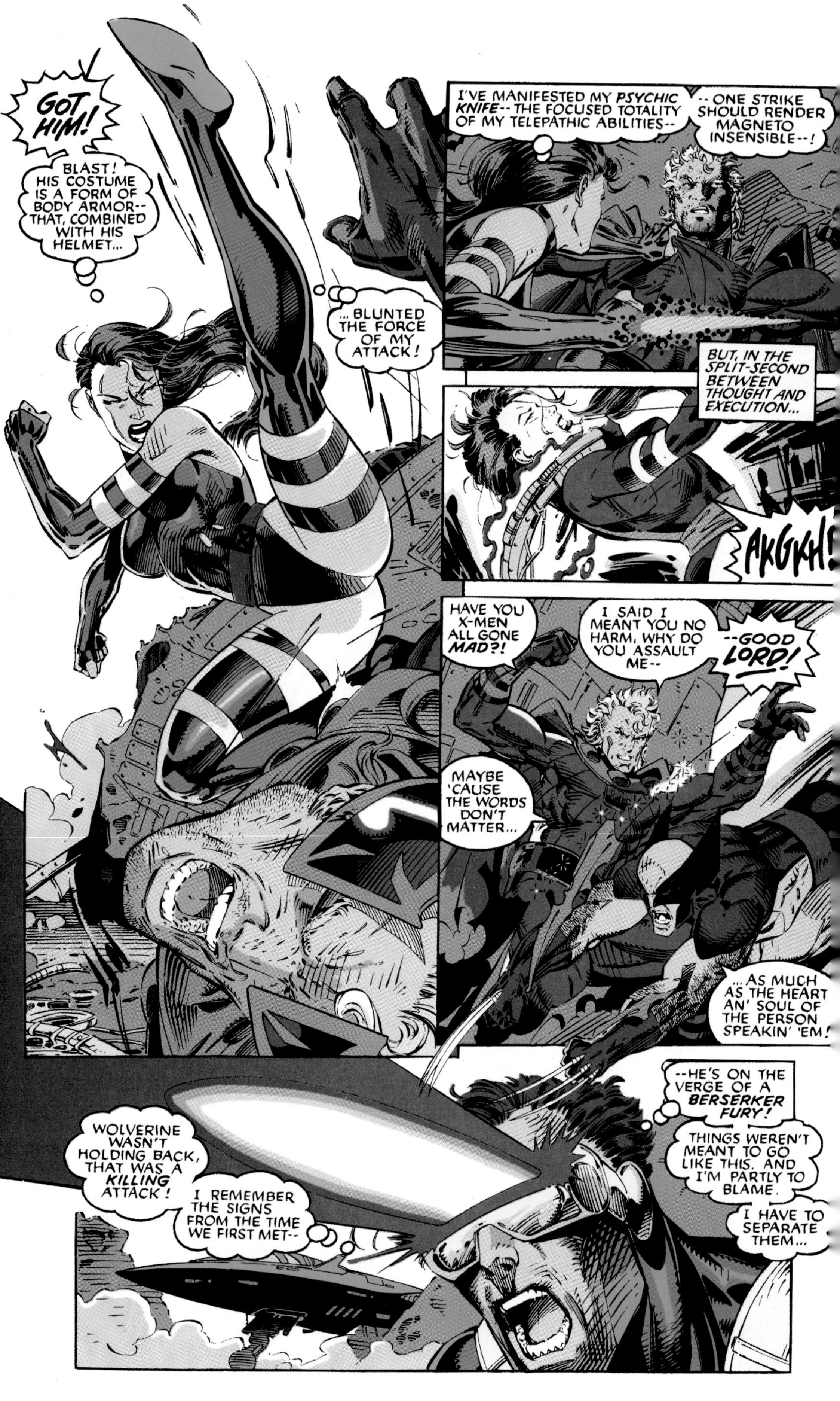
GOT HIM!
BLAST! HIS COSTUME IS A FORM OF BODY ARMOR--THAT, COMBINED WITH HIS HELMET...
...BLUNTED THE FORCE OF MY ATTACK!
I'VE MANIFESTED MY PSYCHIC KNIFE-- THE FOCUSED TOTALITY OF MY TELEPATHIC ABILITIES--
--ONE STRIKE SHOULD RENDER MAGNETO INSENSIBLE--!
BUT, IN THE SPLIT-SECOND BETWEEN THOUGHT AND EXECUTION...
AKGYAH!
HAVE YOU X-MEN ALL GONE MAD?!
I SAID I MEANT YOU NO HARM, WHY DO YOU ASSAULT ME--
--GOOD LORD!
MAYBE 'CAUSE THE WORDS DON'T MATTER...
...AS MUCH AS THE HEART AN' SOUL OF THE PERSON SPEAKIN' 'EM!
WOLVERINE WASN'T HOLDING BACK, THAT WAS A KILLING ATTACK!
I REMEMBER THE SIGNS FROM THE TIME WE FIRST MET--
--HE'S ON THE VERGE OF A BERSERKER FURY!
THINGS WEREN'T MEANT TO GO LIKE THIS, AND I'M PARTLY TO BLAME.
I HAVE TO SEPARATE THEM...

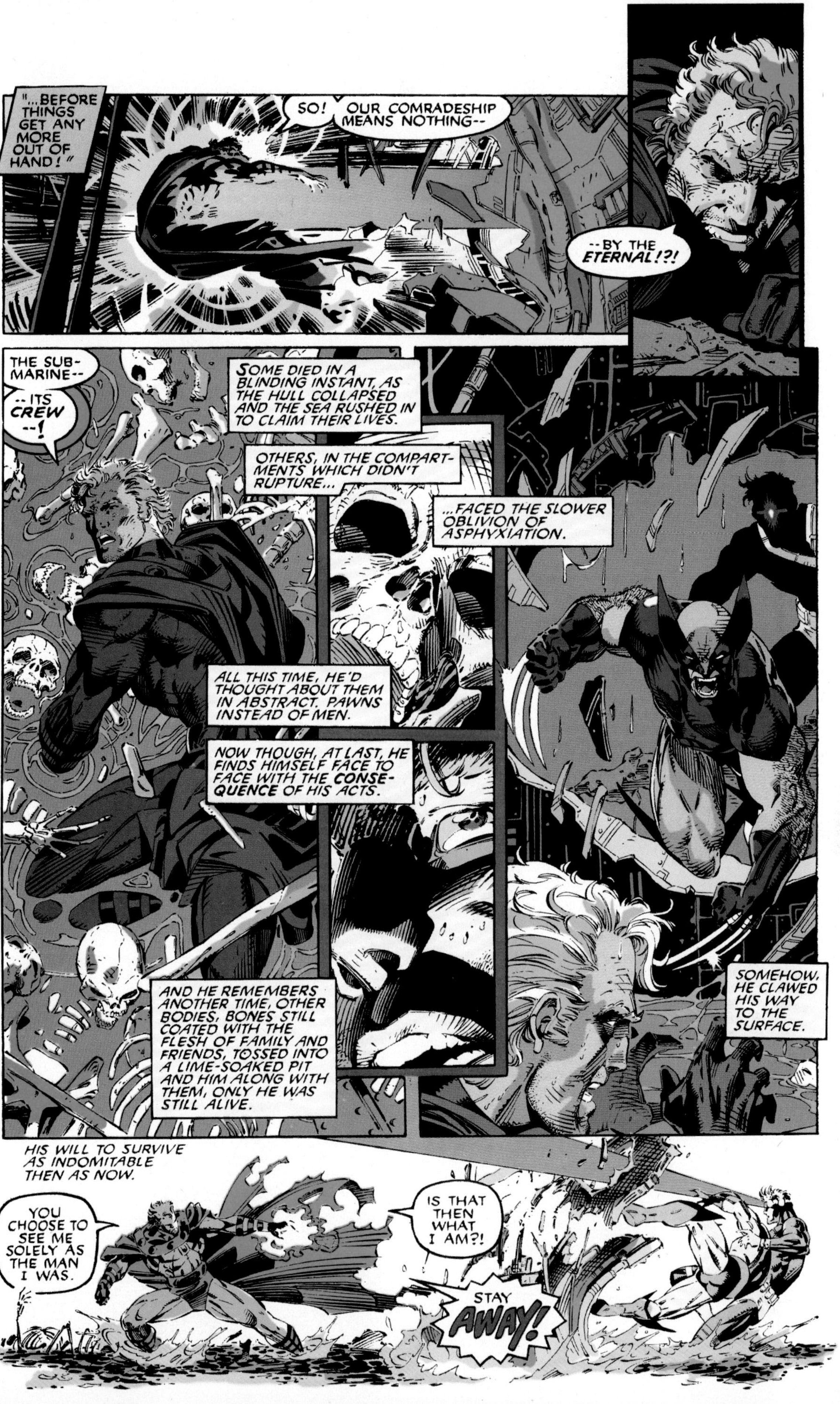
"...BEFORE THINGS GET ANY MORE OUT OF HAND!"
SO!
OUR COMRADESHIP MEANS NOTHING--
--BY THE ETERNAL!?!
THE SUB-MARINE--
--ITS CREW--!
SOME DIED IN A BLINDING INSTANT, AS THE HULL COLLAPSED AND THE SEA RUSHED IN TO CLAIM THEIR LIVES.
OTHERS, IN THE COMPART-MENTS WHICH DIDN'T RUPTURE...
...FACED THE SLOWER OBLIVION OF ASPHYXIATION.
ALL THIS TIME, HE'D THOUGHT ABOUT THEM IN ABSTRACT. PAWNS INSTEAD OF MEN.
NOW THOUGH, AT LAST, HE FINDS HIMSELF FACE TO FACE WITH THE CONSE-QUENCE OF HIS ACTS.
AND HE REMEMBERS ANOTHER TIME, OTHER BODIES, BONES STILL COATED WITH THE FLESH OF FAMILY AND FRIENDS, TOSSED INTO A LIME-SOAKED PIT AND HIM ALONG WITH THEM, ONLY HE WAS STILL ALIVE.
SOMEHOW, HE CLAWED HIS WAY TO THE SURFACE.
HIS WILL TO SURVIVE AS INDOMITABLE THEN AS NOW.
YOU CHOOSE TO SEE ME SOLELY AS THE MAN I WAS.
IS THAT THEN WHAT I AM?!
STAY AWAY!

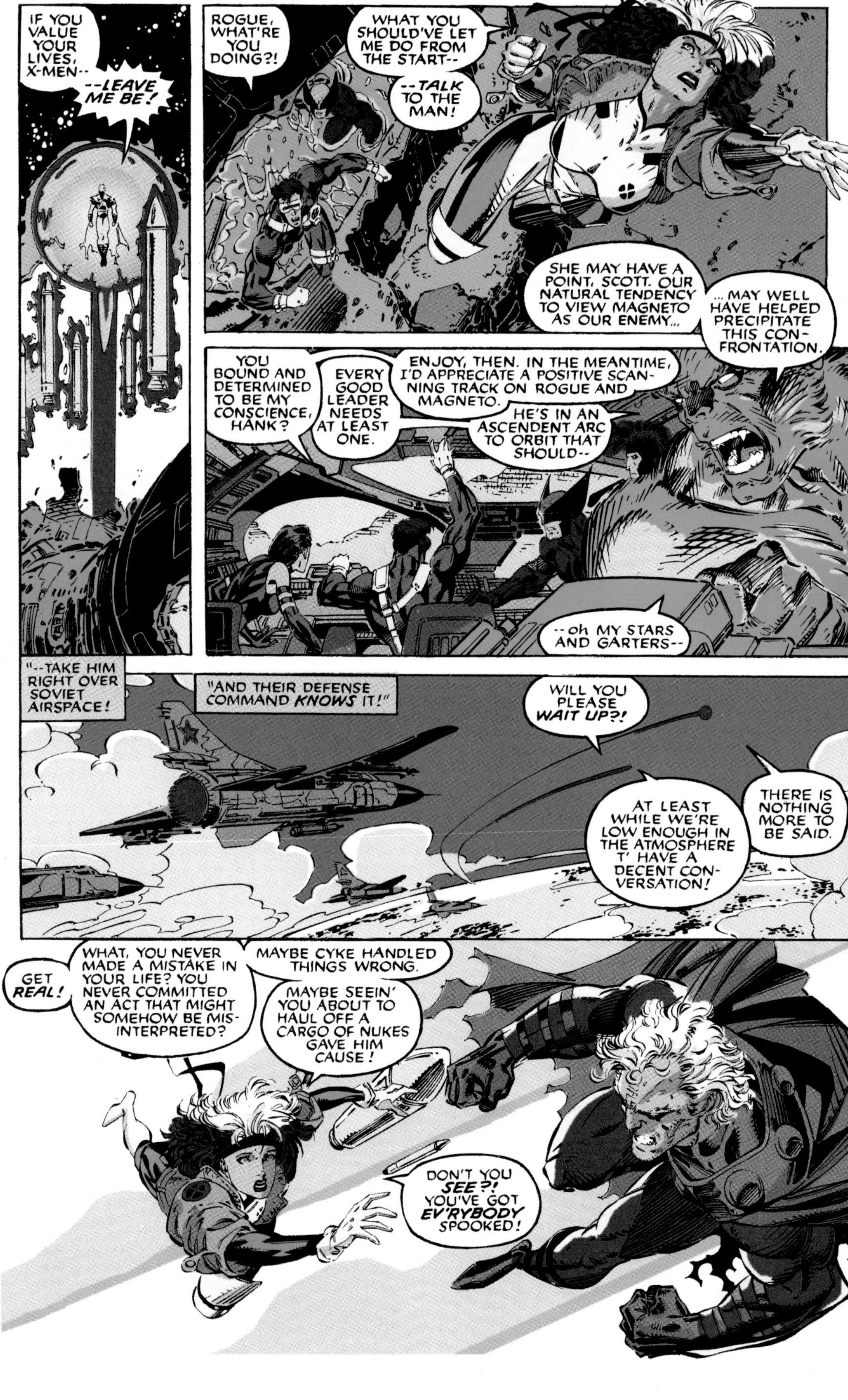

IF YOU VALUE YOUR LIVES, X-MEN--
--LEAVE ME BE!
ROGUE, WHAT'RE YOU DOING?!
WHAT YOU SHOULD'VE LET ME DO FROM THE START--
--TALK TO THE MAN!
SHE MAY HAVE A POINT, SCOTT. OUR NATURAL TENDENCY TO VIEW MAGNETO AS OUR ENEMY...
...MAY WELL HAVE HELPED PRECIPITATE THIS CONFRONTATION.
YOU BOUND AND DETERMINED TO BE MY CONSCIENCE, HANK?
EVERY GOOD LEADER NEEDS AT LEAST ONE.
ENJOY, THEN. IN THE MEANTIME, I'D APPRECIATE A POSITIVE SCANNING TRACK ON ROGUE AND MAGNETO.
HE'S IN AN ASCENDENT ARC TO ORBIT THAT SHOULD--
--oh MY STARS AND GARTERS--
"--TAKE HIM RIGHT OVER SOVIET AIRSPACE!
"AND THEIR DEFENSE COMMAND KNOWS IT!"
WILL YOU PLEASE WAIT UP?!
AT LEAST WHILE WE'RE LOW ENOUGH IN THE ATMOSPHERE T' HAVE A DECENT CONVERSATION!
THERE IS NOTHING MORE TO BE SAID.
MAYBE CYKE HANDLED THINGS WRONG.
MAYBE SEEIN' YOU ABOUT TO HAUL OFF A CARGO OF NUKES GAVE HIM CAUSE!
GET REAL!
WHAT, YOU NEVER MADE A MISTAKE IN YOUR LIFE? YOU NEVER COMMITTED AN ACT THAT MIGHT SOMEHOW BE MISINTERPRETED?
DON'T YOU SEE?! YOU'VE GOT EV'RYBODY SPOOKED!

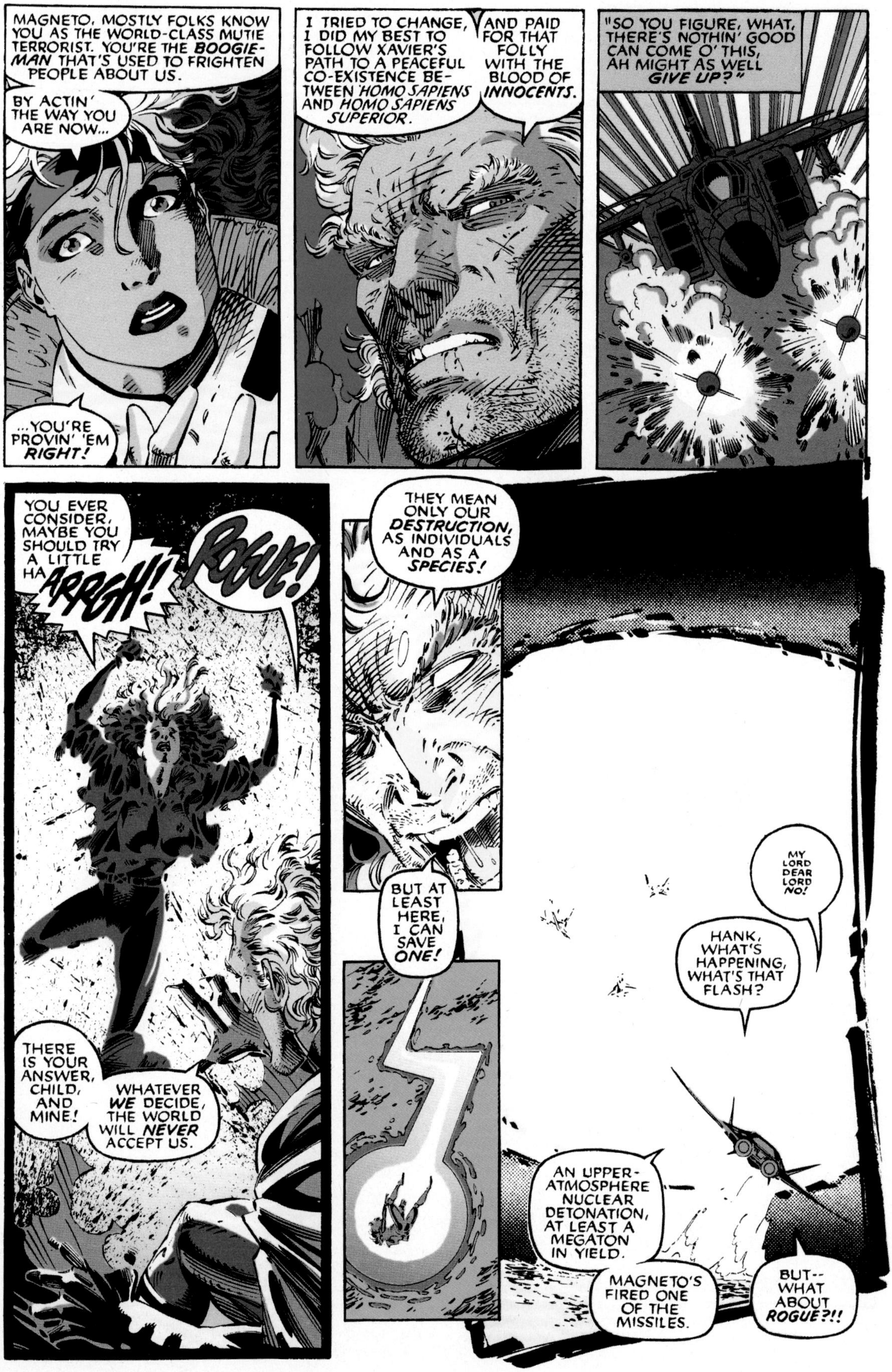

MAGNETO, MOSTLY FOLKS KNOW YOU AS THE WORLD-CLASS MUTIE TERRORIST. YOU'RE THE BOOGIE-MAN THAT'S USED TO FRIGHTEN PEOPLE ABOUT US.
BY ACTIN' THE WAY YOU ARE NOW...
...YOU'RE PROVIN' 'EM RIGHT!
I TRIED TO CHANGE, I DID MY BEST TO FOLLOW XAVIER'S PATH TO A PEACEFUL CO-EXISTENCE BE-TWEEN 'HOMO SAPIENS AND HOMO SAPIENS SUPERIOR.
AND PAID FOR THAT FOLLY WITH THE BLOOD OF INNOCENTS.
"SO YOU FIGURE, WHAT, THERE'S NOTHIN' GOOD CAN COME O' THIS, AH MIGHT AS WELL GIVE UP?"
YOU EVER CONSIDER, MAYBE YOU SHOULD TRY A LITTLE HA
ARRGH!
ROGUE!
THERE IS YOUR ANSWER, CHILD, AND MINE!
WHATEVER WE DECIDE, THE WORLD WILL NEVER ACCEPT US.
THEY MEAN ONLY OUR DESTRUCTION, AS INDIVIDUALS AND AS A SPECIES!
BUT AT LEAST HERE, I CAN SAVE ONE!
MY LORD DEAR LORD NO!
HANK, WHAT'S HAPPENING, WHAT'S THAT FLASH?
AN UPPER-ATMOSPHERE NUCLEAR DETONATION, AT LEAST A MEGATON IN YIELD.
MAGNETO'S FIRED ONE OF THE MISSILES.
BUT-- WHAT ABOUT ROGUE?!!

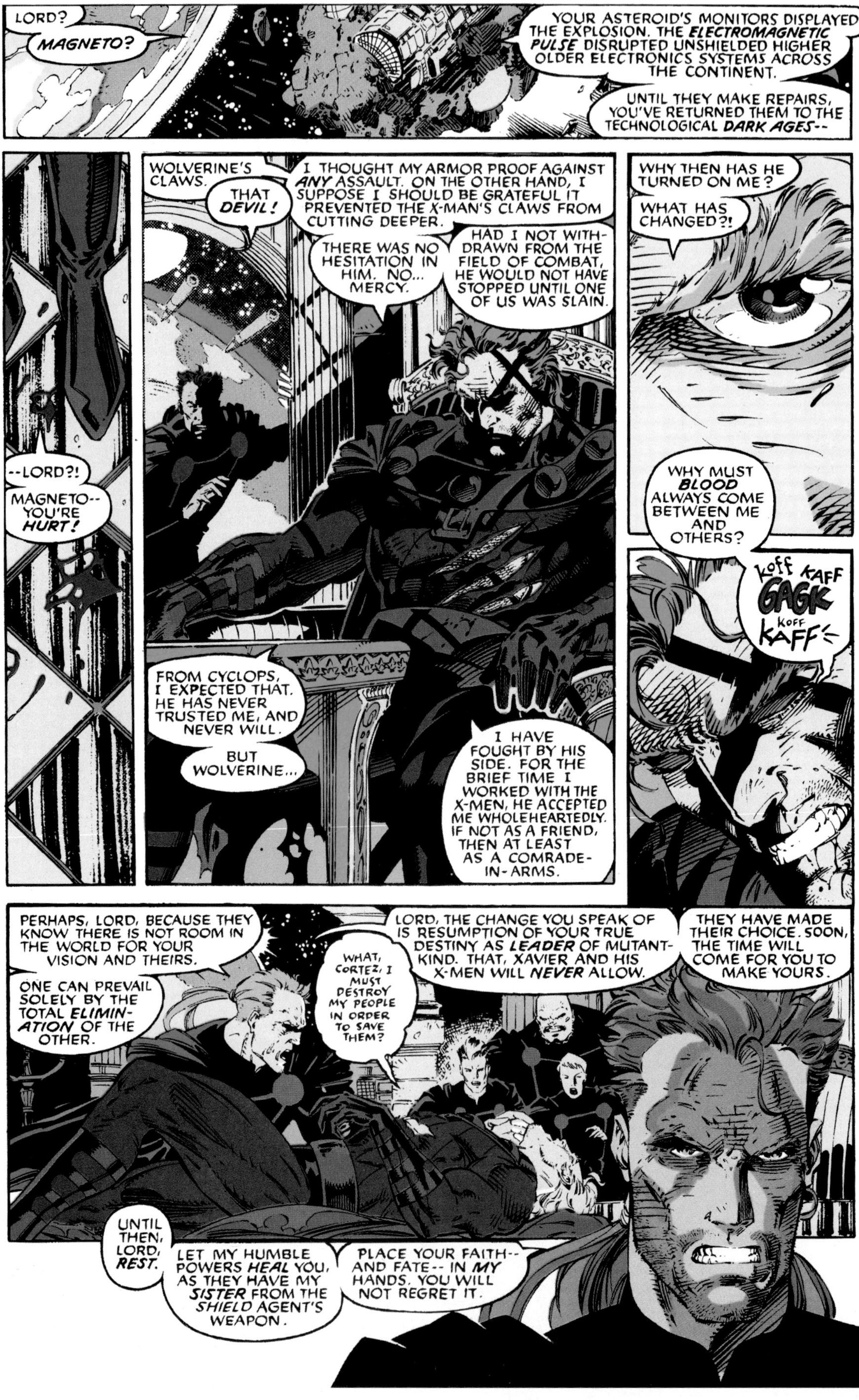
LORD?
MAGNETO?
YOUR ASTEROID'S MONITORS DISPLAYED THE EXPLOSION. THE ELECTROMAGNETIC PULSE DISRUPTED UNSHIELDED HIGHER OLDER ELECTRONICS SYSTEMS ACROSS THE CONTINENT.
UNTIL THEY MAKE REPAIRS, YOU'VE RETURNED THEM TO THE TECHNOLOGICAL DARK AGES--
--LORD?!
MAGNETO-- YOU'RE HURT!
WOLVERINE'S CLAWS.
THAT DEVIL!
I THOUGHT MY ARMOR PROOF AGAINST ANY ASSAULT. ON THE OTHER HAND, I SUPPOSE I SHOULD BE GRATEFUL IT PREVENTED THE X-MAN'S CLAWS FROM CUTTING DEEPER.
THERE WAS NO HESITATION IN HIM. NO... MERCY.
HAD I NOT WITH-DRAWN FROM THE FIELD OF COMBAT, HE WOULD NOT HAVE STOPPED UNTIL ONE OF US WAS SLAIN.
FROM CYCLOPS, I EXPECTED THAT. HE HAS NEVER TRUSTED ME, AND NEVER WILL.
BUT WOLVERINE...
I HAVE FOUGHT BY HIS SIDE. FOR THE BRIEF TIME I WORKED WITH THE X-MEN, HE ACCEPTED ME WHOLEHEARTEDLY. IF NOT AS A FRIEND, THEN AT LEAST AS A COMRADE-IN-ARMS.
WHY THEN HAS HE TURNED ON ME?
WHAT HAS CHANGED?!
WHY MUST BLOOD ALWAYS COME BETWEEN ME AND OTHERS?
KOFF KAFF
GAGK
KOFF
KAFF
PERHAPS, LORD, BECAUSE THEY KNOW THERE IS NOT ROOM IN THE WORLD FOR YOUR VISION AND THEIRS.
ONE CAN PREVAIL SOLELY BY THE TOTAL ELIMINATION OF THE OTHER.
WHAT, CORTEZ, I MUST DESTROY MY PEOPLE IN ORDER TO SAVE THEM?
LORD, THE CHANGE YOU SPEAK OF IS RESUMPTION OF YOUR TRUE DESTINY AS LEADER OF MUTANT-KIND. THAT, XAVIER AND HIS X-MEN WILL NEVER ALLOW.
THEY HAVE MADE THEIR CHOICE. SOON, THE TIME WILL COME FOR YOU TO MAKE YOURS.
UNTIL THEN, LORD, REST.
LET MY HUMBLE POWERS HEAL YOU, AS THEY HAVE MY SISTER FROM THE SHIELD AGENT'S WEAPON.
PLACE YOUR FAITH-- AND FATE-- IN MY HANDS. YOU WILL NOT REGRET IT.

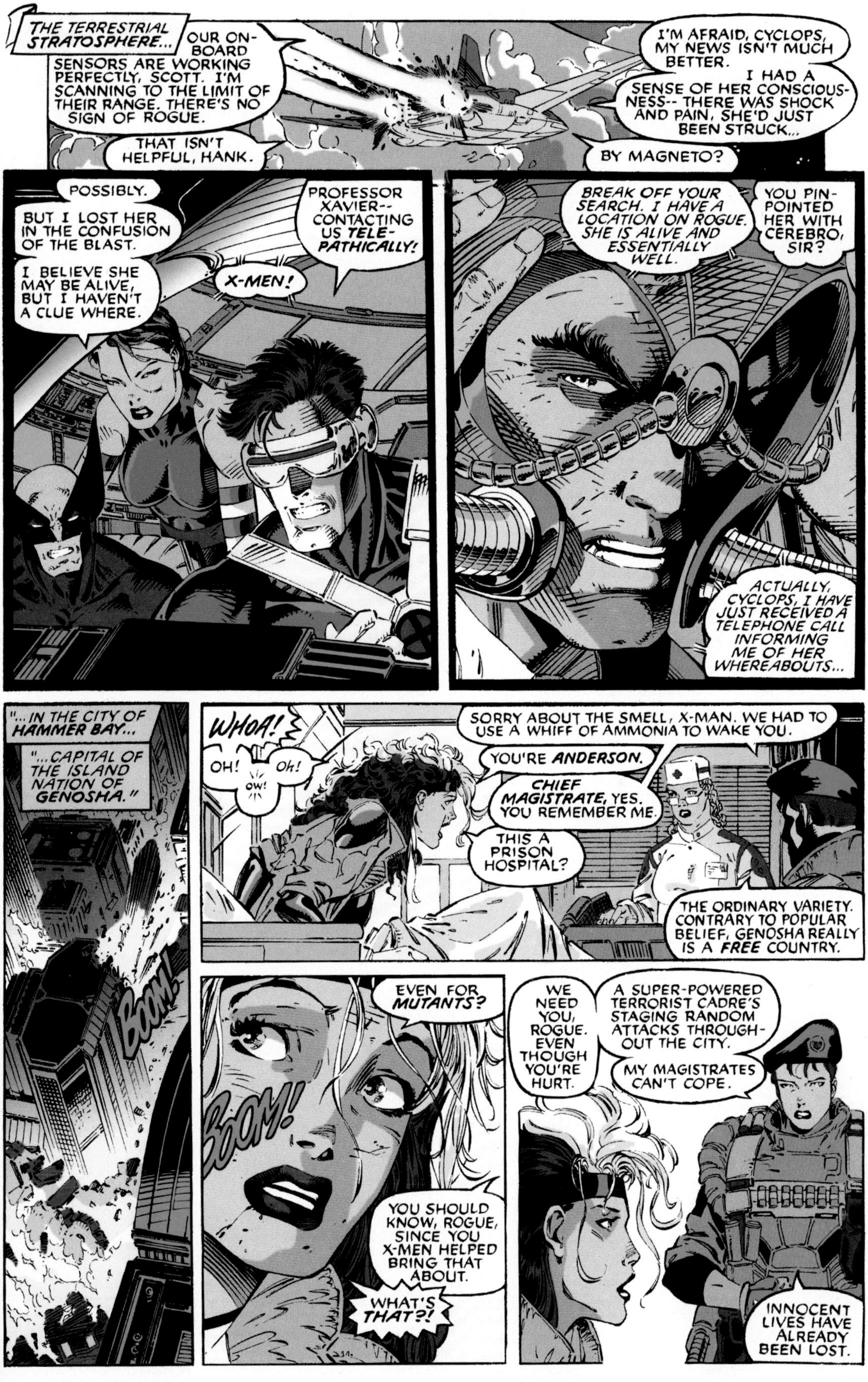
THE TERRESTRIAL STRATOSPHERE...
OUR ON-BOARD SENSORS ARE WORKING PERFECTLY, SCOTT. I'M SCANNING TO THE LIMIT OF THEIR RANGE. THERE'S NO SIGN OF ROGUE.
THAT ISN'T HELPFUL, HANK.
I'M AFRAID, CYCLOPS, MY NEWS ISN'T MUCH BETTER.
I HAD A SENSE OF HER CONSCIOUSNESS-- THERE WAS SHOCK AND PAIN, SHE'D JUST BEEN STRUCK...
BY MAGNETO?
POSSIBLY.
BUT I LOST HER IN THE CONFUSION OF THE BLAST.
I BELIEVE SHE MAY BE ALIVE, BUT I HAVEN'T A CLUE WHERE.
X-MEN!
PROFESSOR XAVIER-- CONTACTING US TELEPATHICALLY!
BREAK OFF YOUR SEARCH. I HAVE A LOCATION ON ROGUE. SHE IS ALIVE AND ESSENTIALLY WELL.
YOU PINPOINTED HER WITH CEREBRO, SIR?
ACTUALLY, CYCLOPS, I HAVE JUST RECEIVED A TELEPHONE CALL INFORMING ME OF HER WHEREABOUTS...
"...IN THE CITY OF HAMMER BAY...
"...CAPITAL OF THE ISLAND NATION OF GENOSHA."
BOOM!
WHOA!
OH!
OW!
Oh!
SORRY ABOUT THE SMELL, X-MAN. WE HAD TO USE A WHIFF OF AMMONIA TO WAKE YOU.
YOU'RE ANDERSON.
CHIEF MAGISTRATE, YES. YOU REMEMBER ME.
THIS A PRISON HOSPITAL?
THE ORDINARY VARIETY. CONTRARY TO POPULAR BELIEF, GENOSHA REALLY IS A FREE COUNTRY.
EVEN FOR MUTANTS?
BOOM!
YOU SHOULD KNOW, ROGUE, SINCE YOU X-MEN HELPED BRING THAT ABOUT.
WHAT'S THAT?!
WE NEED YOU, ROGUE. EVEN THOUGH YOU'RE HURT.
A SUPER-POWERED TERRORIST CADRE'S STAGING RANDOM ATTACKS THROUGHOUT THE CITY.
MY MAGISTRATES CAN'T COPE.
INNOCENT LIVES HAVE ALREADY BEEN LOST.

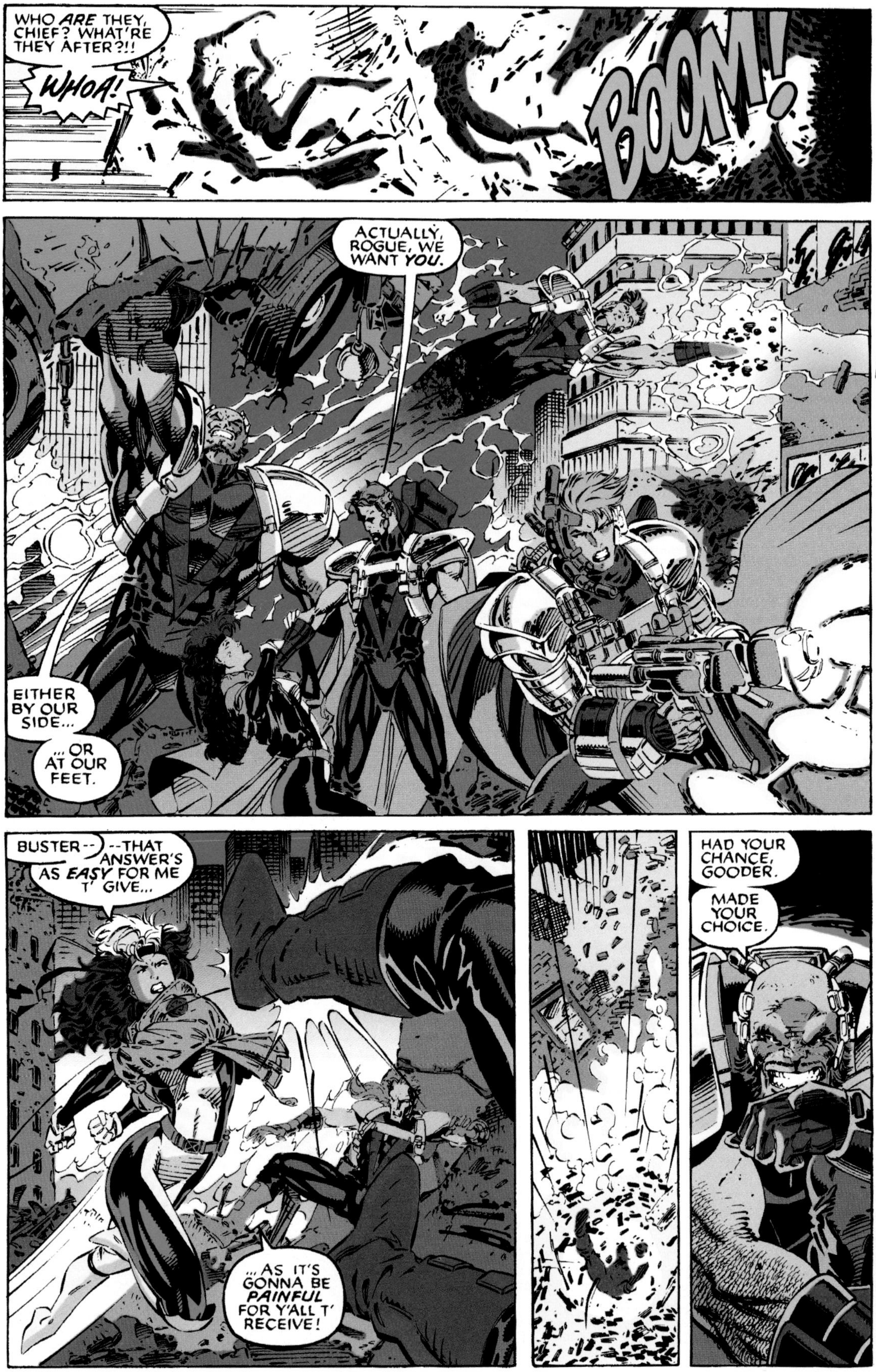
WHO ARE THEY, CHIEF? WHAT'RE THEY AFTER?!!
WHOA!
BOOM!
ACTUALLY, ROGUE, WE WANT YOU.
EITHER BY OUR SIDE...
...OR AT OUR FEET.
BUSTER--
--THAT ANSWER'S AS EASY FOR ME T' GIVE...
...AS IT'S GONNA BE PAINFUL FOR Y'ALL T' RECEIVE!
HAD YOUR CHANCE, GOODER.
MADE YOUR CHOICE.

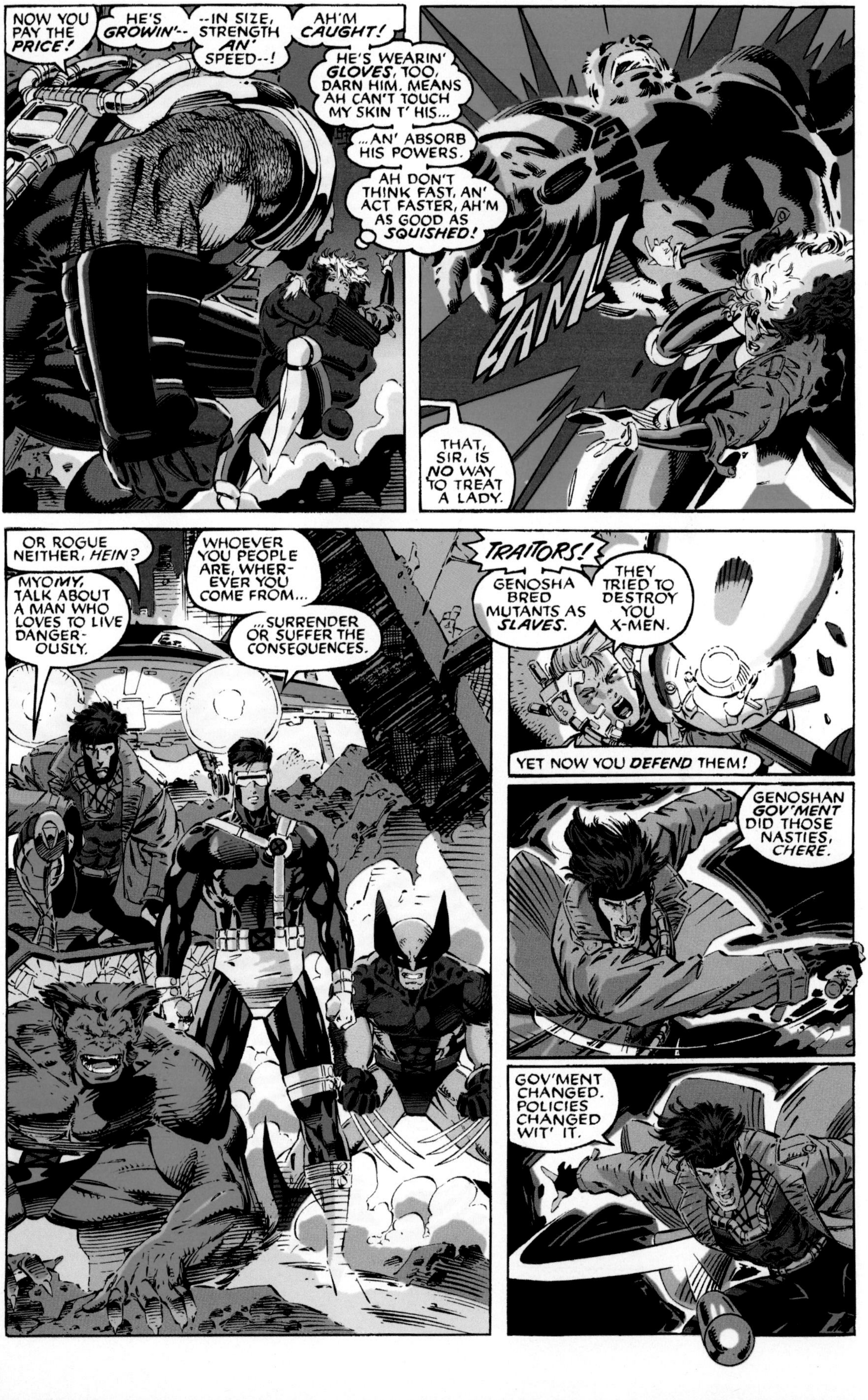
NOW YOU PAY THE *PRICE!*
HE'S *GROWIN'*--
--IN SIZE, STRENGTH *AN'* SPEED--!
AH'M *CAUGHT!*
HE'S WEARIN' *GLOVES*, TOO, DARN HIM. MEANS AH CAN'T TOUCH MY SKIN T' HIS...
...AN' ABSORB HIS POWERS.
AH DON'T THINK FAST, AN' ACT FASTER, AH'M AS GOOD AS *SQUISHED!*
ZAM!
THAT, SIR, IS *NO* WAY TO TREAT A LADY.
OR ROGUE NEITHER, *HEIN?*
MYOMY, TALK ABOUT A MAN WHO LOVES TO LIVE DANGER-OUSLY.
WHOEVER YOU PEOPLE ARE, WHER-EVER YOU COME FROM...
...SURRENDER OR SUFFER THE CONSEQUENCES.
TRAITORS!
GENOSHA BRED MUTANTS AS *SLAVES.*
THEY TRIED TO DESTROY YOU X-MEN.
YET NOW YOU *DEFEND* THEM!
GENOSHAN *GOV'MENT* DID THOSE NASTIES, *CHERE.*
GOV'MENT CHANGED. POLICIES CHANGED WIT' IT.

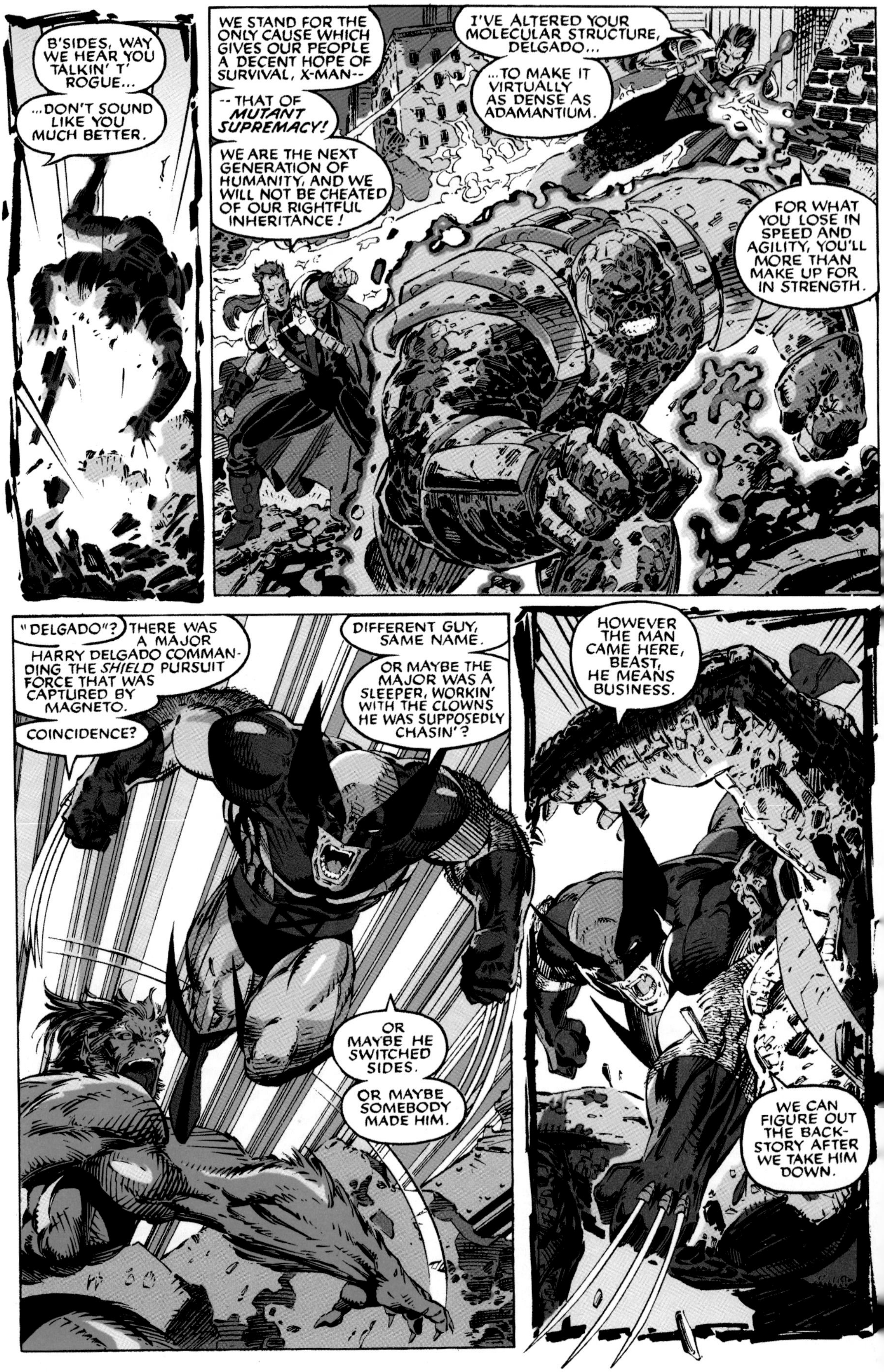
B'SIDES, WAY WE HEAR YOU TALKIN' T' ROGUE...
...DON'T SOUND LIKE YOU MUCH BETTER.
WE STAND FOR THE ONLY CAUSE WHICH GIVES OUR PEOPLE A DECENT HOPE OF SURVIVAL, X-MAN--
--THAT OF *MUTANT SUPREMACY!*
WE ARE THE NEXT GENERATION OF HUMANITY, AND WE WILL NOT BE CHEATED OF OUR RIGHTFUL INHERITANCE!
I'VE ALTERED YOUR MOLECULAR STRUCTURE, DELGADO...
...TO MAKE IT VIRTUALLY AS DENSE AS ADAMANTIUM.
FOR WHAT YOU LOSE IN SPEED AND AGILITY, YOU'LL MORE THAN MAKE UP FOR IN STRENGTH.
"DELGADO"? THERE WAS A MAJOR HARRY DELGADO COMMANDING THE *SHIELD* PURSUIT FORCE THAT WAS CAPTURED BY MAGNETO.
COINCIDENCE?
DIFFERENT GUY, SAME NAME.
OR MAYBE THE MAJOR WAS A SLEEPER, WORKIN' WITH THE CLOWNS HE WAS SUPPOSEDLY CHASIN'?
OR MAYBE HE SWITCHED SIDES.
OR MAYBE SOMEBODY MADE HIM.
HOWEVER THE MAN CAME HERE, BEAST, HE MEANS BUSINESS.
WE CAN FIGURE OUT THE BACK-STORY AFTER WE TAKE HIM DOWN.

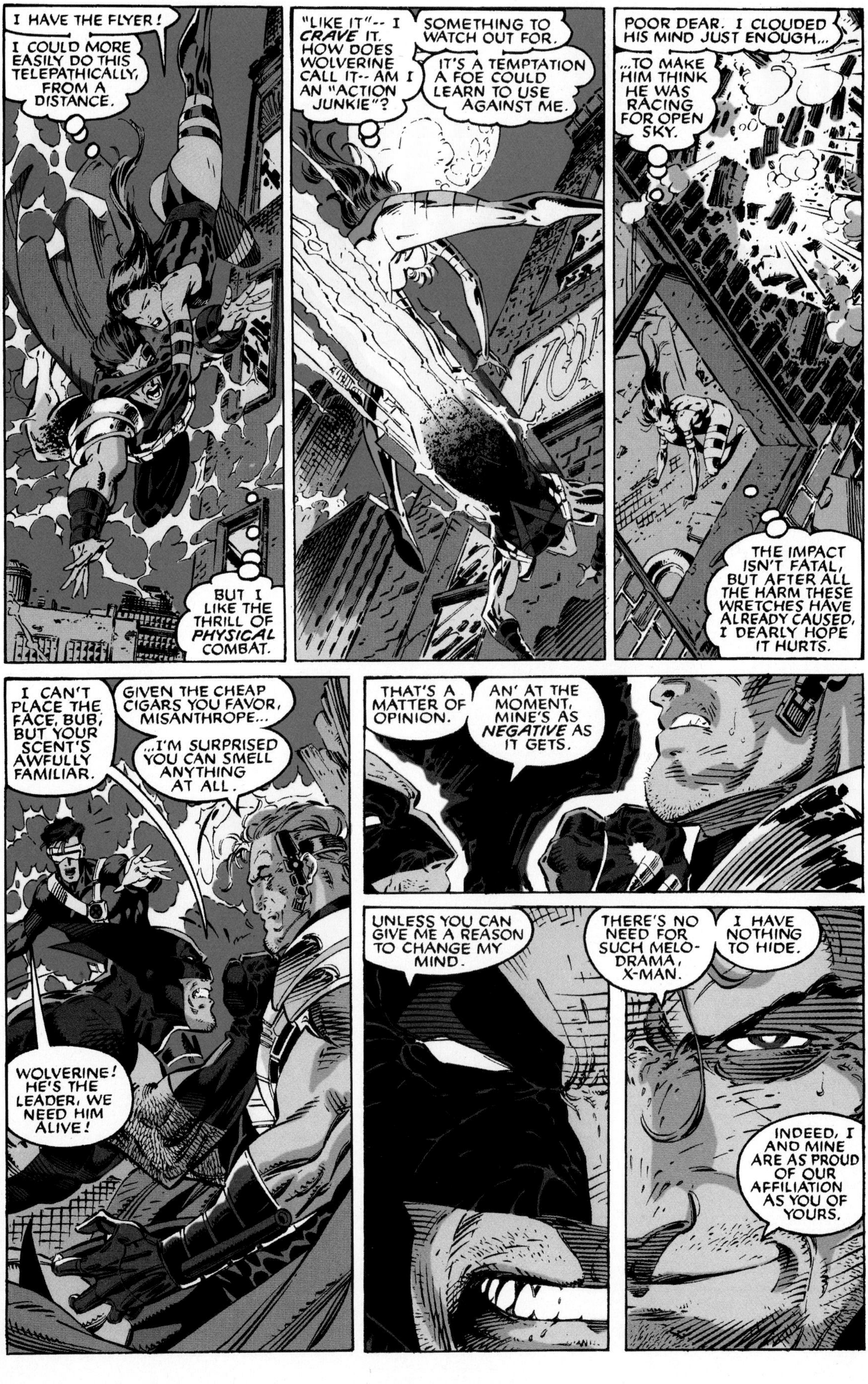
I HAVE THE FLYER!
I COULD MORE EASILY DO THIS TELEPATHICALLY, FROM A DISTANCE.
BUT I LIKE THE THRILL OF *PHYSICAL* COMBAT.
"LIKE IT"-- I *CRAVE* IT. HOW DOES WOLVERINE CALL IT-- AM I AN "ACTION JUNKIE"?
SOMETHING TO WATCH OUT FOR.
IT'S A TEMPTATION A FOE COULD LEARN TO USE AGAINST ME.
POOR DEAR. I CLOUDED HIS MIND JUST ENOUGH...
...TO MAKE HIM THINK HE WAS RACING FOR OPEN SKY.
THE IMPACT ISN'T FATAL, BUT AFTER ALL THE HARM THESE WRETCHES HAVE ALREADY CAUSED, I DEARLY HOPE IT HURTS.
I CAN'T PLACE THE FACE, BUB, BUT YOUR SCENT'S AWFULLY FAMILIAR.
GIVEN THE CHEAP CIGARS YOU FAVOR, MISANTHROPE...
...I'M SURPRISED YOU CAN SMELL ANYTHING AT ALL.
WOLVERINE! HE'S THE LEADER, WE NEED HIM ALIVE!
THAT'S A MATTER OF OPINION.
AN' AT THE MOMENT, MINE'S AS *NEGATIVE* AS IT GETS.
UNLESS YOU CAN GIVE ME A REASON TO CHANGE MY MIND.
THERE'S NO NEED FOR SUCH MELO-DRAMA, X-MAN.
I HAVE NOTHING TO HIDE.
INDEED, I AND MINE ARE AS PROUD OF OUR AFFILIATION AS YOU OF YOURS.

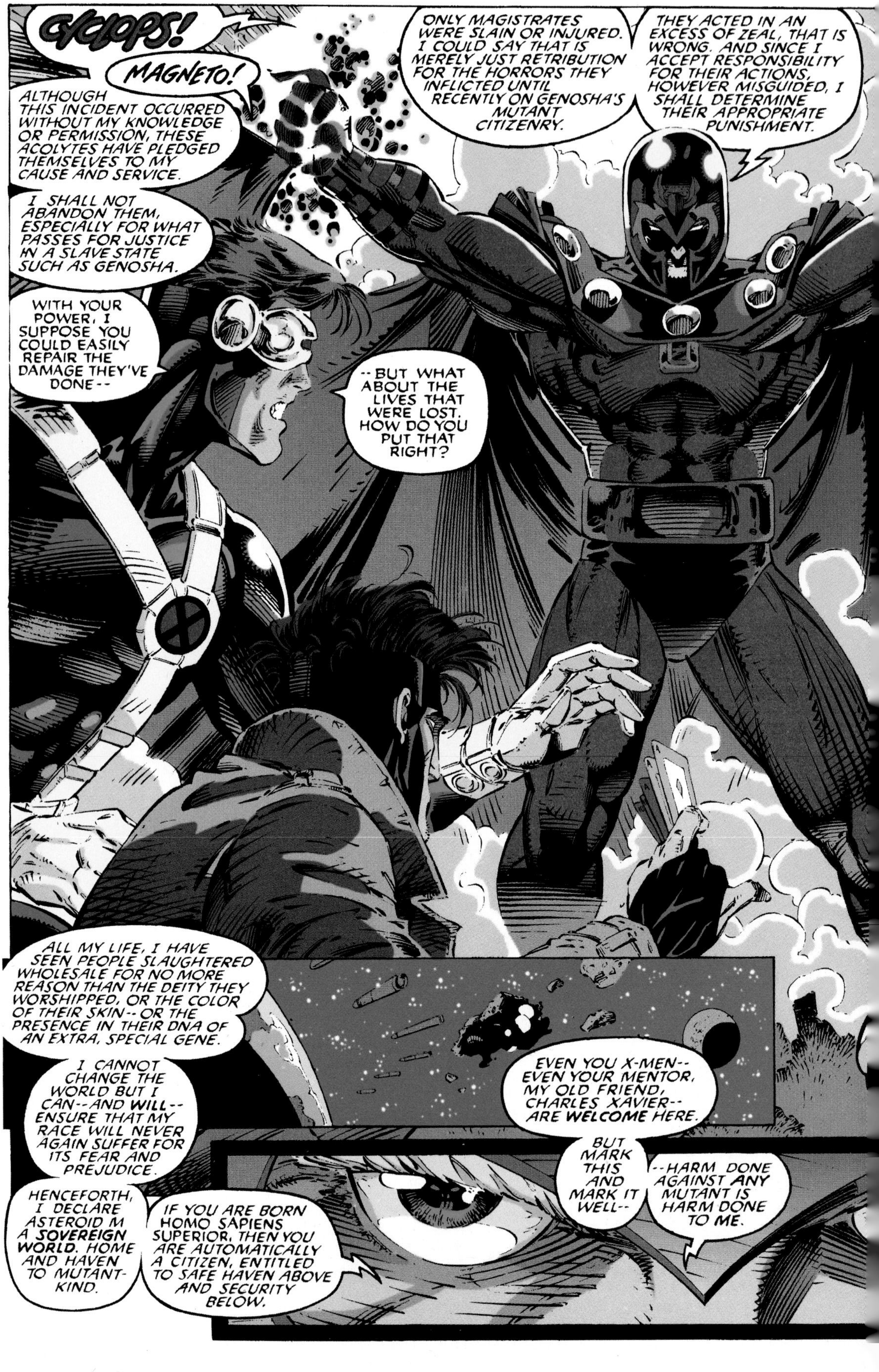
CYCLOPS!
MAGNETO!
ALTHOUGH THIS INCIDENT OCCURRED WITHOUT MY KNOWLEDGE OR PERMISSION, THESE ACOLYTES HAVE PLEDGED THEMSELVES TO MY CAUSE AND SERVICE.
ONLY MAGISTRATES WERE SLAIN OR INJURED. I COULD SAY THAT IS MERELY JUST RETRIBUTION FOR THE HORRORS THEY INFLICTED UNTIL RECENTLY ON GENOSHA'S MUTANT CITIZENRY.
THEY ACTED IN AN EXCESS OF ZEAL, THAT IS WRONG. AND SINCE I ACCEPT RESPONSIBILITY FOR THEIR ACTIONS, HOWEVER MISGUIDED, I SHALL DETERMINE THEIR APPROPRIATE PUNISHMENT.
I SHALL NOT ABANDON THEM, ESPECIALLY FOR WHAT PASSES FOR JUSTICE IN A SLAVE STATE SUCH AS GENOSHA.
WITH YOUR POWER, I SUPPOSE YOU COULD EASILY REPAIR THE DAMAGE THEY'VE DONE--
--BUT WHAT ABOUT THE LIVES THAT WERE LOST. HOW DO YOU PUT THAT RIGHT?
ALL MY LIFE, I HAVE SEEN PEOPLE SLAUGHTERED WHOLESALE FOR NO MORE REASON THAN THE DEITY THEY WORSHIPPED, OR THE COLOR OF THEIR SKIN-- OR THE PRESENCE IN THEIR DNA OF AN EXTRA, SPECIAL GENE.
I CANNOT CHANGE THE WORLD BUT I CAN--AND WILL-- ENSURE THAT MY RACE WILL NEVER AGAIN SUFFER FOR ITS FEAR AND PREJUDICE.
EVEN YOU X-MEN-- EVEN YOUR MENTOR, MY OLD FRIEND, CHARLES XAVIER-- ARE WELCOME HERE.
HENCEFORTH, I DECLARE ASTEROID M A SOVEREIGN WORLD, HOME AND HAVEN TO MUTANT-KIND.
IF YOU ARE BORN HOMO SAPIENS SUPERIOR, THEN YOU ARE AUTOMATICALLY A CITIZEN, ENTITLED TO SAFE HAVEN ABOVE AND SECURITY BELOW.
BUT MARK THIS AND MARK IT WELL--
--HARM DONE AGAINST ANY MUTANT IS HARM DONE TO ME.

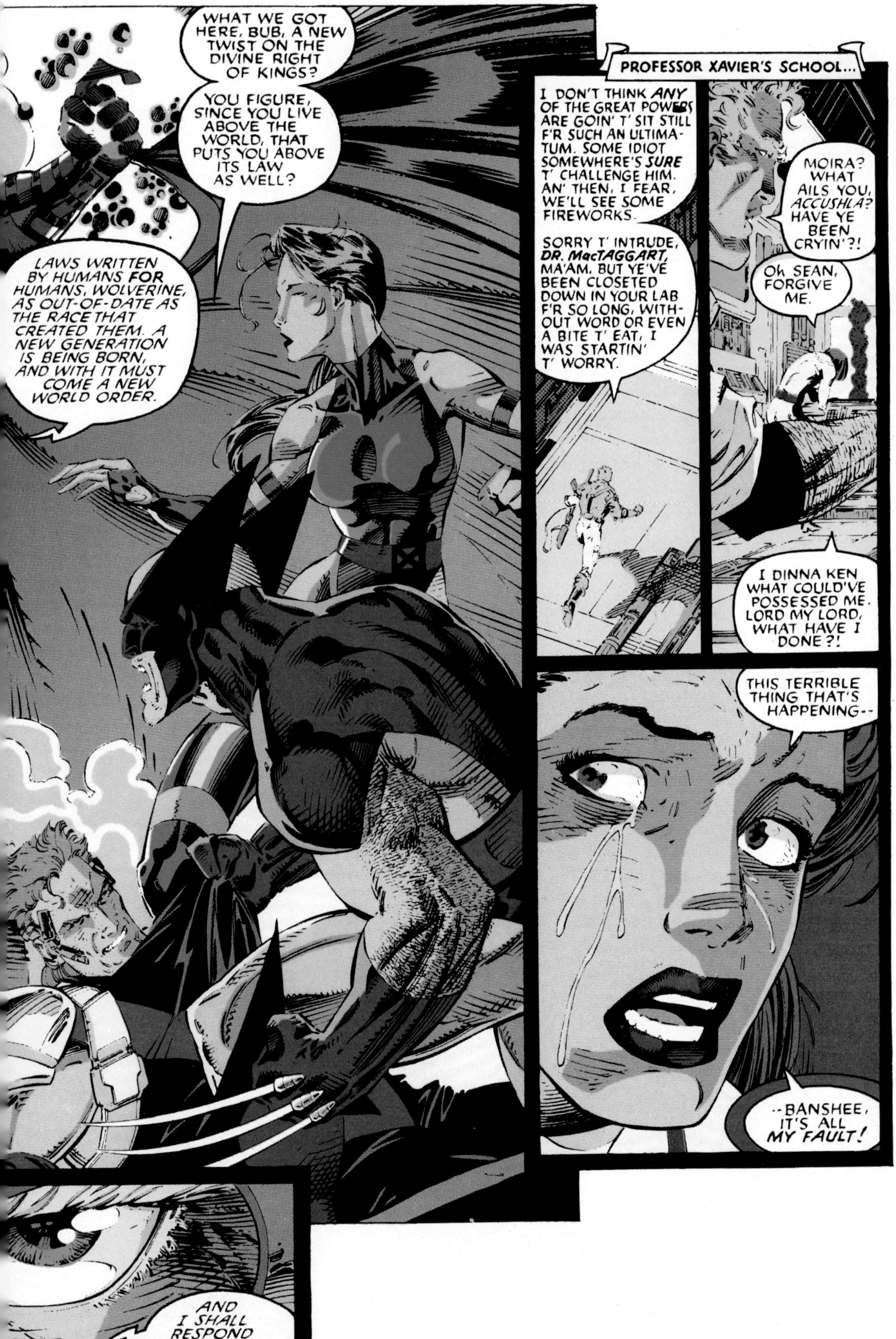
WHAT WE GOT HERE, BUB, A NEW TWIST ON THE DIVINE RIGHT OF KINGS?
YOU FIGURE, SINCE YOU LIVE ABOVE THE WORLD, THAT PUTS YOU ABOVE ITS LAW AS WELL?
LAWS WRITTEN BY HUMANS FOR HUMANS, WOLVERINE, AS OUT-OF-DATE AS THE RACE THAT CREATED THEM. A NEW GENERATION IS BEING BORN, AND WITH IT MUST COME A NEW WORLD ORDER.
AND I SHALL RESPOND ACCORDINGLY.
PROFESSOR XAVIER'S SCHOOL...
I DON'T THINK ANY OF THE GREAT POWERS ARE GOIN' T' SIT STILL F'R SUCH AN ULTIMATUM. SOME IDIOT SOMEWHERE'S SURE T' CHALLENGE HIM. AN' THEN, I FEAR, WE'LL SEE SOME FIREWORKS.
SORRY T' INTRUDE, DR. MacTAGGART, MA'AM. BUT YE'VE BEEN CLOSETED DOWN IN YOUR LAB F'R SO LONG, WITHOUT WORD OR EVEN A BITE T' EAT, I WAS STARTIN' T' WORRY.
MOIRA? WHAT AILS YOU, ACCUSHLA? HAVE YE BEEN CRYIN'?!
Oh SEAN, FORGIVE ME.
I DINNA KEN WHAT COULD'VE POSSESSED ME. LORD MY LORD, WHAT HAVE I DONE?!
THIS TERRIBLE THING THAT'S HAPPENING--
--BANSHEE, IT'S ALL MY FAULT!

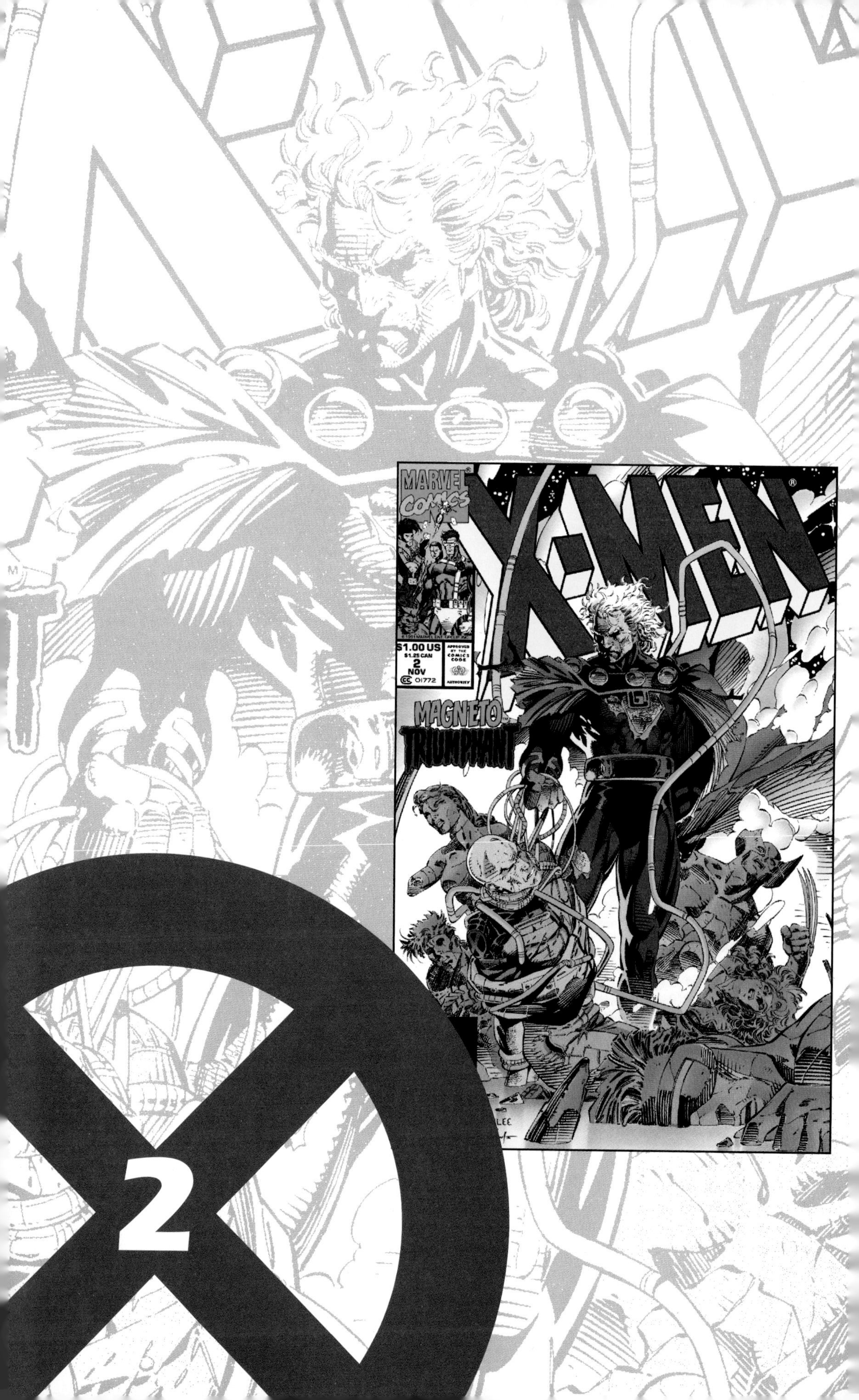
2
MARVEL COMICS
X-MEN
$1.00 US
$1.25 CAN
2
NOV
APPROVED BY THE COMICS CODE AUTHORITY
MAGNETO TRIUMPHANT

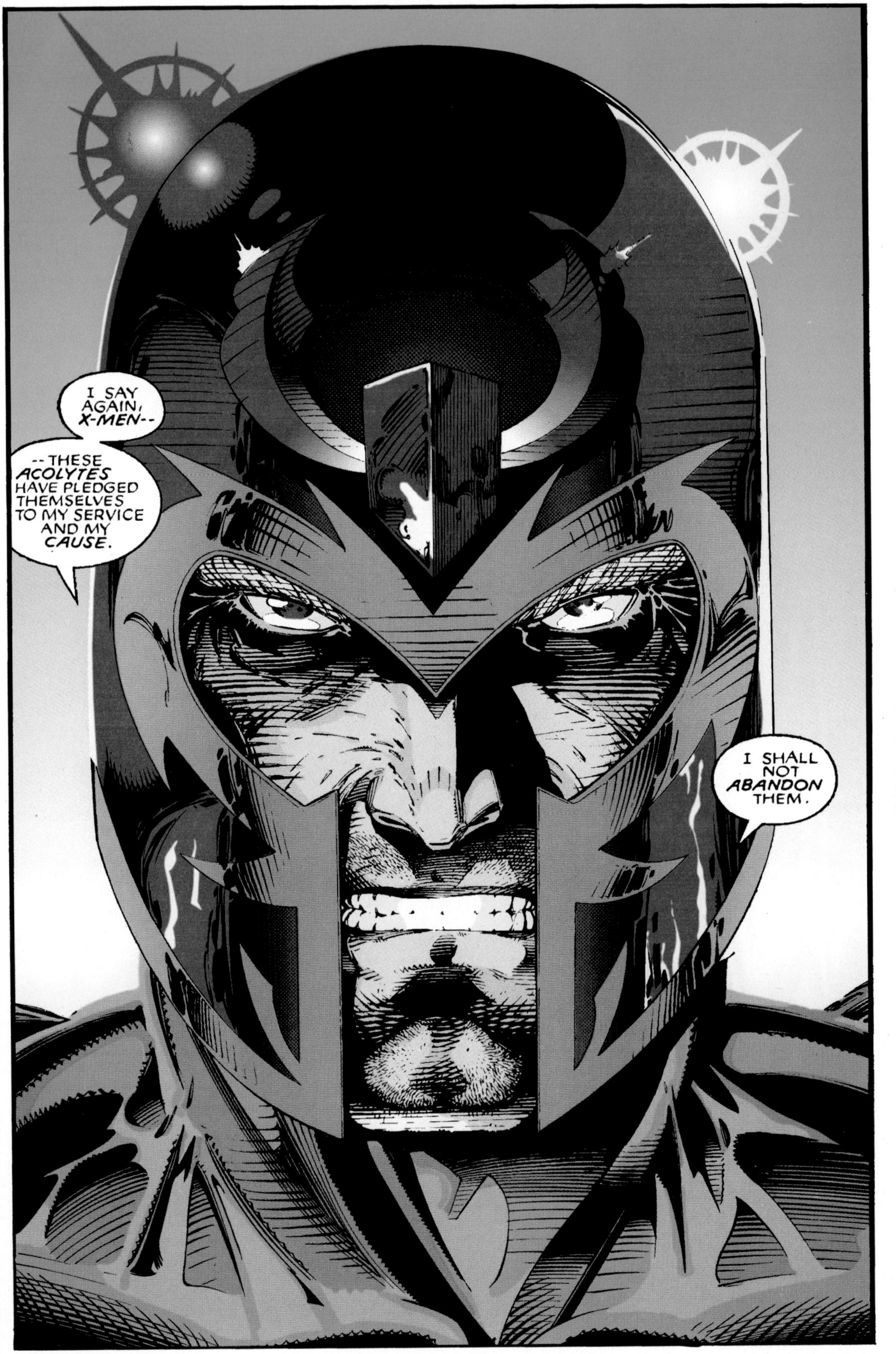
I SAY AGAIN, X-MEN--
--THESE ACOLYTES HAVE PLEDGED THEMSELVES TO MY SERVICE AND MY CAUSE.
I SHALL NOT ABANDON THEM.

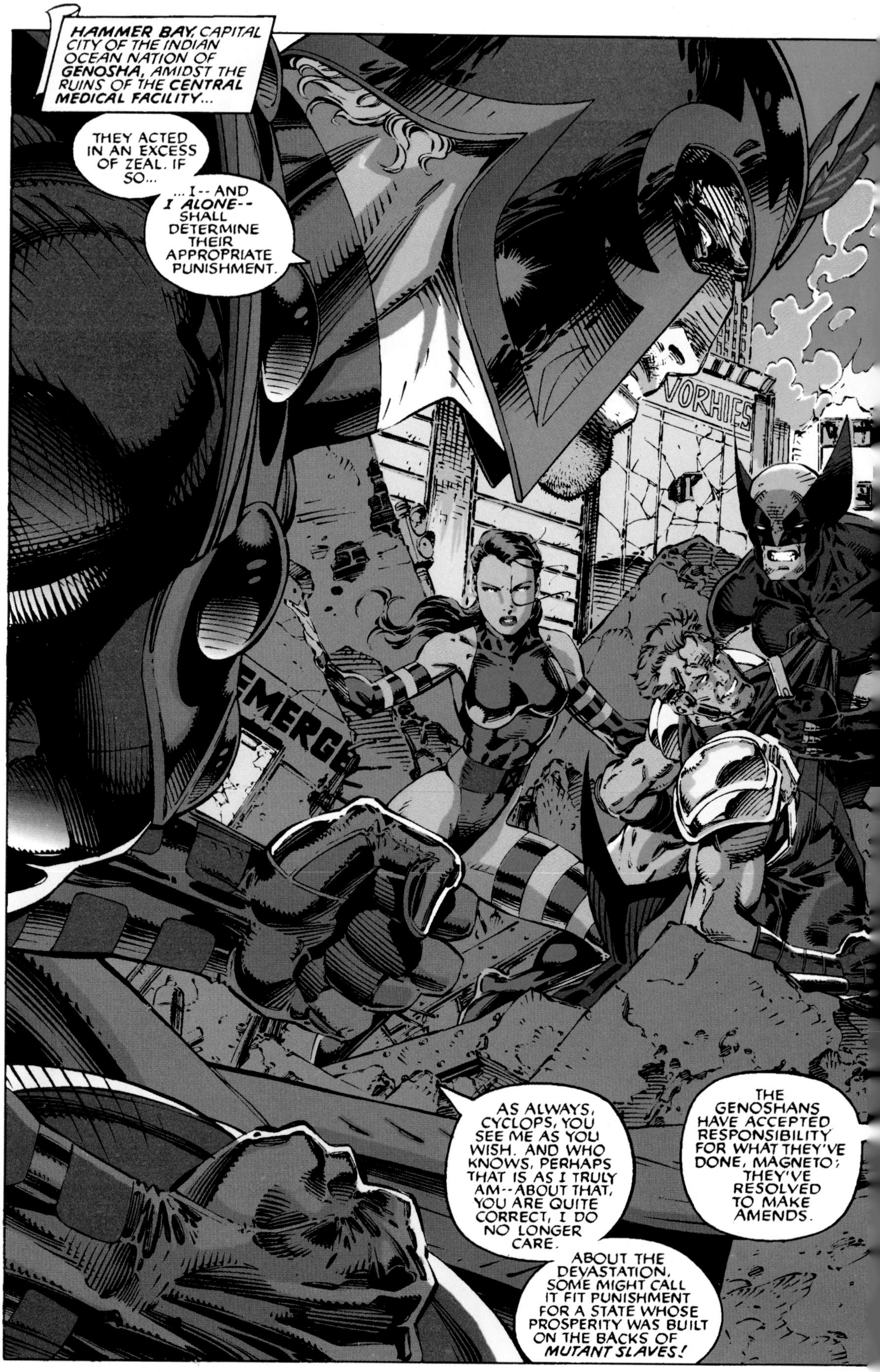
HAMMER BAY, CAPITAL CITY OF THE INDIAN OCEAN NATION OF GENOSHA, AMIDST THE RUINS OF THE CENTRAL MEDICAL FACILITY...
THEY ACTED IN AN EXCESS OF ZEAL. IF SO...
...I--AND I ALONE--SHALL DETERMINE THEIR APPROPRIATE PUNISHMENT.
VORHIES
EMERGE
THE GENOSHANS HAVE ACCEPTED RESPONSIBILITY FOR WHAT THEY'VE DONE, MAGNETO; THEY'VE RESOLVED TO MAKE AMENDS.
AS ALWAYS, CYCLOPS, YOU SEE ME AS YOU WISH. AND WHO KNOWS, PERHAPS THAT IS AS I TRULY AM--ABOUT THAT, YOU ARE QUITE CORRECT, I DO NO LONGER CARE.
ABOUT THE DEVASTATION, SOME MIGHT CALL IT FIT PUNISHMENT FOR A STATE WHOSE PROSPERITY WAS BUILT ON THE BACKS OF MUTANT SLAVES!

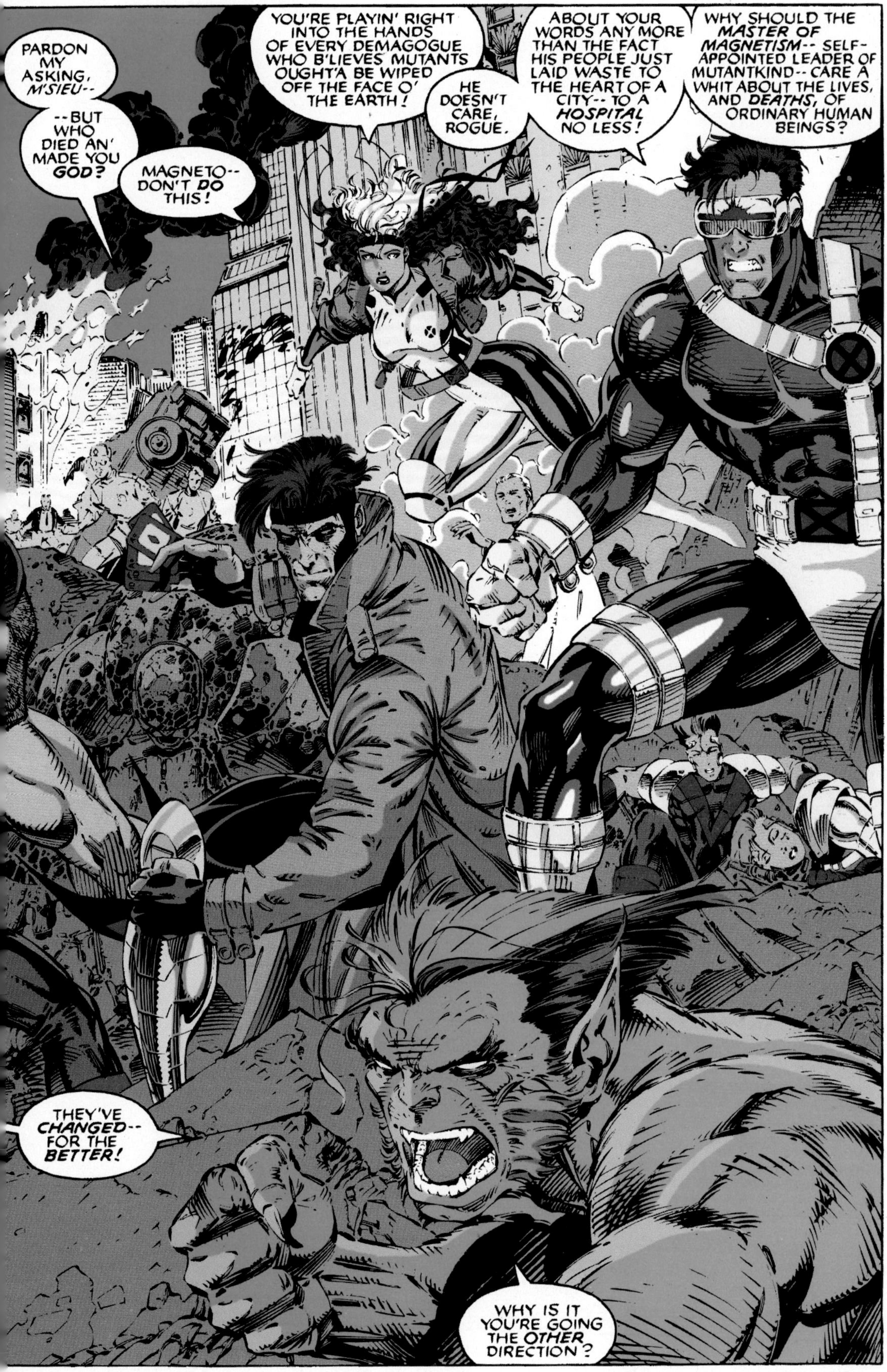
PARDON MY ASKING, M'SIEU--
--BUT WHO DIED AN' MADE YOU GOD?
MAGNETO-- DON'T DO THIS!
YOU'RE PLAYIN' RIGHT INTO THE HANDS OF EVERY DEMAGOGUE WHO B'LIEVES MUTANTS OUGHT'A BE WIPED OFF THE FACE O' THE EARTH!
HE DOESN'T CARE, ROGUE.
ABOUT YOUR WORDS ANY MORE THAN THE FACT HIS PEOPLE JUST LAID WASTE TO THE HEART OF A CITY-- TO A HOSPITAL NO LESS!
WHY SHOULD THE MASTER OF MAGNETISM-- SELF-APPOINTED LEADER OF MUTANTKIND-- CARE A WHIT ABOUT THE LIVES, AND DEATHS, OF ORDINARY HUMAN BEINGS?
THEY'VE CHANGED-- FOR THE BETTER!
WHY IS IT YOU'RE GOING THE OTHER DIRECTION?

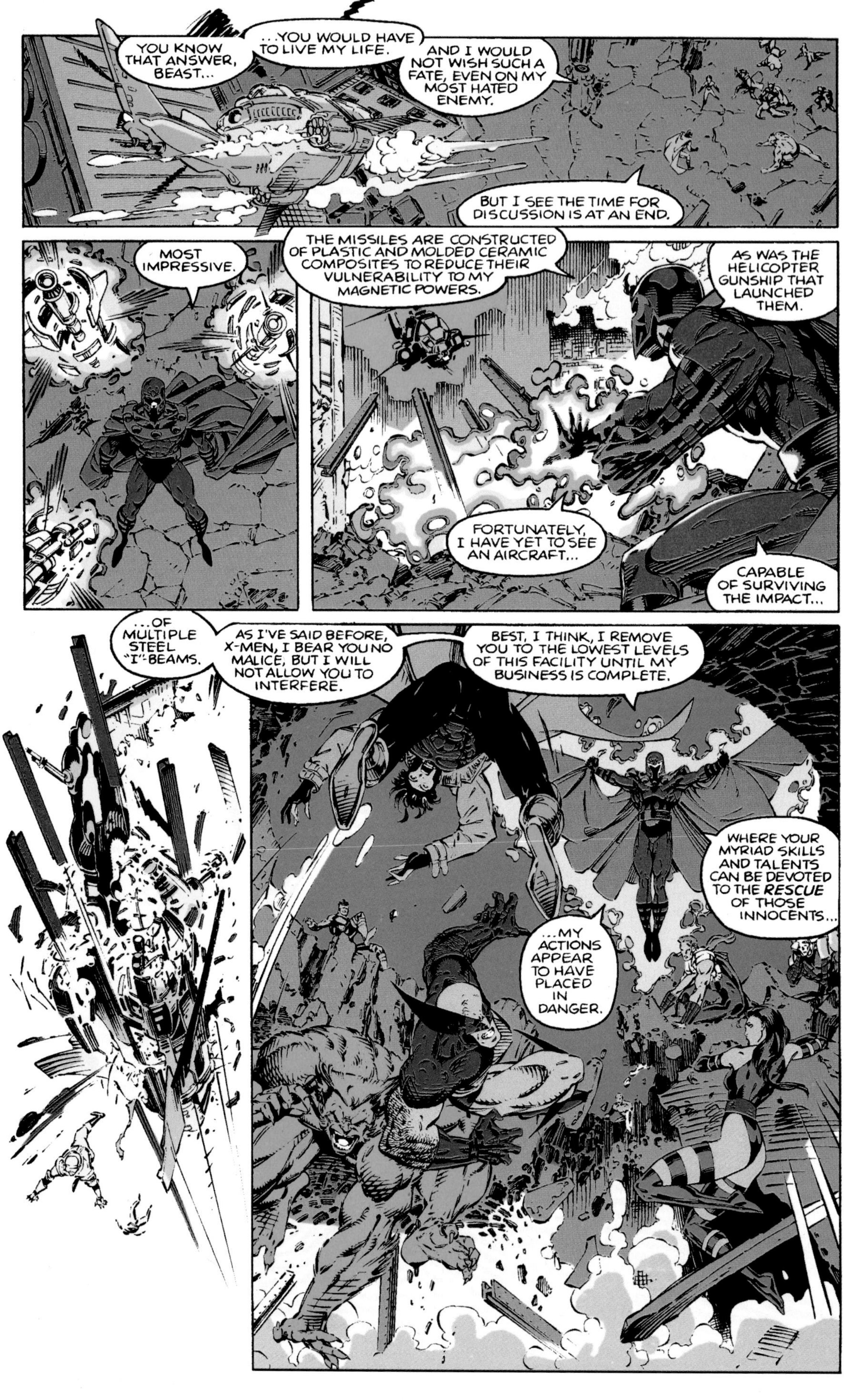
YOU KNOW THAT ANSWER, BEAST...
...YOU WOULD HAVE TO LIVE MY LIFE.
AND I WOULD NOT WISH SUCH A FATE, EVEN ON MY MOST HATED ENEMY.
BUT I SEE THE TIME FOR DISCUSSION IS AT AN END.
MOST IMPRESSIVE.
THE MISSILES ARE CONSTRUCTED OF PLASTIC AND MOLDED CERAMIC COMPOSITES TO REDUCE THEIR VULNERABILITY TO MY MAGNETIC POWERS.
AS WAS THE HELICOPTER GUNSHIP THAT LAUNCHED THEM.
FORTUNATELY, I HAVE YET TO SEE AN AIRCRAFT...
CAPABLE OF SURVIVING THE IMPACT...
...OF MULTIPLE STEEL "I"-BEAMS.
AS I'VE SAID BEFORE, X-MEN, I BEAR YOU NO MALICE, BUT I WILL NOT ALLOW YOU TO INTERFERE.
BEST, I THINK, I REMOVE YOU TO THE LOWEST LEVELS OF THIS FACILITY UNTIL MY BUSINESS IS COMPLETE.
WHERE YOUR MYRIAD SKILLS AND TALENTS CAN BE DEVOTED TO THE RESCUE OF THOSE INNOCENTS...
...MY ACTIONS APPEAR TO HAVE PLACED IN DANGER.

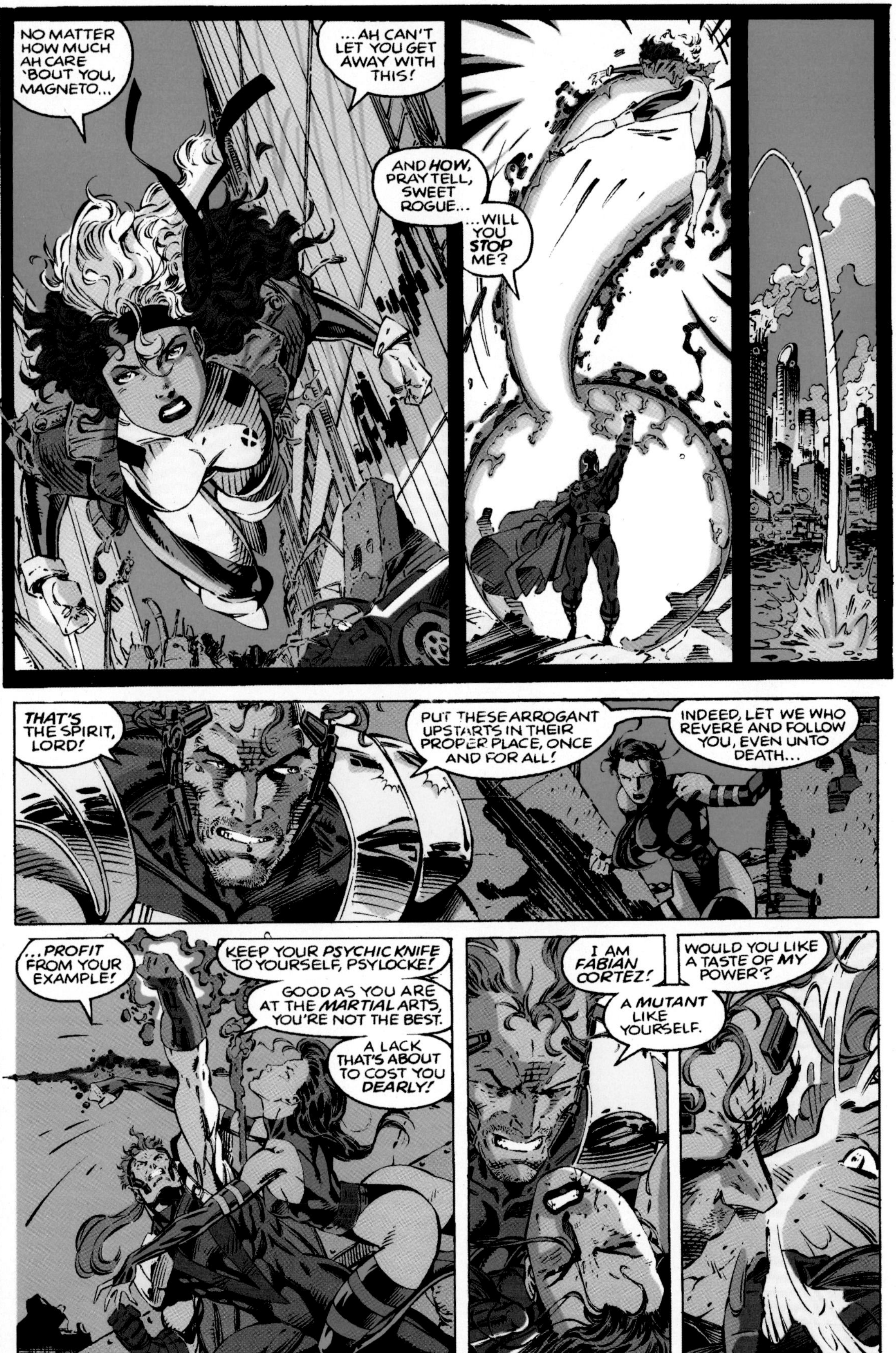
NO MATTER HOW MUCH AH CARE 'BOUT YOU, MAGNETO...
...AH CAN'T LET YOU GET AWAY WITH THIS!
AND HOW, PRAY TELL, SWEET ROGUE...
...WILL YOU STOP ME?
THAT'S THE SPIRIT, LORD!
PUT THESE ARROGANT UPSTARTS IN THEIR PROPER PLACE, ONCE AND FOR ALL!
INDEED, LET WE WHO REVERE AND FOLLOW YOU, EVEN UNTO DEATH...
...PROFIT FROM YOUR EXAMPLE!
KEEP YOUR PSYCHIC KNIFE TO YOURSELF, PSYLOCKE!
GOOD AS YOU ARE AT THE MARTIAL ARTS, YOU'RE NOT THE BEST.
A LACK THAT'S ABOUT TO COST YOU DEARLY!
I AM FABIAN CORTEZ!
A MUTANT LIKE YOURSELF.
WOULD YOU LIKE A TASTE OF MY POWER?

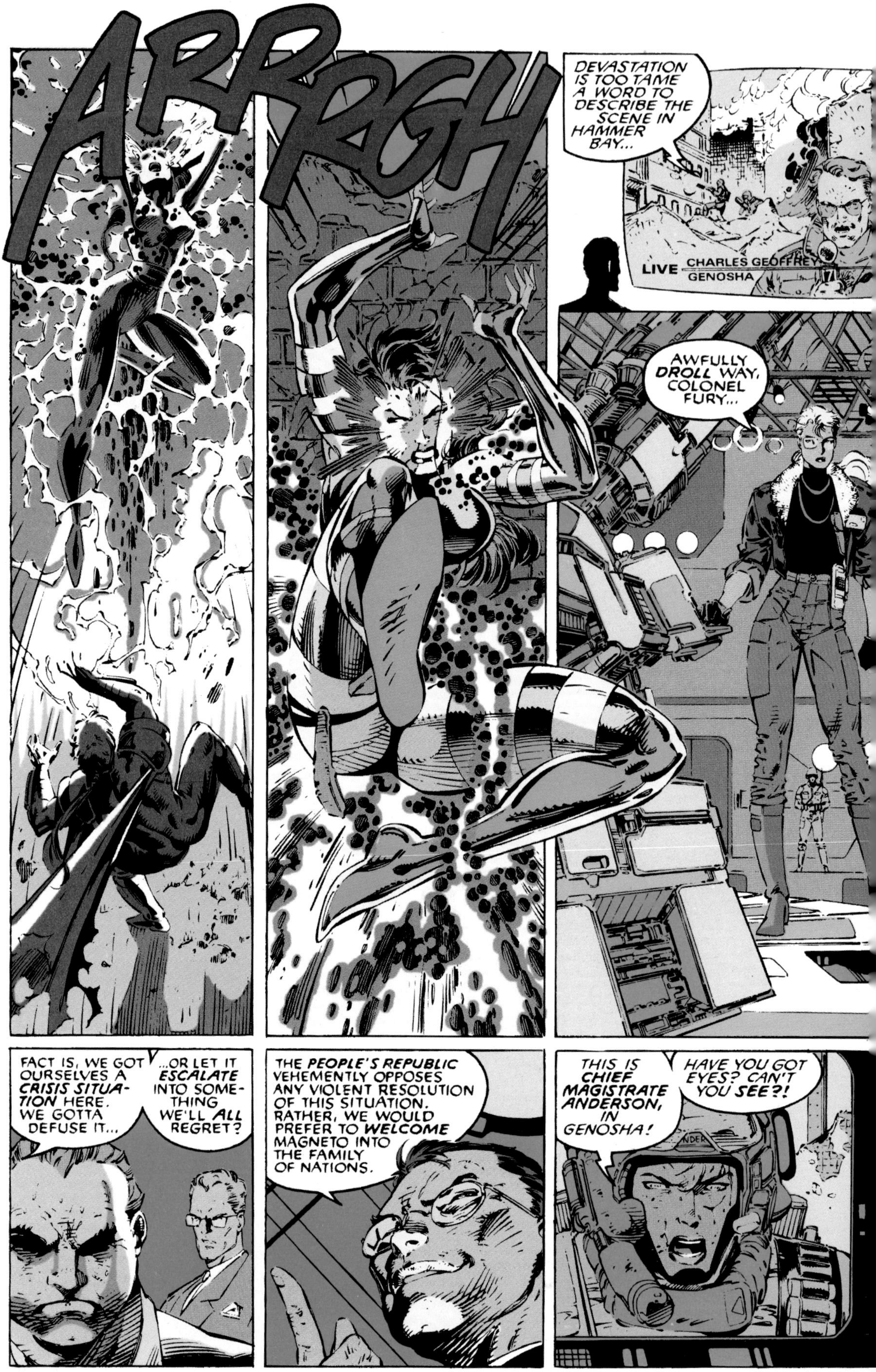
ARRRGH
DEVASTATION IS TOO TAME A WORD TO DESCRIBE THE SCENE IN HAMMER BAY...
LIVE CHARLES GEOFFREY GENOSHA
AWFULLY DROLL WAY, COLONEL FURY...
FACT IS, WE GOT OURSELVES A CRISIS SITUATION HERE. WE GOTTA DEFUSE IT...
...OR LET IT ESCALATE INTO SOMETHING WE'LL ALL REGRET?
THE PEOPLE'S REPUBLIC VEHEMENTLY OPPOSES ANY VIOLENT RESOLUTION OF THIS SITUATION. RATHER, WE WOULD PREFER TO WELCOME MAGNETO INTO THE FAMILY OF NATIONS.
THIS IS CHIEF MAGISTRATE ANDERSON, IN GENOSHA!
HAVE YOU GOT EYES? CAN'T YOU SEE?!

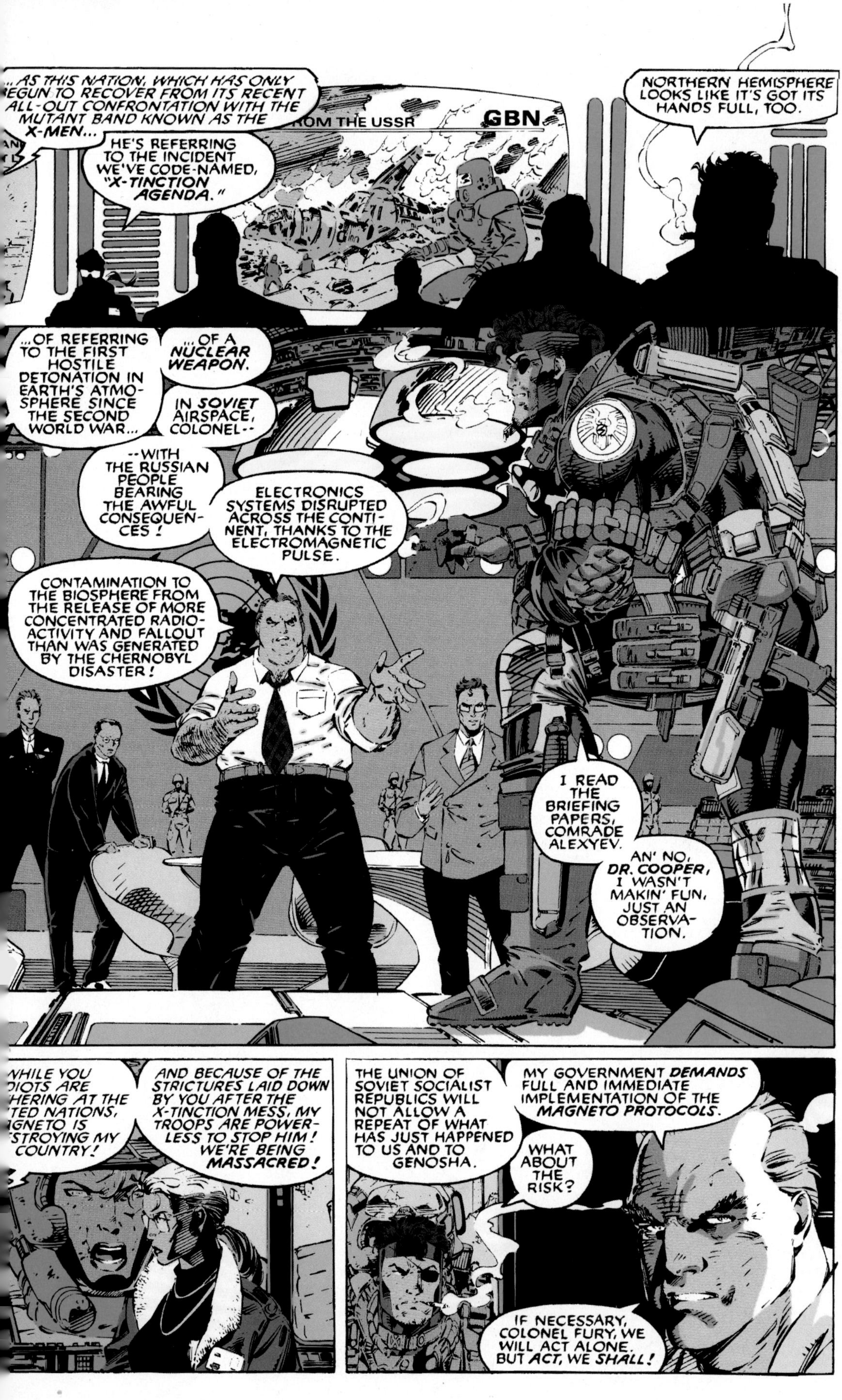

...AS THIS NATION, WHICH HAS ONLY EGUN TO RECOVER FROM ITS RECENT ALL-OUT CONFRONTATION WITH THE MUTANT BAND KNOWN AS THE X-MEN...
ROM THE USSR
GBN
HE'S REFERRING TO THE INCIDENT WE'VE CODE-NAMED, "X-TINCTION AGENDA."
NORTHERN HEMISPHERE LOOKS LIKE IT'S GOT ITS HANDS FULL, TOO.
...OF REFERRING TO THE FIRST HOSTILE DETONATION IN EARTH'S ATMOSPHERE SINCE THE SECOND WORLD WAR...
...OF A NUCLEAR WEAPON.
IN SOVIET AIRSPACE, COLONEL--
--WITH THE RUSSIAN PEOPLE BEARING THE AWFUL CONSEQUENCES!
ELECTRONICS SYSTEMS DISRUPTED ACROSS THE CONTINENT, THANKS TO THE ELECTROMAGNETIC PULSE.
CONTAMINATION TO THE BIOSPHERE FROM THE RELEASE OF MORE CONCENTRATED RADIOACTIVITY AND FALLOUT THAN WAS GENERATED BY THE CHERNOBYL DISASTER!
I READ THE BRIEFING PAPERS, COMRADE ALEXYEV.
AN' NO, DR. COOPER, I WASN'T MAKIN' FUN, JUST AN OBSERVATION.
WHILE YOU DIOTS ARE HERING AT THE TED NATIONS, GNETO IS STROYING MY COUNTRY!
AND BECAUSE OF THE STRICTURES LAID DOWN BY YOU AFTER THE X-TINCTION MESS, MY TROOPS ARE POWERLESS TO STOP HIM! WE'RE BEING MASSACRED!
THE UNION OF SOVIET SOCIALIST REPUBLICS WILL NOT ALLOW A REPEAT OF WHAT HAS JUST HAPPENED TO US AND TO GENOSHA.
MY GOVERNMENT DEMANDS FULL AND IMMEDIATE IMPLEMENTATION OF THE MAGNETO PROTOCOLS.
WHAT ABOUT THE RISK?
IF NECESSARY, COLONEL FURY, WE WILL ACT ALONE. BUT ACT, WE SHALL!

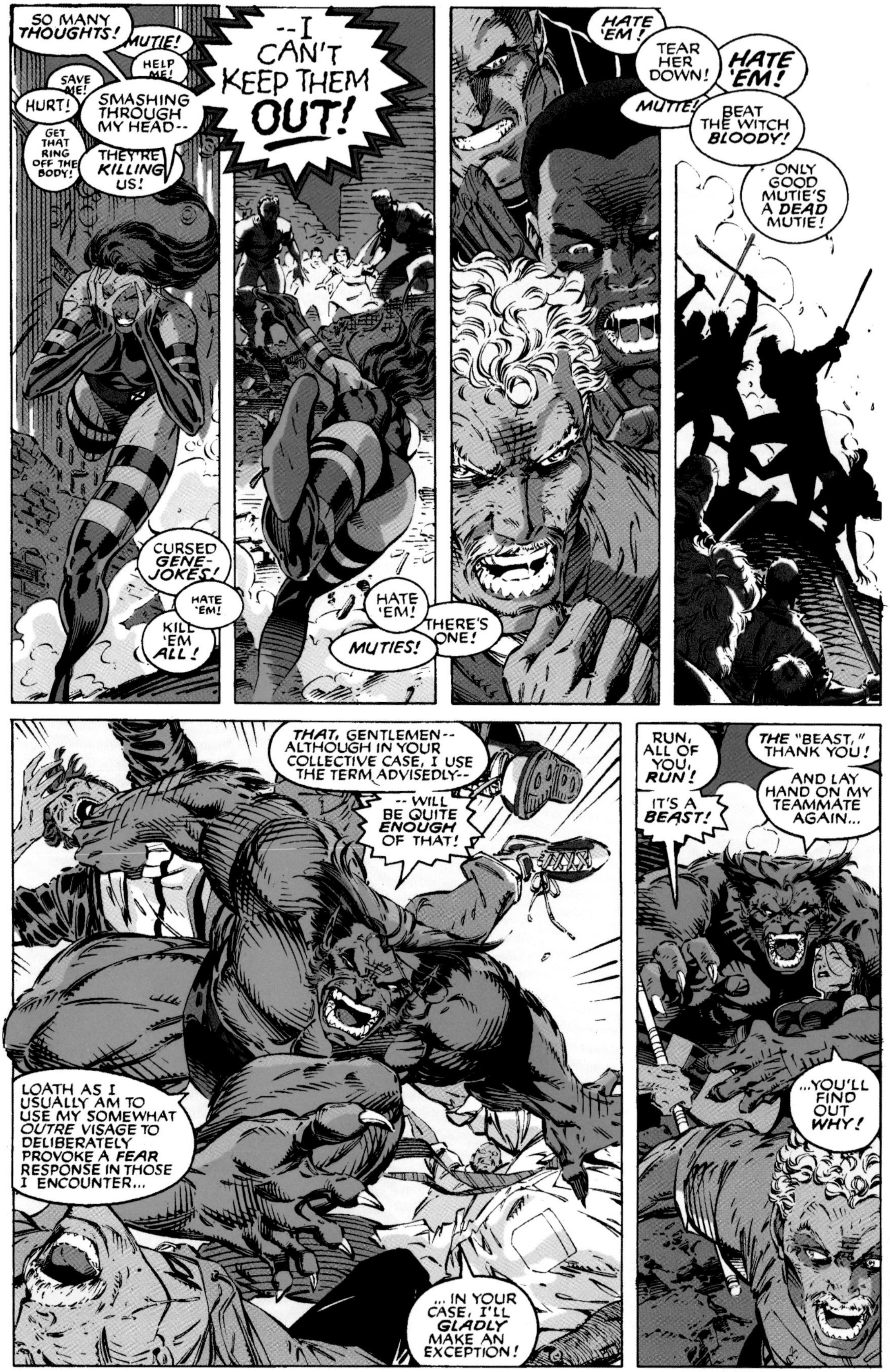
SO MANY THOUGHTS!
MUTIE!
HELP ME!
SAVE ME!
HURT!
SMASHING THROUGH MY HEAD--
GET THAT RING OFF THE BODY!
THEY'RE KILLING US!
--I CAN'T KEEP THEM OUT!
CURSED GENE-JOKES!
HATE 'EM!
KILL 'EM ALL!
HATE 'EM!
THERE'S ONE!
MUTIES!
HATE 'EM!
TEAR HER DOWN!
HATE 'EM!
MUTIE!
BEAT THE WITCH BLOODY!
ONLY GOOD MUTIE'S A DEAD MUTIE!
THAT, GENTLEMEN-- ALTHOUGH IN YOUR COLLECTIVE CASE, I USE THE TERM ADVISEDLY--
-- WILL BE QUITE ENOUGH OF THAT!
LOATH AS I USUALLY AM TO USE MY SOMEWHAT OUTRE VISAGE TO DELIBERATELY PROVOKE A FEAR RESPONSE IN THOSE I ENCOUNTER...
... IN YOUR CASE, I'LL GLADLY MAKE AN EXCEPTION!
RUN, ALL OF YOU, RUN!
IT'S A BEAST!
THE "BEAST," THANK YOU!
AND LAY HAND ON MY TEAMMATE AGAIN...
...YOU'LL FIND OUT WHY!

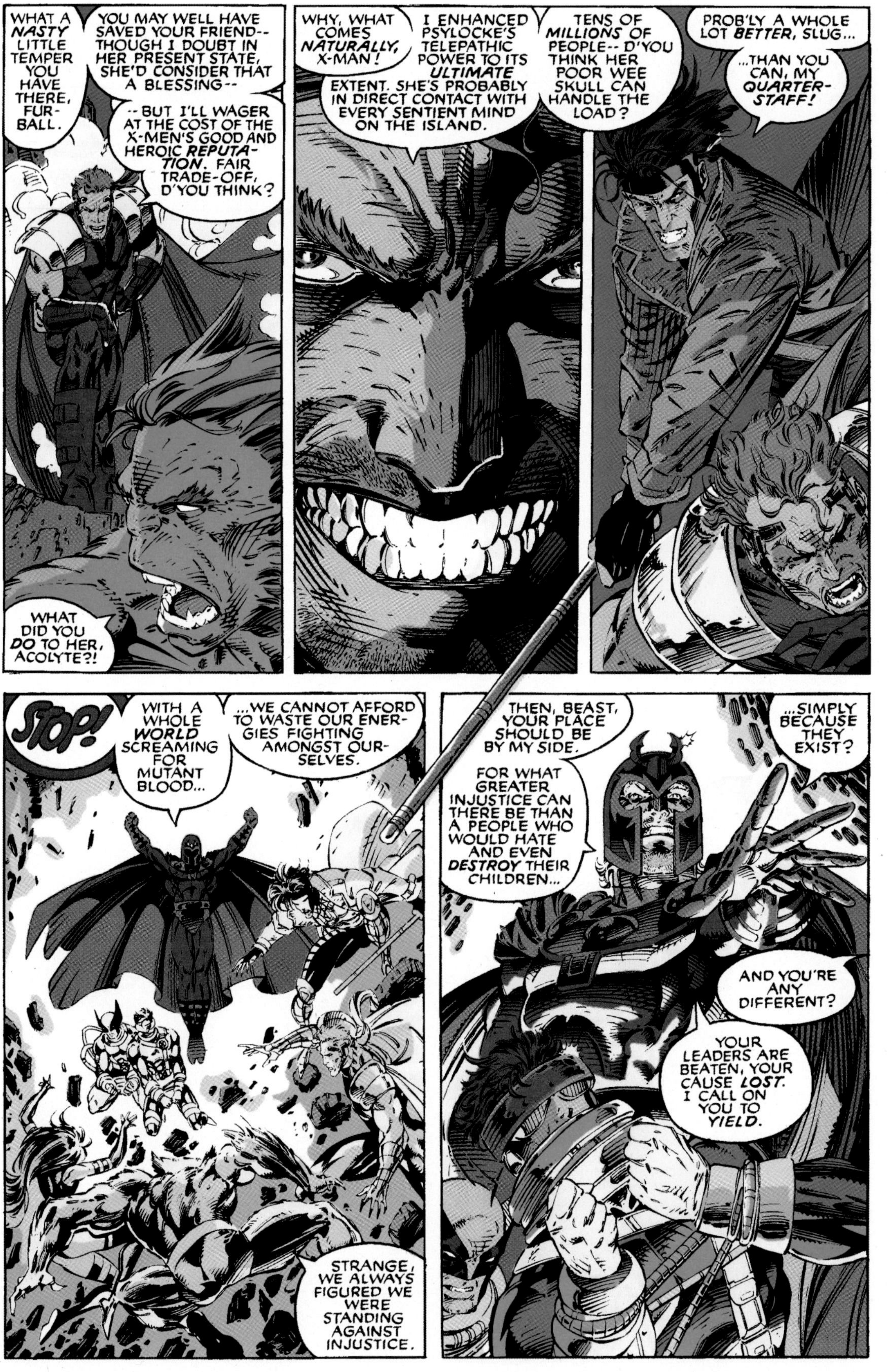
WHAT A NASTY LITTLE TEMPER YOU HAVE THERE, FUR-BALL.
YOU MAY WELL HAVE SAVED YOUR FRIEND-- THOUGH I DOUBT IN HER PRESENT STATE, SHE'D CONSIDER THAT A BLESSING--
--BUT I'LL WAGER AT THE COST OF THE X-MEN'S GOOD AND HEROIC REPUTATION. FAIR TRADE-OFF, D'YOU THINK?
WHAT DID YOU DO TO HER, ACOLYTE?!
WHY, WHAT COMES NATURALLY, X-MAN!
I ENHANCED PSYLOCKE'S TELEPATHIC POWER TO ITS ULTIMATE EXTENT. SHE'S PROBABLY IN DIRECT CONTACT WITH EVERY SENTIENT MIND ON THE ISLAND.
TENS OF MILLIONS OF PEOPLE-- D'YOU THINK HER POOR WEE SKULL CAN HANDLE THE LOAD?
PROB'LY A WHOLE LOT BETTER, SLUG...
...THAN YOU CAN, MY QUARTER-STAFF!
STOP!
WITH A WHOLE WORLD SCREAMING FOR MUTANT BLOOD...
...WE CANNOT AFFORD TO WASTE OUR ENERGIES FIGHTING AMONGST OURSELVES.
STRANGE, WE ALWAYS FIGURED WE WERE STANDING AGAINST INJUSTICE.
THEN, BEAST, YOUR PLACE SHOULD BE BY MY SIDE.
FOR WHAT GREATER INJUSTICE CAN THERE BE THAN A PEOPLE WHO WOULD HATE AND EVEN DESTROY THEIR CHILDREN...
...SIMPLY BECAUSE THEY EXIST?
AND YOU'RE ANY DIFFERENT?
YOUR LEADERS ARE BEATEN, YOUR CAUSE LOST. I CALL ON YOU TO YIELD.

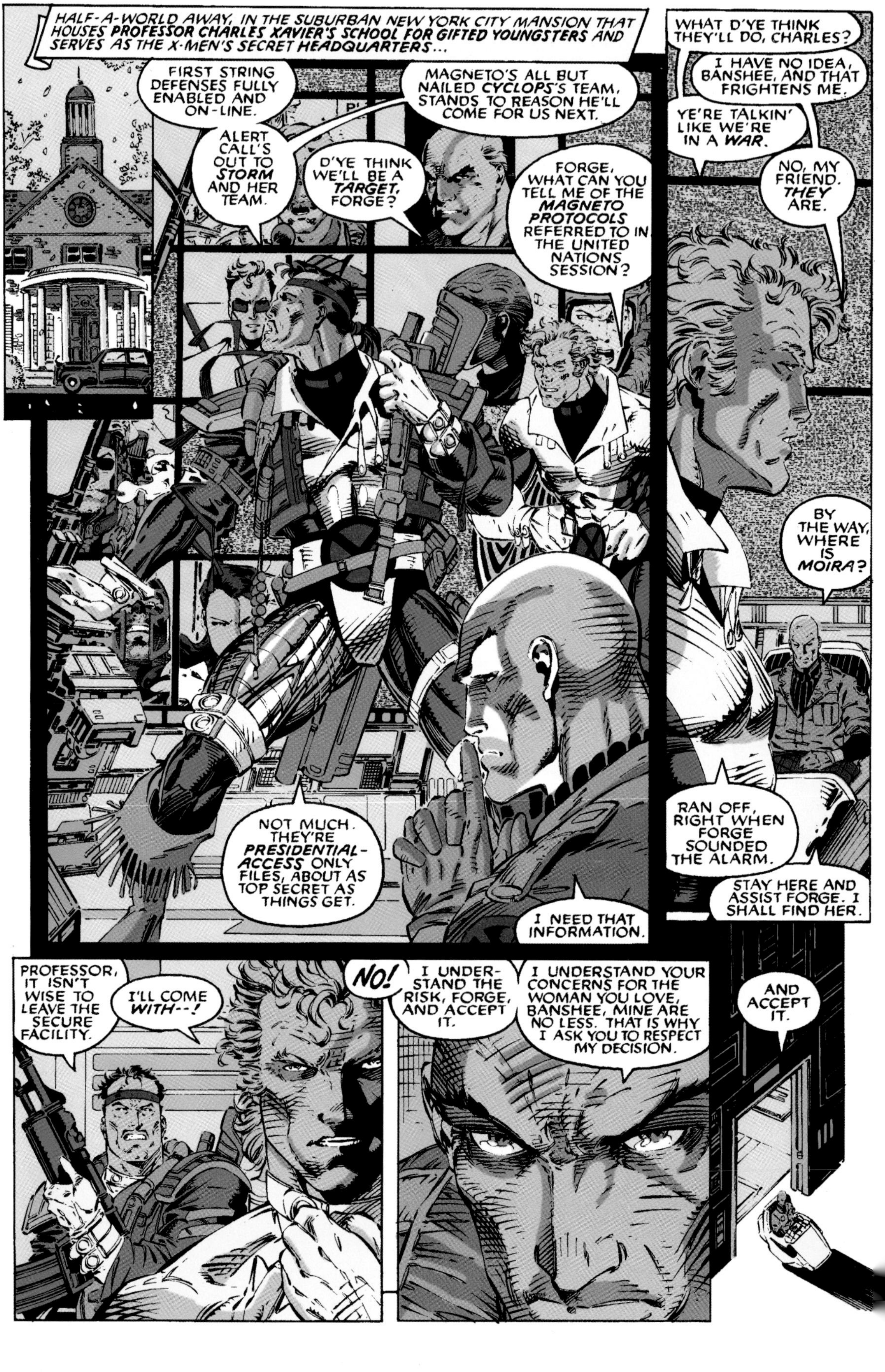
HALF-A-WORLD AWAY, IN THE SUBURBAN NEW YORK CITY MANSION THAT HOUSES PROFESSOR CHARLES XAVIER'S SCHOOL FOR GIFTED YOUNGSTERS AND SERVES AS THE X-MEN'S SECRET HEADQUARTERS...
FIRST STRING DEFENSES FULLY ENABLED AND ON-LINE.
ALERT CALL'S OUT TO STORM AND HER TEAM.
MAGNETO'S ALL BUT NAILED CYCLOPS'S TEAM. STANDS TO REASON HE'LL COME FOR US NEXT.
D'YE THINK WE'LL BE A TARGET, FORGE?
FORGE, WHAT CAN YOU TELL ME OF THE MAGNETO PROTOCOLS REFERRED TO IN THE UNITED NATIONS SESSION?
NOT MUCH. THEY'RE PRESIDENTIAL-ACCESS ONLY FILES, ABOUT AS TOP SECRET AS THINGS GET.
I NEED THAT INFORMATION.
WHAT D'YE THINK THEY'LL DO, CHARLES?
I HAVE NO IDEA, BANSHEE, AND THAT FRIGHTENS ME.
YE'RE TALKIN' LIKE WE'RE IN A WAR.
NO, MY FRIEND. THEY ARE.
BY THE WAY, WHERE IS MOIRA?
RAN OFF, RIGHT WHEN FORGE SOUNDED THE ALARM.
STAY HERE AND ASSIST FORGE. I SHALL FIND HER.
PROFESSOR, IT ISN'T WISE TO LEAVE THE SECURE FACILITY.
I'LL COME WITH--!
NO!
I UNDERSTAND THE RISK, FORGE, AND ACCEPT IT.
I UNDERSTAND YOUR CONCERNS FOR THE WOMAN YOU LOVE, BANSHEE, MINE ARE NO LESS. THAT IS WHY I ASK YOU TO RESPECT MY DECISION.
AND ACCEPT IT.

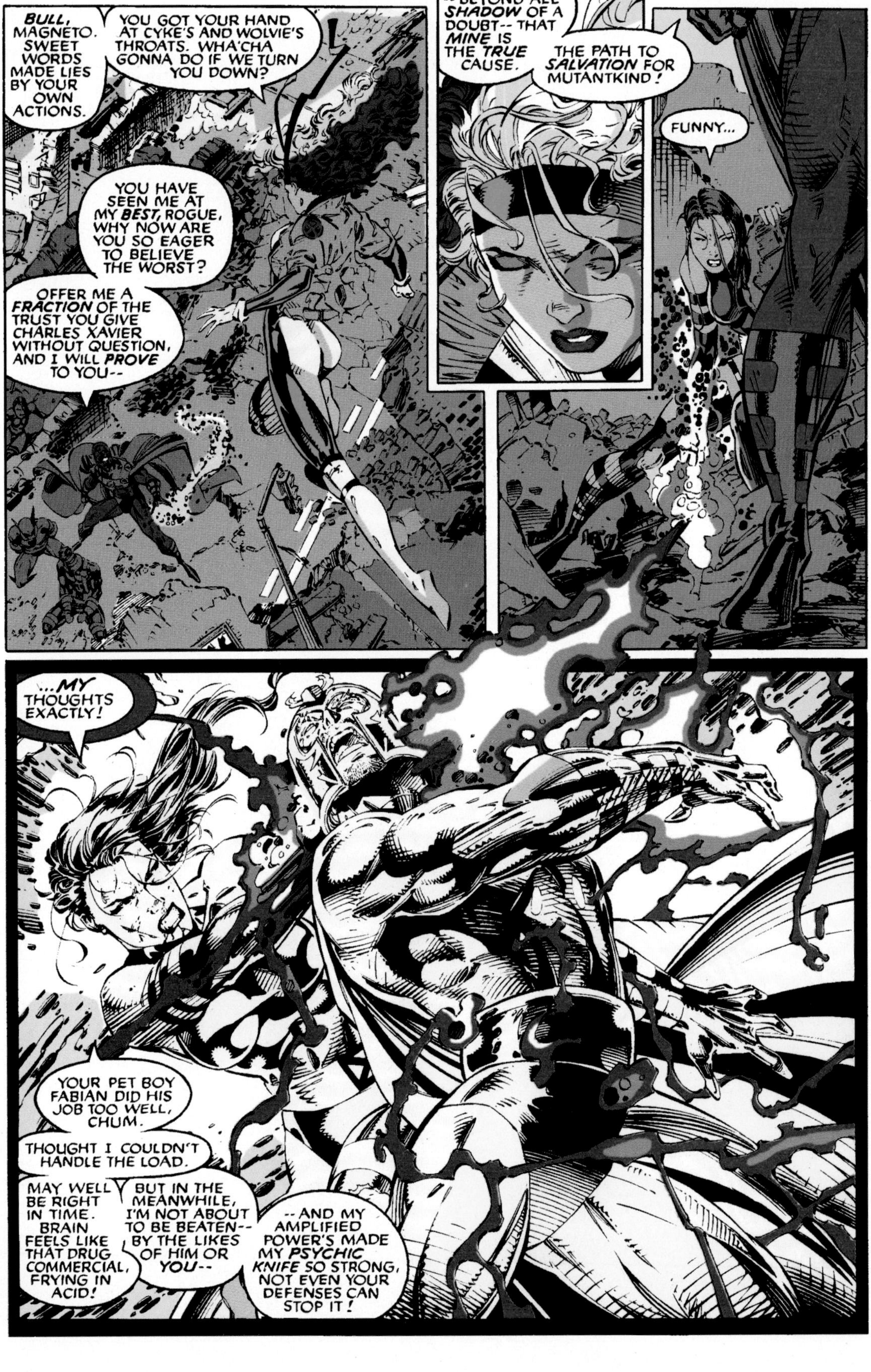
BULL, MAGNETO. SWEET WORDS MADE LIES BY YOUR OWN ACTIONS.
YOU GOT YOUR HAND AT CYKE'S AND WOLVIE'S THROATS. WHA'CHA GONNA DO IF WE TURN YOU DOWN?
YOU HAVE SEEN ME AT MY BEST, ROGUE. WHY NOW ARE YOU SO EAGER TO BELIEVE THE WORST?
OFFER ME A FRACTION OF THE TRUST YOU GIVE CHARLES XAVIER WITHOUT QUESTION, AND I WILL PROVE TO YOU--
--BEYOND ALL SHADOW OF A DOUBT-- THAT MINE IS THE TRUE CAUSE.
THE PATH TO SALVATION FOR MUTANTKIND!
FUNNY...
...MY THOUGHTS EXACTLY!
YOUR PET BOY FABIAN DID HIS JOB TOO WELL, CHUM.
THOUGHT I COULDN'T HANDLE THE LOAD.
MAY WELL BE RIGHT IN TIME. BRAIN FEELS LIKE THAT DRUG COMMERCIAL, FRYING IN ACID!
BUT IN THE MEANWHILE, I'M NOT ABOUT TO BE BEATEN-- BY THE LIKES OF HIM OR YOU--
--AND MY AMPLIFIED POWER'S MADE MY PSYCHIC KNIFE SO STRONG, NOT EVEN YOUR DEFENSES CAN STOP IT!

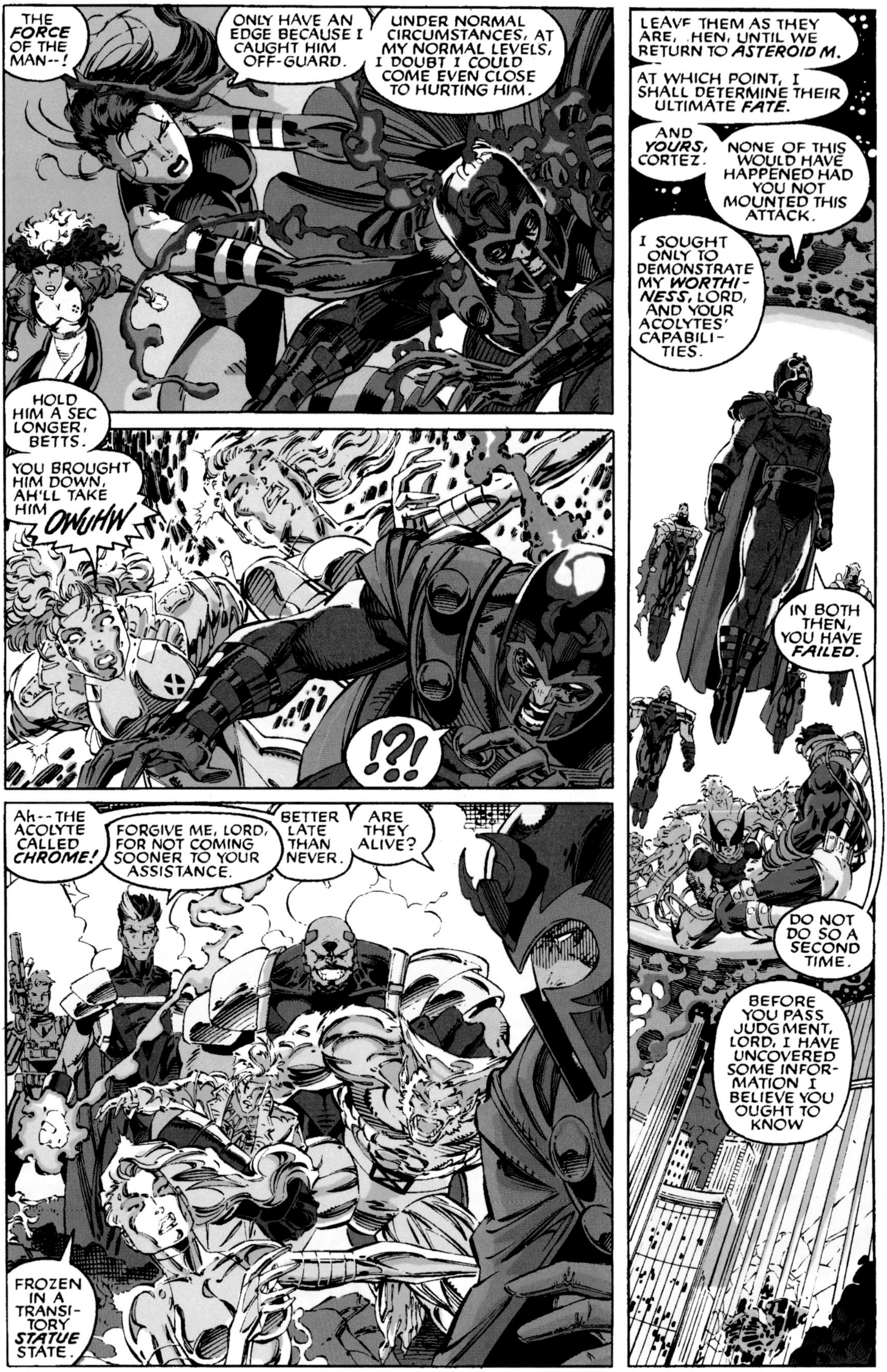
THE FORCE OF THE MAN--!
ONLY HAVE AN EDGE BECAUSE I CAUGHT HIM OFF-GUARD.
UNDER NORMAL CIRCUMSTANCES, AT MY NORMAL LEVELS, I DOUBT I COULD COME EVEN CLOSE TO HURTING HIM.
HOLD HIM A SEC LONGER, BETTS.
YOU BROUGHT HIM DOWN, AH'LL TAKE HIM
OWUHW
!?!
Ah--THE ACOLYTE CALLED CHROME!
FORGIVE ME, LORD, FOR NOT COMING SOONER TO YOUR ASSISTANCE.
BETTER LATE THAN NEVER.
ARE THEY ALIVE?
FROZEN IN A TRANSITORY STATUE STATE.
LEAVE THEM AS THEY ARE, THEN, UNTIL WE RETURN TO ASTEROID M.
AT WHICH POINT, I SHALL DETERMINE THEIR ULTIMATE FATE.
AND YOURS, CORTEZ.
NONE OF THIS WOULD HAVE HAPPENED HAD YOU NOT MOUNTED THIS ATTACK.
I SOUGHT ONLY TO DEMONSTRATE MY WORTHINESS, LORD, AND YOUR ACOLYTES' CAPABILITIES.
IN BOTH THEN, YOU HAVE FAILED.
DO NOT DO SO A SECOND TIME.
BEFORE YOU PASS JUDGMENT, LORD, I HAVE UNCOVERED SOME INFORMATION I BELIEVE YOU OUGHT TO KNOW

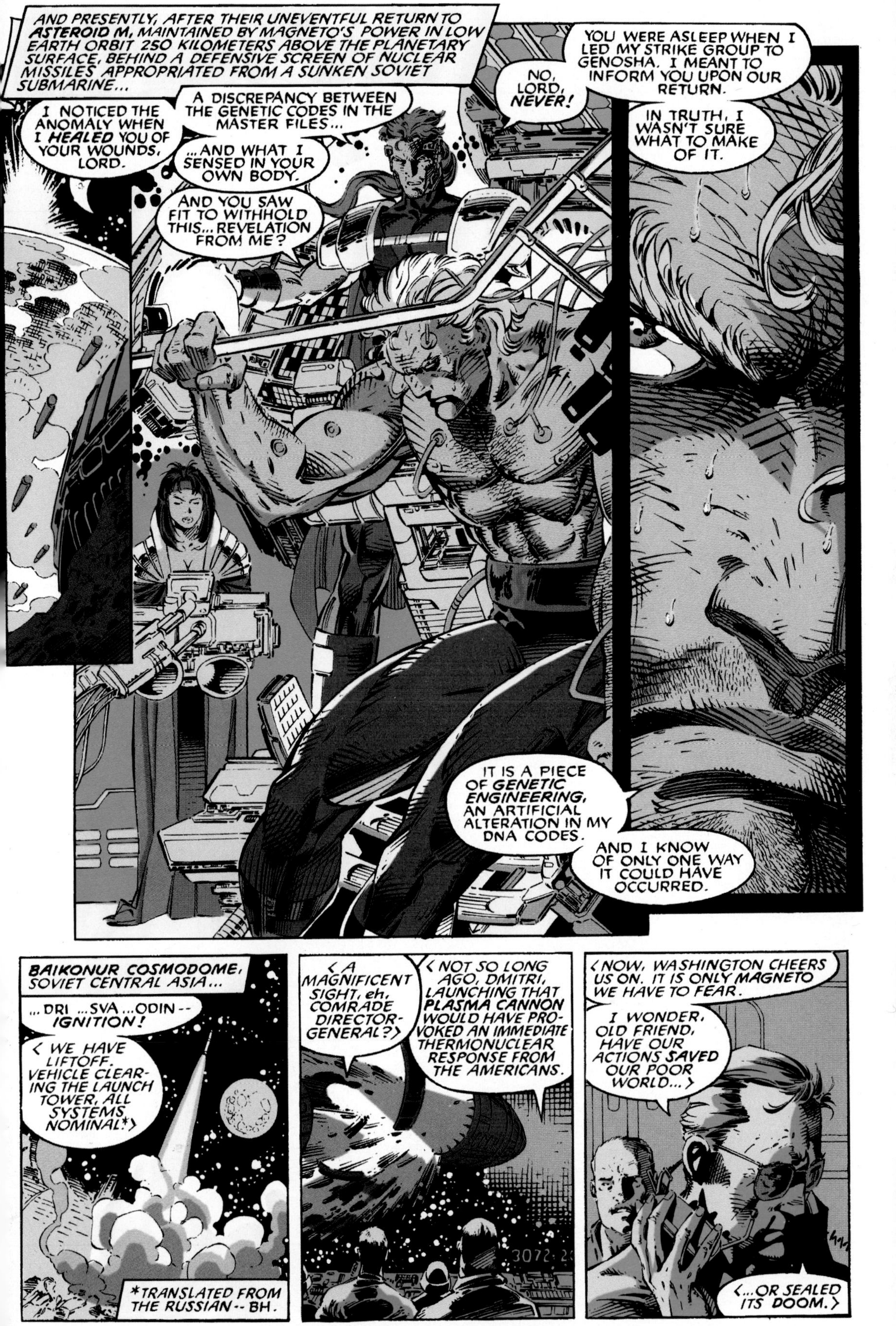
AND PRESENTLY, AFTER THEIR UNEVENTFUL RETURN TO ASTEROID M, MAINTAINED BY MAGNETO'S POWER IN LOW EARTH ORBIT 250 KILOMETERS ABOVE THE PLANETARY SURFACE, BEHIND A DEFENSIVE SCREEN OF NUCLEAR MISSILES APPROPRIATED FROM A SUNKEN SOVIET SUBMARINE...
I NOTICED THE ANOMALY WHEN I HEALED YOU OF YOUR WOUNDS, LORD.
A DISCREPANCY BETWEEN THE GENETIC CODES IN THE MASTER FILES...
...AND WHAT I SENSED IN YOUR OWN BODY.
AND YOU SAW FIT TO WITHHOLD THIS... REVELATION FROM ME?
NO, LORD, NEVER!
YOU WERE ASLEEP WHEN I LED MY STRIKE GROUP TO GENOSHA. I MEANT TO INFORM YOU UPON OUR RETURN.
IN TRUTH, I WASN'T SURE WHAT TO MAKE OF IT.
IT IS A PIECE OF GENETIC ENGINEERING, AN ARTIFICIAL ALTERATION IN MY DNA CODES.
AND I KNOW OF ONLY ONE WAY IT COULD HAVE OCCURRED.
BAIKONUR COSMODOME, SOVIET CENTRAL ASIA...
... DRI ... SVA ... ODIN -- IGNITION!
< WE HAVE LIFTOFF. VEHICLE CLEARING THE LAUNCH TOWER, ALL SYSTEMS NOMINAL!* >
*TRANSLATED FROM THE RUSSIAN -- BH.
< A MAGNIFICENT SIGHT, eh, COMRADE DIRECTOR-GENERAL? >
< NOT SO LONG AGO, DMITRI, LAUNCHING THAT PLASMA CANNON WOULD HAVE PROVOKED AN IMMEDIATE THERMONUCLEAR RESPONSE FROM THE AMERICANS.
< NOW, WASHINGTON CHEERS US ON. IT IS ONLY MAGNETO WE HAVE TO FEAR.
I WONDER, OLD FRIEND, HAVE OUR ACTIONS SAVED OUR POOR WORLD... >
< ...OR SEALED ITS DOOM. >

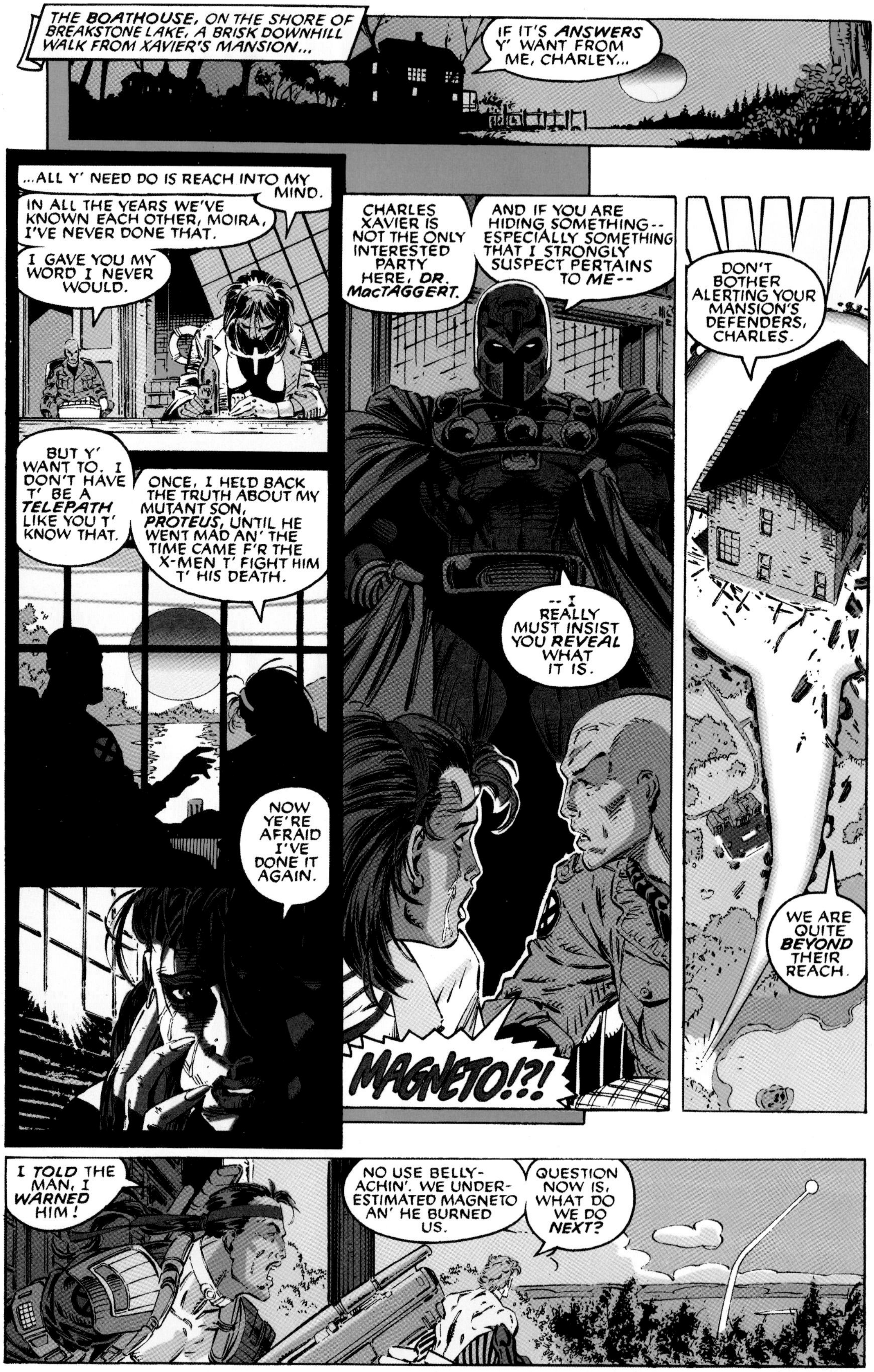
THE BOATHOUSE, ON THE SHORE OF BREAKSTONE LAKE, A BRISK DOWNHILL WALK FROM XAVIER'S MANSION...
IF IT'S ANSWERS Y' WANT FROM ME, CHARLEY...
...ALL Y' NEED DO IS REACH INTO MY MIND.
IN ALL THE YEARS WE'VE KNOWN EACH OTHER, MOIRA, I'VE NEVER DONE THAT.
I GAVE YOU MY WORD I NEVER WOULD.
BUT Y' WANT TO. I DON'T HAVE T' BE A TELEPATH LIKE YOU T' KNOW THAT.
ONCE, I HELD BACK THE TRUTH ABOUT MY MUTANT SON, PROTEUS, UNTIL HE WENT MAD AN' THE TIME CAME F'R THE X-MEN T' FIGHT HIM T' HIS DEATH.
NOW YE'RE AFRAID I'VE DONE IT AGAIN.
CHARLES XAVIER IS NOT THE ONLY INTERESTED PARTY HERE, DR. MacTAGGERT.
AND IF YOU ARE HIDING SOMETHING-- ESPECIALLY SOMETHING THAT I STRONGLY SUSPECT PERTAINS TO ME--
--I REALLY MUST INSIST YOU REVEAL WHAT IT IS.
MAGNETO!?!
DON'T BOTHER ALERTING YOUR MANSION'S DEFENDERS, CHARLES.
WE ARE QUITE BEYOND THEIR REACH.
I TOLD THE MAN, I WARNED HIM!
NO USE BELLY-ACHIN'. WE UNDER-ESTIMATED MAGNETO AN' HE BURNED US.
QUESTION NOW IS, WHAT DO WE DO NEXT?

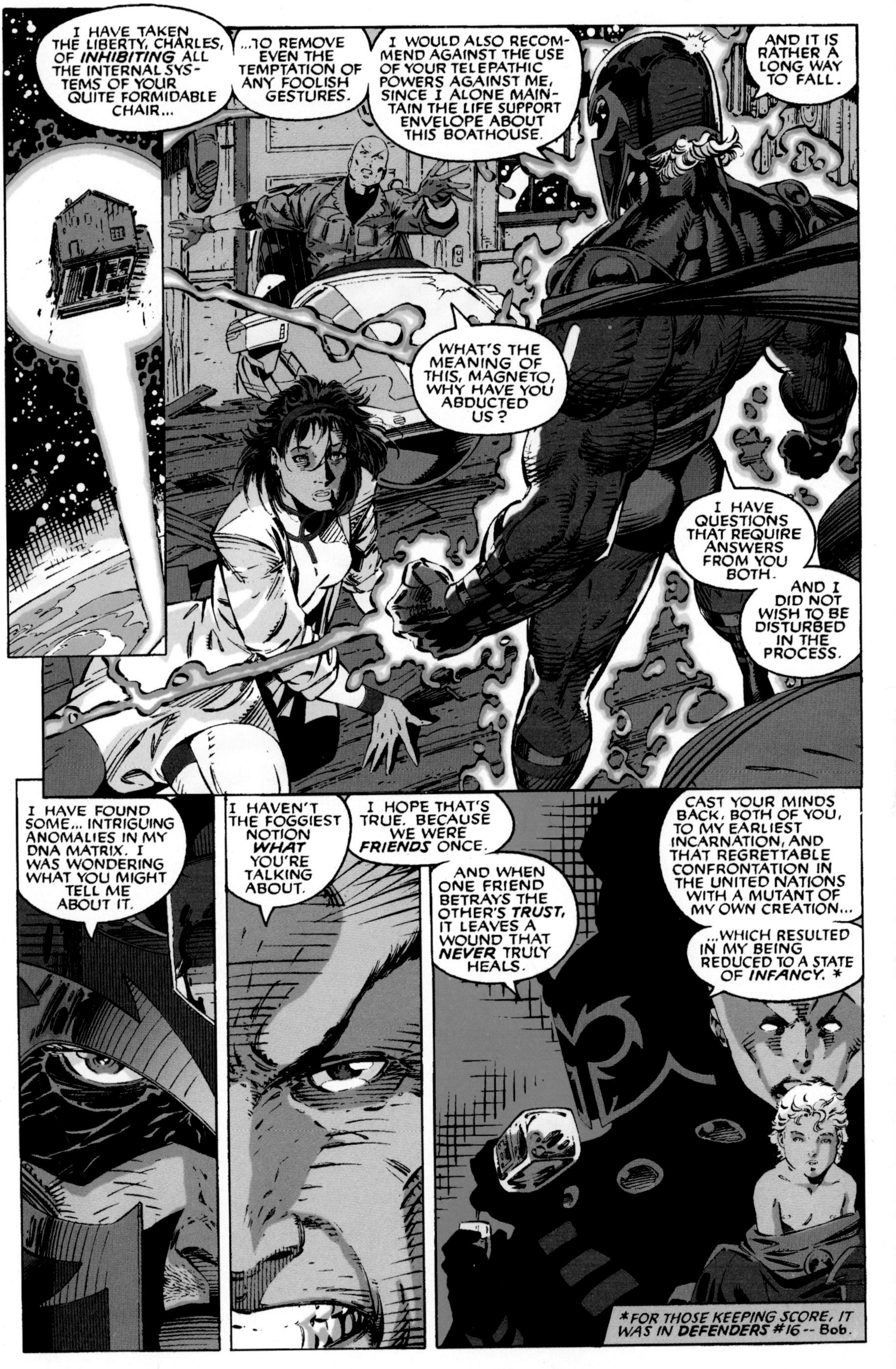
I HAVE TAKEN THE LIBERTY, CHARLES, OF INHIBITING ALL THE INTERNAL SYSTEMS OF YOUR QUITE FORMIDABLE CHAIR...
...TO REMOVE EVEN THE TEMPTATION OF ANY FOOLISH GESTURES.
I WOULD ALSO RECOMMEND AGAINST THE USE OF YOUR TELEPATHIC POWERS AGAINST ME, SINCE I ALONE MAINTAIN THE LIFE SUPPORT ENVELOPE ABOUT THIS BOATHOUSE.
AND IT IS RATHER A LONG WAY TO FALL.
WHAT'S THE MEANING OF THIS, MAGNETO, WHY HAVE YOU ABDUCTED US?
I HAVE QUESTIONS THAT REQUIRE ANSWERS FROM YOU BOTH.
AND I DID NOT WISH TO BE DISTURBED IN THE PROCESS.
I HAVE FOUND SOME... INTRIGUING ANOMALIES IN MY DNA MATRIX. I WAS WONDERING WHAT YOU MIGHT TELL ME ABOUT IT.
I HAVEN'T THE FOGGIEST NOTION WHAT YOU'RE TALKING ABOUT.
I HOPE THAT'S TRUE. BECAUSE WE WERE FRIENDS ONCE.
AND WHEN ONE FRIEND BETRAYS THE OTHER'S TRUST, IT LEAVES A WOUND THAT NEVER TRULY HEALS.
CAST YOUR MINDS BACK, BOTH OF YOU, TO MY EARLIEST INCARNATION, AND THAT REGRETTABLE CONFRONTATION IN THE UNITED NATIONS WITH A MUTANT OF MY OWN CREATION...
...WHICH RESULTED IN MY BEING REDUCED TO A STATE OF INFANCY. *
*FOR THOSE KEEPING SCORE, IT WAS IN DEFENDERS #16 -- Bob.

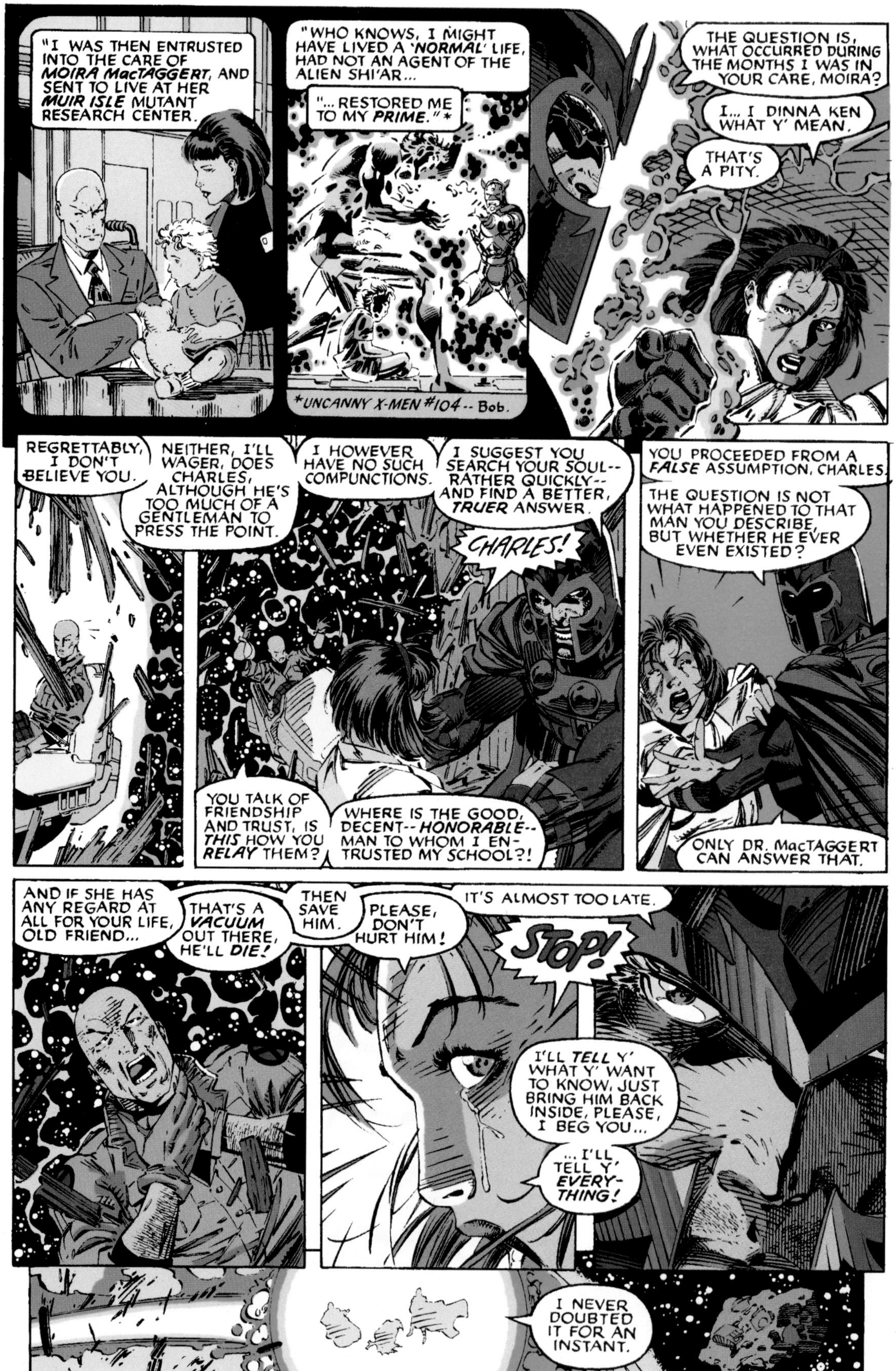
"I WAS THEN ENTRUSTED INTO THE CARE OF MOIRA MacTAGGERT, AND SENT TO LIVE AT HER MUIR ISLE MUTANT RESEARCH CENTER.
"WHO KNOWS, I MIGHT HAVE LIVED A 'NORMAL' LIFE, HAD NOT AN AGENT OF THE ALIEN SHI'AR...
"...RESTORED ME TO MY PRIME." *
*UNCANNY X-MEN #104 -- Bob.
THE QUESTION IS, WHAT OCCURRED DURING THE MONTHS I WAS IN YOUR CARE, MOIRA?
I... I DINNA KEN WHAT Y' MEAN.
THAT'S A PITY.
REGRETTABLY, I DON'T BELIEVE YOU.
NEITHER, I'LL WAGER, DOES CHARLES, ALTHOUGH HE'S TOO MUCH OF A GENTLEMAN TO PRESS THE POINT.
I HOWEVER HAVE NO SUCH COMPUNCTIONS.
I SUGGEST YOU SEARCH YOUR SOUL-- RATHER QUICKLY-- AND FIND A BETTER, TRUER ANSWER.
CHARLES!
YOU TALK OF FRIENDSHIP AND TRUST, IS THIS HOW YOU RELAY THEM?
WHERE IS THE GOOD, DECENT-- HONORABLE-- MAN TO WHOM I ENTRUSTED MY SCHOOL?!
YOU PROCEEDED FROM A FALSE ASSUMPTION, CHARLES.
THE QUESTION IS NOT WHAT HAPPENED TO THAT MAN YOU DESCRIBE, BUT WHETHER HE EVER EVEN EXISTED?
ONLY DR. MacTAGGERT CAN ANSWER THAT.
AND IF SHE HAS ANY REGARD AT ALL FOR YOUR LIFE, OLD FRIEND...
THAT'S A VACUUM OUT THERE, HE'LL DIE!
THEN SAVE HIM.
PLEASE, DON'T HURT HIM!
IT'S ALMOST TOO LATE.
STOP!
I'LL TELL Y' WHAT Y' WANT TO KNOW. JUST BRING HIM BACK INSIDE, PLEASE, I BEG YOU...
...I'LL, TELL Y' EVERYTHING!
I NEVER DOUBTED IT FOR AN INSTANT.

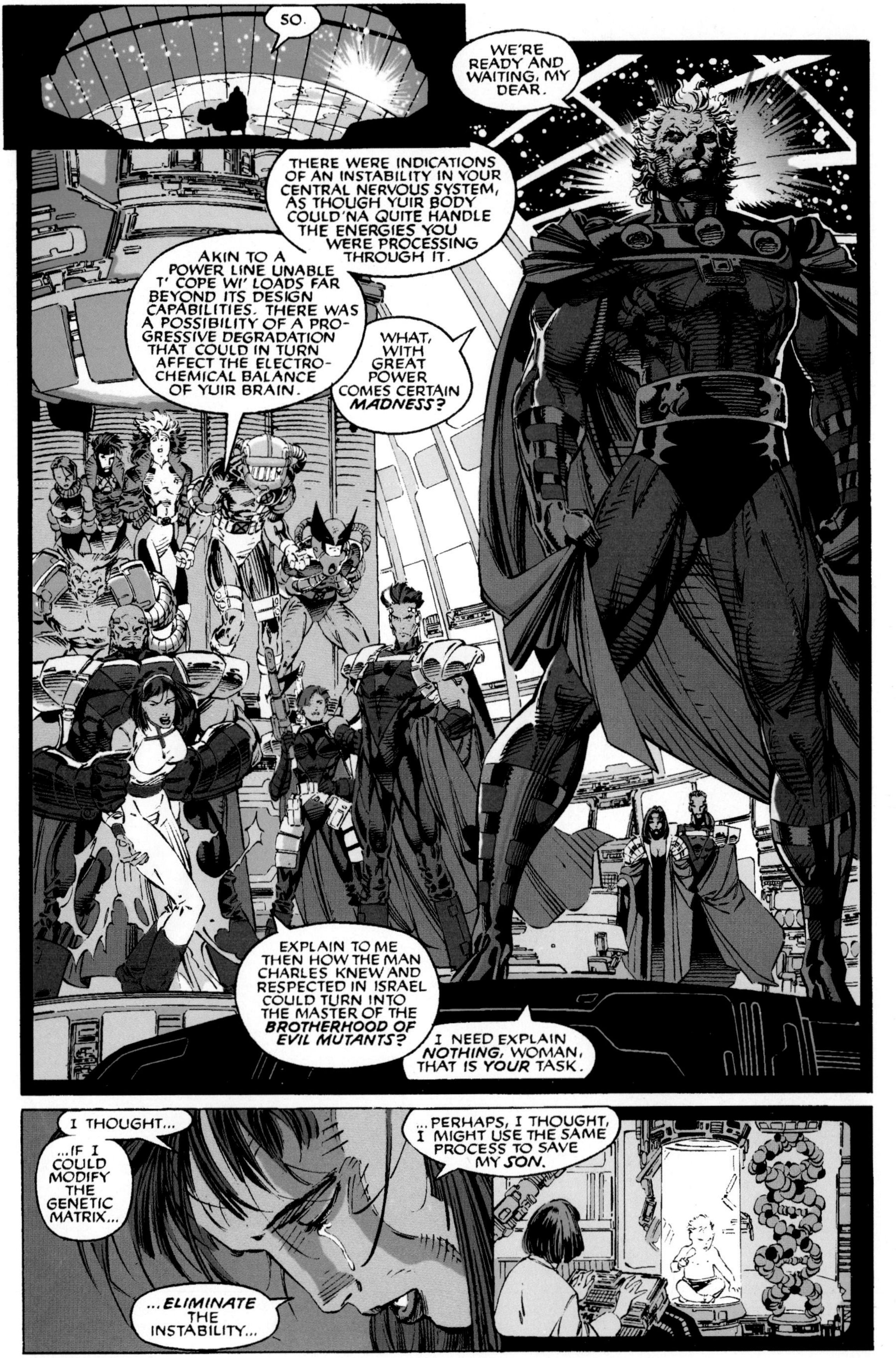
SO.
WE'RE READY AND WAITING, MY DEAR.
THERE WERE INDICATIONS OF AN INSTABILITY IN YOUR CENTRAL NERVOUS SYSTEM, AS THOUGH YUIR BODY COULD'NA QUITE HANDLE THE ENERGIES YOU WERE PROCESSING THROUGH IT.
AKIN TO A POWER LINE UNABLE T' COPE WI' LOADS FAR BEYOND ITS DESIGN CAPABILITIES. THERE WAS A POSSIBILITY OF A PROGRESSIVE DEGRADATION THAT COULD IN TURN AFFECT THE ELECTRO-CHEMICAL BALANCE OF YUIR BRAIN.
WHAT, WITH GREAT POWER COMES CERTAIN ***MADNESS?***
EXPLAIN TO ME THEN HOW THE MAN CHARLES KNEW AND RESPECTED IN ISRAEL COULD TURN INTO THE MASTER OF THE ***BROTHERHOOD OF EVIL MUTANTS?***
I NEED EXPLAIN ***NOTHING,*** WOMAN, THAT IS ***YOUR*** TASK.
I THOUGHT...
...IF I COULD MODIFY THE GENETIC MATRIX...
...***ELIMINATE*** THE INSTABILITY...
...PERHAPS, I THOUGHT, I MIGHT USE THE SAME PROCESS TO SAVE MY ***SON.***

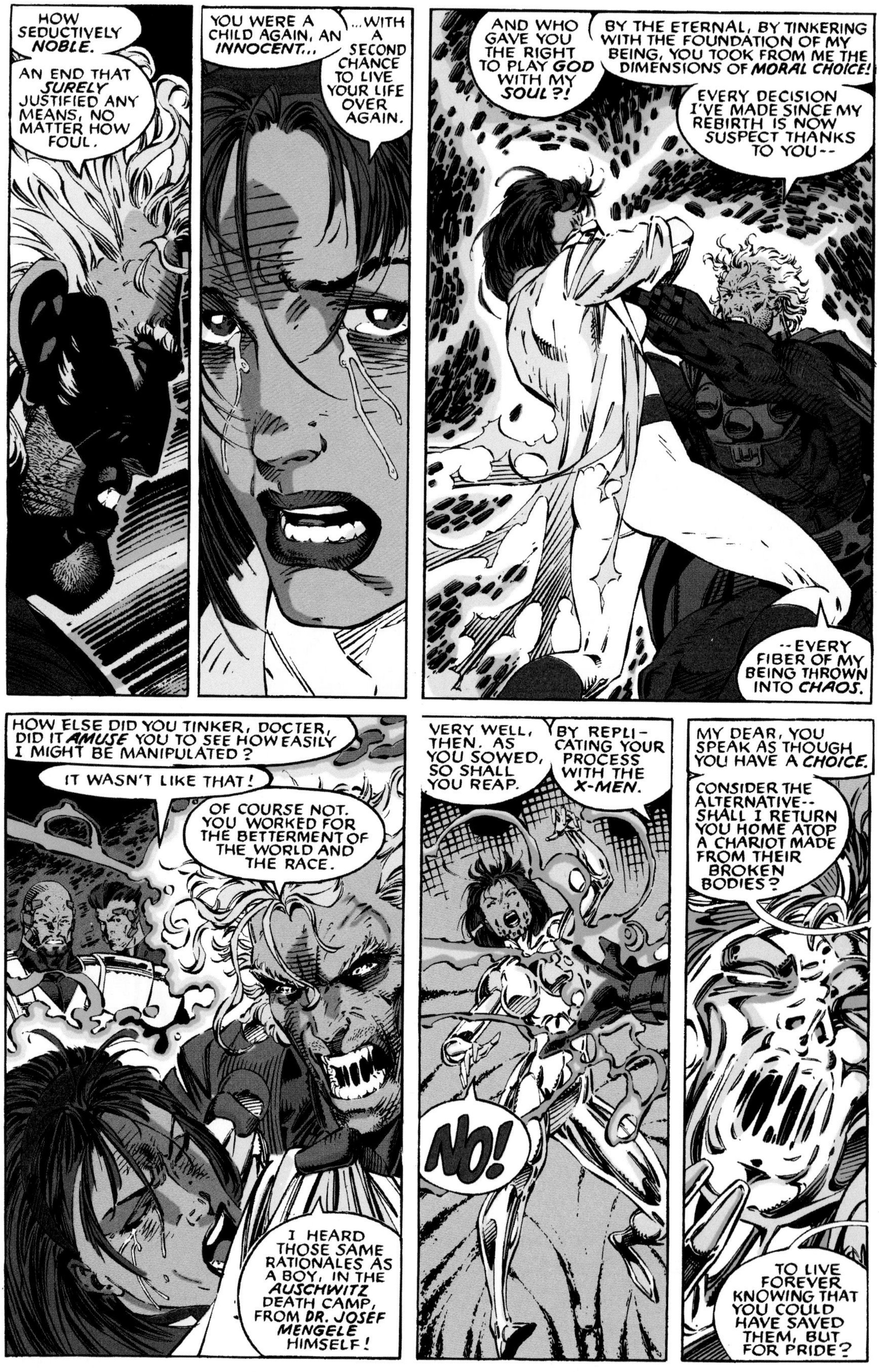
HOW SEDUCTIVELY NOBLE.
AN END THAT SURELY JUSTIFIED ANY MEANS, NO MATTER HOW FOUL.
YOU WERE A CHILD AGAIN, AN INNOCENT...
...WITH A SECOND CHANCE TO LIVE YOUR LIFE OVER AGAIN.
AND WHO GAVE YOU THE RIGHT TO PLAY GOD WITH MY SOUL?!
BY THE ETERNAL, BY TINKERING WITH THE FOUNDATION OF MY BEING, YOU TOOK FROM ME THE DIMENSIONS OF MORAL CHOICE!
EVERY DECISION I'VE MADE SINCE MY REBIRTH IS NOW SUSPECT THANKS TO YOU--
--EVERY FIBER OF MY BEING THROWN INTO CHAOS.
HOW ELSE DID YOU TINKER, DOCTER, DID IT AMUSE YOU TO SEE HOW EASILY I MIGHT BE MANIPULATED?
IT WASN'T LIKE THAT!
OF COURSE NOT. YOU WORKED FOR THE BETTERMENT OF THE WORLD AND THE RACE.
I HEARD THOSE SAME RATIONALES AS A BOY, IN THE AUSCHWITZ DEATH CAMP, FROM DR. JOSEF MENGELE HIMSELF!
VERY WELL, THEN. AS YOU SOWED, SO SHALL YOU REAP.
BY REPLICATING YOUR PROCESS WITH THE X-MEN.
NO!
MY DEAR, YOU SPEAK AS THOUGH YOU HAVE A CHOICE.
CONSIDER THE ALTERNATIVE-- SHALL I RETURN YOU HOME ATOP A CHARIOT MADE FROM THEIR BROKEN BODIES?
TO LIVE FOREVER KNOWING THAT YOU COULD HAVE SAVED THEM, BUT FOR PRIDE?

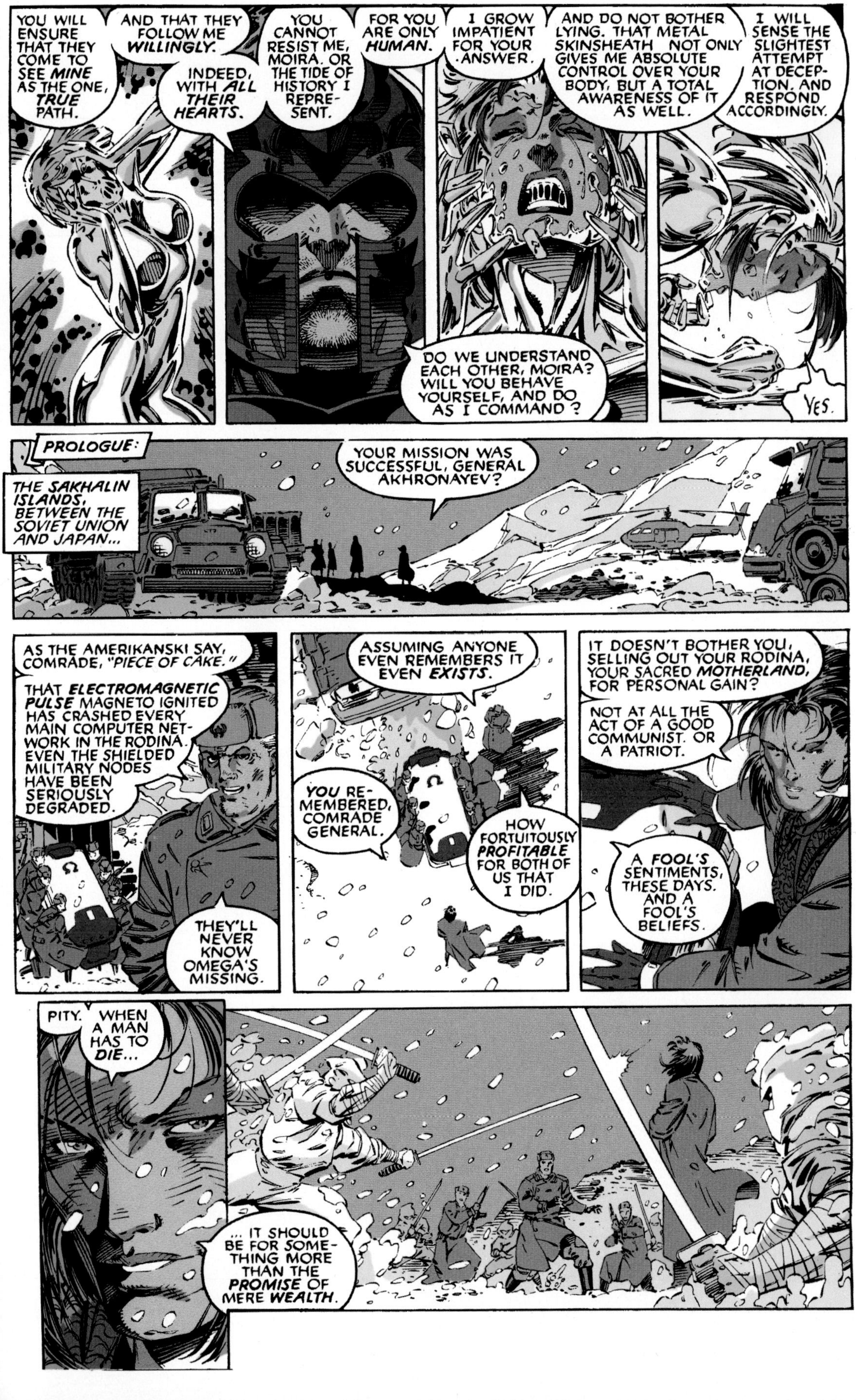

YOU WILL ENSURE THAT THEY COME TO SEE *MINE* AS THE ONE, *TRUE* PATH.
AND THAT THEY FOLLOW ME *WILLINGLY*.
INDEED, WITH *ALL THEIR HEARTS*.
YOU CANNOT RESIST ME, MOIRA. OR THE TIDE OF HISTORY I REPRESENT.
FOR YOU ARE ONLY *HUMAN*.
I GROW IMPATIENT FOR YOUR ANSWER.
AND DO NOT BOTHER LYING. THAT METAL SKINSHEATH NOT ONLY GIVES ME ABSOLUTE CONTROL OVER YOUR BODY, BUT A TOTAL AWARENESS OF IT AS WELL.
I WILL SENSE THE SLIGHTEST ATTEMPT AT DECEPTION. AND RESPOND ACCORDINGLY.
DO WE UNDERSTAND EACH OTHER, MOIRA? WILL YOU BEHAVE YOURSELF, AND DO AS I COMMAND?
YES.
PROLOGUE:
THE SAKHALIN ISLANDS, BETWEEN THE SOVIET UNION AND JAPAN...
YOUR MISSION WAS SUCCESSFUL, GENERAL AKHRONAYEV?
AS THE AMERIKANSKI SAY, COMRADE, "PIECE OF CAKE."
THAT *ELECTROMAGNETIC PULSE* MAGNETO IGNITED HAS CRASHED EVERY MAIN COMPUTER NETWORK IN THE RODINA. EVEN THE SHIELDED MILITARY NODES HAVE BEEN SERIOUSLY DEGRADED.
THEY'LL NEVER KNOW OMEGA'S MISSING.
ASSUMING ANYONE EVEN REMEMBERS IT EVEN *EXISTS*.
YOU REMEMBERED, COMRADE GENERAL.
HOW FORTUITOUSLY *PROFITABLE* FOR BOTH OF US THAT I DID.
IT DOESN'T BOTHER YOU, SELLING OUT YOUR RODINA, YOUR SACRED *MOTHERLAND*, FOR PERSONAL GAIN?
NOT AT ALL THE ACT OF A GOOD COMMUNIST. OR A PATRIOT.
A *FOOL'S* SENTIMENTS, THESE DAYS. AND A FOOL'S BELIEFS.
PITY.
WHEN A MAN HAS TO *DIE*...
... IT SHOULD BE FOR SOMETHING MORE THAN THE *PROMISE* OF MERE *WEALTH*.

CURSE YOU, MATSUO TSURAYABA-- --WE HAD AN AGREEMENT!

WHICH I HAVE HONORED, TO THE LETTER.

IN RETURN FOR THE DELIVERY OF A CERTAIN ITEM, I HAVE PAID YOU A CERTAIN PRICE. NOTHING WAS EVER SAID ABOUT HOW LONG YOU MIGHT ENJOY IT.

GOOD-BYE, GENERAL.

OUR BUSINESS IS NOW CONCLUDED.

LATER, ASTEROID M.

PROFESSOR XAVIER!

CYCLOPS?!

ARE YOU ALL RIGHT, SIR?

MUCH THE BETTER, LAD, FOR SEEING ALL OF YOU AGAIN.

NEITHER MAGNETO NOR HIS ACOLYTES ARE AWARE OF YOUR ESCAPE.

HAVE YOU A PLAN FOR DEALING WITH THEM AND EFFECTING OUR RETURN TO EARTH--

--OR... HAVE YOU ALREADY DONE SO?

NO, PROFESSOR, NOTHING LIKE THAT AT ALL.

WE'VE COME TO TELL YOU THAT WE'VE JOINED MAGNETO.

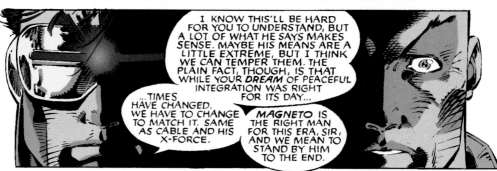

I KNOW THIS'LL BE HARD FOR YOU TO UNDERSTAND, BUT A LOT OF WHAT HE SAYS MAKES SENSE. MAYBE HIS MEANS ARE A LITTLE EXTREME, BUT I THINK WE CAN TEMPER THEM. THE PLAIN FACT, THOUGH, IS THAT WHILE YOUR DREAM OF PEACEFUL INTEGRATION WAS RIGHT FOR ITS DAY...

...TIMES HAVE CHANGED. WE HAVE TO CHANGE TO MATCH IT. SAME AS CABLE AND HIS X-FORCE.

MAGNETO IS THE RIGHT MAN FOR THIS ERA, SIR, AND WE MEAN TO STAND BY HIM TO THE END.

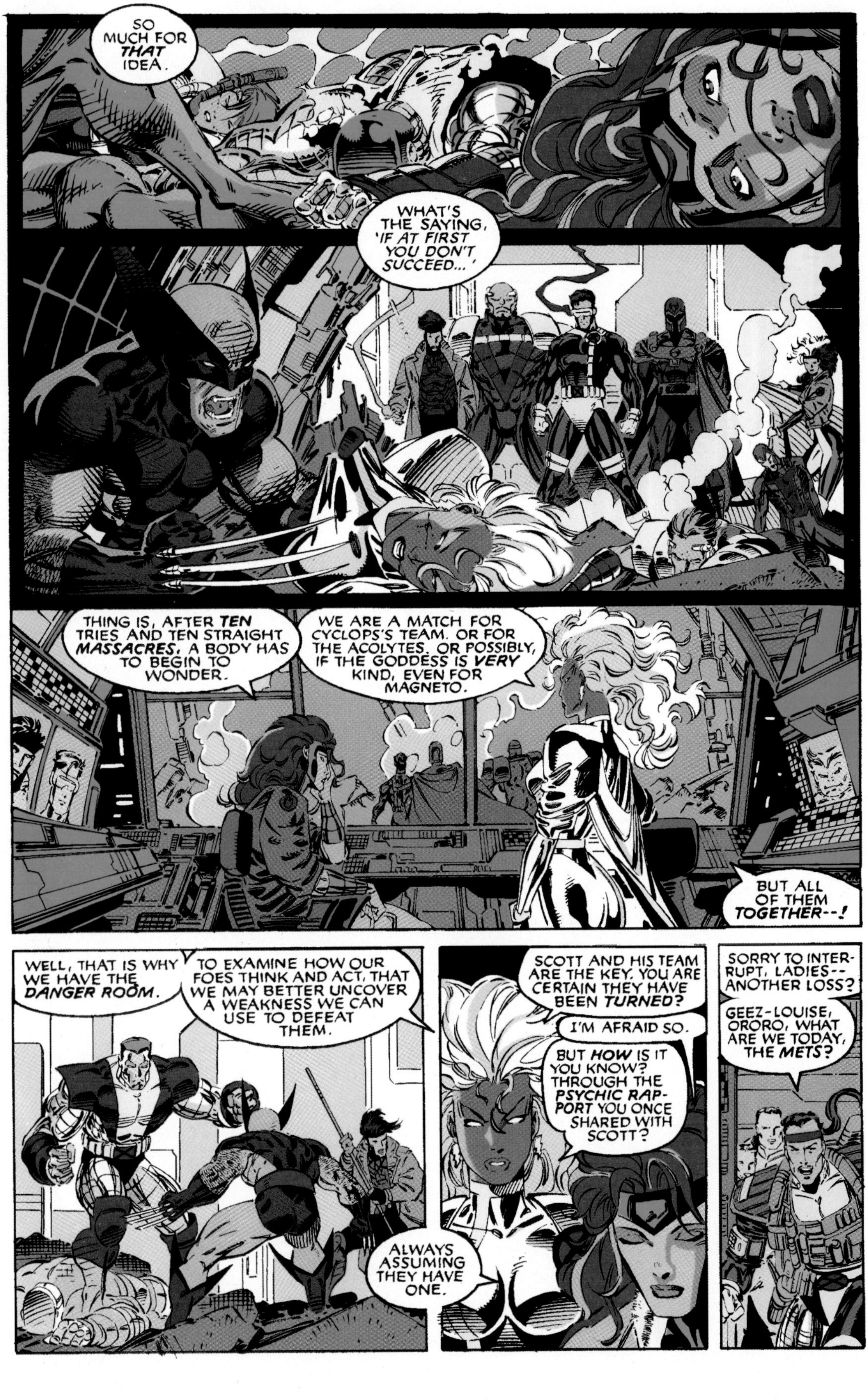
SO MUCH FOR THAT IDEA.
WHAT'S THE SAYING, 'IF AT FIRST YOU DON'T SUCCEED...'
THING IS, AFTER TEN TRIES AND TEN STRAIGHT MASSACRES, A BODY HAS TO BEGIN TO WONDER.
WE ARE A MATCH FOR CYCLOPS'S TEAM. OR FOR THE ACOLYTES. OR POSSIBLY, IF THE GODDESS IS VERY KIND, EVEN FOR MAGNETO.
BUT ALL OF THEM TOGETHER--!
WELL, THAT IS WHY WE HAVE THE DANGER ROOM.
TO EXAMINE HOW OUR FOES THINK AND ACT, THAT WE MAY BETTER UNCOVER A WEAKNESS WE CAN USE TO DEFEAT THEM.
ALWAYS ASSUMING THEY HAVE ONE.
SCOTT AND HIS TEAM ARE THE KEY. YOU ARE CERTAIN THEY HAVE BEEN TURNED?
I'M AFRAID SO.
BUT HOW IS IT YOU KNOW? THROUGH THE PSYCHIC RAPPORT YOU ONCE SHARED WITH SCOTT?
SORRY TO INTERRUPT, LADIES-- ANOTHER LOSS?
GEEZ-LOUISE, ORORO, WHAT ARE WE TODAY, THE METS?

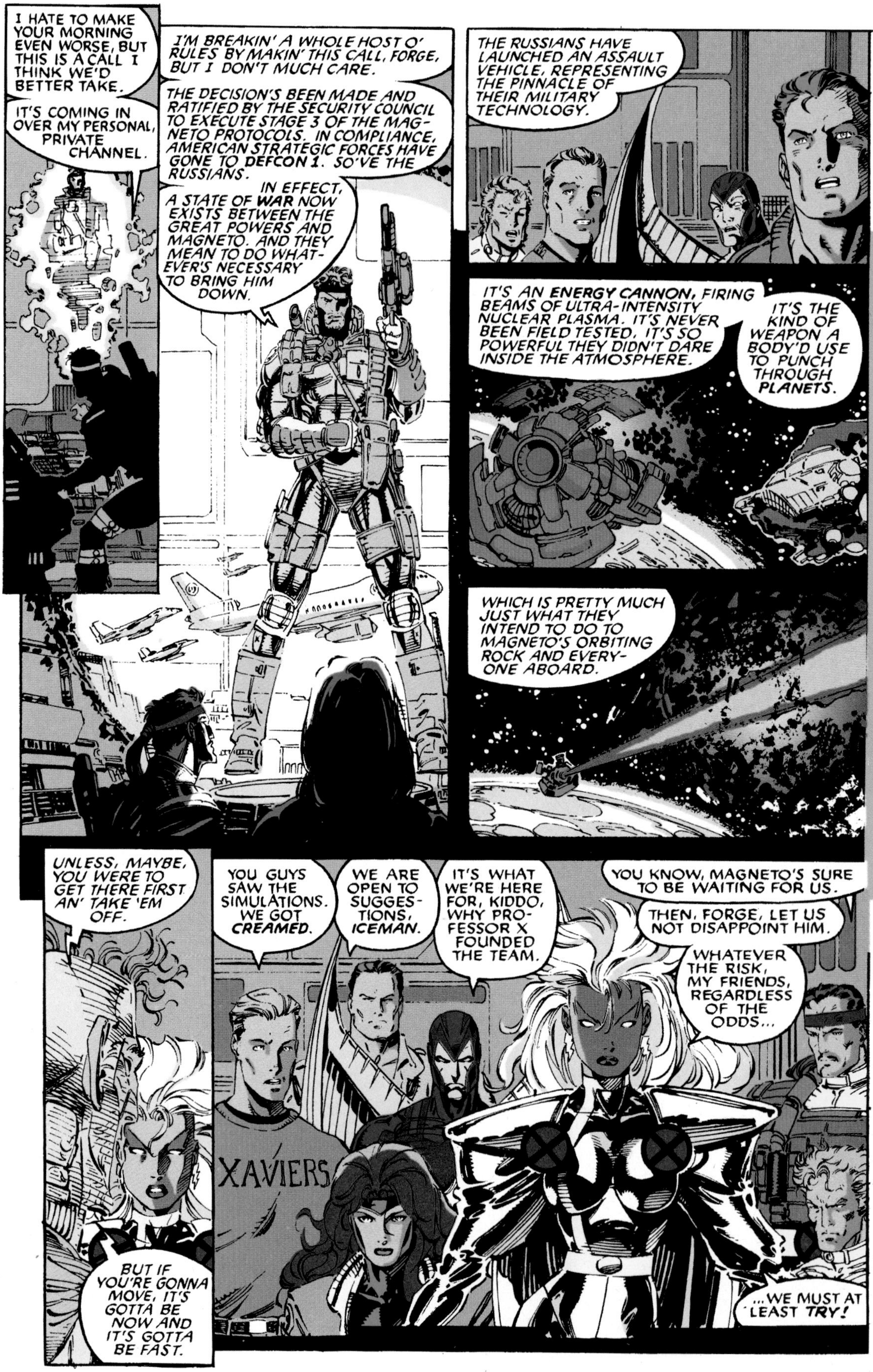
I HATE TO MAKE YOUR MORNING EVEN WORSE, BUT THIS IS A CALL I THINK WE'D BETTER TAKE.
IT'S COMING IN OVER MY PERSONAL, PRIVATE CHANNEL.
I'M BREAKIN' A WHOLE HOST O' RULES BY MAKIN' THIS CALL, FORGE, BUT I DON'T MUCH CARE.
THE DECISION'S BEEN MADE AND RATIFIED BY THE SECURITY COUNCIL TO EXECUTE STAGE 3 OF THE MAGNETO PROTOCOLS. IN COMPLIANCE, AMERICAN STRATEGIC FORCES HAVE GONE TO DEFCON 1. SO'VE THE RUSSIANS.
IN EFFECT, A STATE OF WAR NOW EXISTS BETWEEN THE GREAT POWERS AND MAGNETO. AND THEY MEAN TO DO WHATEVER'S NECESSARY TO BRING HIM DOWN.
THE RUSSIANS HAVE LAUNCHED AN ASSAULT VEHICLE, REPRESENTING THE PINNACLE OF THEIR MILITARY TECHNOLOGY.
IT'S AN ENERGY CANNON, FIRING BEAMS OF ULTRA-INTENSITY NUCLEAR PLASMA. IT'S NEVER BEEN FIELD TESTED. IT'S SO POWERFUL THEY DIDN'T DARE INSIDE THE ATMOSPHERE.
IT'S THE KIND OF WEAPON A BODY'D USE TO PUNCH THROUGH PLANETS.
WHICH IS PRETTY MUCH JUST WHAT THEY INTEND TO DO TO MAGNETO'S ORBITING ROCK AND EVERYONE ABOARD.
UNLESS, MAYBE, YOU WERE TO GET THERE FIRST AN' TAKE 'EM OFF.
BUT IF YOU'RE GONNA MOVE, IT'S GOTTA BE NOW AND IT'S GOTTA BE FAST.
YOU GUYS SAW THE SIMULATIONS. WE GOT CREAMED.
WE ARE OPEN TO SUGGESTIONS, ICEMAN.
IT'S WHAT WE'RE HERE FOR, KIDDO, WHY PROFESSOR X FOUNDED THE TEAM.
YOU KNOW, MAGNETO'S SURE TO BE WAITING FOR US.
THEN, FORGE, LET US NOT DISAPPOINT HIM.
WHATEVER THE RISK, MY FRIENDS, REGARDLESS OF THE ODDS...
...WE MUST AT LEAST TRY!
XAVIERS

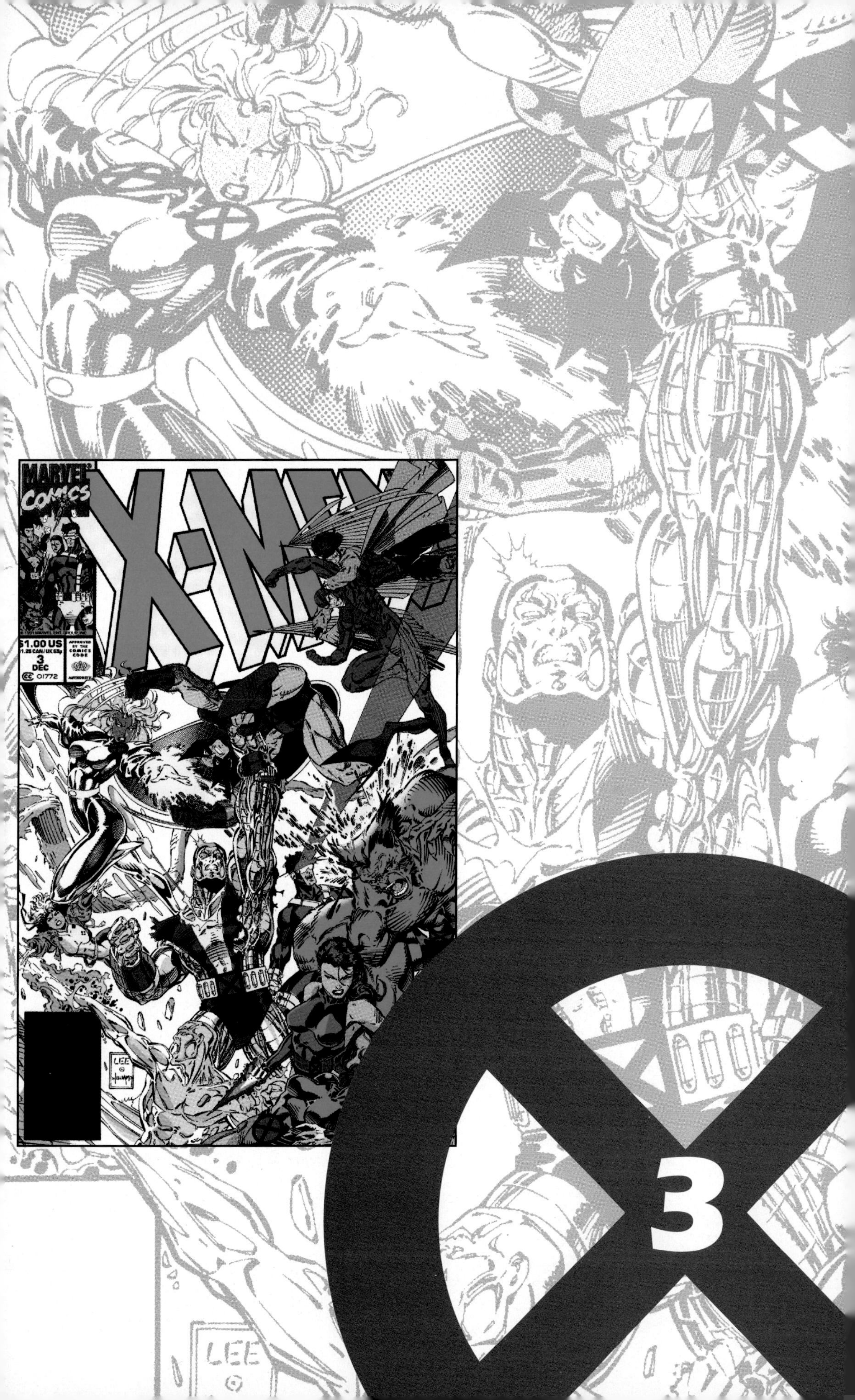
MARVEL COMICS
$1.00 US
3
DEC
LEE
3

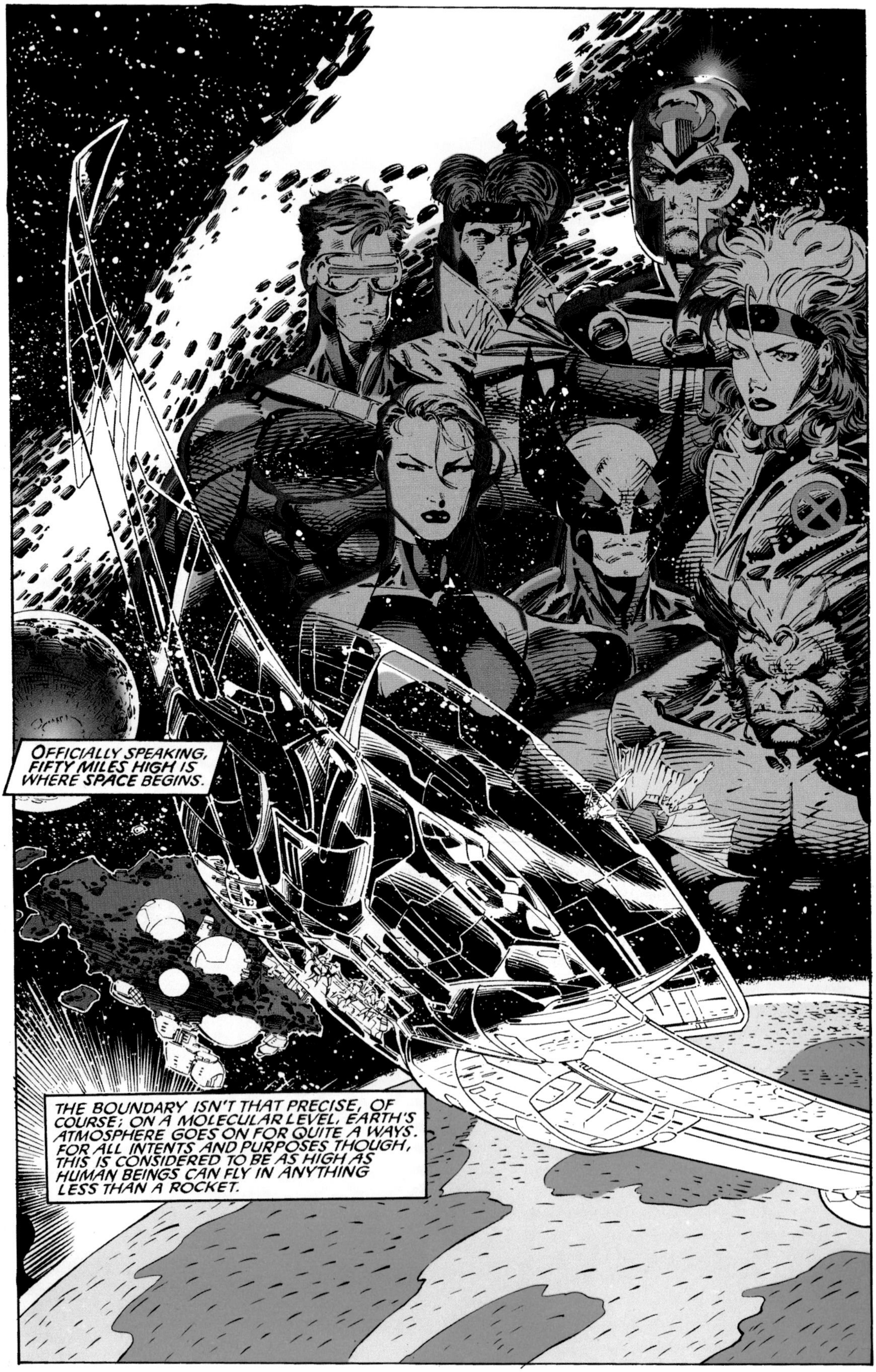
OFFICIALLY SPEAKING, FIFTY MILES HIGH IS WHERE SPACE BEGINS.
THE BOUNDARY ISN'T THAT PRECISE, OF COURSE; ON A MOLECULAR LEVEL, EARTH'S ATMOSPHERE GOES ON FOR QUITE A WAYS. FOR ALL INTENTS AND PURPOSES THOUGH, THIS IS CONSIDERED TO BE AS HIGH AS HUMAN BEINGS CAN FLY IN ANYTHING LESS THAN A ROCKET.

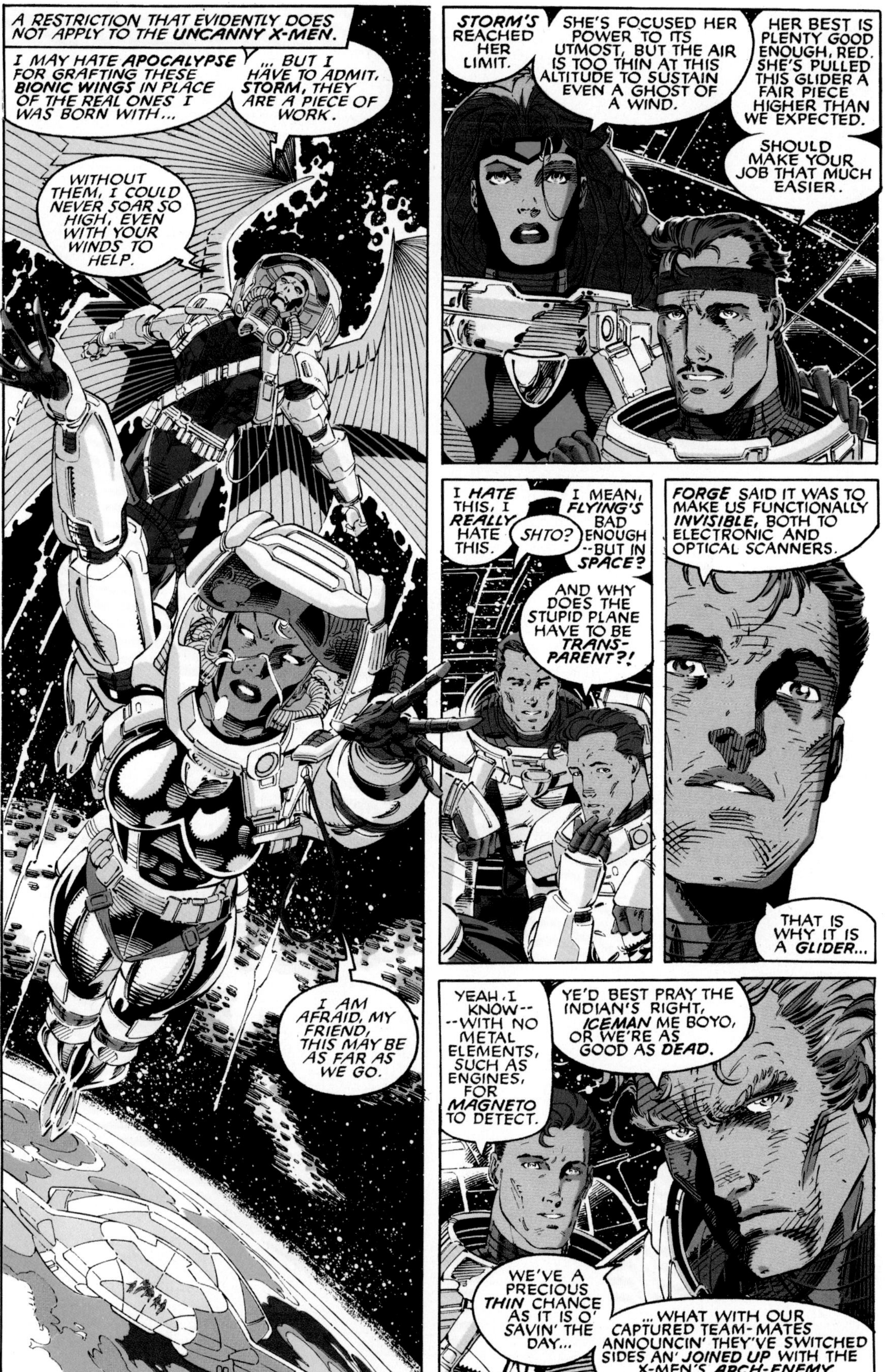
A RESTRICTION THAT EVIDENTLY DOES NOT APPLY TO THE UNCANNY X-MEN.
I MAY HATE APOCALYPSE FOR GRAFTING THESE BIONIC WINGS IN PLACE OF THE REAL ONES I WAS BORN WITH...
...BUT I HAVE TO ADMIT, STORM, THEY ARE A PIECE OF WORK.
WITHOUT THEM, I COULD NEVER SOAR SO HIGH, EVEN WITH YOUR WINDS TO HELP.
I AM AFRAID, MY FRIEND, THIS MAY BE AS FAR AS WE GO.
STORM'S REACHED HER LIMIT.
SHE'S FOCUSED HER POWER TO ITS UTMOST, BUT THE AIR IS TOO THIN AT THIS ALTITUDE TO SUSTAIN EVEN A GHOST OF A WIND.
HER BEST IS PLENTY GOOD ENOUGH, RED. SHE'S PULLED THIS GLIDER A FAIR PIECE HIGHER THAN WE EXPECTED.
SHOULD MAKE YOUR JOB THAT MUCH EASIER.
I HATE THIS, I REALLY HATE THIS.
SHTO?
I MEAN, FLYING'S BAD ENOUGH --BUT IN SPACE?
AND WHY DOES THE STUPID PLANE HAVE TO BE TRANS-PARENT?!
FORGE SAID IT WAS TO MAKE US FUNCTIONALLY INVISIBLE, BOTH TO ELECTRONIC AND OPTICAL SCANNERS.
THAT IS WHY IT IS A GLIDER...
YEAH, I KNOW-- --WITH NO METAL ELEMENTS, SUCH AS ENGINES, FOR MAGNETO TO DETECT.
YE'D BEST PRAY THE INDIAN'S RIGHT, ICEMAN ME BOYO, OR WE'RE AS GOOD AS DEAD.
WE'VE A PRECIOUS THIN CHANCE AS IT IS O' SAVIN' THE DAY...
...WHAT WITH OUR CAPTURED TEAM-MATES ANNOUNCIN' THEY'VE SWITCHED SIDES AN' JOINED UP WITH THE X-MEN'S ARCH-ENEMY.

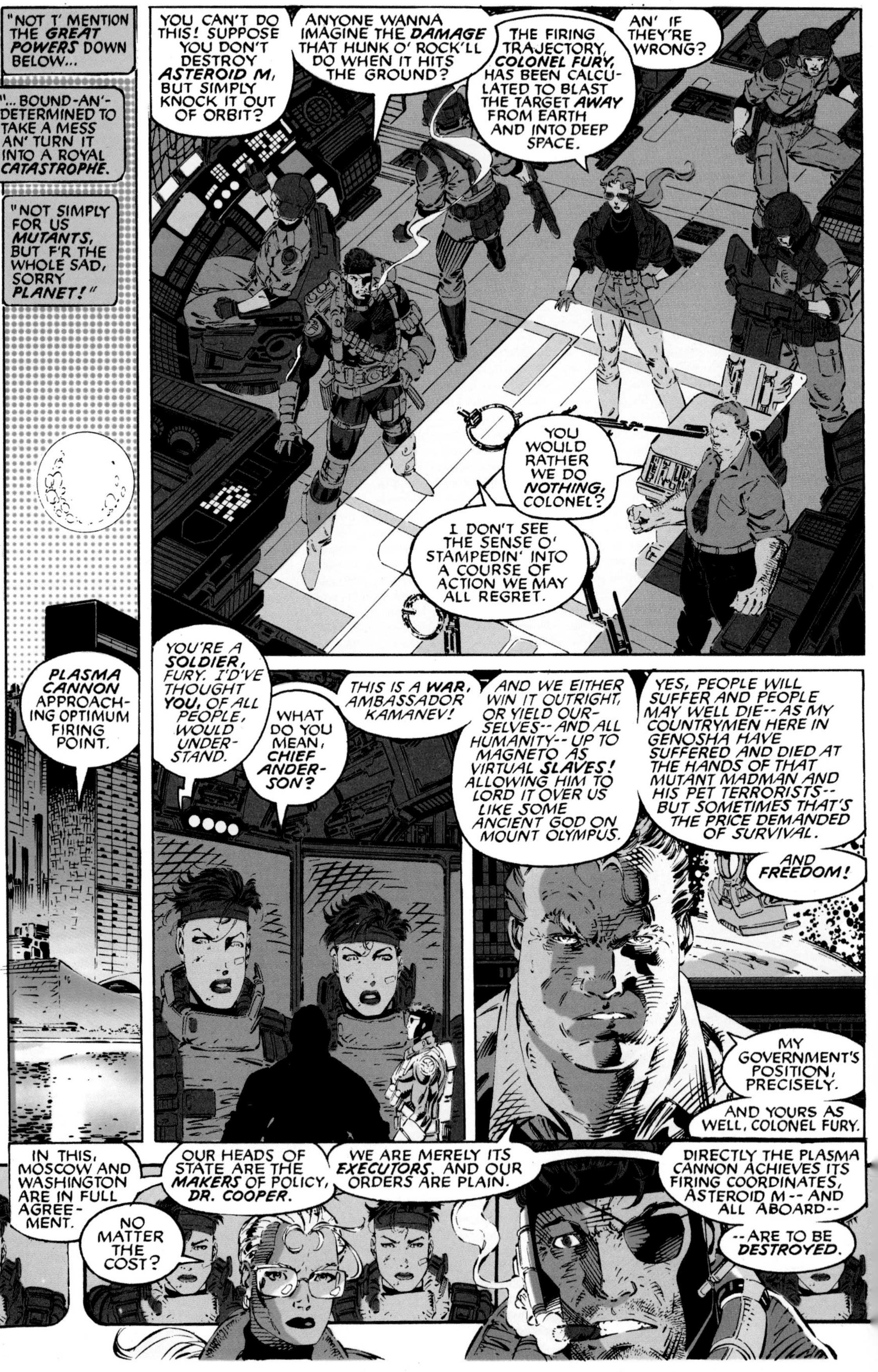
"NOT T' MENTION THE GREAT POWERS DOWN BELOW...
"...BOUND-AN'-DETERMINED TO TAKE A MESS AN' TURN IT INTO A ROYAL CATASTROPHE.
"NOT SIMPLY FOR US MUTANTS, BUT F'R THE WHOLE SAD, SORRY PLANET!"
YOU CAN'T DO THIS! SUPPOSE YOU DON'T DESTROY ASTEROID M, BUT SIMPLY KNOCK IT OUT OF ORBIT?
ANYONE WANNA IMAGINE THE DAMAGE THAT HUNK O' ROCK'LL DO WHEN IT HITS THE GROUND?
THE FIRING TRAJECTORY, COLONEL FURY, HAS BEEN CALCULATED TO BLAST THE TARGET AWAY FROM EARTH AND INTO DEEP SPACE.
AN' IF THEY'RE WRONG?
YOU WOULD RATHER WE DO NOTHING, COLONEL?
I DON'T SEE THE SENSE O' STAMPEDIN' INTO A COURSE OF ACTION WE MAY ALL REGRET.
PLASMA CANNON APPROACHING OPTIMUM FIRING POINT.
YOU'RE A SOLDIER, FURY. I'D'VE THOUGHT YOU, OF ALL PEOPLE, WOULD UNDERSTAND.
WHAT DO YOU MEAN, CHIEF ANDERSON?
THIS IS A WAR, AMBASSADOR KAMANEV!
AND WE EITHER WIN IT OUTRIGHT, OR YIELD OURSELVES-- AND ALL HUMANITY-- UP TO MAGNETO AS VIRTUAL SLAVES! ALLOWING HIM TO LORD IT OVER US LIKE SOME ANCIENT GOD ON MOUNT OLYMPUS.
YES, PEOPLE WILL SUFFER AND PEOPLE MAY WELL DIE-- AS MY COUNTRYMEN HERE IN GENOSHA HAVE SUFFERED AND DIED AT THE HANDS OF THAT MUTANT MADMAN AND HIS PET TERRORISTS-- BUT SOMETIMES THAT'S THE PRICE DEMANDED OF SURVIVAL.
AND FREEDOM!
MY GOVERNMENT'S POSITION, PRECISELY.
AND YOURS AS WELL, COLONEL FURY.
IN THIS, MOSCOW AND WASHINGTON ARE IN FULL AGREEMENT.
NO MATTER THE COST?
OUR HEADS OF STATE ARE THE MAKERS OF POLICY, DR. COOPER.
WE ARE MERELY ITS EXECUTORS. AND OUR ORDERS ARE PLAIN.
DIRECTLY THE PLASMA CANNON ACHIEVES ITS FIRING COORDINATES, ASTEROID M -- AND ALL ABOARD--
--ARE TO BE DESTROYED.

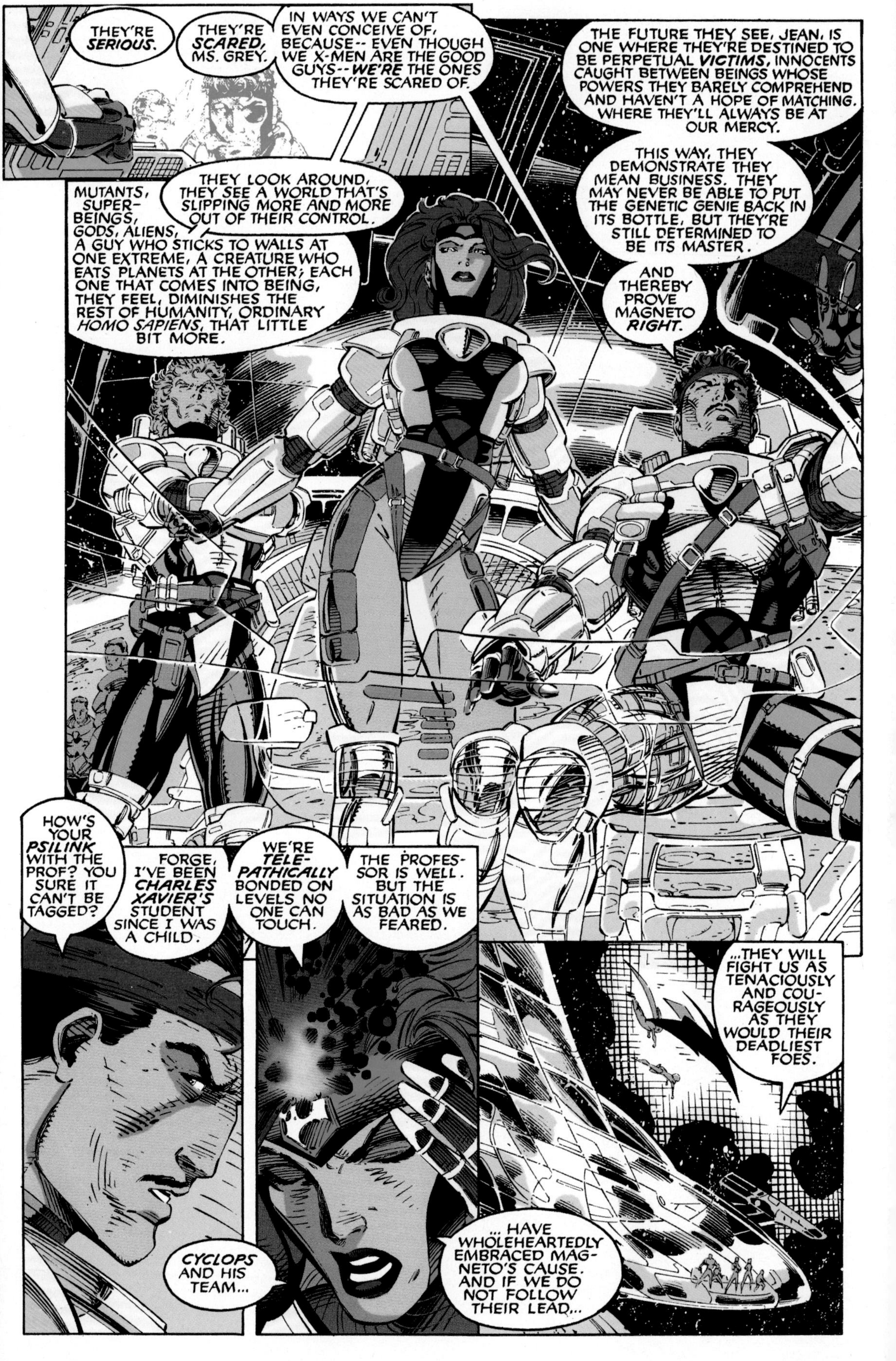
THEY'RE SERIOUS.
THEY'RE SCARED, MS. GREY.
IN WAYS WE CAN'T EVEN CONCEIVE OF, BECAUSE-- EVEN THOUGH WE X-MEN ARE THE GOOD GUYS-- WE'RE THE ONES THEY'RE SCARED OF.
THE FUTURE THEY SEE, JEAN, IS ONE WHERE THEY'RE DESTINED TO BE PERPETUAL VICTIMS, INNOCENTS CAUGHT BETWEEN BEINGS WHOSE POWERS THEY BARELY COMPREHEND AND HAVEN'T A HOPE OF MATCHING. WHERE THEY'LL ALWAYS BE AT OUR MERCY.
THEY LOOK AROUND, THEY SEE A WORLD THAT'S SLIPPING MORE AND MORE OUT OF THEIR CONTROL.
MUTANTS, SUPER-BEINGS, GODS, ALIENS, A GUY WHO STICKS TO WALLS AT ONE EXTREME, A CREATURE WHO EATS PLANETS AT THE OTHER; EACH ONE THAT COMES INTO BEING, THEY FEEL, DIMINISHES THE REST OF HUMANITY, ORDINARY HOMO SAPIENS, THAT LITTLE BIT MORE.
THIS WAY, THEY DEMONSTRATE THEY MEAN BUSINESS. THEY MAY NEVER BE ABLE TO PUT THE GENETIC GENIE BACK IN ITS BOTTLE, BUT THEY'RE STILL DETERMINED TO BE ITS MASTER.
AND THEREBY PROVE MAGNETO RIGHT.
HOW'S YOUR PSILINK WITH THE PROF? YOU SURE IT CAN'T BE TAGGED?
FORGE, I'VE BEEN CHARLES XAVIER'S STUDENT SINCE I WAS A CHILD.
WE'RE TELE-PATHICALLY BONDED ON LEVELS NO ONE CAN TOUCH.
THE PROFES-SOR IS WELL. BUT THE SITUATION IS AS BAD AS WE FEARED.
CYCLOPS AND HIS TEAM...
... HAVE WHOLEHEARTEDLY EMBRACED MAG-NETO'S CAUSE. AND IF WE DO NOT FOLLOW THEIR LEAD...
...THEY WILL FIGHT US AS TENACIOUSLY AND COU-RAGEOUSLY AS THEY WOULD THEIR DEADLIEST FOES.

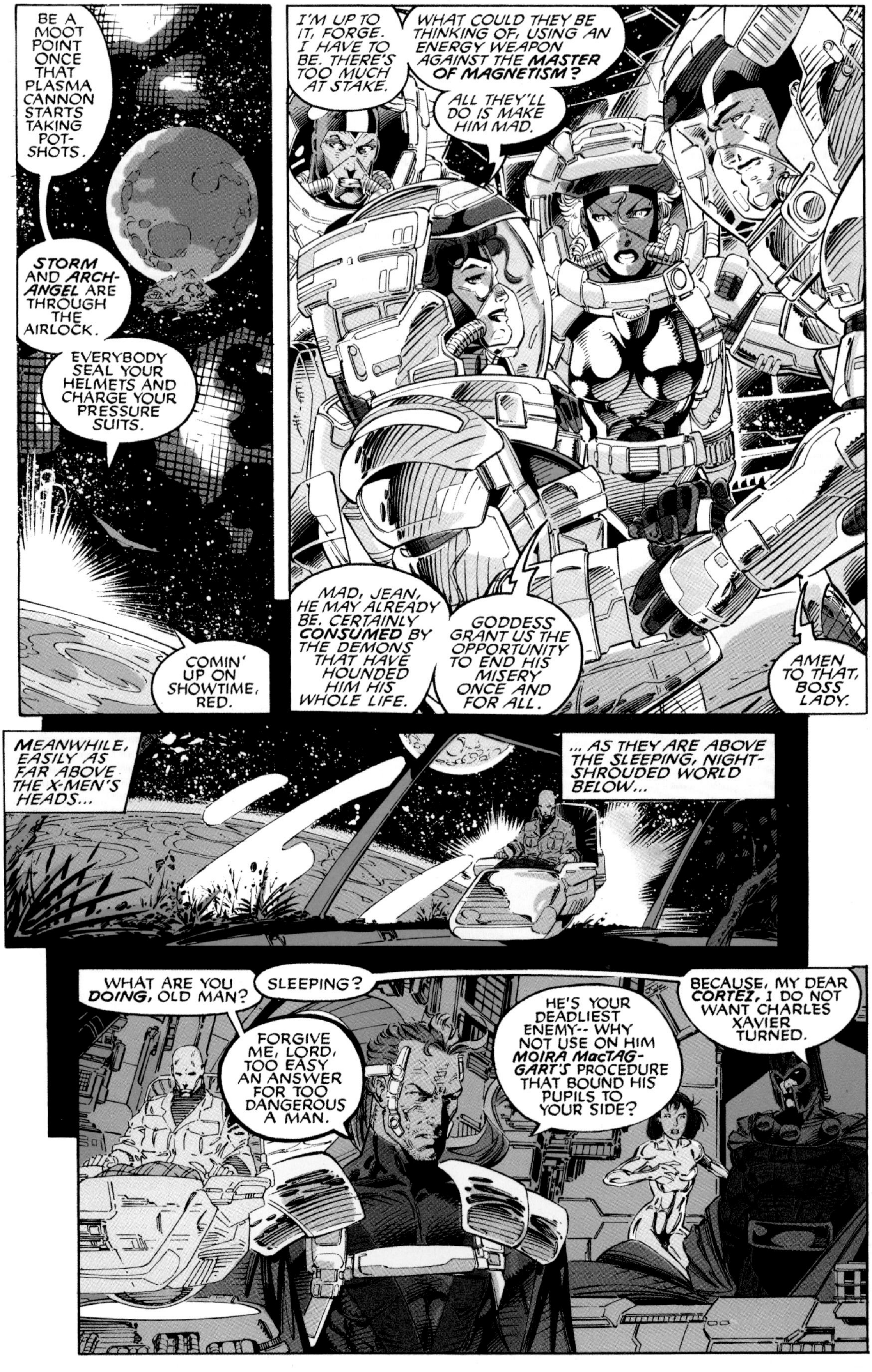
BE A MOOT POINT ONCE THAT PLASMA CANNON STARTS TAKING POT-SHOTS.
STORM AND ARCH-ANGEL ARE THROUGH THE AIRLOCK.
EVERYBODY SEAL YOUR HELMETS AND CHARGE YOUR PRESSURE SUITS.
COMIN' UP ON SHOWTIME, RED.
I'M UP TO IT, FORGE. I HAVE TO BE. THERE'S TOO MUCH AT STAKE.
WHAT COULD THEY BE THINKING OF, USING AN ENERGY WEAPON AGAINST THE MASTER OF MAGNETISM?
ALL THEY'LL DO IS MAKE HIM MAD.
MAD, JEAN, HE MAY ALREADY BE. CERTAINLY CONSUMED BY THE DEMONS THAT HAVE HOUNDED HIM HIS WHOLE LIFE.
GODDESS GRANT US THE OPPORTUNITY TO END HIS MISERY ONCE AND FOR ALL.
AMEN TO THAT, BOSS LADY.
MEANWHILE, EASILY AS FAR ABOVE THE X-MEN'S HEADS...
...AS THEY ARE ABOVE THE SLEEPING, NIGHT-SHROUDED WORLD BELOW...
WHAT ARE YOU DOING, OLD MAN?
SLEEPING?
FORGIVE ME, LORD, TOO EASY AN ANSWER FOR TOO DANGEROUS A MAN.
HE'S YOUR DEADLIEST ENEMY-- WHY NOT USE ON HIM MOIRA MacTAGGART'S PROCEDURE THAT BOUND HIS PUPILS TO YOUR SIDE?
BECAUSE, MY DEAR CORTEZ, I DO NOT WANT CHARLES XAVIER TURNED.

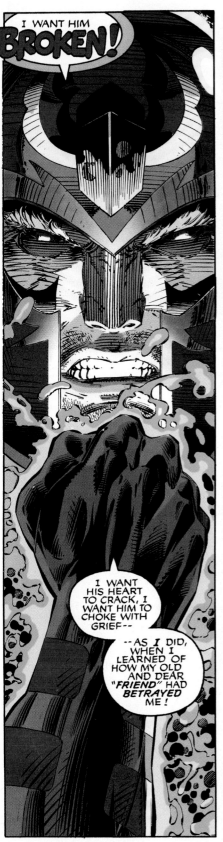

I WANT HIM **BROKEN!**

I WANT HIS HEART TO CRACK, I WANT HIM TO CHOKE WITH GRIEF--

--AS *I* DID, WHEN I LEARNED OF HOW MY OLD AND DEAR *"FRIEND"* HAD *BETRAYED* ME!

NO!

WILL Y' NAE LISTEN, EVEN NOW? CHARLES HAD *NOTHING* T'DO WITH WHAT HAPPENED, MAGNETO!

IT WAS *ME*, ACTIN' ON MY OWN, TRYIN' T' FIND A MEANS O' SAVIN' YOUR SOUL--!

I HAVE TOLD YOU, *WOMAN*--

--AND WILL NOT DO SO AGAIN--

--YOU WILL SPEAK WHEN SPOKEN TO.

MGMP*GK!*

AND *NEVER* ON THIS SUBJECT, DO YOU *HEAR?!*

YOU *DARE* CALL YOURSELF A *HUMAN* BEING?!

I WAS A *BABY*, Dr. MacTAGGART, ENTRUSTED *HELPLESS* TO YOUR CHARGE.

YET YOU BETRAYED EVERY CODE OF HONOR AND DECENCY-- EVEN YOUR OWN HIPPOCRATIC OATH AS A PHYSICIAN--

--TO ALTER MY GENETIC STRUCTURE.

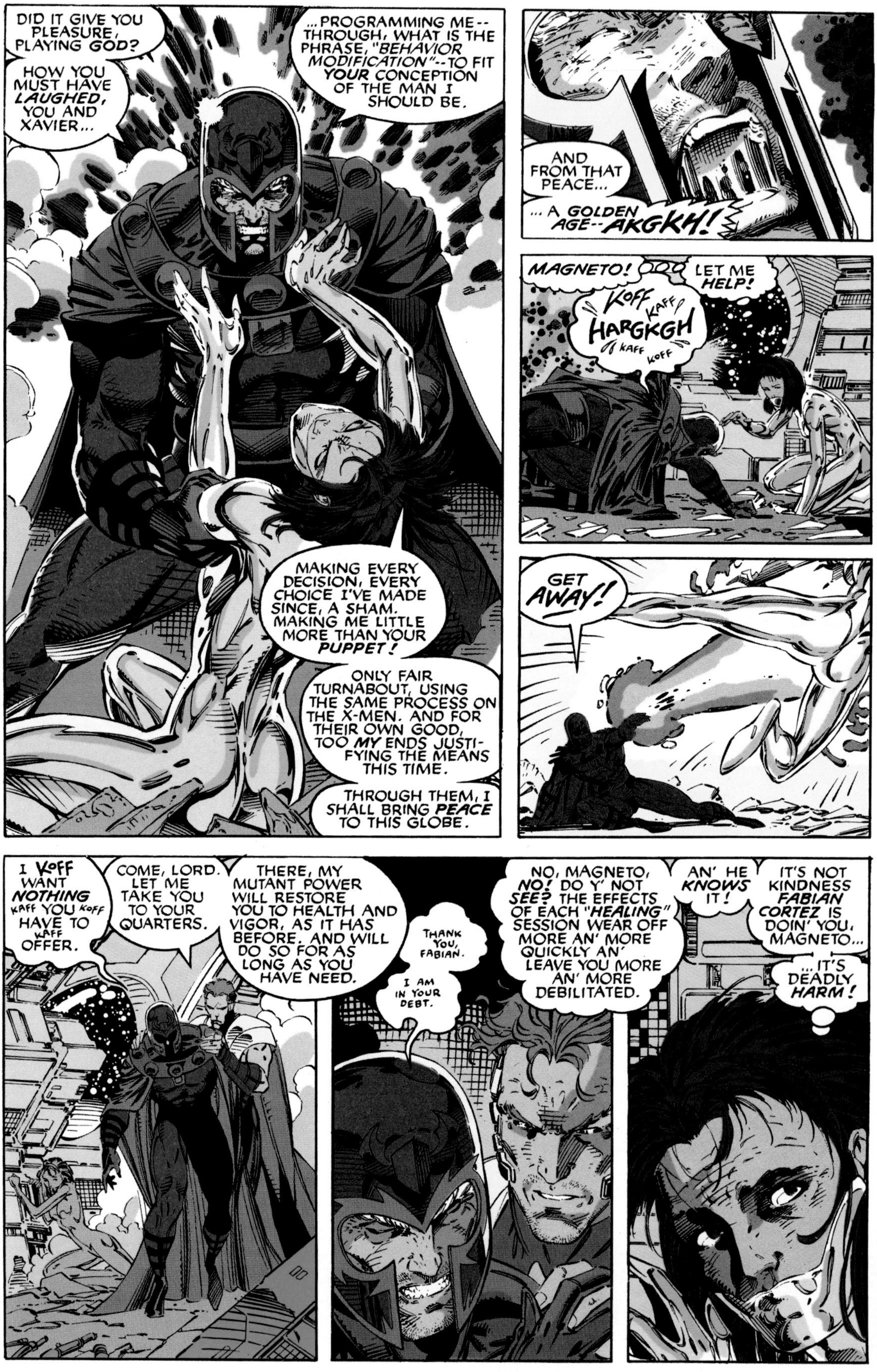
DID IT GIVE YOU PLEASURE, PLAYING GOD?
HOW YOU MUST HAVE LAUGHED, YOU AND XAVIER...
...PROGRAMMING ME--THROUGH, WHAT IS THE PHRASE, "BEHAVIOR MODIFICATION"--TO FIT YOUR CONCEPTION OF THE MAN I SHOULD BE.
MAKING EVERY DECISION, EVERY CHOICE I'VE MADE SINCE, A SHAM. MAKING ME LITTLE MORE THAN YOUR PUPPET!
ONLY FAIR TURNABOUT, USING THE SAME PROCESS ON THE X-MEN. AND FOR THEIR OWN GOOD, TOO MY ENDS JUSTI-FYING THE MEANS THIS TIME.
THROUGH THEM, I SHALL BRING PEACE TO THIS GLOBE.
AND FROM THAT PEACE...
... A GOLDEN AGE--AKGKH!
MAGNETO!
LET ME HELP!
KOFF KAFF HARGKGH KAFF KOFF
GET AWAY!
I KOFF WANT NOTHING KAFF YOU KOFF HAVE TO KAFF OFFER.
COME, LORD. LET ME TAKE YOU TO YOUR QUARTERS.
THERE, MY MUTANT POWER WILL RESTORE YOU TO HEALTH AND VIGOR, AS IT HAS BEFORE. AND WILL DO SO FOR AS LONG AS YOU HAVE NEED.
THANK YOU, FABIAN.
I AM IN YOUR DEBT.
NO, MAGNETO, NO! DO Y' NOT SEE? THE EFFECTS OF EACH "HEALING" SESSION WEAR OFF MORE AN' MORE QUICKLY AN' LEAVE YOU MORE AN' MORE DEBILITATED.
AN' HE KNOWS IT!
IT'S NOT KINDNESS FABIAN CORTEZ IS DOIN' YOU, MAGNETO...
...IT'S DEADLY HARM!

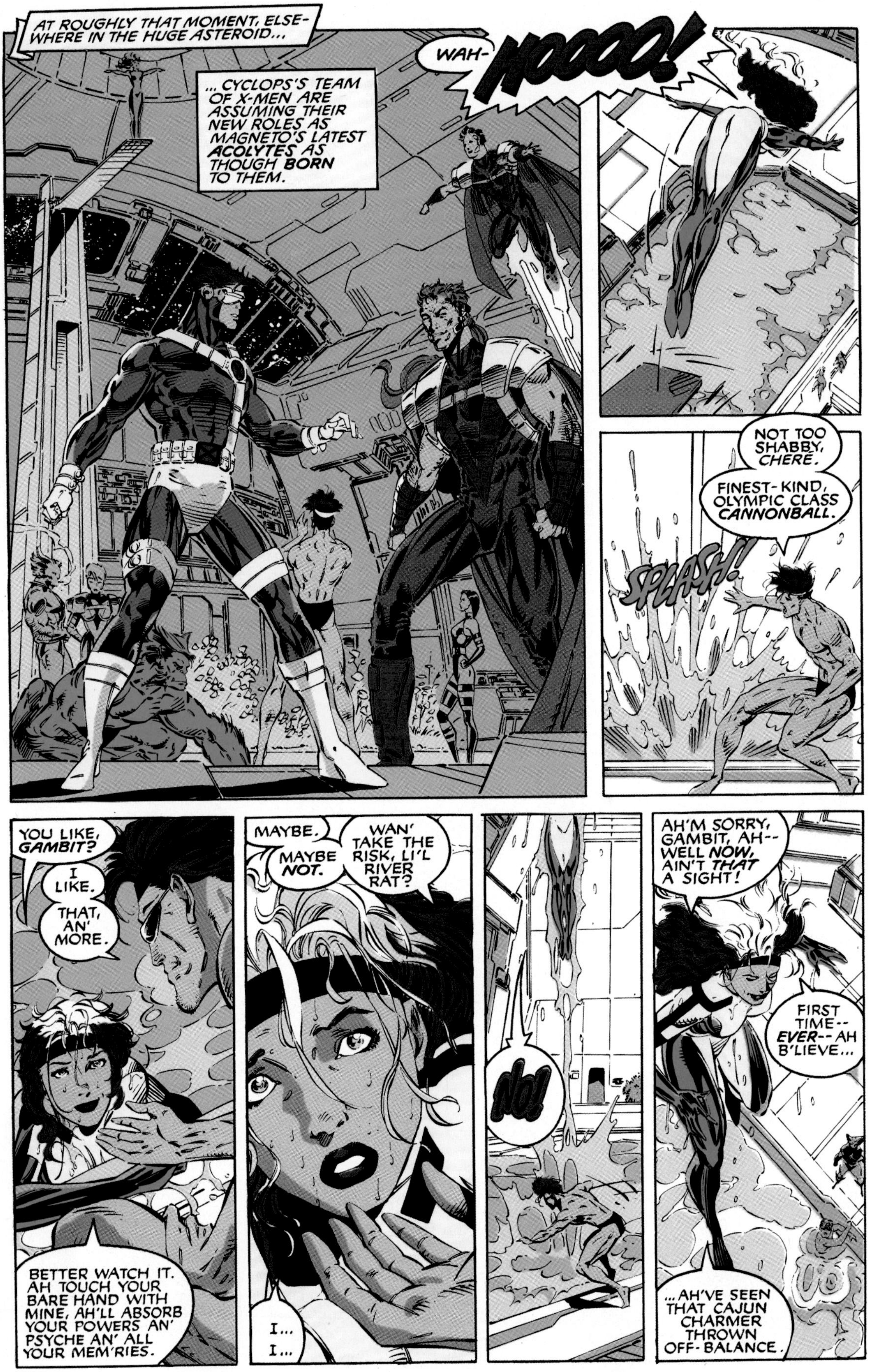

AT ROUGHLY THAT MOMENT, ELSEWHERE IN THE HUGE ASTEROID...
...CYCLOPS'S TEAM OF X-MEN ARE ASSUMING THEIR NEW ROLES AS MAGNETO'S LATEST ACOLYTES AS THOUGH BORN TO THEM.
WAH-HOOOOO!
NOT TOO SHABBY, CHERE.
FINEST-KIND, OLYMPIC CLASS CANNONBALL.
SPLASH!
YOU LIKE, GAMBIT?
I LIKE.
THAT, AN' MORE.
BETTER WATCH IT. AH TOUCH YOUR BARE HAND WITH MINE, AH'LL ABSORB YOUR POWERS AN' PSYCHE AN' ALL YOUR MEM'RIES.
MAYBE.
MAYBE NOT.
WAN' TAKE THE RISK, LI'L RIVER RAT?
I...
I...
NO!
AH'M SORRY, GAMBIT, AH-- WELL NOW, AIN'T THAT A SIGHT!
FIRST TIME-- EVER-- AH B'LIEVE...
...AH'VE SEEN THAT CAJUN CHARMER THROWN OFF-BALANCE.

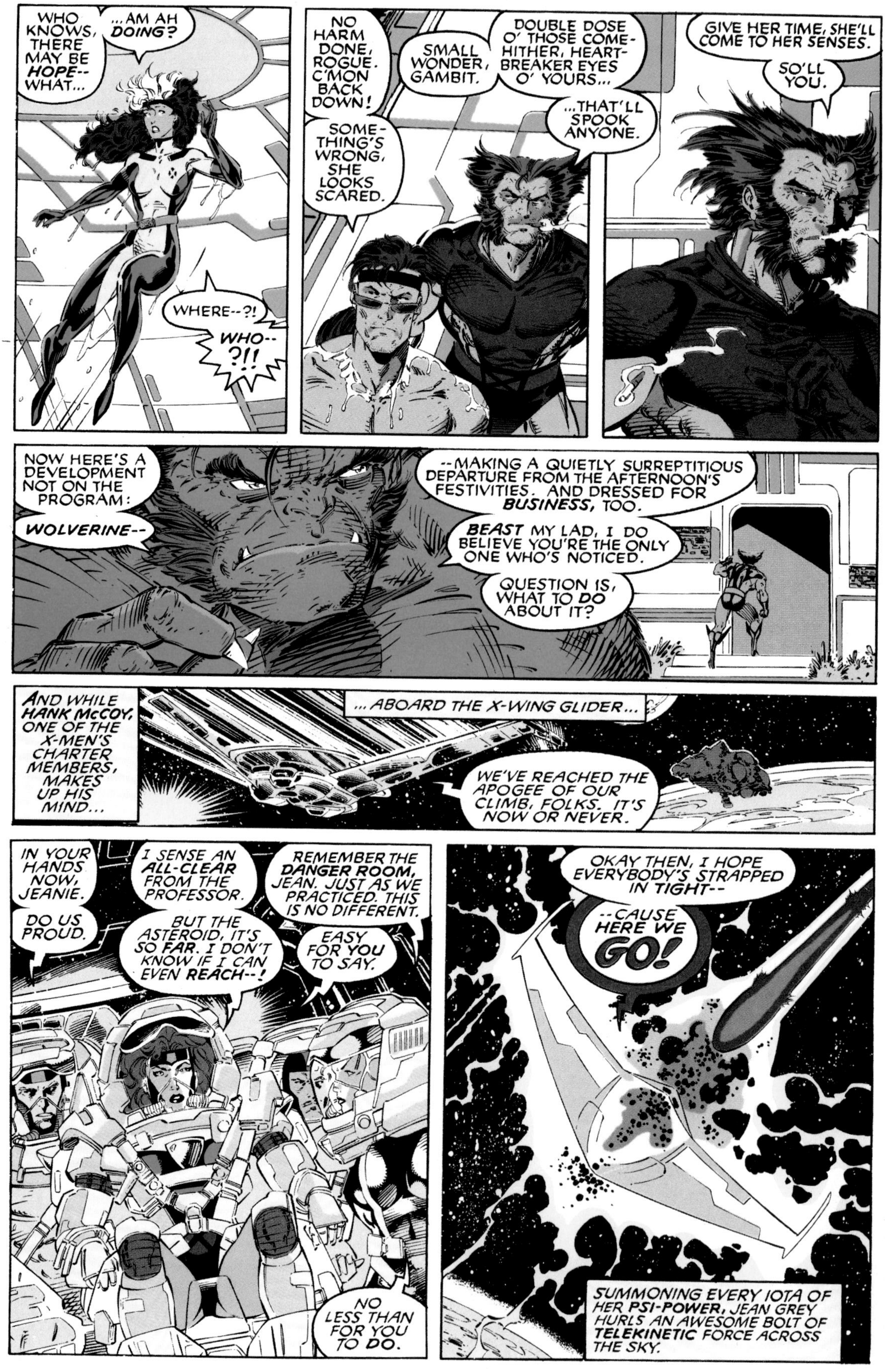
WHO KNOWS, THERE MAY BE HOPE-- WHAT...
...AM AH DOING?
WHERE--?!
WHO--?!!
NO HARM DONE, ROGUE. C'MON BACK DOWN!
SOMETHING'S WRONG, SHE LOOKS SCARED.
SMALL WONDER, GAMBIT.
DOUBLE DOSE O' THOSE COME-HITHER, HEART-BREAKER EYES O' YOURS...
...THAT'LL SPOOK ANYONE.
GIVE HER TIME, SHE'LL COME TO HER SENSES.
SO'LL YOU.
NOW HERE'S A DEVELOPMENT NOT ON THE PROGRAM:
WOLVERINE--
--MAKING A QUIETLY SURREPTITIOUS DEPARTURE FROM THE AFTERNOON'S FESTIVITIES. AND DRESSED FOR BUSINESS, TOO.
BEAST MY LAD, I DO BELIEVE YOU'RE THE ONLY ONE WHO'S NOTICED.
QUESTION IS, WHAT TO DO ABOUT IT?
AND WHILE HANK McCOY, ONE OF THE X-MEN'S CHARTER MEMBERS, MAKES UP HIS MIND...
...ABOARD THE X-WING GLIDER...
WE'VE REACHED THE APOGEE OF OUR CLIMB, FOLKS. IT'S NOW OR NEVER.
IN YOUR HANDS NOW, JEANIE.
DO US PROUD.
I SENSE AN ALL-CLEAR FROM THE PROFESSOR.
BUT THE ASTEROID, IT'S SO FAR. I DON'T KNOW IF I CAN EVEN REACH--!
REMEMBER THE DANGER ROOM, JEAN. JUST AS WE PRACTICED. THIS IS NO DIFFERENT.
EASY FOR YOU TO SAY.
NO LESS THAN FOR YOU TO DO.
OKAY THEN, I HOPE EVERYBODY'S STRAPPED IN TIGHT--
--CAUSE HERE WE GO!
SUMMONING EVERY IOTA OF HER PSI-POWER, JEAN GREY HURLS AN AWESOME BOLT OF TELEKINETIC FORCE ACROSS THE SKY.

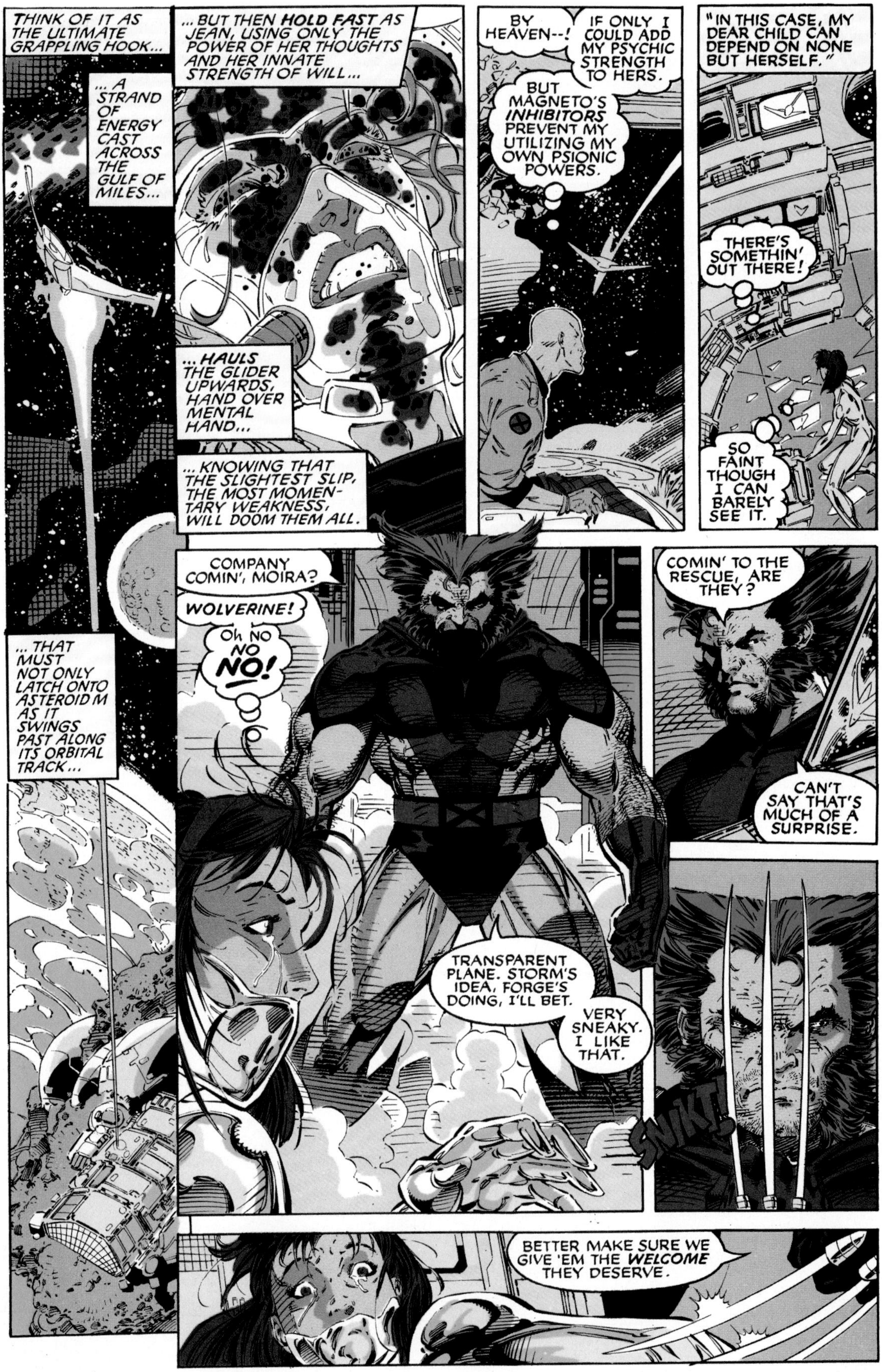
THINK OF IT AS THE ULTIMATE GRAPPLING HOOK...
... A STRAND OF ENERGY CAST ACROSS THE GULF OF MILES...
... BUT THEN HOLD FAST AS JEAN, USING ONLY THE POWER OF HER THOUGHTS AND HER INNATE STRENGTH OF WILL...
... HAULS THE GLIDER UPWARDS, HAND OVER MENTAL HAND...
... KNOWING THAT THE SLIGHTEST SLIP, THE MOST MOMENTARY WEAKNESS, WILL DOOM THEM ALL.
BY HEAVEN--!
IF ONLY I COULD ADD MY PSYCHIC STRENGTH TO HERS.
BUT MAGNETO'S INHIBITORS PREVENT MY UTILIZING MY OWN PSIONIC POWERS.
"IN THIS CASE, MY DEAR CHILD CAN DEPEND ON NONE BUT HERSELF."
THERE'S SOMETHIN' OUT THERE!
SO FAINT THOUGH I CAN BARELY SEE IT.
... THAT MUST NOT ONLY LATCH ONTO ASTEROID M AS IT SWINGS PAST ALONG ITS ORBITAL TRACK...
COMPANY COMIN', MOIRA?
WOLVERINE!
Oh NO NO NO!
TRANSPARENT PLANE. STORM'S IDEA, FORGE'S DOING, I'LL BET.
VERY SNEAKY. I LIKE THAT.
COMIN' TO THE RESCUE, ARE THEY?
CAN'T SAY THAT'S MUCH OF A SURPRISE.
SNIKT!
BETTER MAKE SURE WE GIVE 'EM THE WELCOME THEY DESERVE.

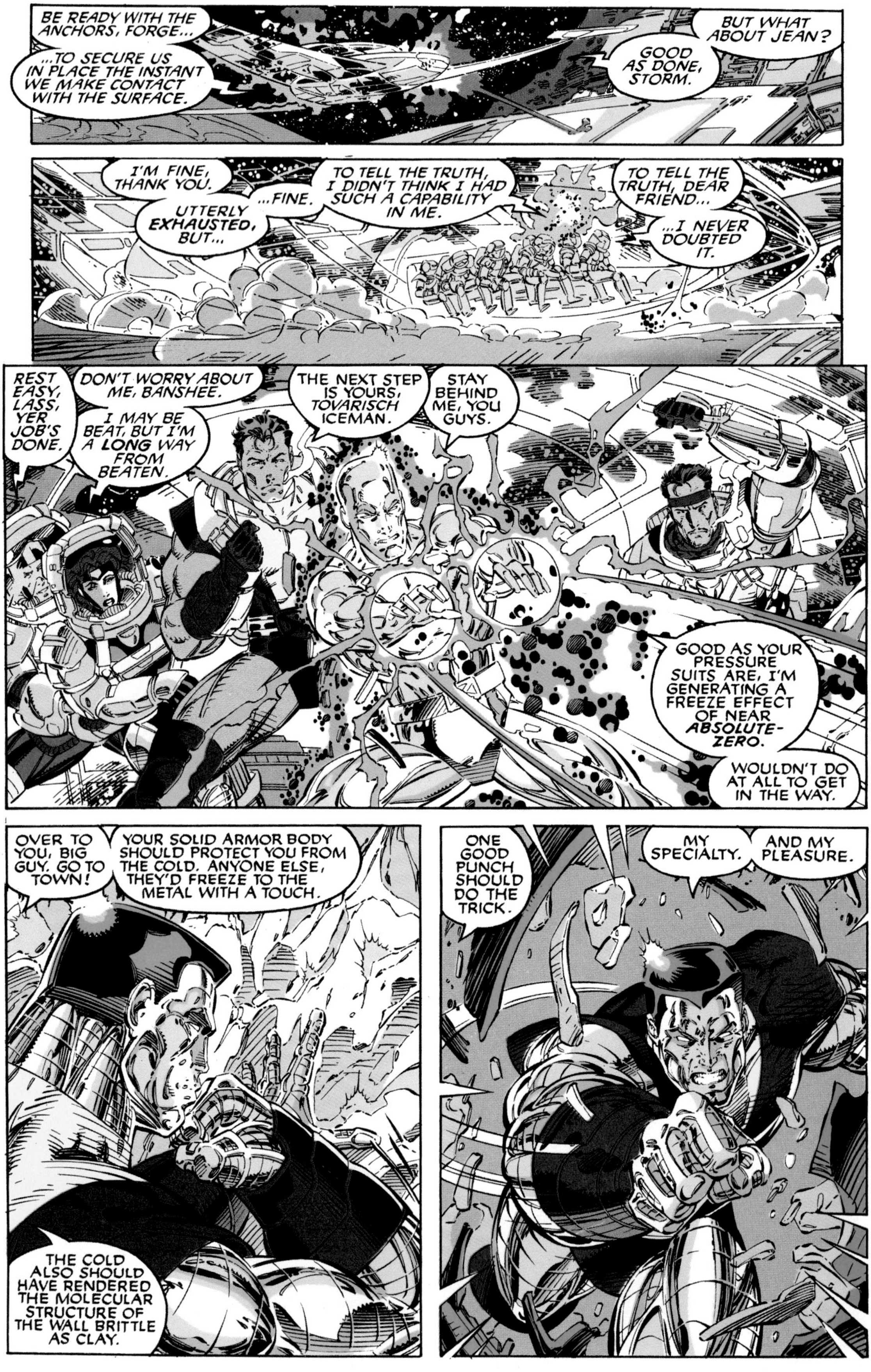

BE READY WITH THE ANCHORS, FORGE...
...TO SECURE US IN PLACE THE INSTANT WE MAKE CONTACT WITH THE SURFACE.
GOOD AS DONE, STORM.
BUT WHAT ABOUT JEAN?
I'M FINE, THANK YOU.
UTTERLY EXHAUSTED, BUT...
...FINE.
TO TELL THE TRUTH, I DIDN'T THINK I HAD SUCH A CAPABILITY IN ME.
TO TELL THE TRUTH, DEAR FRIEND...
...I NEVER DOUBTED IT.
REST EASY, LASS, YER JOB'S DONE.
DON'T WORRY ABOUT ME, BANSHEE.
I MAY BE BEAT, BUT I'M A LONG WAY FROM BEATEN.
THE NEXT STEP IS YOURS, TOVARISCH ICEMAN.
STAY BEHIND ME, YOU GUYS.
GOOD AS YOUR PRESSURE SUITS ARE, I'M GENERATING A FREEZE EFFECT OF NEAR ABSOLUTE-ZERO.
WOULDN'T DO AT ALL TO GET IN THE WAY.
OVER TO YOU, BIG GUY. GO TO TOWN!
YOUR SOLID ARMOR BODY SHOULD PROTECT YOU FROM THE COLD. ANYONE ELSE, THEY'D FREEZE TO THE METAL WITH A TOUCH.
THE COLD ALSO SHOULD HAVE RENDERED THE MOLECULAR STRUCTURE OF THE WALL BRITTLE AS CLAY.
ONE GOOD PUNCH SHOULD DO THE TRICK.
MY SPECIALTY.
AND MY PLEASURE.

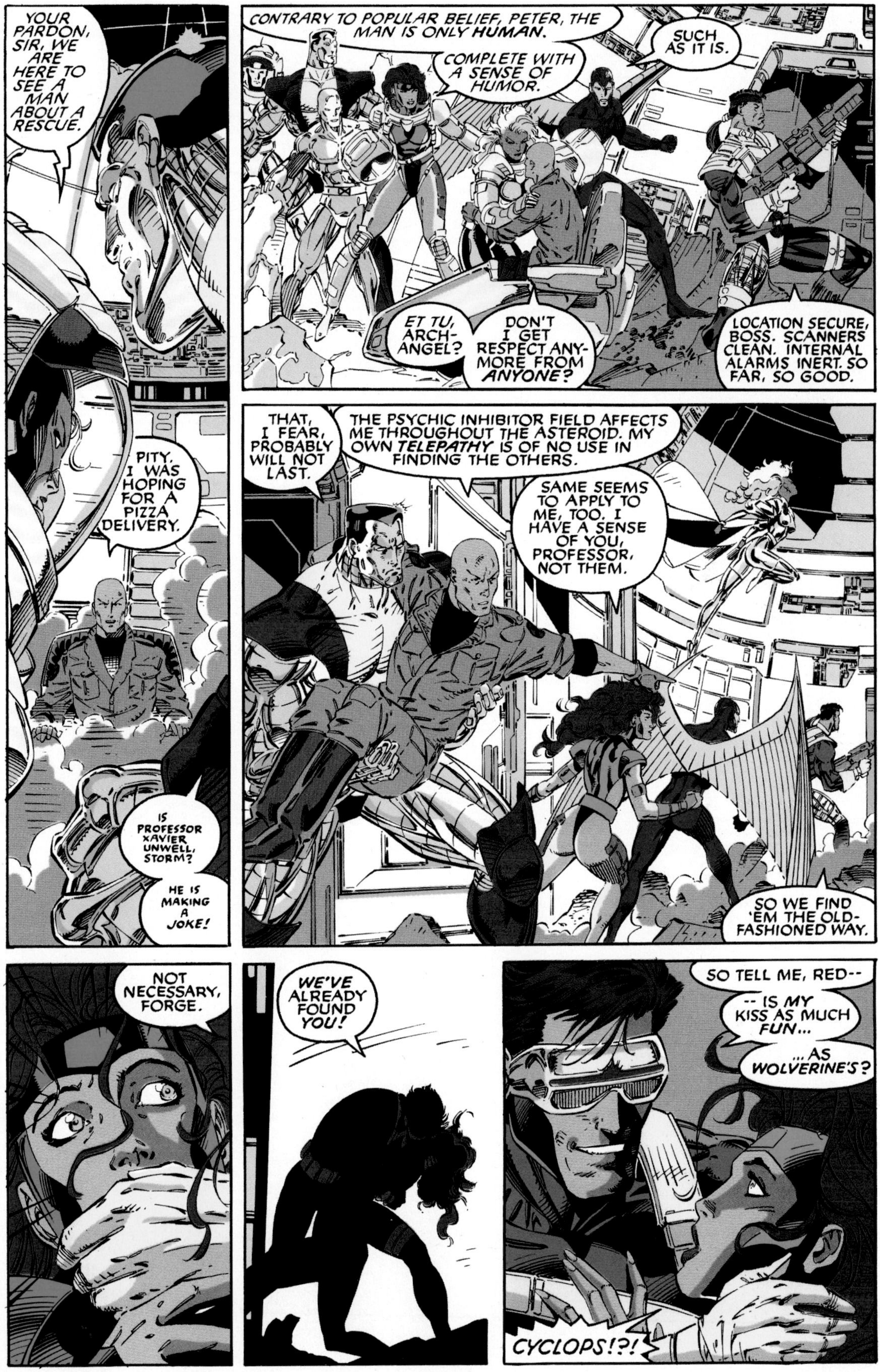
YOUR PARDON, SIR, WE ARE HERE TO SEE A MAN ABOUT A RESCUE.
CONTRARY TO POPULAR BELIEF, PETER, THE MAN IS ONLY HUMAN.
COMPLETE WITH A SENSE OF HUMOR.
SUCH AS IT IS.
ET TU, ARCHANGEL?
DON'T I GET RESPECT ANYMORE FROM ANYONE?
LOCATION SECURE, BOSS. SCANNERS CLEAN. INTERNAL ALARMS INERT. SO FAR, SO GOOD.
PITY. I WAS HOPING FOR A PIZZA DELIVERY.
IS PROFESSOR XAVIER UNWELL, STORM?
HE IS MAKING A JOKE!
THAT, I FEAR, PROBABLY WILL NOT LAST.
THE PSYCHIC INHIBITOR FIELD AFFECTS ME THROUGHOUT THE ASTEROID. MY OWN TELEPATHY IS OF NO USE IN FINDING THE OTHERS.
SAME SEEMS TO APPLY TO ME, TOO. I HAVE A SENSE OF YOU, PROFESSOR, NOT THEM.
SO WE FIND 'EM THE OLD-FASHIONED WAY.
NOT NECESSARY, FORGE.
WE'VE ALREADY FOUND YOU!
SO TELL ME, RED--
-- IS MY KISS AS MUCH FUN...
...AS WOLVERINE'S?
CYCLOPS!?!

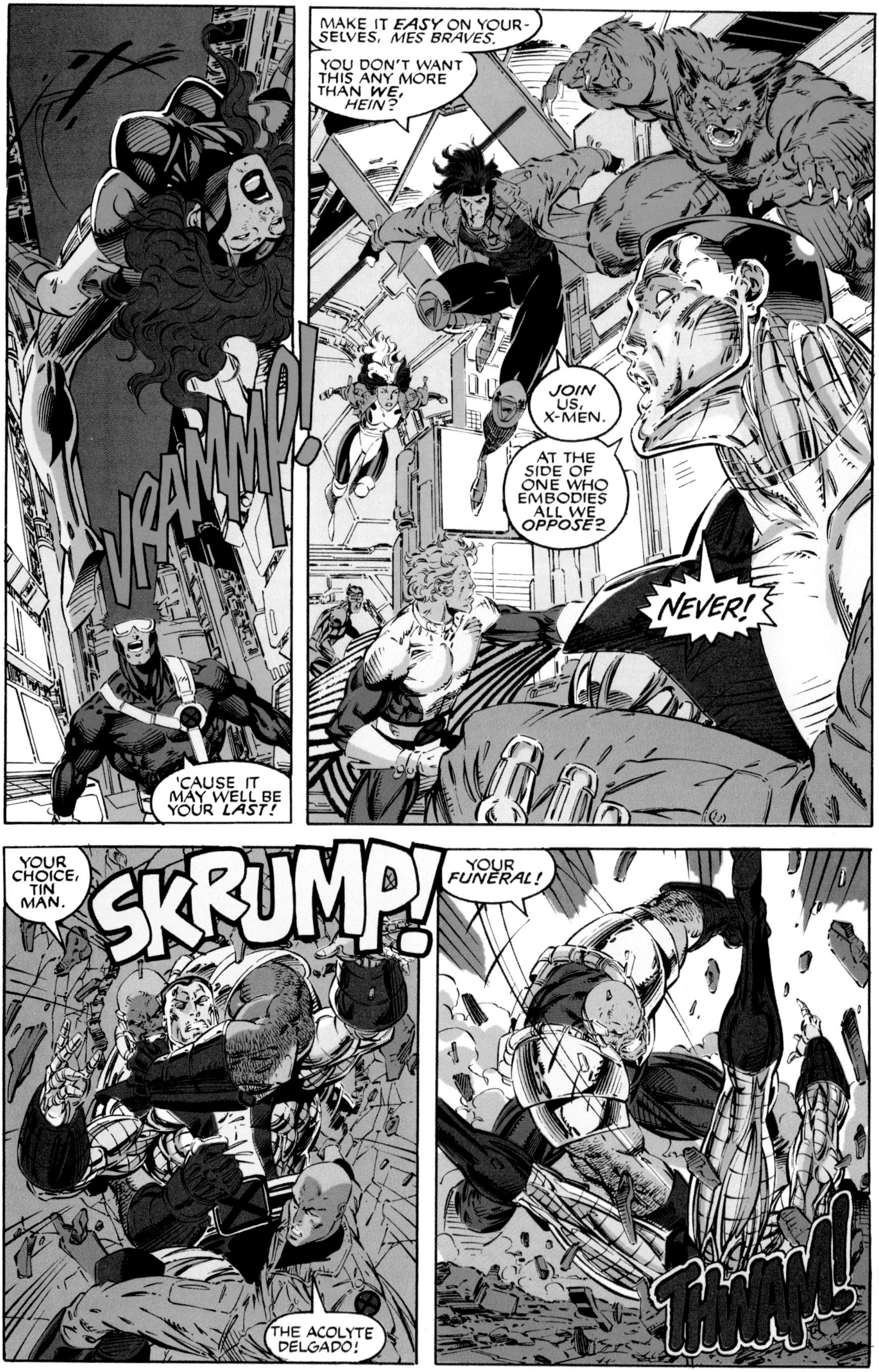

VRAMMP!
'CAUSE IT MAY WELL BE YOUR LAST!
MAKE IT EASY ON YOURSELVES, MES BRAVES.
YOU DON'T WANT THIS ANY MORE THAN WE, HEIN?
JOIN US, X-MEN.
AT THE SIDE OF ONE WHO EMBODIES ALL WE OPPOSE?
NEVER!
YOUR CHOICE, TIN MAN.
SKRUMP!
THE ACOLYTE DELGADO!
YOUR FUNERAL!
THWAM!

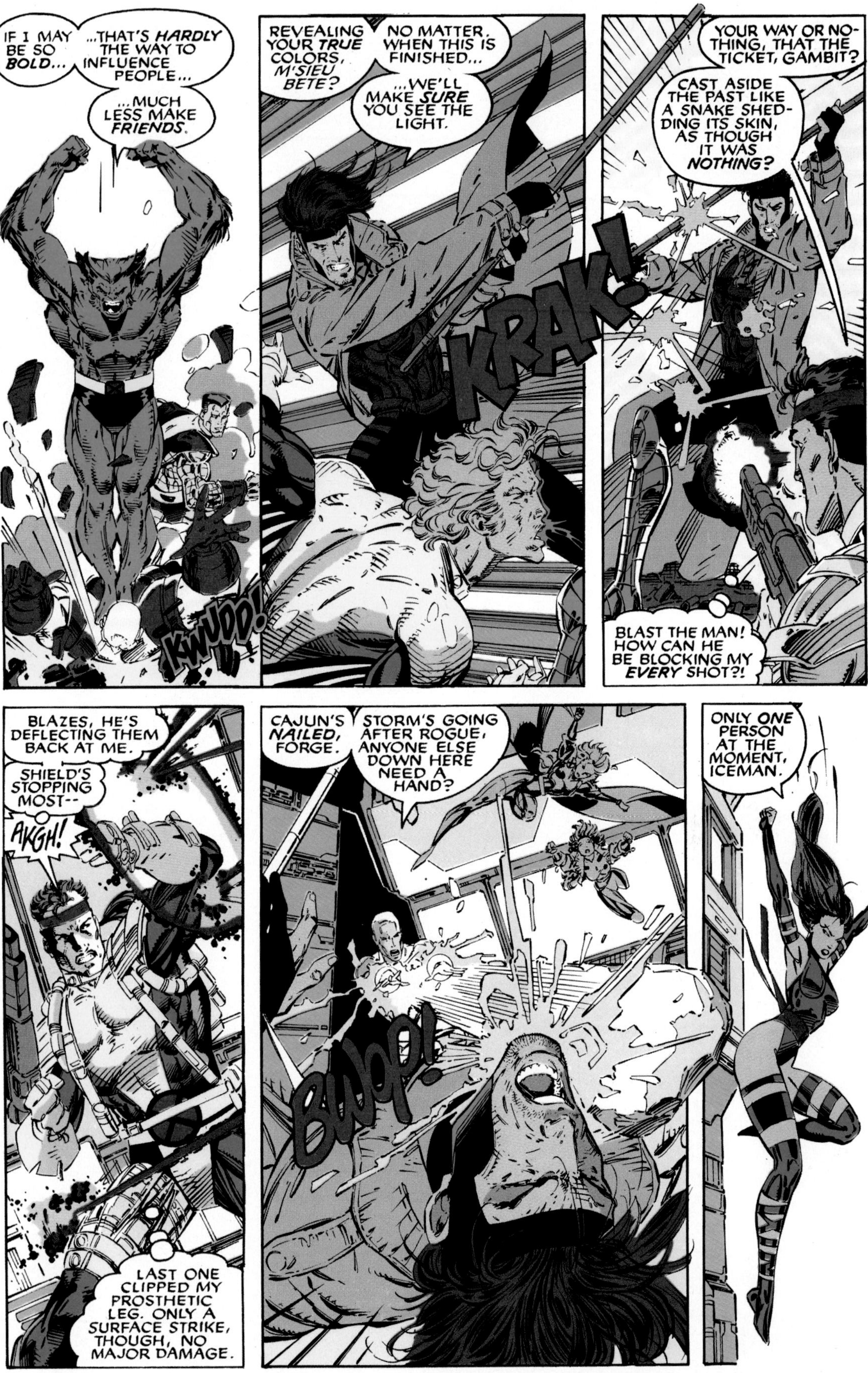
IF I MAY BE SO BOLD...
...THAT'S HARDLY THE WAY TO INFLUENCE PEOPLE...
...MUCH LESS MAKE FRIENDS.
KWUDD!
REVEALING YOUR TRUE COLORS, M'SIEU BETE?
NO MATTER. WHEN THIS IS FINISHED...
...WE'LL MAKE SURE YOU SEE THE LIGHT.
KRAK!
YOUR WAY OR NOTHING, THAT THE TICKET, GAMBIT?
CAST ASIDE THE PAST LIKE A SNAKE SHEDDING ITS SKIN, AS THOUGH IT WAS NOTHING?
BLAST THE MAN! HOW CAN HE BE BLOCKING MY EVERY SHOT?!
BLAZES, HE'S DEFLECTING THEM BACK AT ME.
SHIELD'S STOPPING MOST--
AKGH!
LAST ONE CLIPPED MY PROSTHETIC LEG. ONLY A SURFACE STRIKE, THOUGH, NO MAJOR DAMAGE.
CAJUN'S NAILED, FORGE.
STORM'S GOING AFTER ROGUE, ANYONE ELSE DOWN HERE NEED A HAND?
BUDOP!
ONLY ONE PERSON AT THE MOMENT, ICEMAN.

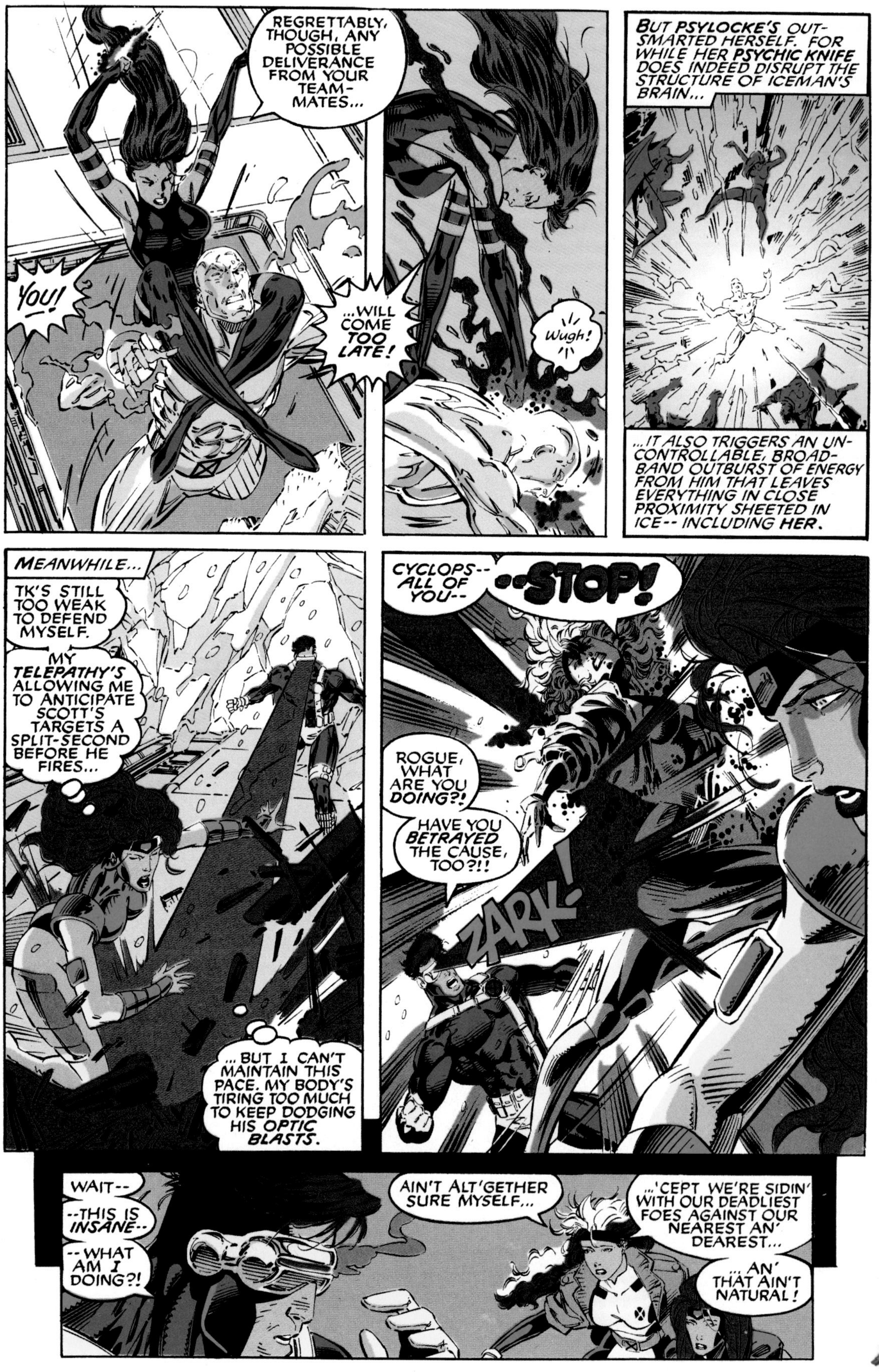
REGRETTABLY, THOUGH, ANY POSSIBLE DELIVERANCE FROM YOUR TEAM-MATES...
YOU!
...WILL COME TOO LATE!
Wugh!
BUT PSYLOCKE'S OUT-SMARTED HERSELF. FOR WHILE HER PSYCHIC KNIFE DOES INDEED DISRUPT THE STRUCTURE OF ICEMAN'S BRAIN...
...IT ALSO TRIGGERS AN UN-CONTROLLABLE, BROAD-BAND OUTBURST OF ENERGY FROM HIM THAT LEAVES EVERYTHING IN CLOSE PROXIMITY SHEETED IN ICE -- INCLUDING HER.
MEANWHILE...
TK'S STILL TOO WEAK TO DEFEND MYSELF.
MY TELEPATHY'S ALLOWING ME TO ANTICIPATE SCOTT'S TARGETS A SPLIT-SECOND BEFORE HE FIRES...
...BUT I CAN'T MAINTAIN THIS PACE. MY BODY'S TIRING TOO MUCH TO KEEP DODGING HIS OPTIC BLASTS.
CYCLOPS-- ALL OF YOU--
--STOP!
ROGUE, WHAT ARE YOU DOING?!
HAVE YOU BETRAYED THE CAUSE, TOO?!!
ZARK!
WAIT--
--THIS IS INSANE--
--WHAT AM I DOING?!
AIN'T ALT'GETHER SURE MYSELF...
...'CEPT WE'RE SIDIN' WITH OUR DEADLIEST FOES AGAINST OUR NEAREST AN' DEAREST...
...AN' THAT AIN'T NATURAL!

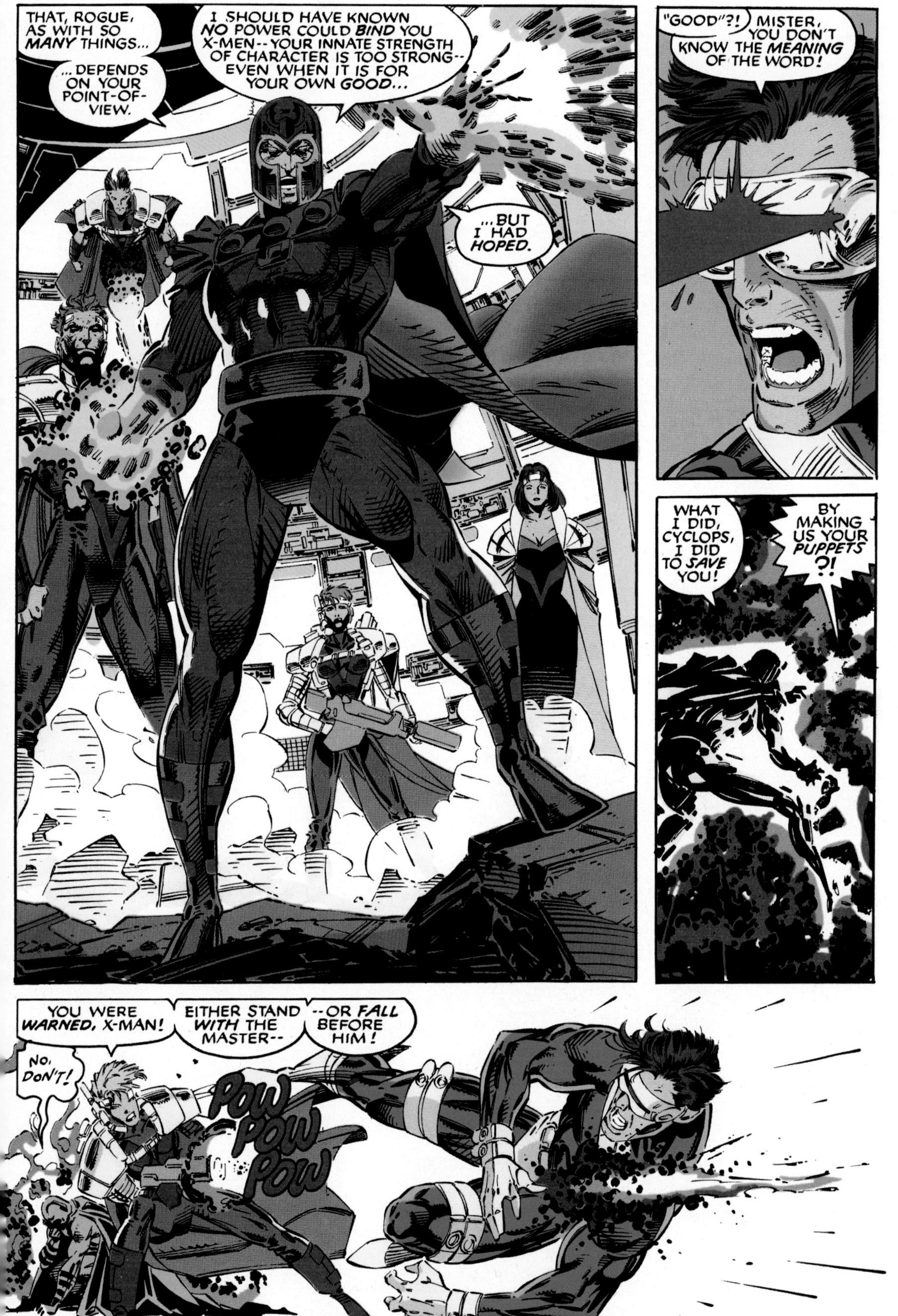
THAT, ROGUE, AS WITH SO MANY THINGS...
...DEPENDS ON YOUR POINT-OF-VIEW.
I SHOULD HAVE KNOWN NO POWER COULD BIND YOU X-MEN--YOUR INNATE STRENGTH OF CHARACTER IS TOO STRONG--EVEN WHEN IT IS FOR YOUR OWN GOOD...
...BUT I HAD HOPED.
"GOOD"?! MISTER, YOU DON'T KNOW THE MEANING OF THE WORD!
WHAT I DID, CYCLOPS, I DID TO SAVE YOU!
BY MAKING US YOUR PUPPETS?!
YOU WERE WARNED, X-MAN!
EITHER STAND WITH THE MASTER--
--OR FALL BEFORE HIM!
NO, DON'T!
POW POW POW

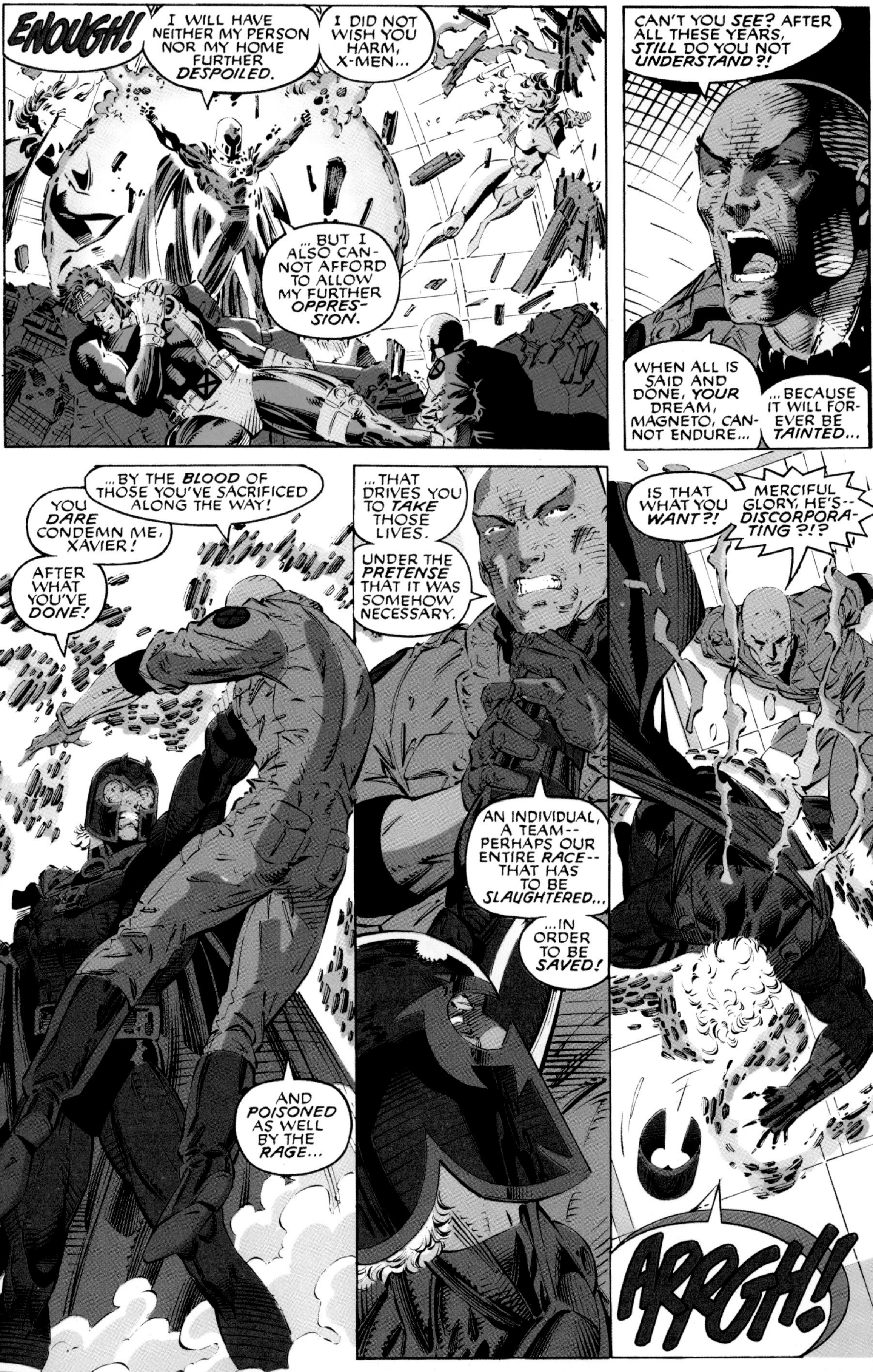
ENOUGH!
I WILL HAVE NEITHER MY PERSON NOR MY HOME FURTHER DESPOILED.
I DID NOT WISH YOU HARM, X-MEN...
...BUT I ALSO CANNOT AFFORD TO ALLOW MY FURTHER OPPRESSION.
CAN'T YOU SEE? AFTER ALL THESE YEARS, STILL DO YOU NOT UNDERSTAND?!
WHEN ALL IS SAID AND DONE, YOUR DREAM, MAGNETO, CANNOT ENDURE...
...BECAUSE IT WILL FOREVER BE TAINTED...
...BY THE BLOOD OF THOSE YOU'VE SACRIFICED ALONG THE WAY!
YOU DARE CONDEMN ME, XAVIER!
AFTER WHAT YOU'VE DONE!
AND POISONED AS WELL BY THE RAGE...
...THAT DRIVES YOU TO TAKE THOSE LIVES.
UNDER THE PRETENSE THAT IT WAS SOMEHOW NECESSARY.
AN INDIVIDUAL, A TEAM-- PERHAPS OUR ENTIRE RACE-- THAT HAS TO BE SLAUGHTERED...
...IN ORDER TO BE SAVED!
IS THAT WHAT YOU WANT?!
MERCIFUL GLORY, HE'S-- DISCORPORATING?!?
ARRGH!!

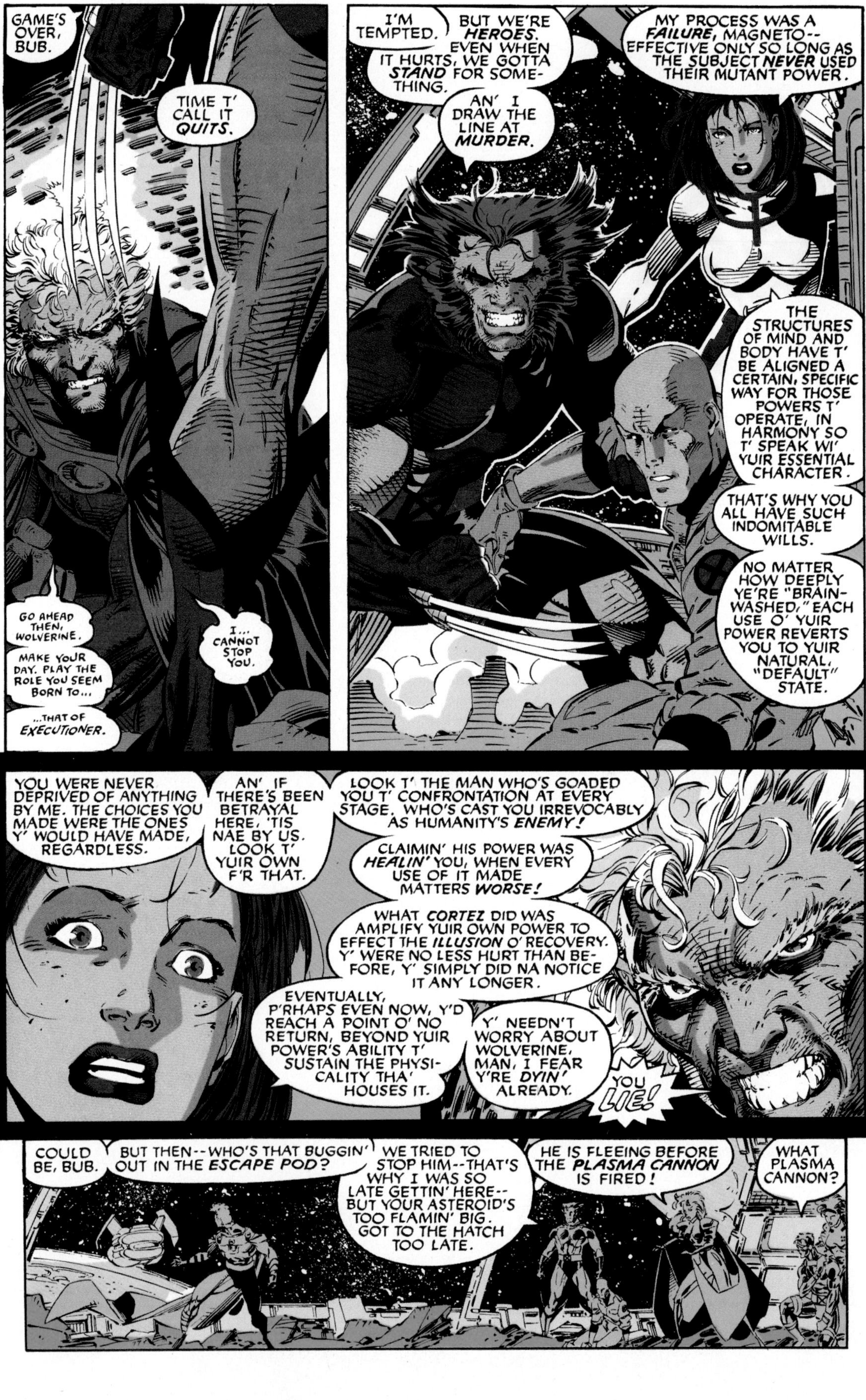

GAME'S OVER, BUB.
TIME T' CALL IT *QUITS*.
I'M TEMPTED.
BUT WE'RE *HEROES*. EVEN WHEN IT HURTS, WE GOTTA *STAND* FOR SOMETHING.
AN' I DRAW THE LINE AT *MURDER*.
MY PROCESS WAS A *FAILURE*, MAGNETO-- EFFECTIVE ONLY SO LONG AS THE SUBJECT *NEVER* USED THEIR MUTANT POWER.
THE STRUCTURES OF MIND AND BODY HAVE T' BE ALIGNED A CERTAIN, SPECIFIC WAY FOR THOSE POWERS T' OPERATE, IN HARMONY SO T' SPEAK WI' YUIR ESSENTIAL CHARACTER.
THAT'S WHY YOU ALL HAVE SUCH INDOMITABLE WILLS.
NO MATTER HOW DEEPLY YE'RE "BRAIN-WASHED," EACH USE O' YUIR POWER REVERTS YOU TO YUIR NATURAL, "DEFAULT" STATE.
GO AHEAD THEN, WOLVERINE.
MAKE YOUR DAY. PLAY THE ROLE YOU SEEM BORN TO...
...THAT OF *EXECUTIONER*.
I... CANNOT STOP YOU.
YOU WERE NEVER DEPRIVED OF ANYTHING BY ME. THE CHOICES YOU MADE WERE THE ONES Y' WOULD HAVE MADE, REGARDLESS.
AN' IF THERE'S BEEN BETRAYAL HERE, 'TIS NAE BY US. LOOK T' YUIR OWN F'R THAT.
LOOK T' THE MAN WHO'S GOADED YOU T' CONFRONTATION AT EVERY STAGE. WHO'S CAST YOU IRREVOCABLY AS HUMANITY'S *ENEMY*!
CLAIMIN' HIS POWER WAS *HEALIN'* YOU, WHEN EVERY USE OF IT MADE MATTERS *WORSE*!
WHAT *CORTEZ* DID WAS AMPLIFY YUIR OWN POWER TO EFFECT THE *ILLUSION* O' RECOVERY. Y' WERE NO LESS HURT THAN BEFORE, Y' SIMPLY DID NA NOTICE IT ANY LONGER.
EVENTUALLY, P'RHAPS EVEN NOW, Y'D REACH A POINT O' NO RETURN, BEYOND YUIR POWER'S ABILITY T' SUSTAIN THE PHYSICALITY THA' HOUSES IT.
Y' NEEDN'T WORRY ABOUT WOLVERINE, MAN, I FEAR Y'RE *DYIN'* ALREADY.
YOU *LIE!*
COULD BE, BUB.
BUT THEN--WHO'S THAT BUGGIN' OUT IN THE *ESCAPE POD*?
WE TRIED TO STOP HIM--THAT'S WHY I WAS SO LATE GETTIN' HERE--BUT YOUR ASTEROID'S TOO FLAMIN' BIG. GOT TO THE HATCH TOO LATE.
HE IS FLEEING BEFORE THE *PLASMA CANNON* IS FIRED!
WHAT PLASMA CANNON?

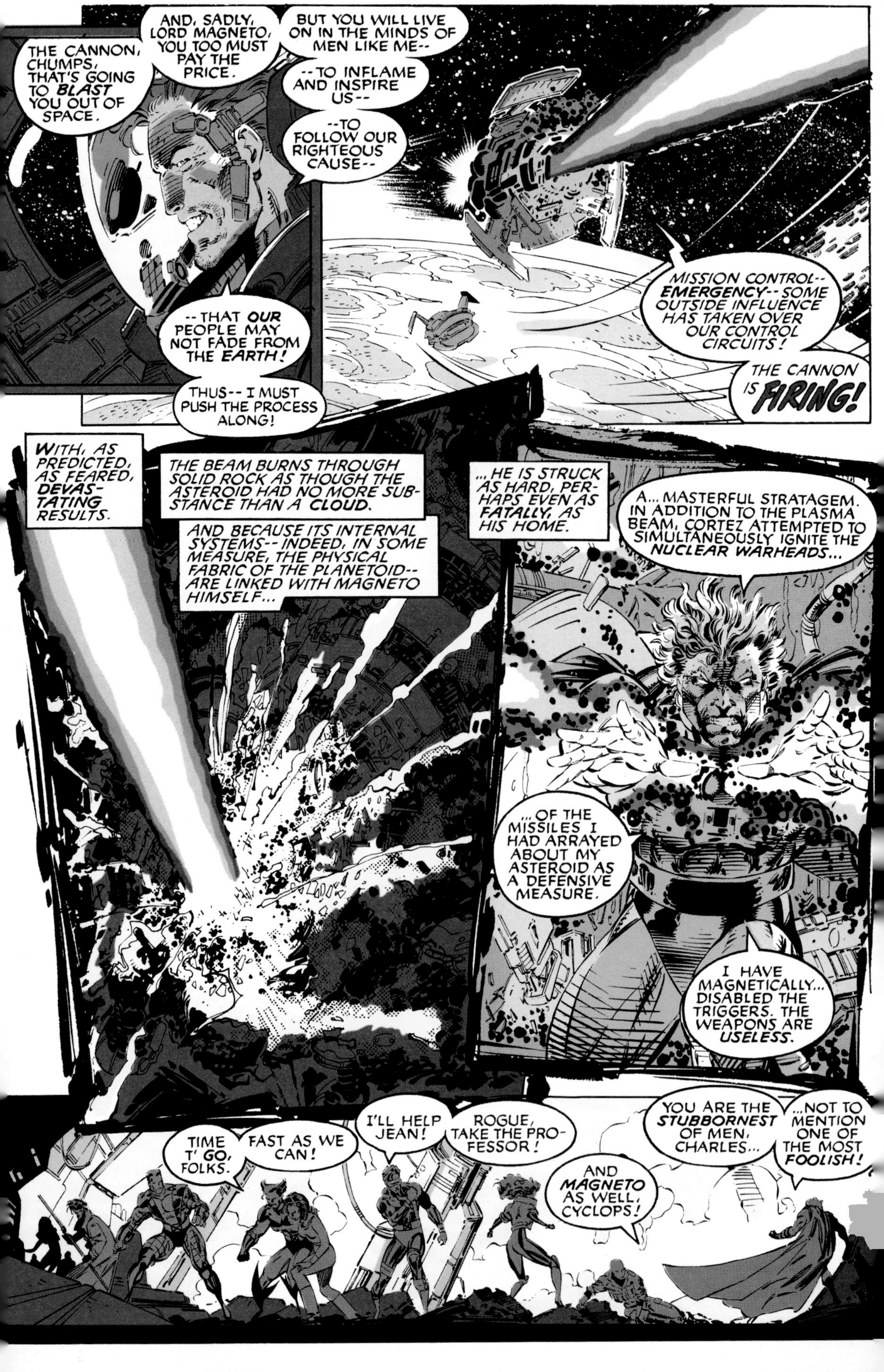

THE CANNON, CHUMPS, THAT'S GOING TO BLAST YOU OUT OF SPACE.
AND, SADLY, LORD MAGNETO, YOU TOO MUST PAY THE PRICE.
BUT YOU WILL LIVE ON IN THE MINDS OF MEN LIKE ME--
--TO INFLAME AND INSPIRE US--
--TO FOLLOW OUR RIGHTEOUS CAUSE--
--THAT OUR PEOPLE MAY NOT FADE FROM THE EARTH!
THUS--I MUST PUSH THE PROCESS ALONG!
MISSION CONTROL-- EMERGENCY--SOME OUTSIDE INFLUENCE HAS TAKEN OVER OUR CONTROL CIRCUITS!
THE CANNON IS FIRING!
WITH, AS PREDICTED, AS FEARED, DEVASTATING RESULTS.
THE BEAM BURNS THROUGH SOLID ROCK AS THOUGH THE ASTEROID HAD NO MORE SUBSTANCE THAN A CLOUD.
AND BECAUSE ITS INTERNAL SYSTEMS--INDEED, IN SOME MEASURE, THE PHYSICAL FABRIC OF THE PLANETOID--ARE LINKED WITH MAGNETO HIMSELF...
...HE IS STRUCK AS HARD, PERHAPS EVEN AS FATALLY, AS HIS HOME.
A... MASTERFUL STRATAGEM. IN ADDITION TO THE PLASMA BEAM, CORTEZ ATTEMPTED TO SIMULTANEOUSLY IGNITE THE NUCLEAR WARHEADS...
...OF THE MISSILES I HAD ARRAYED ABOUT MY ASTEROID AS A DEFENSIVE MEASURE.
I HAVE MAGNETICALLY... DISABLED THE TRIGGERS. THE WEAPONS ARE USELESS.
TIME T' GO, FOLKS.
FAST AS WE CAN!
I'LL HELP JEAN!
ROGUE, TAKE THE PROFESSOR!
AND MAGNETO AS WELL, CYCLOPS!
YOU ARE THE STUBBORNEST OF MEN, CHARLES...
...NOT TO MENTION ONE OF THE MOST FOOLISH!

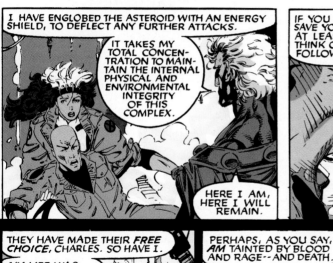

I HAVE ENGLOBED THE ASTEROID WITH AN ENERGY SHIELD, TO DEFLECT ANY FURTHER ATTACKS.

IT TAKES MY TOTAL CONCENTRATION TO MAINTAIN THE INTERNAL PHYSICAL AND ENVIRONMENTAL INTEGRITY OF THIS COMPLEX.

HERE I AM, HERE I WILL REMAIN.

IF YOU WON'T SAVE YOURSELF, AT LEAST THINK OF YOUR FOLLOWERS.

THERE'S ROOM IN THE X-WING, COME WITH US, I BEG YOU!

NO.

THEY HAVE MADE THEIR *FREE CHOICE,* CHARLES. SO HAVE I.

MY LIFE WAS SHAPED BY FORCES AND EVENTS NONE OF YOU CAN POSSIBLY UNDERSTAND.

YOU SPEAK TO THE *BEST* IN HUMANITY. I HAVE ENDURED THE *WORST.*

YOU *IMAGINE* THE REALITY OF THE *HOLOCAUST,* OF THE NAZI *DEATH CAMPS.* I GREW UP IN ONE.

PERHAPS, AS YOU SAY, I *AM* TAINTED BY BLOOD AND RAGE-- AND DEATH.

BUT PERHAPS AS WELL, THAT BLOOD AND RAGE AND DEATH COMPRISE THE *ARMOR* THAT WILL *SUSTAIN* ME AND THOSE WHO STAND BY ME THROUGH THE ORDEAL TO COME.

THE PAST IS PROLOGUE, OLD FRIEND. AND THE FUTURE I BEHOLD FOR YOU IS...

...WAR.

WE HAVE ALREADY *CHOSEN* OUR PATH.

CHOSEN *WHAT--* A LEGACY TO OUR CHILDREN OF UNENDING *CONFLICT?*

ARE YOUR HEART AND SOUL SO *BLACK?*

PROFESSOR, WE GOTTA *GO!*

IT'S NO USE TALKIN', AH SEE THAT NOW.

Y'ALL MAY USE THE SAME WORDS, BUT YOU DON'T SPEAK THE SAME LANGUAGE. AH WONDER IF Y'EVER DID.

LEAVE ME *BE,* ROGUE! I WON'T *PERMIT* THIS!

THAT DECISION, CHARLES, IS NOT YOURS TO MAKE.

FAREWELL, MY OLD FRIEND.

WHATEVER COMES, I AND MINE WILL NOT GO LIKE LAMBS TO THE SLAUGHTER-- BUT LIKE *TIGERS.*

WE'RE ABOARD, STORM! HATCH IS SEALED TIGHT!

GET US *OUTTA* HERE!

--NO!

NO-- *MAGNETO--* THIS ISN'T THE ANSWER, IT ISN'T THE WAY--

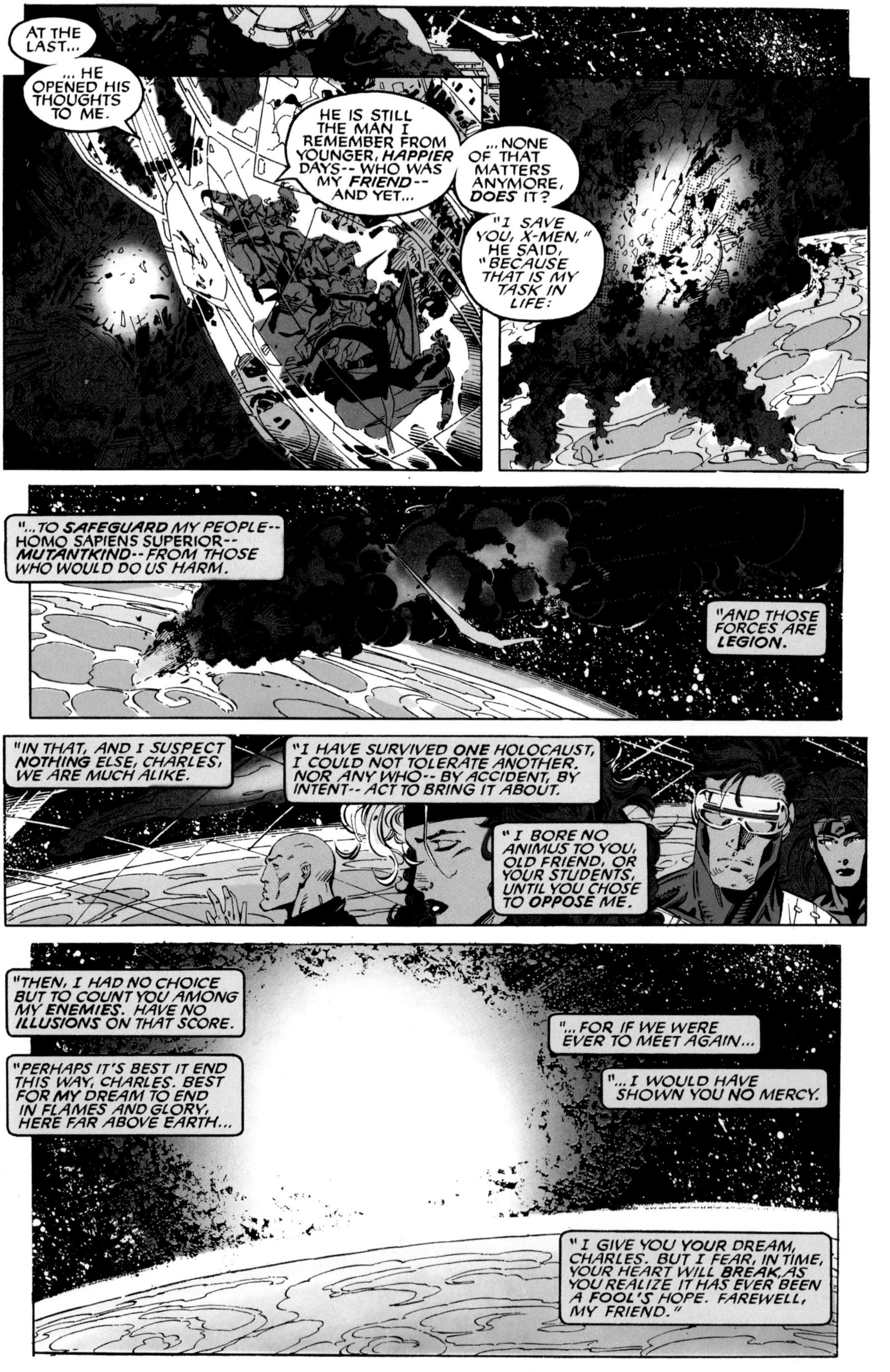
AT THE LAST...
... HE OPENED HIS THOUGHTS TO ME.
HE IS STILL THE MAN I REMEMBER FROM YOUNGER, HAPPIER DAYS-- WHO WAS MY FRIEND-- AND YET...
... NONE OF THAT MATTERS ANYMORE, DOES IT?
"I SAVE YOU, X-MEN," HE SAID, "BECAUSE THAT IS MY TASK IN LIFE:
"...TO SAFEGUARD MY PEOPLE-- HOMO SAPIENS SUPERIOR-- MUTANTKIND-- FROM THOSE WHO WOULD DO US HARM.
"AND THOSE FORCES ARE LEGION.
"IN THAT, AND I SUSPECT NOTHING ELSE, CHARLES, WE ARE MUCH ALIKE.
"I HAVE SURVIVED ONE HOLOCAUST, I COULD NOT TOLERATE ANOTHER. NOR ANY WHO-- BY ACCIDENT, BY INTENT-- ACT TO BRING IT ABOUT.
"I BORE NO ANIMUS TO YOU, OLD FRIEND, OR YOUR STUDENTS, UNTIL YOU CHOSE TO OPPOSE ME.
"THEN, I HAD NO CHOICE BUT TO COUNT YOU AMONG MY ENEMIES. HAVE NO ILLUSIONS ON THAT SCORE.
"PERHAPS IT'S BEST IT END THIS WAY, CHARLES. BEST FOR MY DREAM TO END IN FLAMES AND GLORY, HERE FAR ABOVE EARTH...
"...FOR IF WE WERE EVER TO MEET AGAIN...
"...I WOULD HAVE SHOWN YOU NO MERCY.
"I GIVE YOU YOUR DREAM, CHARLES. BUT I FEAR, IN TIME, YOUR HEART WILL BREAK, AS YOU REALIZE IT HAS EVER BEEN A FOOL'S HOPE. FAREWELL, MY FRIEND."

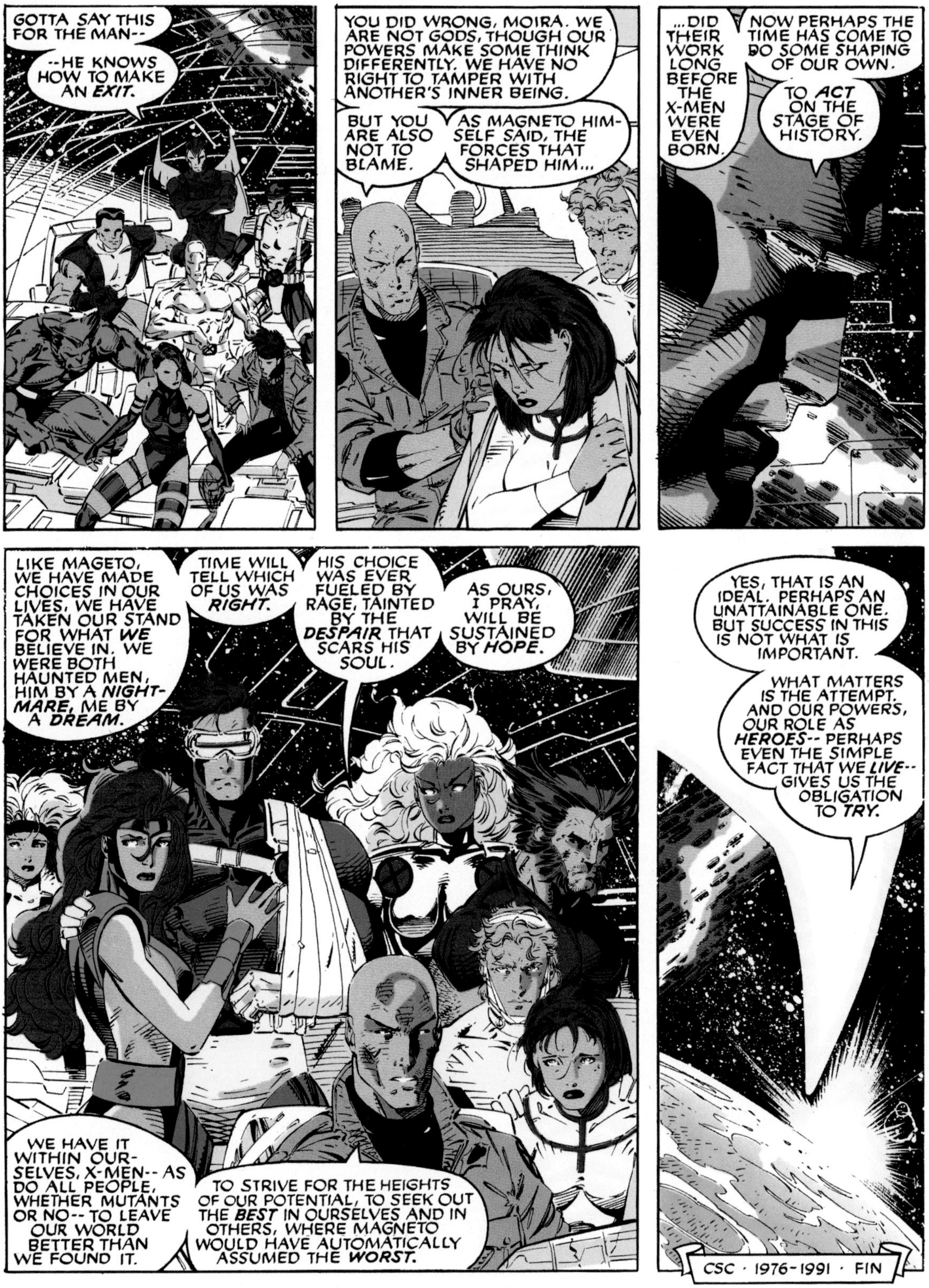

GOTTA SAY THIS FOR THE MAN--
--HE KNOWS HOW TO MAKE AN EXIT.
YOU DID WRONG, MOIRA. WE ARE NOT GODS, THOUGH OUR POWERS MAKE SOME THINK DIFFERENTLY. WE HAVE NO RIGHT TO TAMPER WITH ANOTHER'S INNER BEING.
BUT YOU ARE ALSO NOT TO BLAME.
AS MAGNETO HIMSELF SAID, THE FORCES THAT SHAPED HIM...
...DID THEIR WORK LONG BEFORE THE X-MEN WERE EVEN BORN.
NOW PERHAPS THE TIME HAS COME TO DO SOME SHAPING OF OUR OWN.
TO ACT ON THE STAGE OF HISTORY.
LIKE MAGETO, WE HAVE MADE CHOICES IN OUR LIVES, WE HAVE TAKEN OUR STAND FOR WHAT WE BELIEVE IN. WE WERE BOTH HAUNTED MEN, HIM BY A NIGHTMARE, ME BY A DREAM.
TIME WILL TELL WHICH OF US WAS RIGHT.
HIS CHOICE WAS EVER FUELED BY RAGE, TAINTED BY THE DESPAIR THAT SCARS HIS SOUL.
AS OURS, I PRAY, WILL BE SUSTAINED BY HOPE.
WE HAVE IT WITHIN OURSELVES, X-MEN-- AS DO ALL PEOPLE, WHETHER MUTANTS OR NO-- TO LEAVE OUR WORLD BETTER THAN WE FOUND IT.
TO STRIVE FOR THE HEIGHTS OF OUR POTENTIAL, TO SEEK OUT THE BEST IN OURSELVES AND IN OTHERS, WHERE MAGNETO WOULD HAVE AUTOMATICALLY ASSUMED THE WORST.
YES, THAT IS AN IDEAL. PERHAPS AN UNATTAINABLE ONE. BUT SUCCESS IN THIS IS NOT WHAT IS IMPORTANT.
WHAT MATTERS IS THE ATTEMPT. AND OUR POWERS, OUR ROLE AS HEROES-- PERHAPS EVEN THE SIMPLE FACT THAT WE LIVE-- GIVES US THE OBLIGATION TO TRY.
CSC · 1976-1991 · FIN

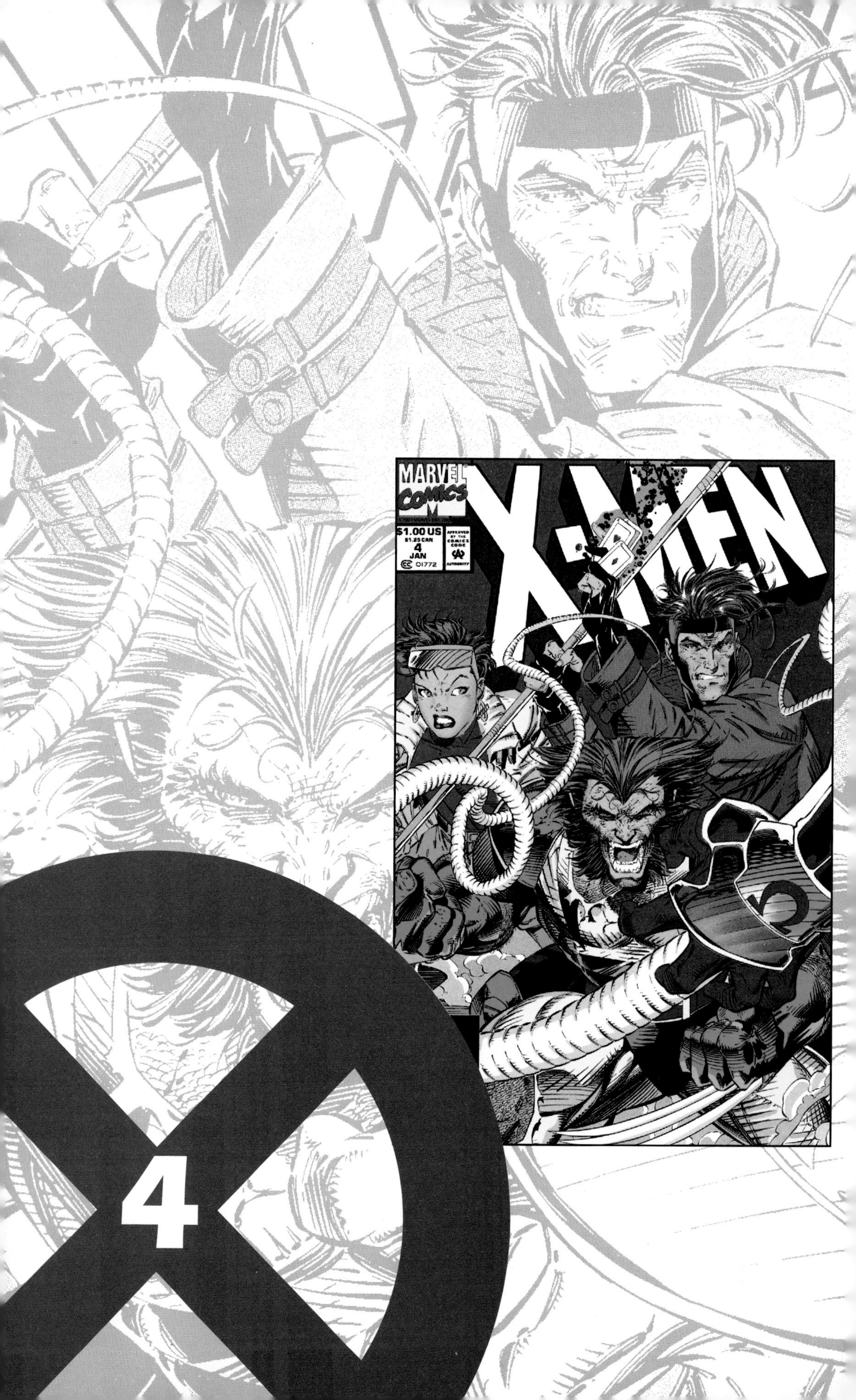

MARVEL COMICS
X-MEN
$1.00 US
$1.25 CAN
4
JAN
APPROVED BY THE COMICS CODE AUTHORITY
01772
4

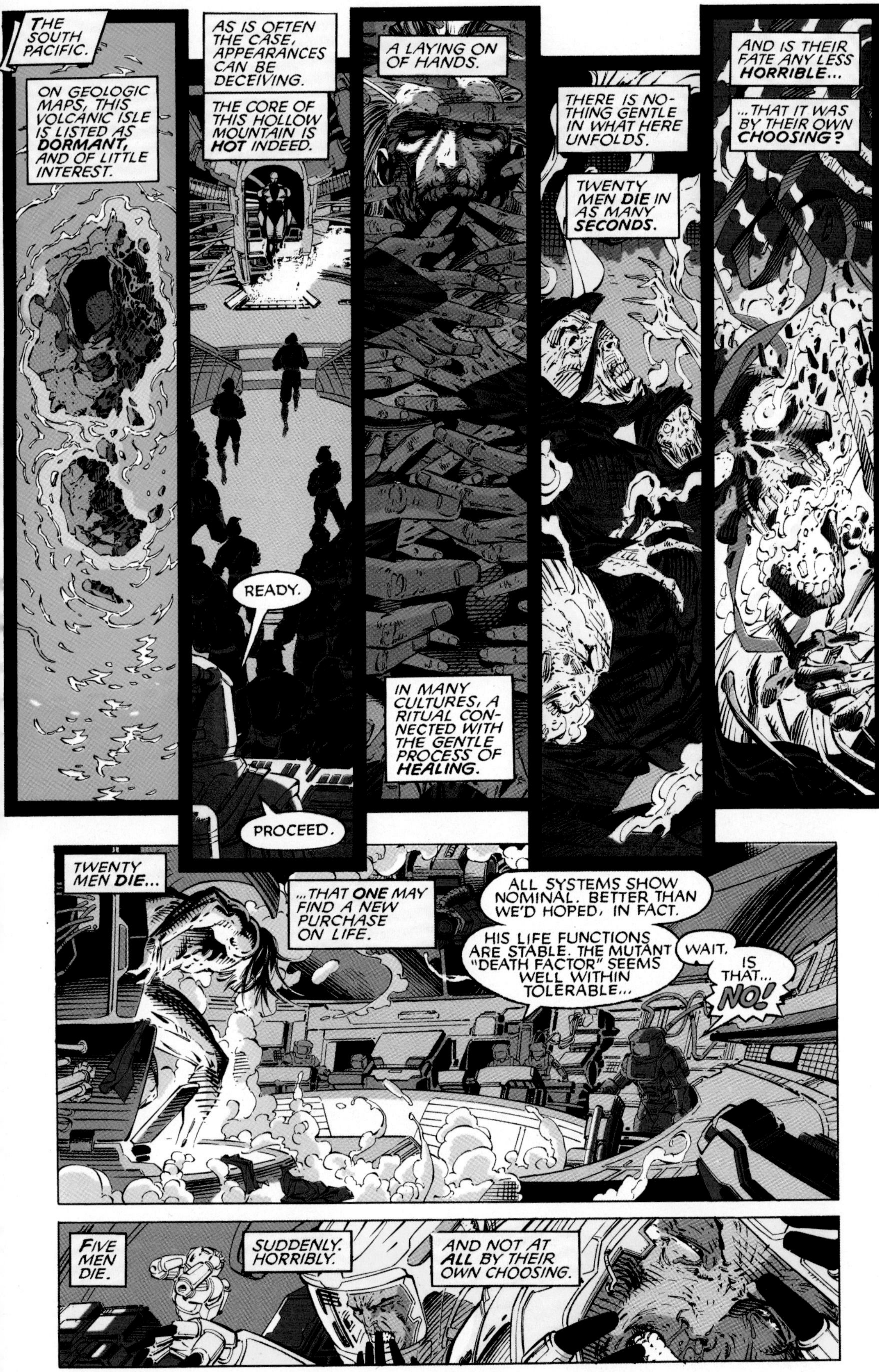

THE SOUTH PACIFIC.
ON GEOLOGIC MAPS, THIS VOLCANIC ISLE IS LISTED AS DORMANT, AND OF LITTLE INTEREST.
AS IS OFTEN THE CASE, APPEARANCES CAN BE DECEIVING.
THE CORE OF THIS HOLLOW MOUNTAIN IS HOT INDEED.
READY.
PROCEED.
A LAYING ON OF HANDS.
IN MANY CULTURES, A RITUAL CONNECTED WITH THE GENTLE PROCESS OF HEALING.
THERE IS NOTHING GENTLE IN WHAT HERE UNFOLDS.
TWENTY MEN DIE IN AS MANY SECONDS.
AND IS THEIR FATE ANY LESS HORRIBLE...
...THAT IT WAS BY THEIR OWN CHOOSING?
TWENTY MEN DIE...
...THAT ONE MAY FIND A NEW PURCHASE ON LIFE.
ALL SYSTEMS SHOW NOMINAL. BETTER THAN WE'D HOPED, IN FACT.
HIS LIFE FUNCTIONS ARE STABLE. THE MUTANT "DEATH FACTOR" SEEMS WELL WITHIN TOLERABLE...
WAIT. IS THAT... NO!
FIVE MEN DIE.
SUDDENLY. HORRIBLY.
AND NOT AT ALL BY THEIR OWN CHOOSING.

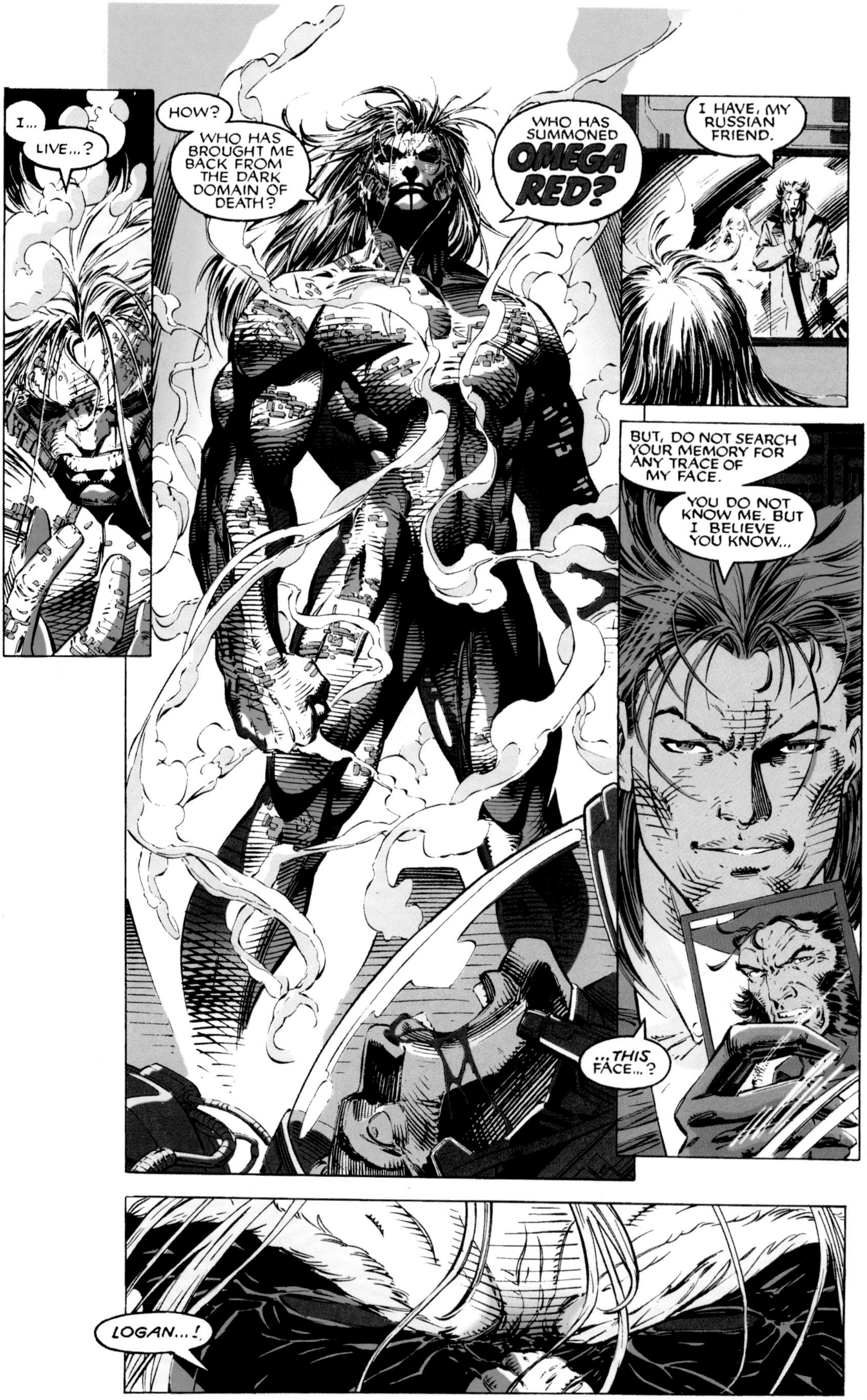
I... LIVE...?
HOW? WHO HAS BROUGHT ME BACK FROM THE DARK DOMAIN OF DEATH?
WHO HAS SUMMONED OMEGA RED?
I HAVE, MY RUSSIAN FRIEND.
BUT, DO NOT SEARCH YOUR MEMORY FOR ANY TRACE OF MY FACE.
YOU DO NOT KNOW ME. BUT I BELIEVE YOU KNOW...
...THIS FACE...?
LOGAN...!

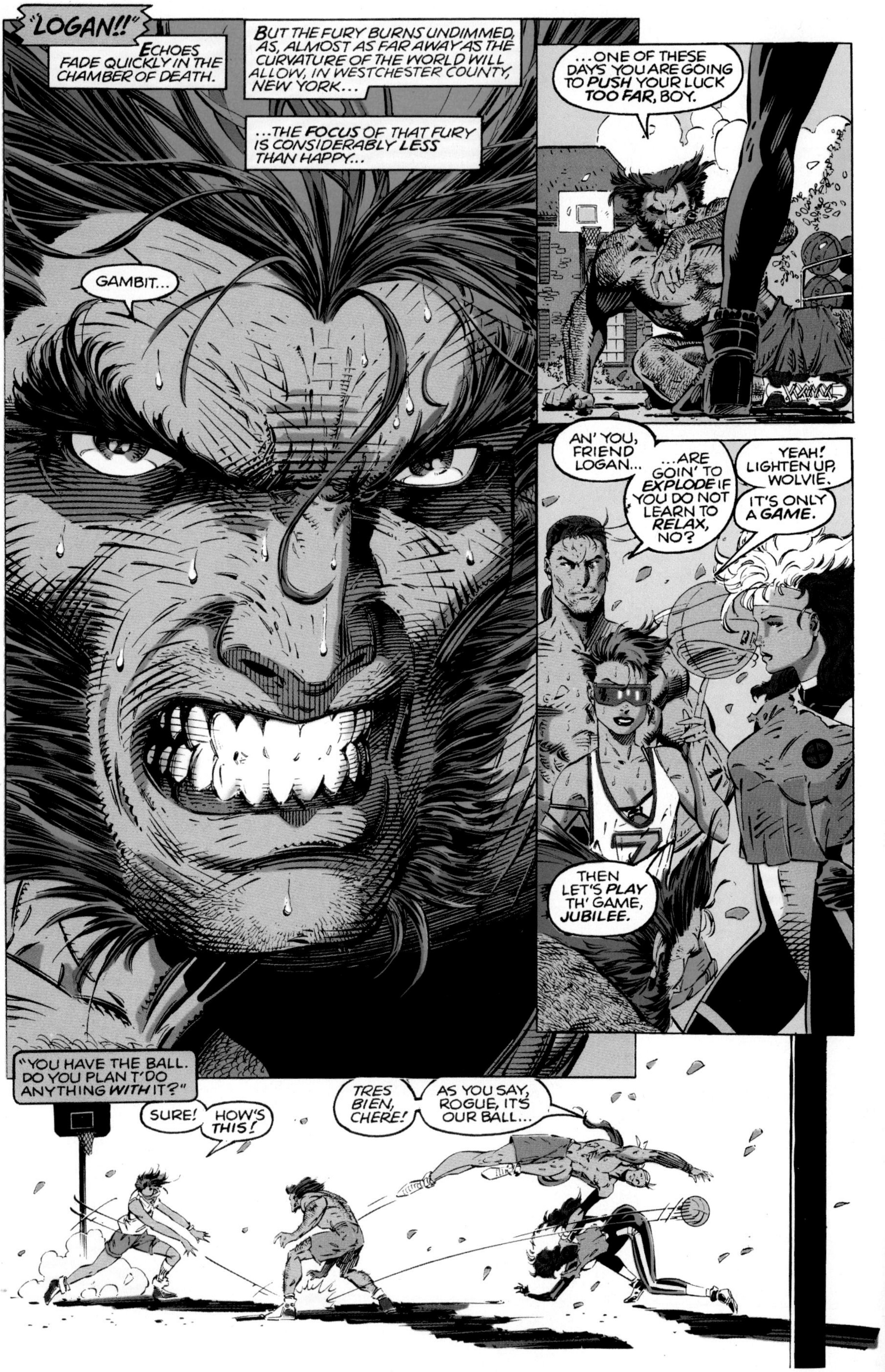
"LOGAN!!"
ECHOES FADE QUICKLY IN THE CHAMBER OF DEATH.
BUT THE FURY BURNS UNDIMMED, AS, ALMOST AS FAR AWAY AS THE CURVATURE OF THE WORLD WILL ALLOW, IN WESTCHESTER COUNTY, NEW YORK...
...THE FOCUS OF THAT FURY IS CONSIDERABLY LESS THAN HAPPY...
GAMBIT...
...ONE OF THESE DAYS YOU ARE GOING TO PUSH YOUR LUCK TOO FAR, BOY.
AN' YOU, FRIEND LOGAN...
...ARE GOIN' TO EXPLODE IF YOU DO NOT LEARN TO RELAX, NO?
YEAH! LIGHTEN UP, WOLVIE.
IT'S ONLY A GAME.
THEN LET'S PLAY TH' GAME, JUBILEE.
"YOU HAVE THE BALL. DO YOU PLAN T'DO ANYTHING WITH IT?"
SURE!
HOW'S THIS!
AS YOU SAY, ROGUE, IT'S OUR BALL...
TRES BIEN, CHERE!

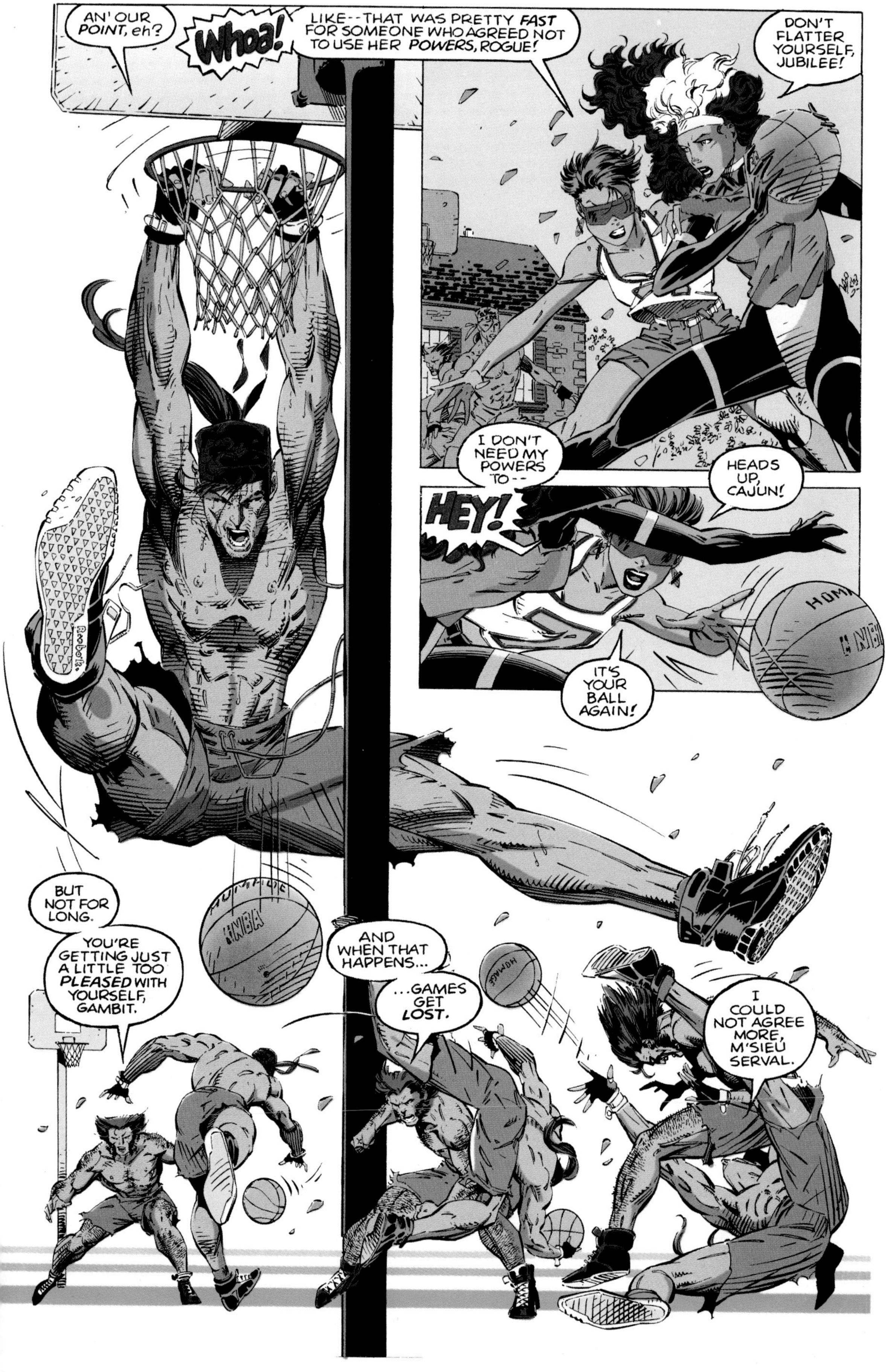

AN' OUR POINT, eh?
Whoa!
LIKE--THAT WAS PRETTY FAST FOR SOMEONE WHO AGREED NOT TO USE HER POWERS, ROGUE!
DON'T FLATTER YOURSELF, JUBILEE!
I DON'T NEED MY POWERS TO--
HEY!
HEADS UP, CAJUN!
IT'S YOUR BALL AGAIN!
BUT NOT FOR LONG.
YOU'RE GETTING JUST A LITTLE TOO PLEASED WITH YOURSELF, GAMBIT.
AND WHEN THAT HAPPENS...
...GAMES GET LOST.
I COULD NOT AGREE MORE, M'SIEU SERVAL.

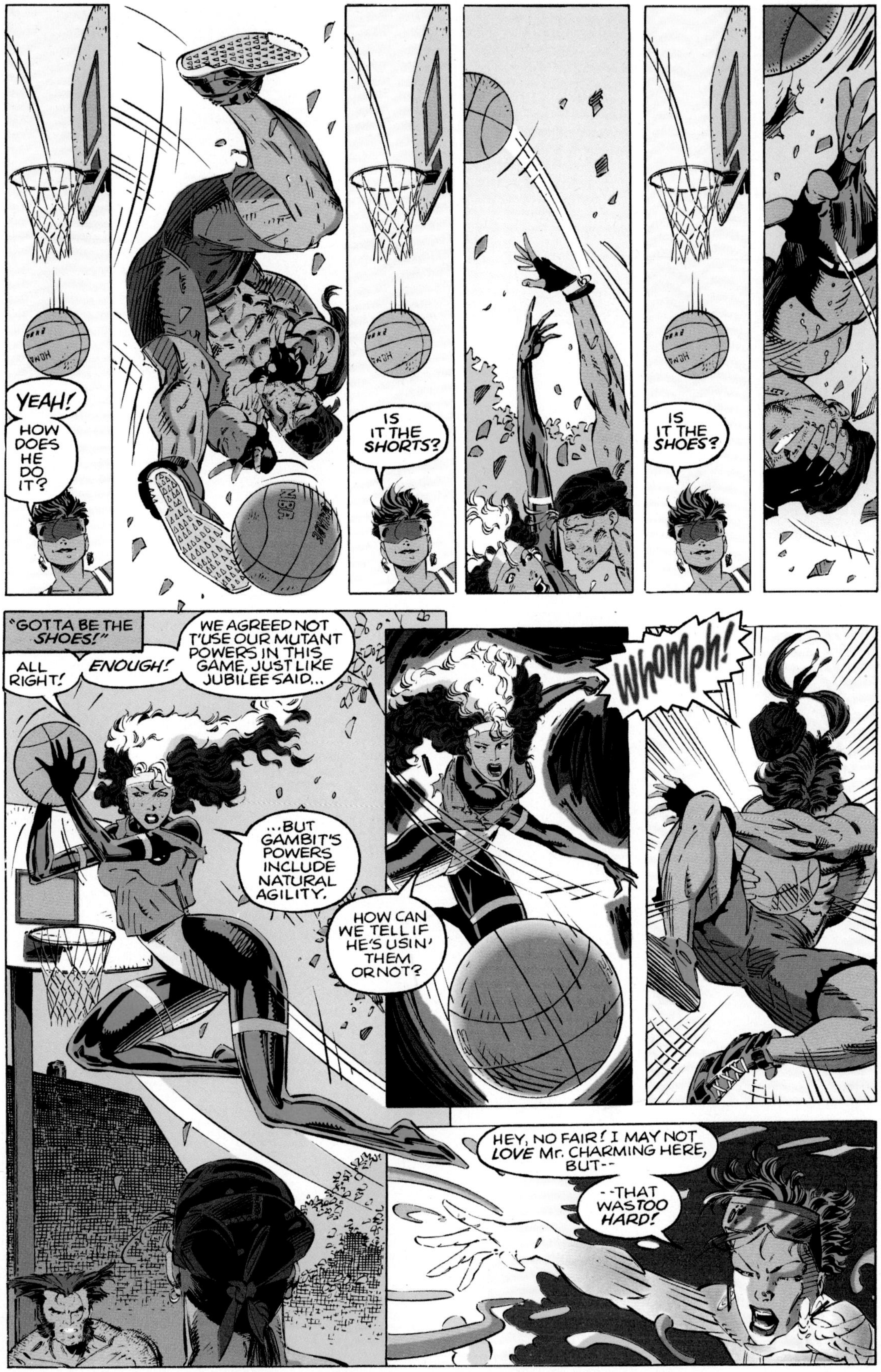
YEAH!
HOW DOES HE DO IT?
IS IT THE SHORTS?
IS IT THE SHOES?
"GOTTA BE THE SHOES!"
ALL RIGHT!
ENOUGH!
WE AGREED NOT T'USE OUR MUTANT POWERS IN THIS GAME, JUST LIKE JUBILEE SAID...
...BUT GAMBIT'S POWERS INCLUDE NATURAL AGILITY.
HOW CAN WE TELL IF HE'S USIN' THEM OR NOT?
WHOMPH!
HEY, NO FAIR! I MAY NOT LOVE Mr. CHARMING HERE, BUT--
--THAT WASTOO HARD!

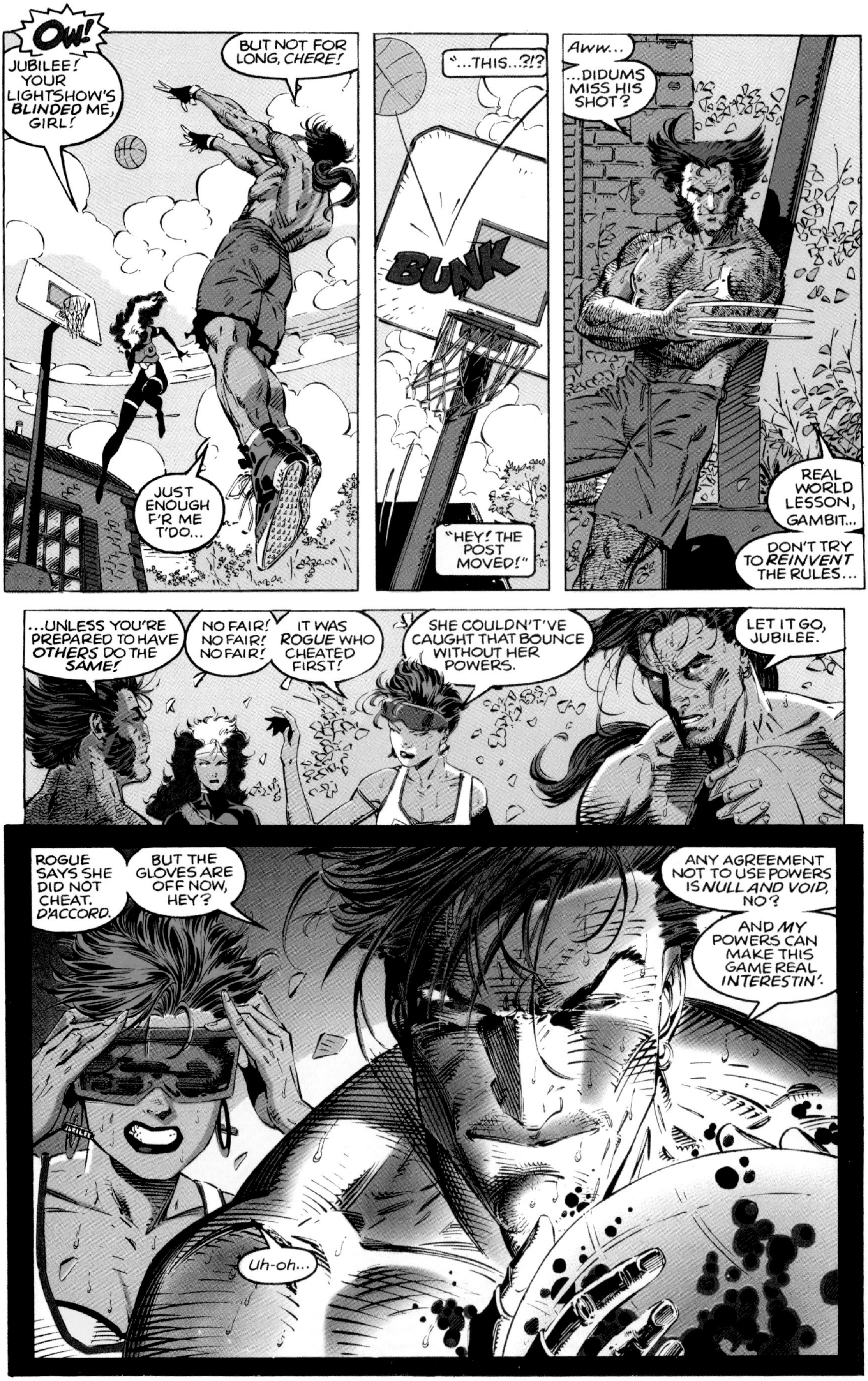
OW!
JUBILEE! YOUR LIGHTSHOW'S BLINDED ME, GIRL!
BUT NOT FOR LONG, CHERE!
JUST ENOUGH F'R ME T'DO...
"...THIS...?!?
BUNK
"HEY! THE POST MOVED!"
Aww...
...DIDUMS MISS HIS SHOT?
REAL WORLD LESSON, GAMBIT...
DON'T TRY TO REINVENT THE RULES...
...UNLESS YOU'RE PREPARED TO HAVE OTHERS DO THE SAME!
NO FAIR! NO FAIR! NO FAIR!
IT WAS ROGUE WHO CHEATED FIRST!
SHE COULDN'T'VE CAUGHT THAT BOUNCE WITHOUT HER POWERS.
LET IT GO, JUBILEE.
ROGUE SAYS SHE DID NOT CHEAT. D'ACCORD.
BUT THE GLOVES ARE OFF NOW, HEY?
ANY AGREEMENT NOT TO USE POWERS IS NULL AND VOID, NO?
AND MY POWERS CAN MAKE THIS GAME REAL INTERESTIN'.
Uh-oh...

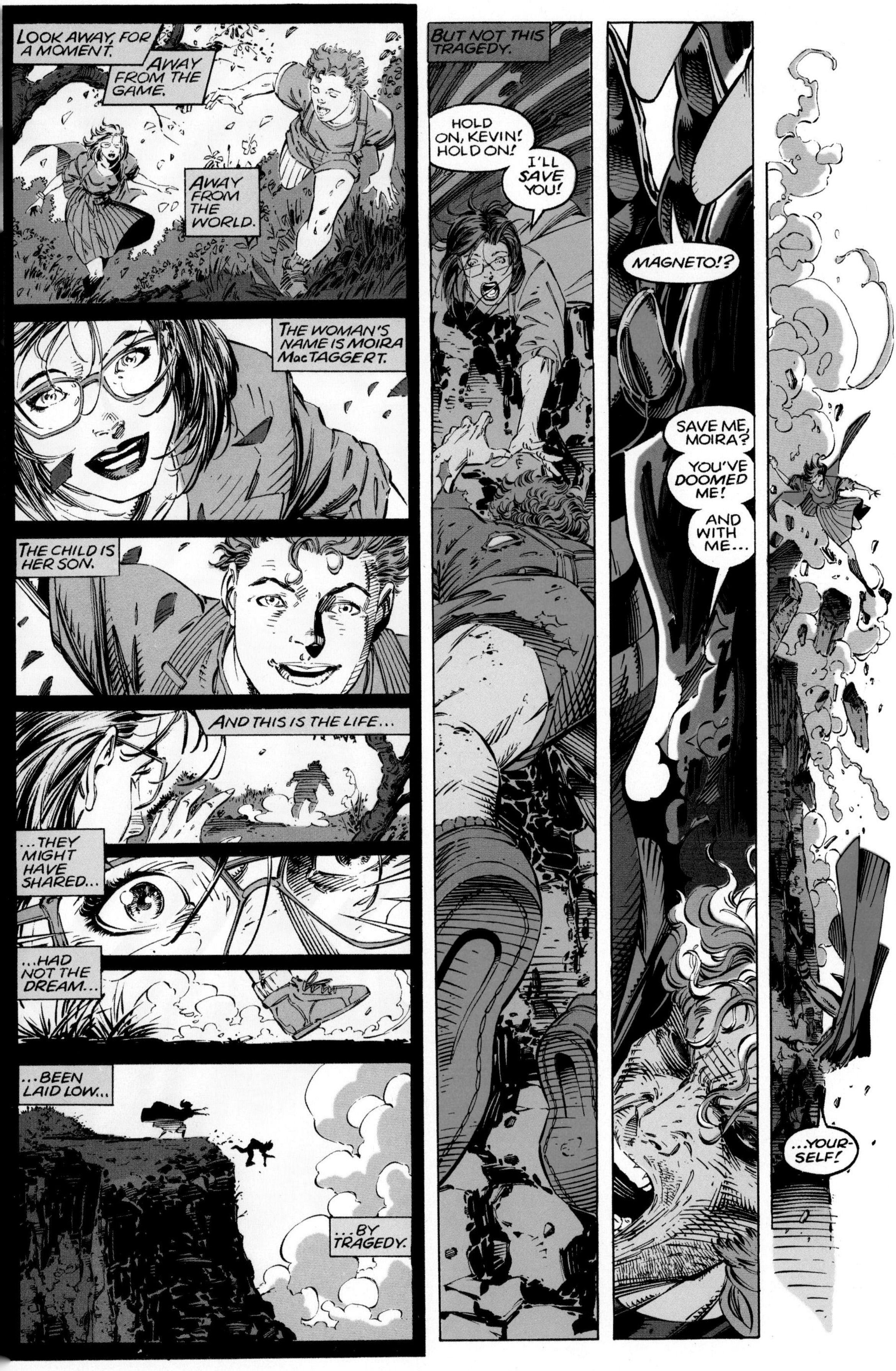
LOOK AWAY, FOR A MOMENT.
AWAY FROM THE GAME.
AWAY FROM THE WORLD.
THE WOMAN'S NAME IS MOIRA MacTAGGERT.
THE CHILD IS HER SON.
AND THIS IS THE LIFE...
...THEY MIGHT HAVE SHARED...
...HAD NOT THE DREAM...
...BEEN LAID LOW...
...BY TRAGEDY.
BUT NOT THIS TRAGEDY.
HOLD ON, KEVIN! HOLD ON!
I'LL SAVE YOU!
MAGNETO!?
SAVE ME, MOIRA?
YOU'VE DOOMED ME!
AND WITH ME...
...YOURSELF!

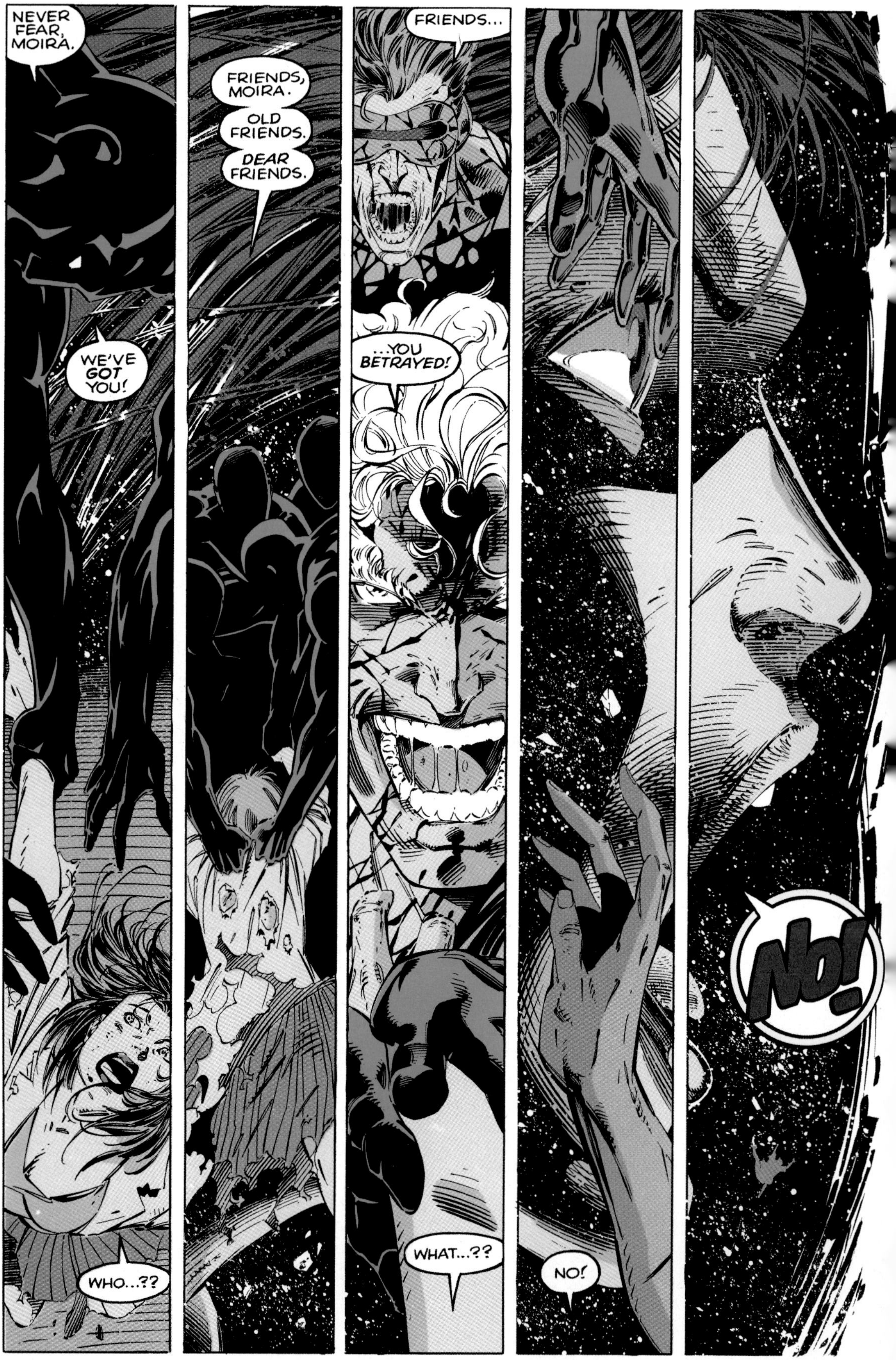
NEVER FEAR, MOIRA.
WE'VE GOT YOU!
WHO...??
FRIENDS, MOIRA.
OLD FRIENDS.
DEAR FRIENDS.
FRIENDS...
...YOU BETRAYED!
WHAT...??
NO!
No!

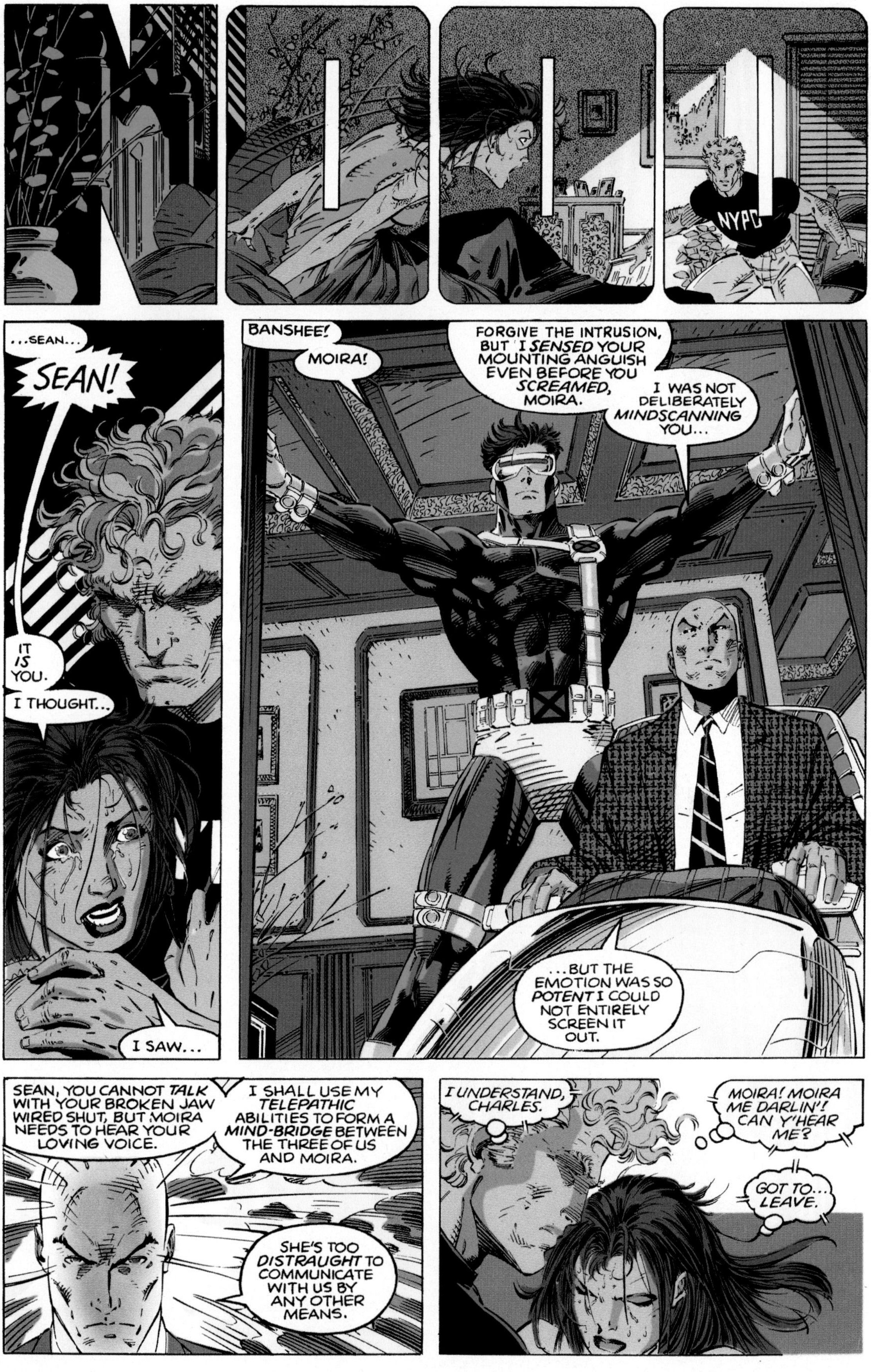

...SEAN...
SEAN!
IT IS YOU.
I THOUGHT...
I SAW...
BANSHEE!
MOIRA!
FORGIVE THE INTRUSION, BUT I SENSED YOUR MOUNTING ANGUISH EVEN BEFORE YOU SCREAMED, MOIRA.
I WAS NOT DELIBERATELY MINDSCANNING YOU...
...BUT THE EMOTION WAS SO POTENT I COULD NOT ENTIRELY SCREEN IT OUT.
SEAN, YOU CANNOT TALK WITH YOUR BROKEN JAW WIRED SHUT, BUT MOIRA NEEDS TO HEAR YOUR LOVING VOICE.
I SHALL USE MY TELEPATHIC ABILITIES TO FORM A MIND-BRIDGE BETWEEN THE THREE OF US AND MOIRA.
SHE'S TOO DISTRAUGHT TO COMMUNICATE WITH US BY ANY OTHER MEANS.
I UNDERSTAND, CHARLES.
MOIRA! MOIRA ME DARLIN'! CAN Y'HEAR ME?
GOT TO... LEAVE.

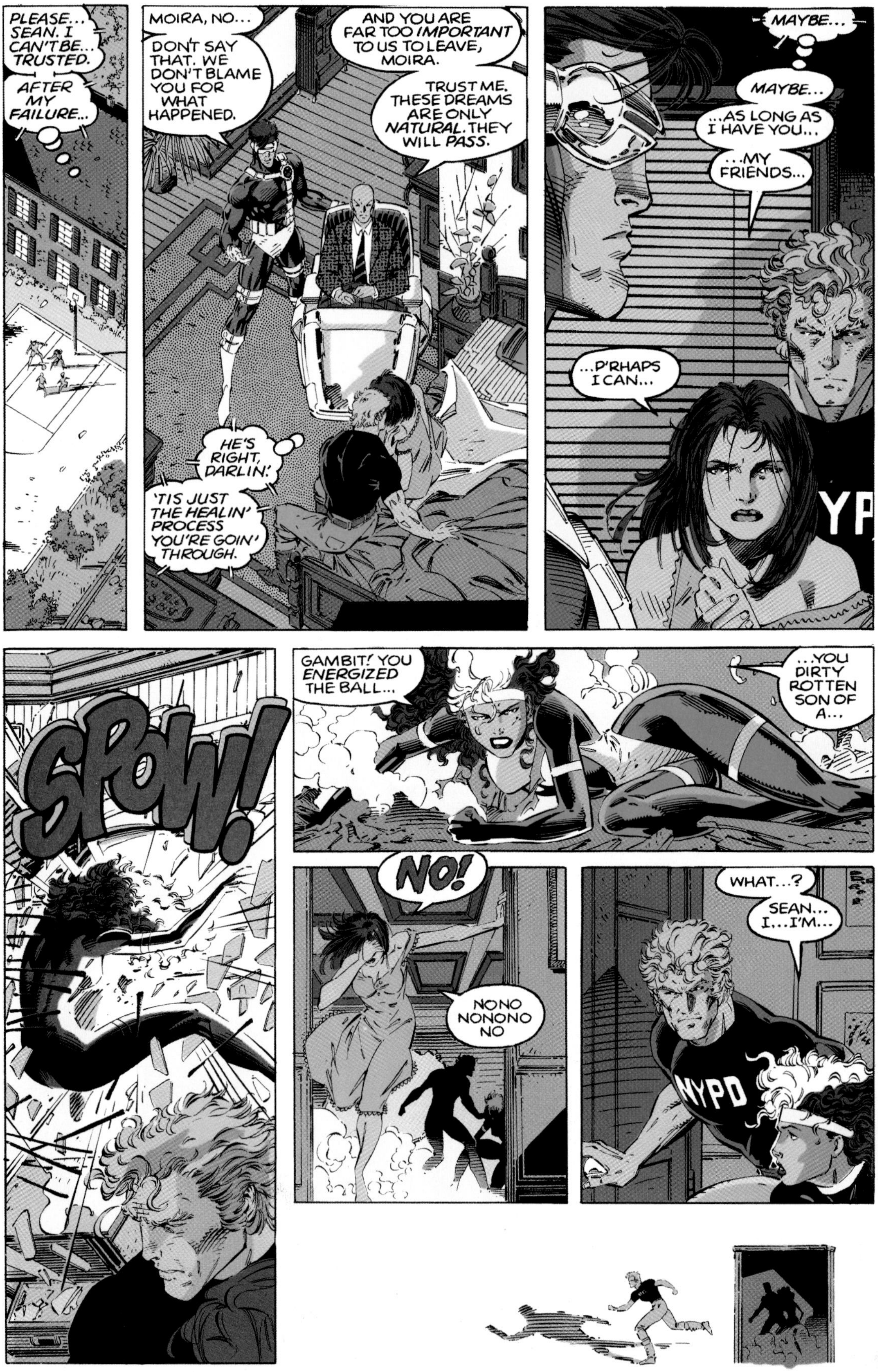
PLEASE... SEAN. I CAN'T BE... TRUSTED.
AFTER MY FAILURE...
MOIRA, NO...
DON'T SAY THAT. WE DON'T BLAME YOU FOR WHAT HAPPENED.
AND YOU ARE FAR TOO IMPORTANT TO US TO LEAVE, MOIRA.
TRUST ME. THESE DREAMS ARE ONLY NATURAL. THEY WILL PASS.
HE'S RIGHT, DARLIN'.
'TIS JUST THE HEALIN' PROCESS YOU'RE GOIN' THROUGH.
MAYBE...
MAYBE...
...AS LONG AS I HAVE YOU...
...MY FRIENDS...
...P'RHAPS I CAN...
NYPD
SPOW!
GAMBIT! YOU ENERGIZED THE BALL...
...YOU DIRTY ROTTEN SON OF A...
NO!
NONO NONONO NO
WHAT...?
SEAN... I...I'M...
NYPD

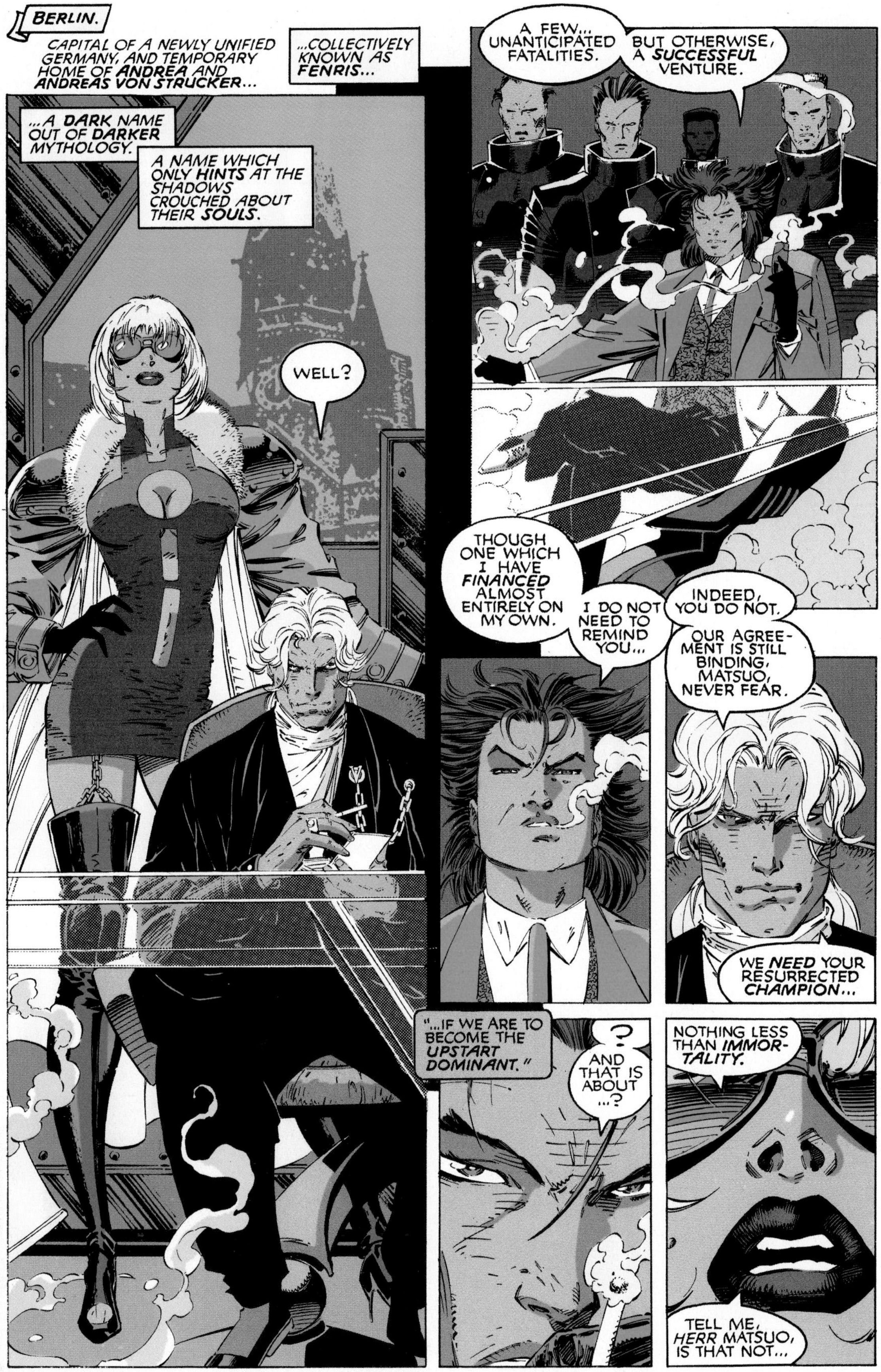
BERLIN.
CAPITAL OF A NEWLY UNIFIED GERMANY, AND TEMPORARY HOME OF ANDREA AND ANDREAS VON STRUCKER...
...COLLECTIVELY KNOWN AS FENRIS...
...A DARK NAME OUT OF DARKER MYTHOLOGY.
A NAME WHICH ONLY HINTS AT THE SHADOWS CROUCHED ABOUT THEIR SOULS.
WELL?
A FEW... UNANTICIPATED FATALITIES.
BUT OTHERWISE, A SUCCESSFUL VENTURE.
THOUGH ONE WHICH I HAVE FINANCED ALMOST ENTIRELY ON MY OWN.
I DO NOT NEED TO REMIND YOU...
INDEED, YOU DO NOT.
OUR AGREEMENT IS STILL BINDING, MATSUO, NEVER FEAR.
WE NEED YOUR RESURRECTED CHAMPION...
"...IF WE ARE TO BECOME THE UPSTART DOMINANT."
?
AND THAT IS ABOUT ...?
NOTHING LESS THAN IMMORTALITY.
TELL ME, HERR MATSUO, IS THAT NOT...

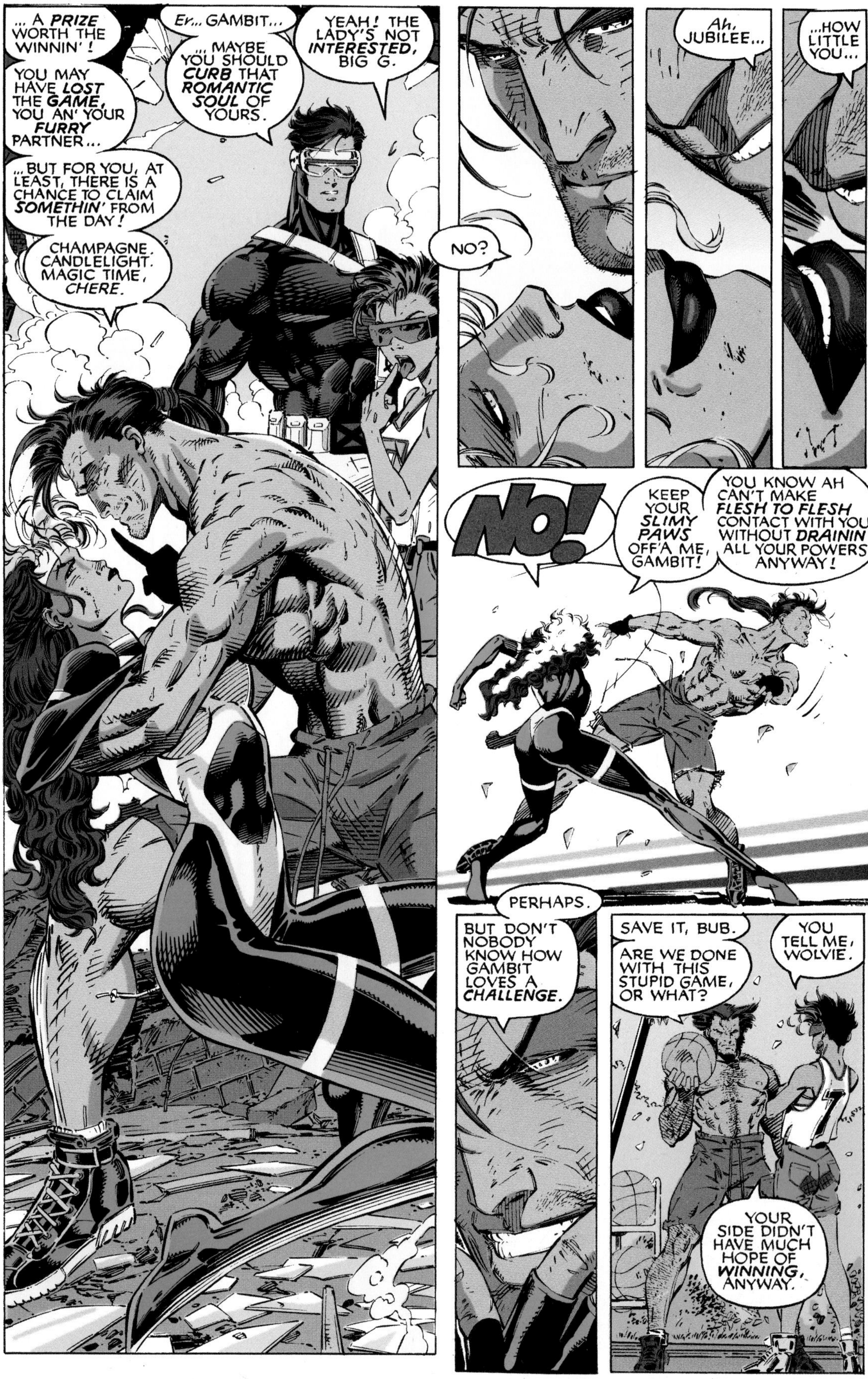
...A PRIZE WORTH THE WINNIN'!
YOU MAY HAVE LOST THE GAME, YOU AN' YOUR FURRY PARTNER...
...BUT FOR YOU, AT LEAST, THERE IS A CHANCE TO CLAIM SOMETHIN' FROM THE DAY!
CHAMPAGNE. CANDLELIGHT. MAGIC TIME, CHERE.
Er... GAMBIT...
...MAYBE YOU SHOULD CURB THAT ROMANTIC SOUL OF YOURS.
YEAH! THE LADY'S NOT INTERESTED, BIG G.
NO?
Ah, JUBILEE...
...HOW LITTLE YOU...
NO!
KEEP YOUR SLIMY PAWS OFF'A ME, GAMBIT!
YOU KNOW AH CAN'T MAKE FLESH TO FLESH CONTACT WITH YOU WITHOUT DRAININ' ALL YOUR POWERS ANYWAY!
PERHAPS.
BUT DON'T NOBODY KNOW HOW GAMBIT LOVES A CHALLENGE.
SAVE IT, BUB.
ARE WE DONE WITH THIS STUPID GAME, OR WHAT?
YOU TELL ME, WOLVIE.
YOUR SIDE DIDN'T HAVE MUCH HOPE OF WINNING, ANYWAY.

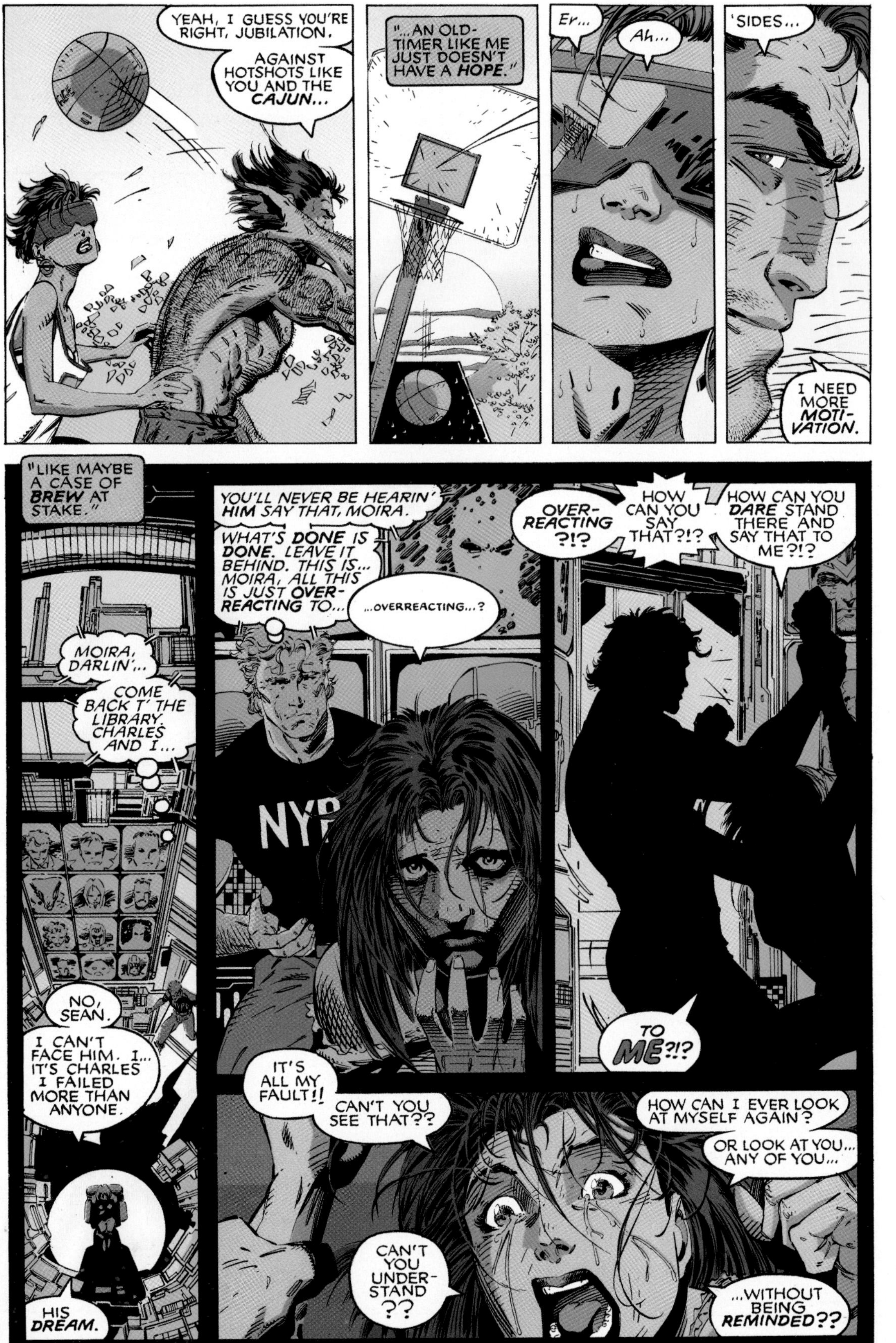

YEAH, I GUESS YOU'RE RIGHT, JUBILATION.
AGAINST HOTSHOTS LIKE YOU AND THE CAJUN...
"...AN OLD-TIMER LIKE ME JUST DOESN'T HAVE A HOPE."
Er...
Ah...
'SIDES...
I NEED MORE MOTI-VATION.
"LIKE MAYBE A CASE OF BREW AT STAKE."
MOIRA, DARLIN'...
COME BACK T' THE LIBRARY. CHARLES AND I...
NO, SEAN.
I CAN'T FACE HIM. I... IT'S CHARLES I FAILED MORE THAN ANYONE.
HIS DREAM.
YOU'LL NEVER BE HEARIN' HIM SAY THAT, MOIRA.
WHAT'S DONE IS DONE. LEAVE IT BEHIND. THIS IS... MOIRA, ALL THIS IS JUST OVER-REACTING TO...
...OVERREACTING...?
OVER-REACTING ?!?
HOW CAN YOU SAY THAT?!?
HOW CAN YOU DARE STAND THERE AND SAY THAT TO ME?!?
TO ME?!?
IT'S ALL MY FAULT!!
CAN'T YOU SEE THAT??
CAN'T YOU UNDER-STAND ??
HOW CAN I EVER LOOK AT MYSELF AGAIN?
OR LOOK AT YOU... ANY OF YOU...
...WITHOUT BEING REMINDED??

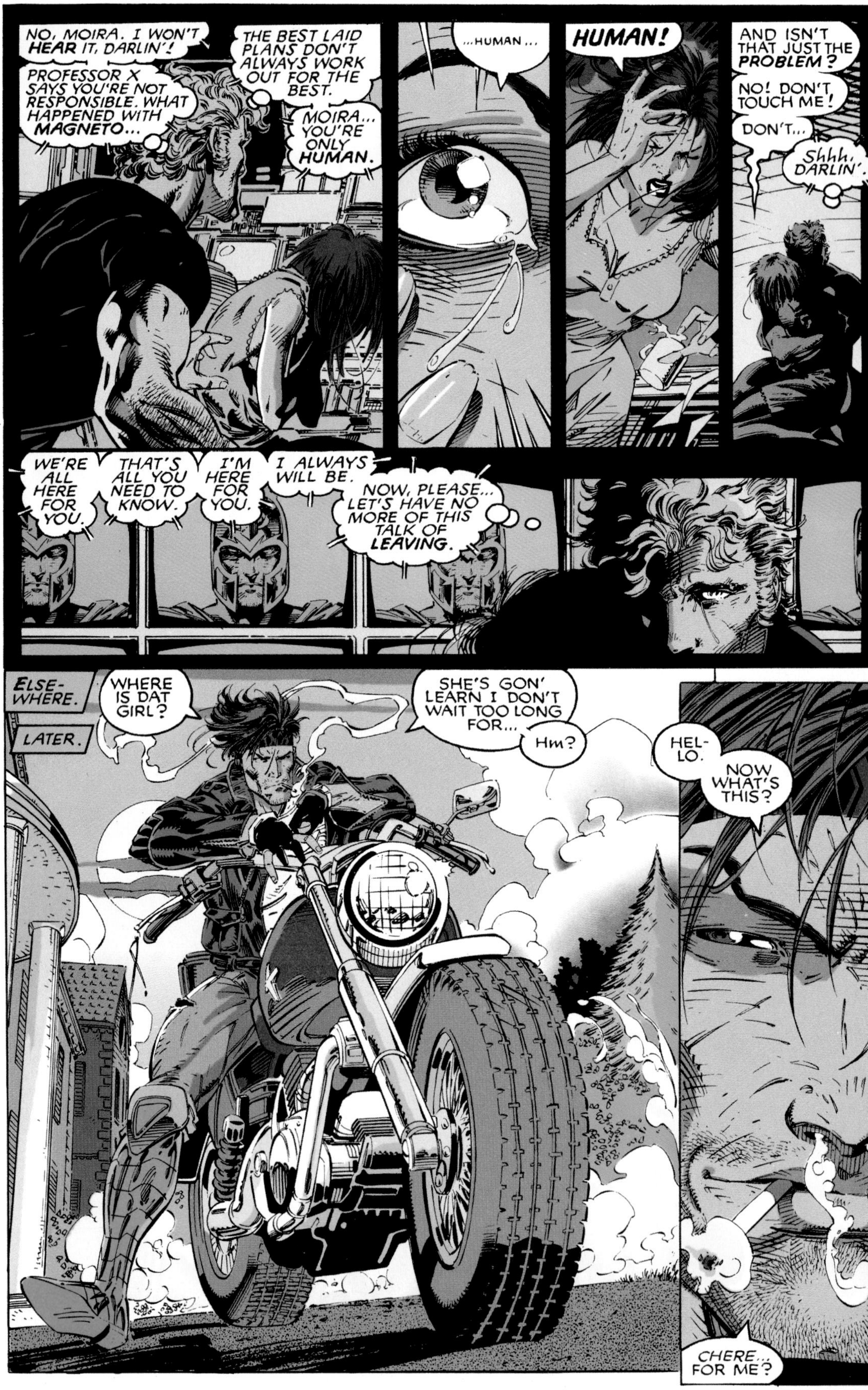
NO, MOIRA. I WON'T HEAR IT, DARLIN'!
PROFESSOR X SAYS YOU'RE NOT RESPONSIBLE. WHAT HAPPENED WITH MAGNETO...
THE BEST LAID PLANS DON'T ALWAYS WORK OUT FOR THE BEST.
MOIRA... YOU'RE ONLY HUMAN.
...HUMAN...
HUMAN!
AND ISN'T THAT JUST THE PROBLEM?
NO! DON'T TOUCH ME!
DON'T...
Shhh, DARLIN'.
WE'RE ALL HERE FOR YOU.
THAT'S ALL YOU NEED TO KNOW.
I'M HERE FOR YOU.
I ALWAYS WILL BE.
NOW, PLEASE... LET'S HAVE NO MORE OF THIS TALK OF LEAVING.
ELSE-WHERE.
LATER.
WHERE IS DAT GIRL?
SHE'S GON' LEARN I DON'T WAIT TOO LONG FOR...
Hm?
HEL-LO.
NOW WHAT'S THIS?
CHERE... FOR ME?

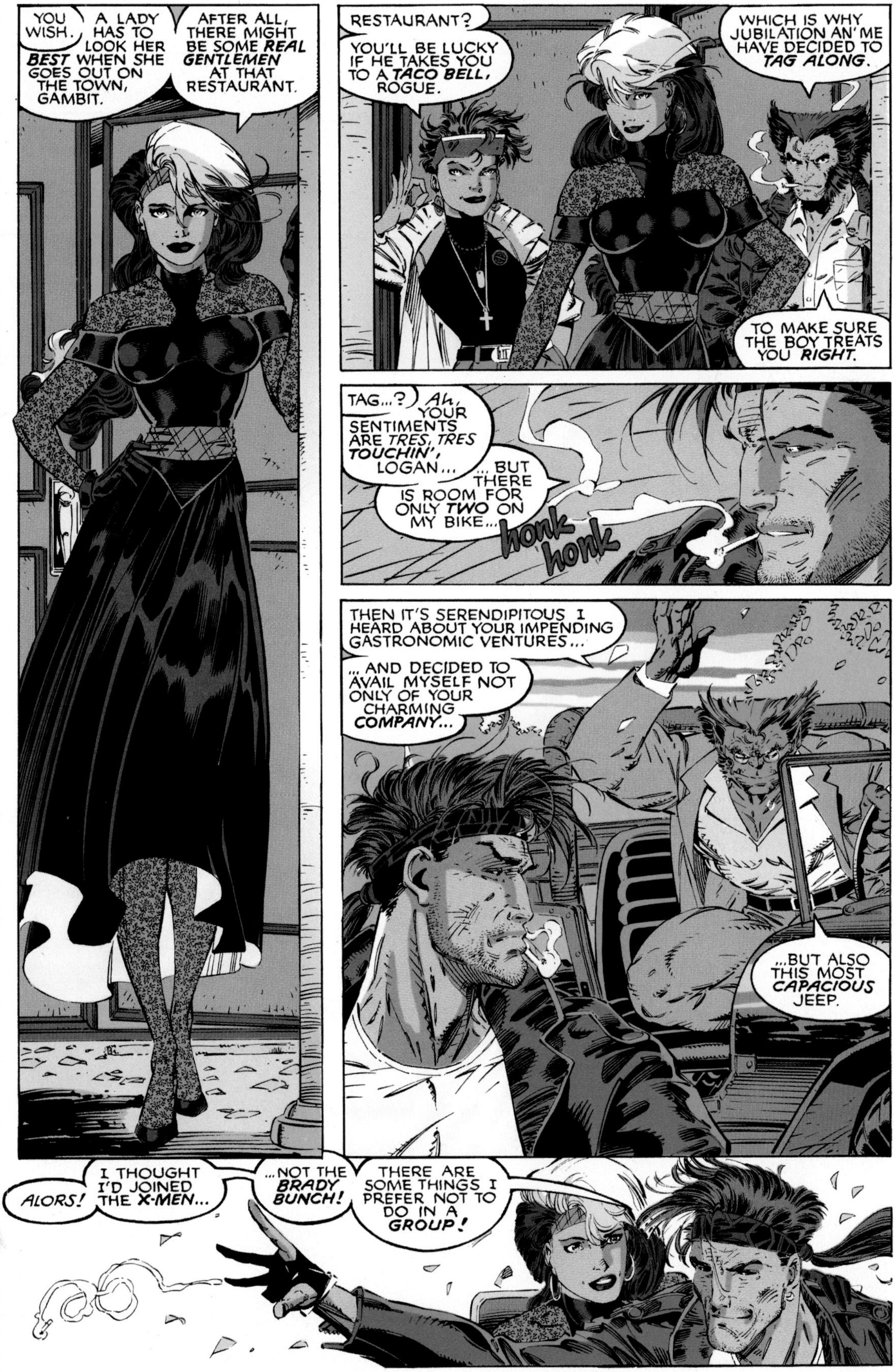
YOU WISH.
A LADY HAS TO LOOK HER BEST WHEN SHE GOES OUT ON THE TOWN, GAMBIT.
AFTER ALL, THERE MIGHT BE SOME REAL GENTLEMEN AT THAT RESTAURANT.
RESTAURANT?
YOU'LL BE LUCKY IF HE TAKES YOU TO A TACO BELL, ROGUE.
WHICH IS WHY JUBILATION AN' ME HAVE DECIDED TO TAG ALONG.
TO MAKE SURE THE BOY TREATS YOU RIGHT.
TAG...?
Ah, YOUR SENTIMENTS ARE TRES, TRES TOUCHIN', LOGAN...
... BUT THERE IS ROOM FOR ONLY TWO ON MY BIKE...
honk honk
THEN IT'S SERENDIPITOUS I HEARD ABOUT YOUR IMPENDING GASTRONOMIC VENTURES...
... AND DECIDED TO AVAIL MYSELF NOT ONLY OF YOUR CHARMING COMPANY...
...BUT ALSO THIS MOST CAPACIOUS JEEP.
ALORS!
I THOUGHT I'D JOINED THE X-MEN...
...NOT THE BRADY BUNCH!
THERE ARE SOME THINGS I PREFER NOT TO DO IN A GROUP!

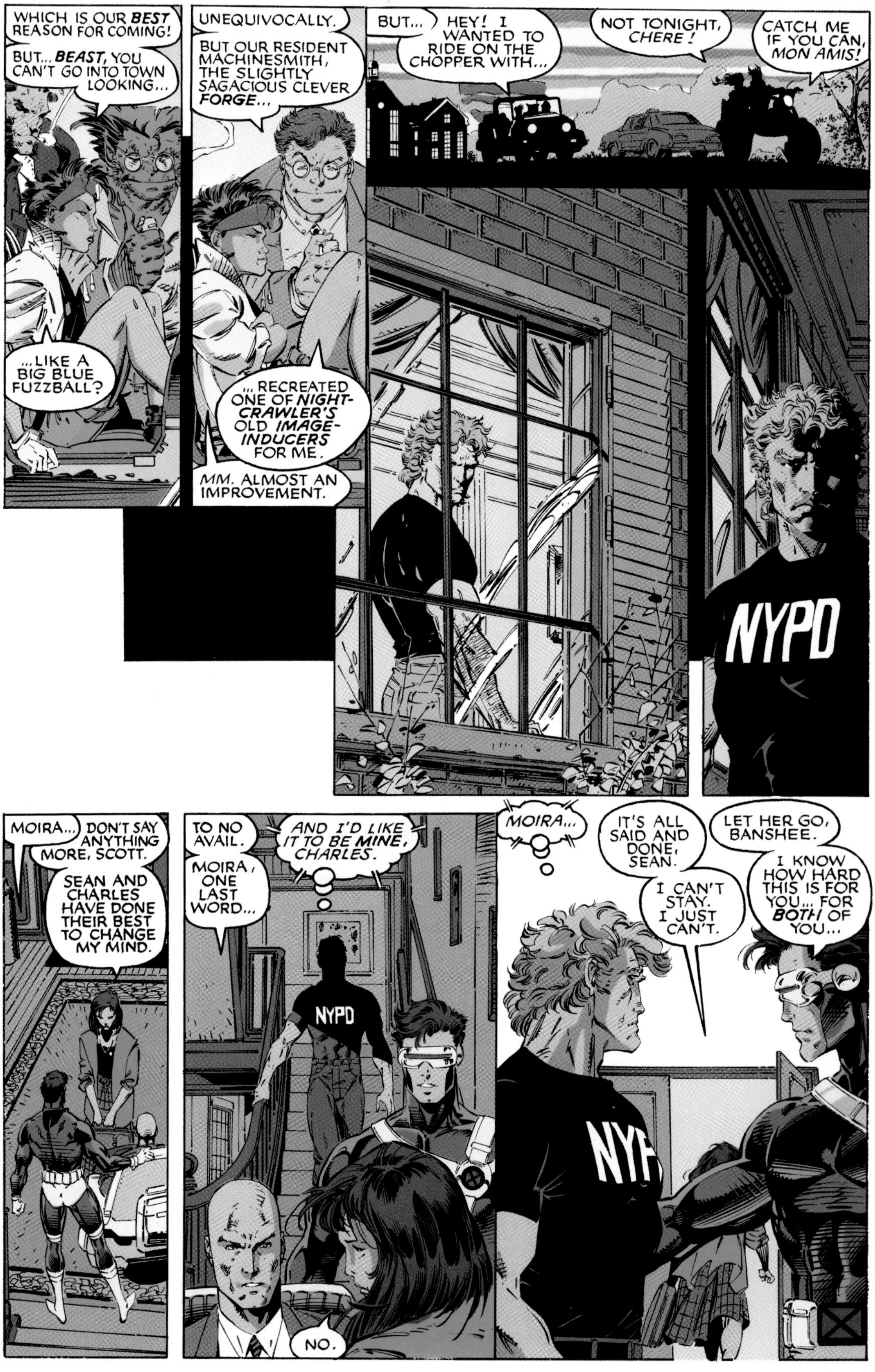
WHICH IS OUR BEST REASON FOR COMING!
BUT... BEAST, YOU CAN'T GO INTO TOWN LOOKING...
...LIKE A BIG BLUE FUZZBALL?
UNEQUIVOCALLY.
BUT OUR RESIDENT MACHINESMITH, THE SLIGHTLY SAGACIOUS CLEVER FORGE...
...RECREATED ONE OF NIGHTCRAWLER'S OLD IMAGE-INDUCERS FOR ME.
MM. ALMOST AN IMPROVEMENT.
BUT...
HEY! I WANTED TO RIDE ON THE CHOPPER WITH...
NOT TONIGHT, CHERE!
CATCH ME IF YOU CAN, MON AMIS!
NYPD
MOIRA...
DON'T SAY ANYTHING MORE, SCOTT.
SEAN AND CHARLES HAVE DONE THEIR BEST TO CHANGE MY MIND.
TO NO AVAIL.
AND I'D LIKE IT TO BE MINE, CHARLES.
MOIRA, ONE LAST WORD...
NYPD
NO.
MOIRA...
IT'S ALL SAID AND DONE, SEAN.
I CAN'T STAY. I JUST CAN'T.
LET HER GO, BANSHEE.
I KNOW HOW HARD THIS IS FOR YOU... FOR BOTH OF YOU...

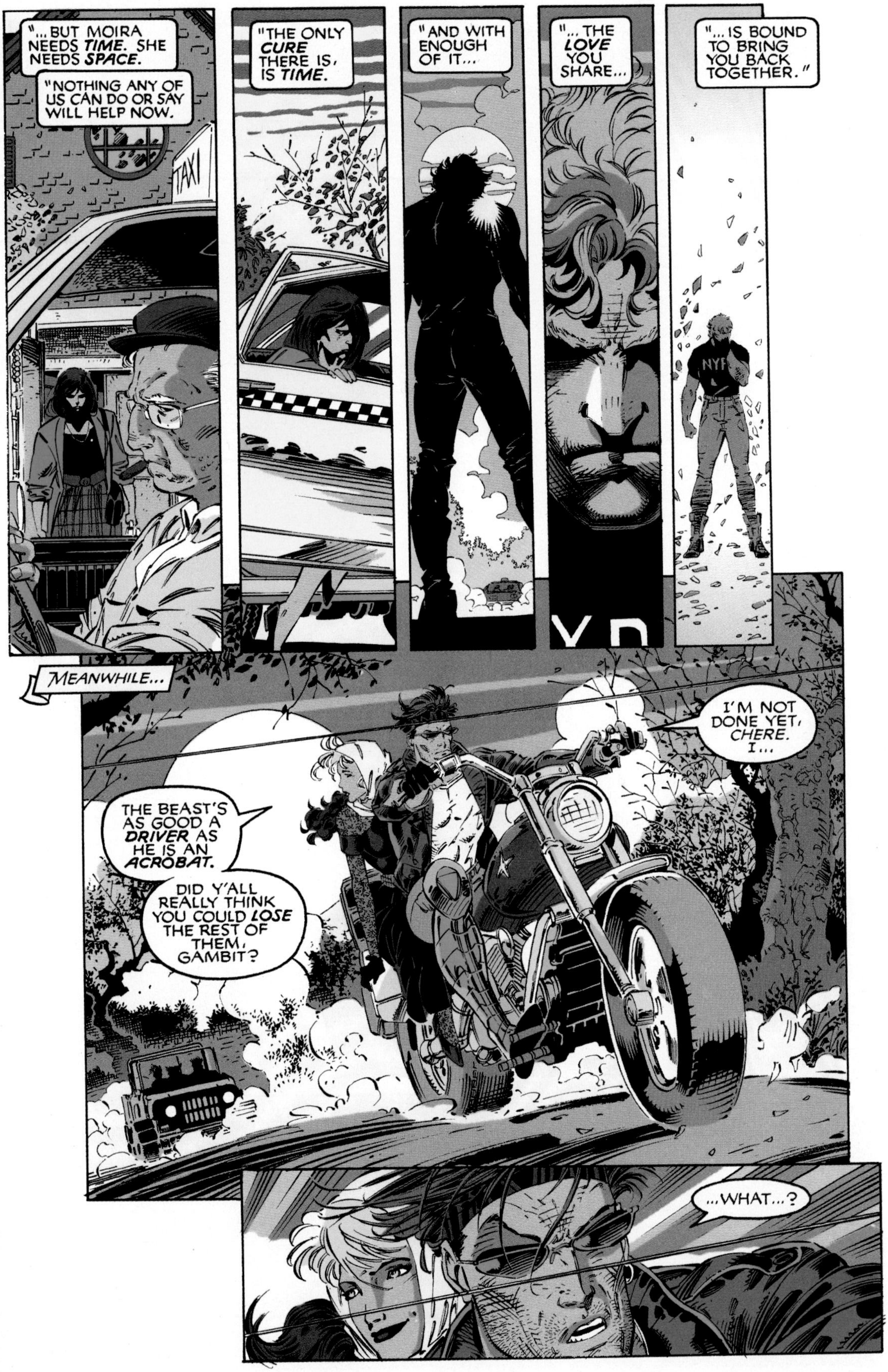
"...BUT MOIRA NEEDS TIME. SHE NEEDS SPACE.
"NOTHING ANY OF US CAN DO OR SAY WILL HELP NOW.
TAXI
"THE ONLY CURE THERE IS, IS TIME.
"AND WITH ENOUGH OF IT...
"...THE LOVE YOU SHARE...
"...IS BOUND TO BRING YOU BACK TOGETHER."
NYPD
MEANWHILE...
I'M NOT DONE YET, CHERE. I...
THE BEAST'S AS GOOD A DRIVER AS HE IS AN ACROBAT.
DID Y'ALL REALLY THINK YOU COULD LOSE THE REST OF THEM, GAMBIT?
...WHAT...?

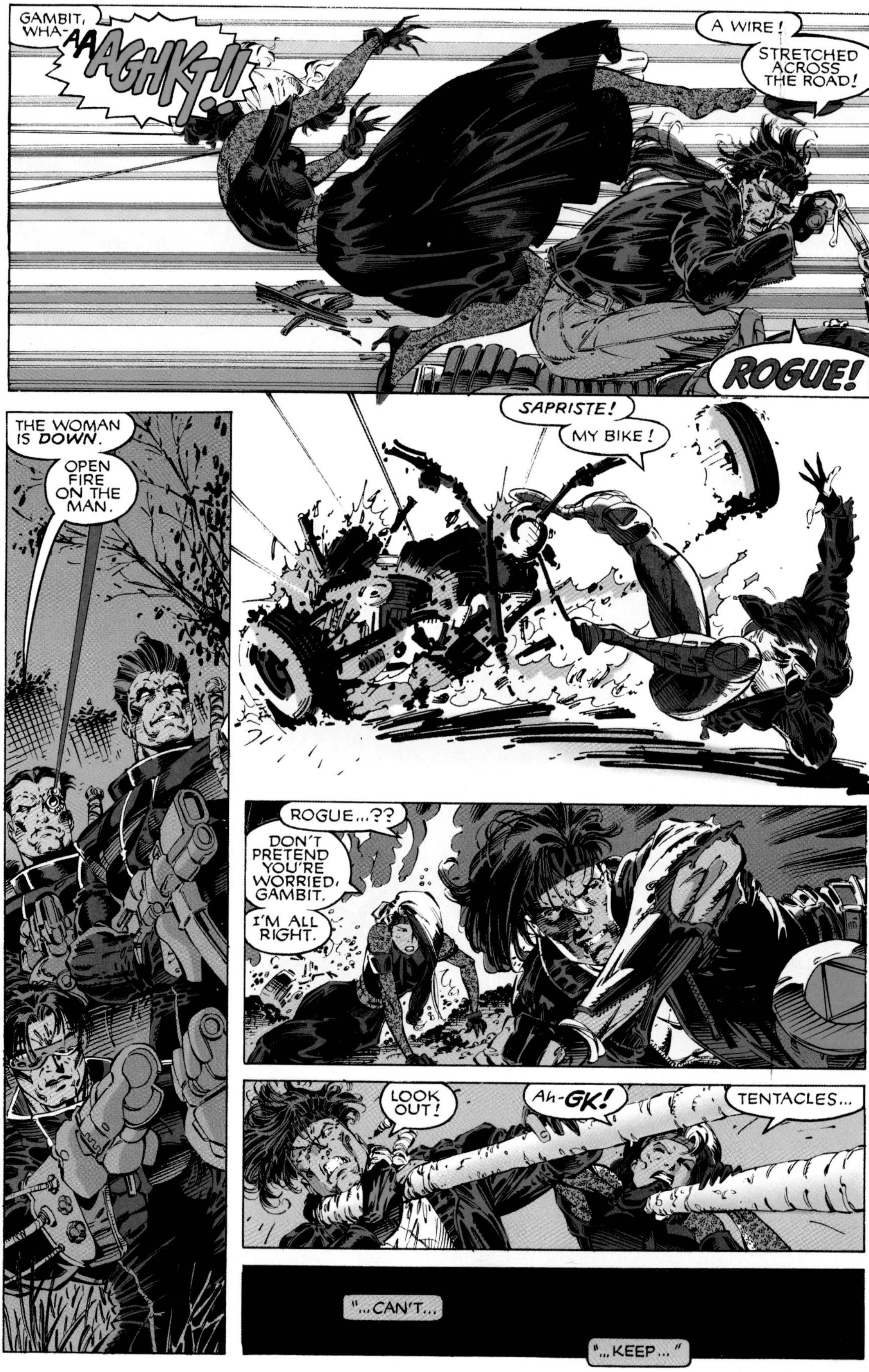
GAMBIT, WHA-
AAAAGHKT!!
A WIRE!
STRETCHED ACROSS THE ROAD!
ROGUE!
THE WOMAN IS DOWN.
OPEN FIRE ON THE MAN.
SAPRISTE!
MY BIKE!
ROGUE...??
DON'T PRETEND YOU'RE WORRIED, GAMBIT.
I'M ALL RIGHT.
LOOK OUT!
Ah-GK!
TENTACLES...
"...CAN'T...
"...KEEP..."

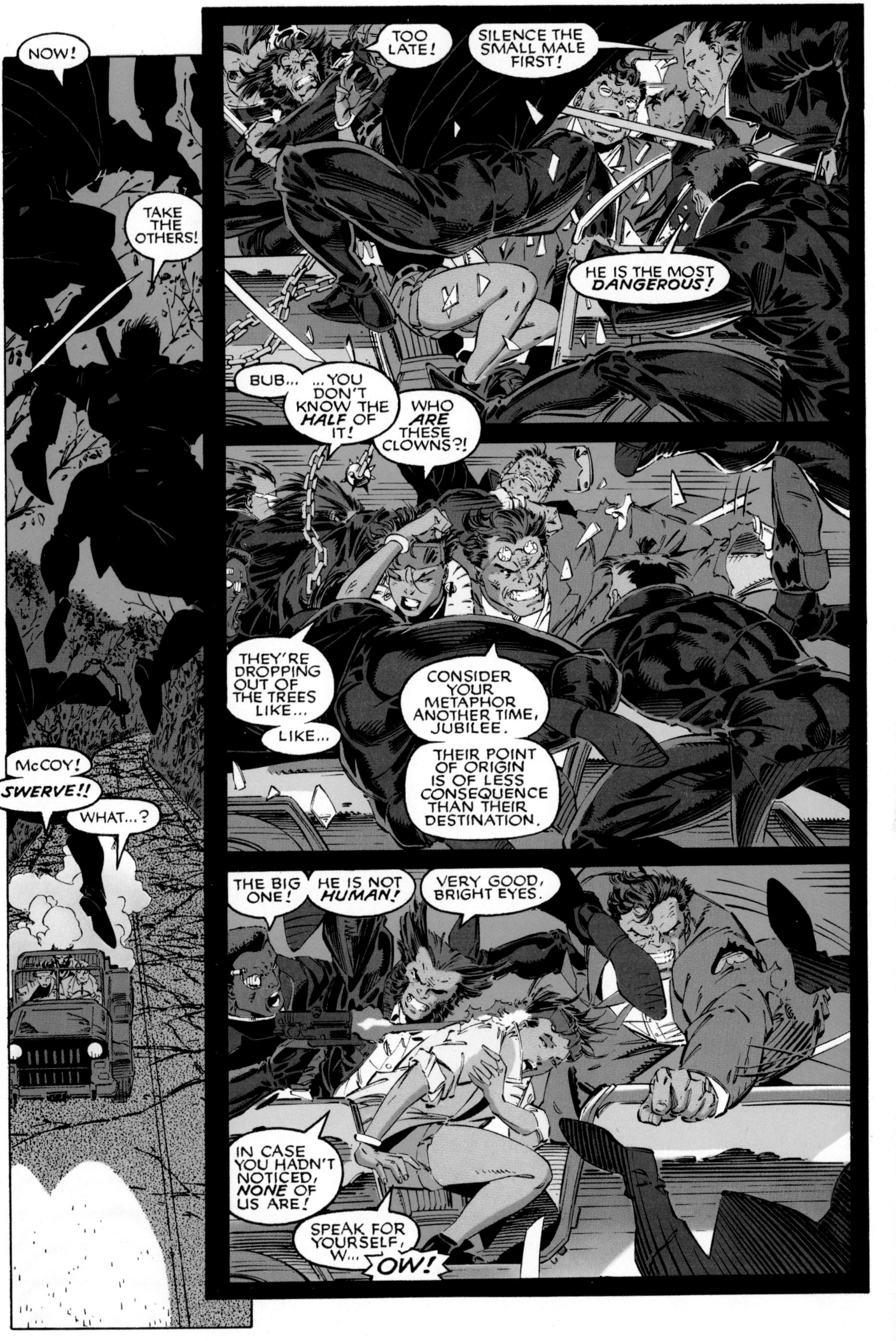
NOW!
TAKE THE OTHERS!
McCOY! SWERVE!!
WHAT...?
TOO LATE!
SILENCE THE SMALL MALE FIRST!
HE IS THE MOST DANGEROUS!
BUB... ...YOU DON'T KNOW THE HALF OF IT!
WHO ARE THESE CLOWNS?!
THEY'RE DROPPING OUT OF THE TREES LIKE...
LIKE...
CONSIDER YOUR METAPHOR ANOTHER TIME, JUBILEE.
THEIR POINT OF ORIGIN IS OF LESS CONSEQUENCE THAN THEIR DESTINATION.
THE BIG ONE!
HE IS NOT HUMAN!
VERY GOOD, BRIGHT EYES.
IN CASE YOU HADN'T NOTICED, NONE OF US ARE!
SPEAK FOR YOURSELF, W...
OW!

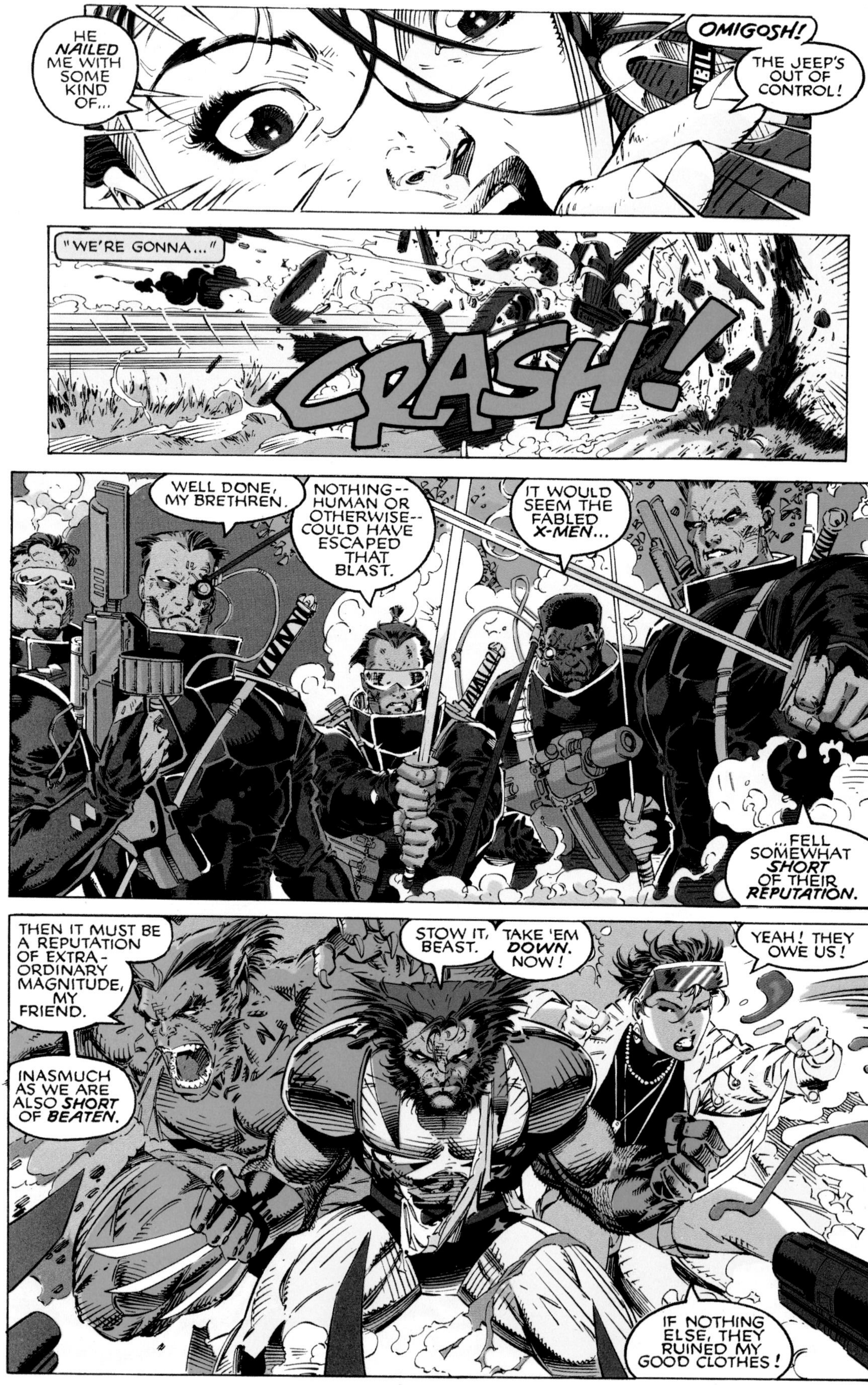
HE NAILED ME WITH SOME KIND OF...
OMIGOSH!
THE JEEP'S OUT OF CONTROL!
"WE'RE GONNA..."
CRASH!
WELL DONE, MY BRETHREN.
NOTHING-- HUMAN OR OTHERWISE-- COULD HAVE ESCAPED THAT BLAST.
IT WOULD SEEM THE FABLED X-MEN...
...FELL SOMEWHAT SHORT OF THEIR REPUTATION.
THEN IT MUST BE A REPUTATION OF EXTRA-ORDINARY MAGNITUDE, MY FRIEND.
INASMUCH AS WE ARE ALSO SHORT OF BEATEN.
STOW IT, BEAST.
TAKE 'EM DOWN. NOW!
YEAH! THEY OWE US!
IF NOTHING ELSE, THEY RUINED MY GOOD CLOTHES!

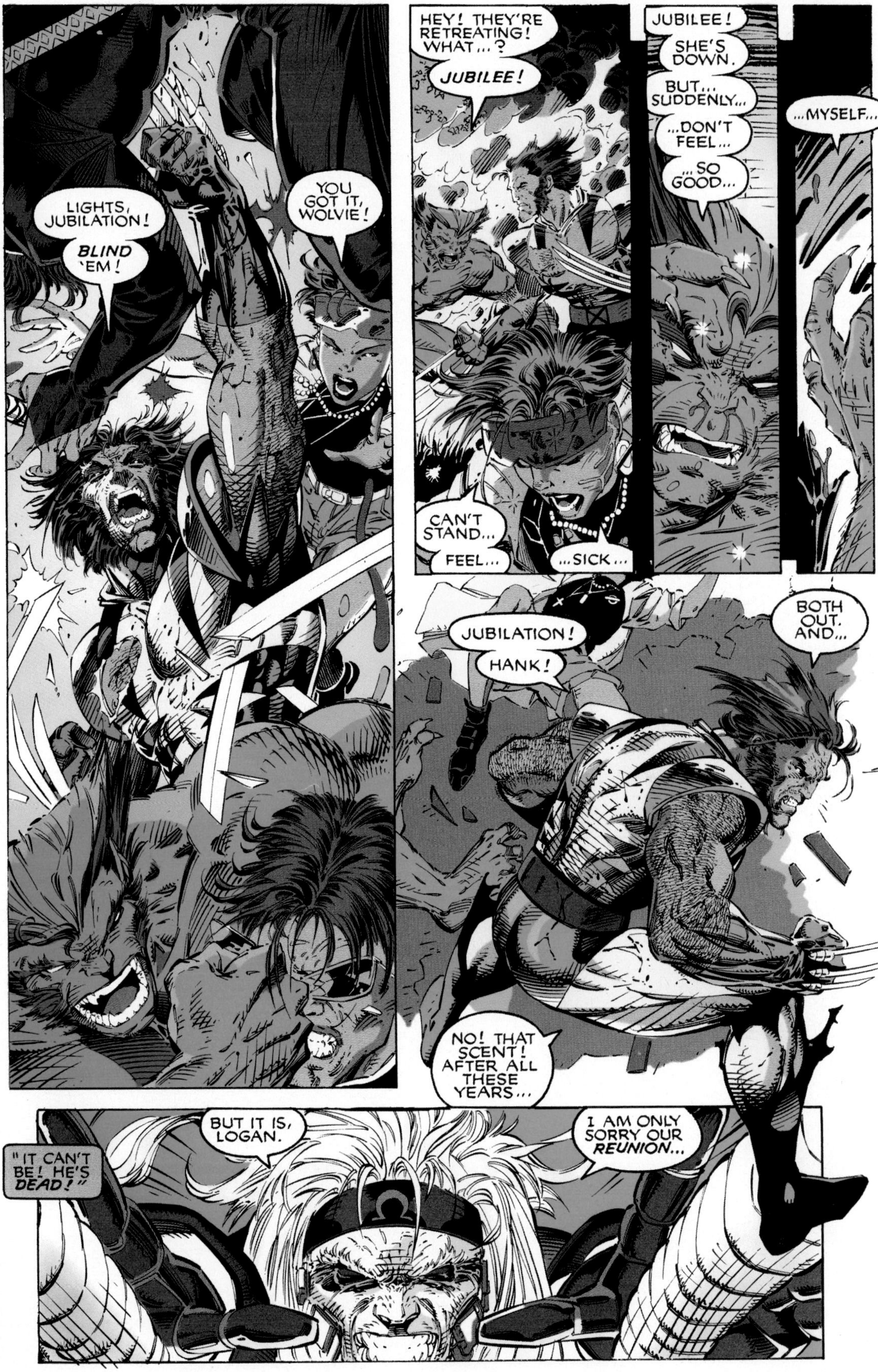
LIGHTS, JUBILATION!
BLIND 'EM!
YOU GOT IT, WOLVIE!
HEY! THEY'RE RETREATING! WHAT...?
JUBILEE!
CAN'T STAND...
FEEL...
...SICK...
JUBILEE!
SHE'S DOWN.
BUT... SUDDENLY...
...DON'T FEEL...
...SO GOOD...
...MYSELF...
JUBILATION!
HANK!
BOTH OUT. AND...
NO! THAT SCENT! AFTER ALL THESE YEARS...
"IT CAN'T BE! HE'S DEAD!"
BUT IT IS, LOGAN.
I AM ONLY SORRY OUR REUNION...

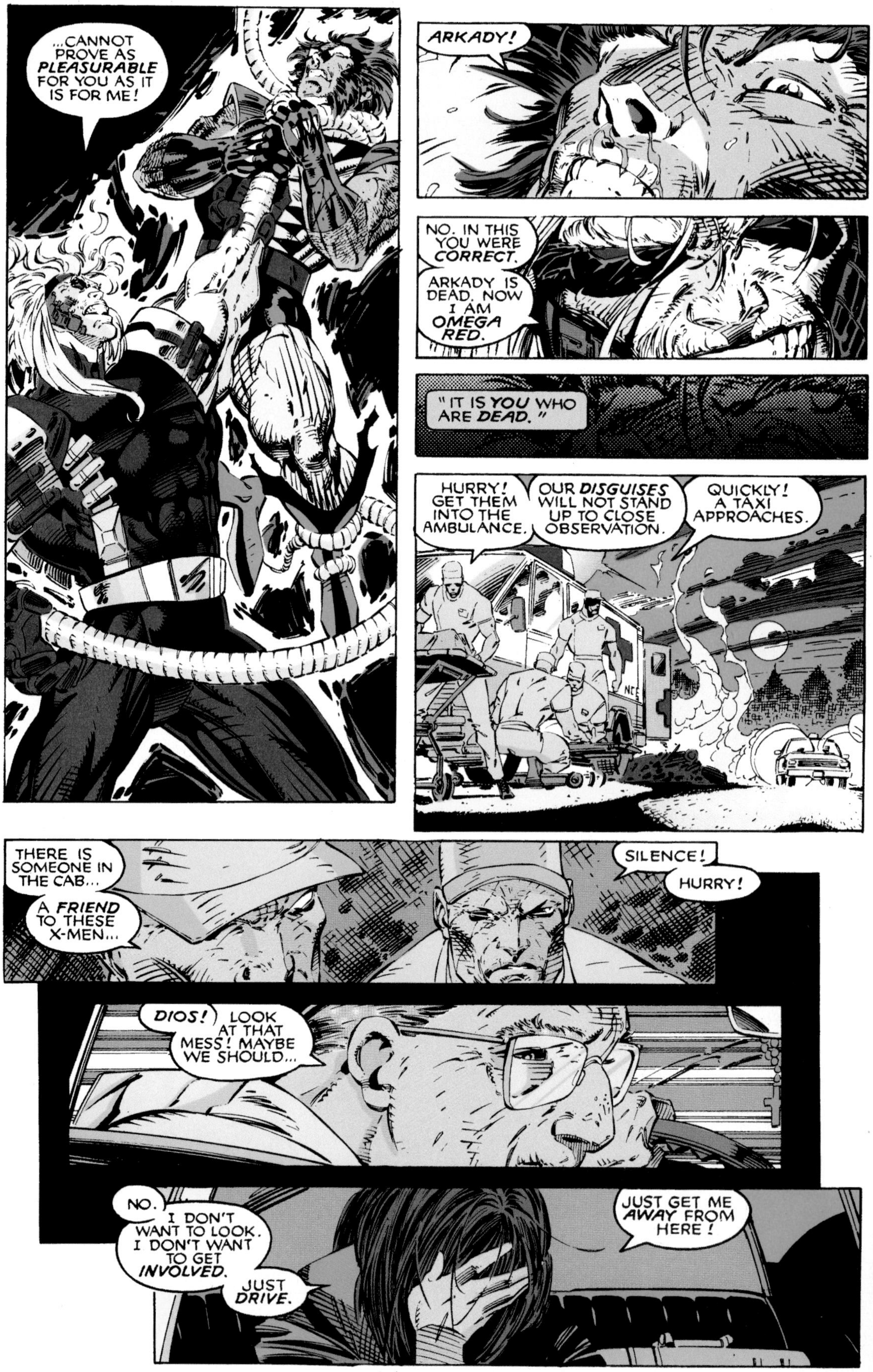

...CANNOT PROVE AS PLEASURABLE FOR YOU AS IT IS FOR ME!
ARKADY!
NO. IN THIS YOU WERE CORRECT.
ARKADY IS DEAD. NOW I AM OMEGA RED.
"IT IS YOU WHO ARE DEAD."
HURRY! GET THEM INTO THE AMBULANCE.
OUR DISGUISES WILL NOT STAND UP TO CLOSE OBSERVATION.
QUICKLY! A TAXI APPROACHES.
THERE IS SOMEONE IN THE CAB...
A FRIEND TO THESE X-MEN...
SILENCE!
HURRY!
DIOS! LOOK AT THAT MESS! MAYBE WE SHOULD...
NO.
I DON'T WANT TO LOOK. I DON'T WANT TO GET INVOLVED.
JUST DRIVE.
JUST GET ME AWAY FROM HERE!

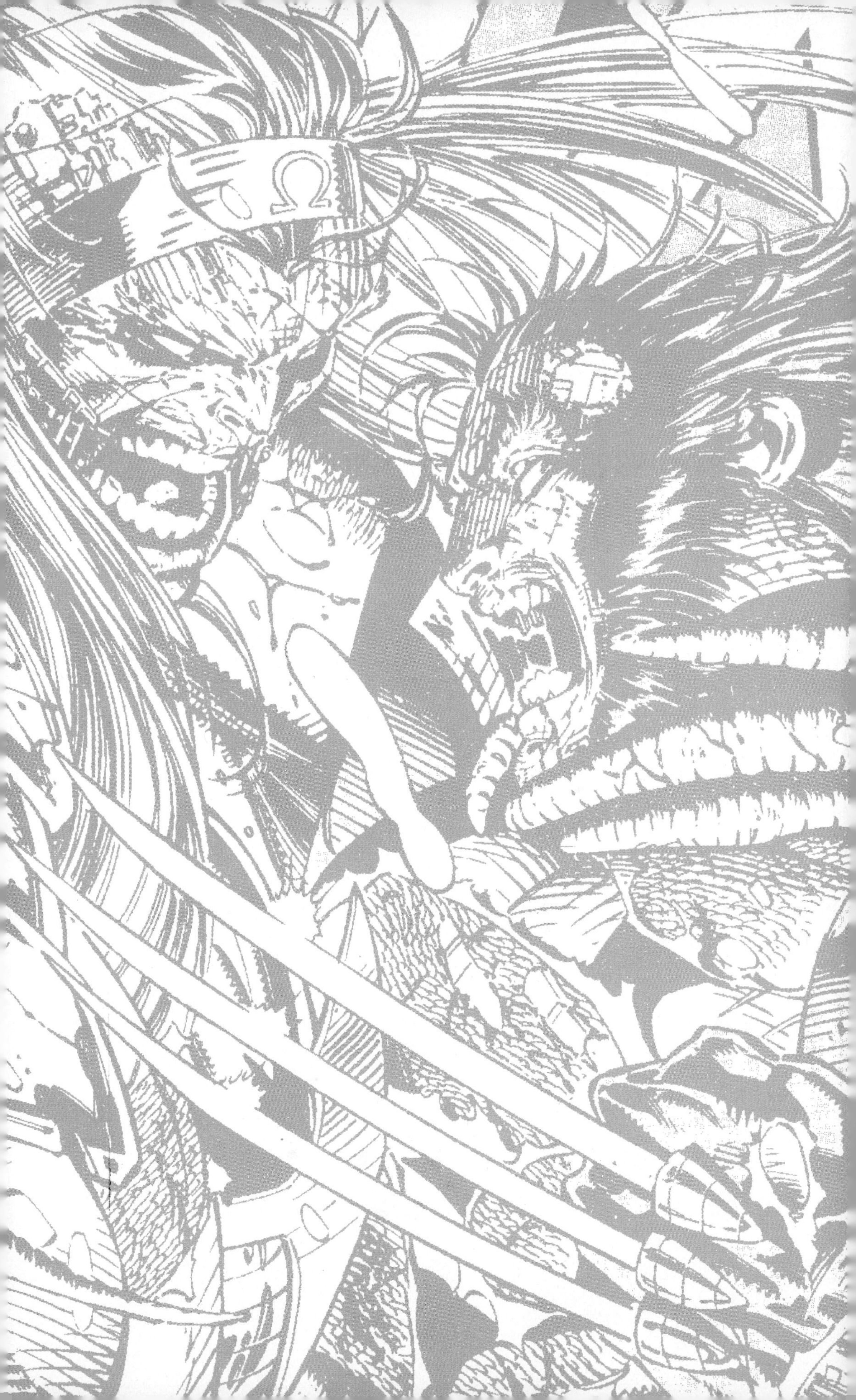

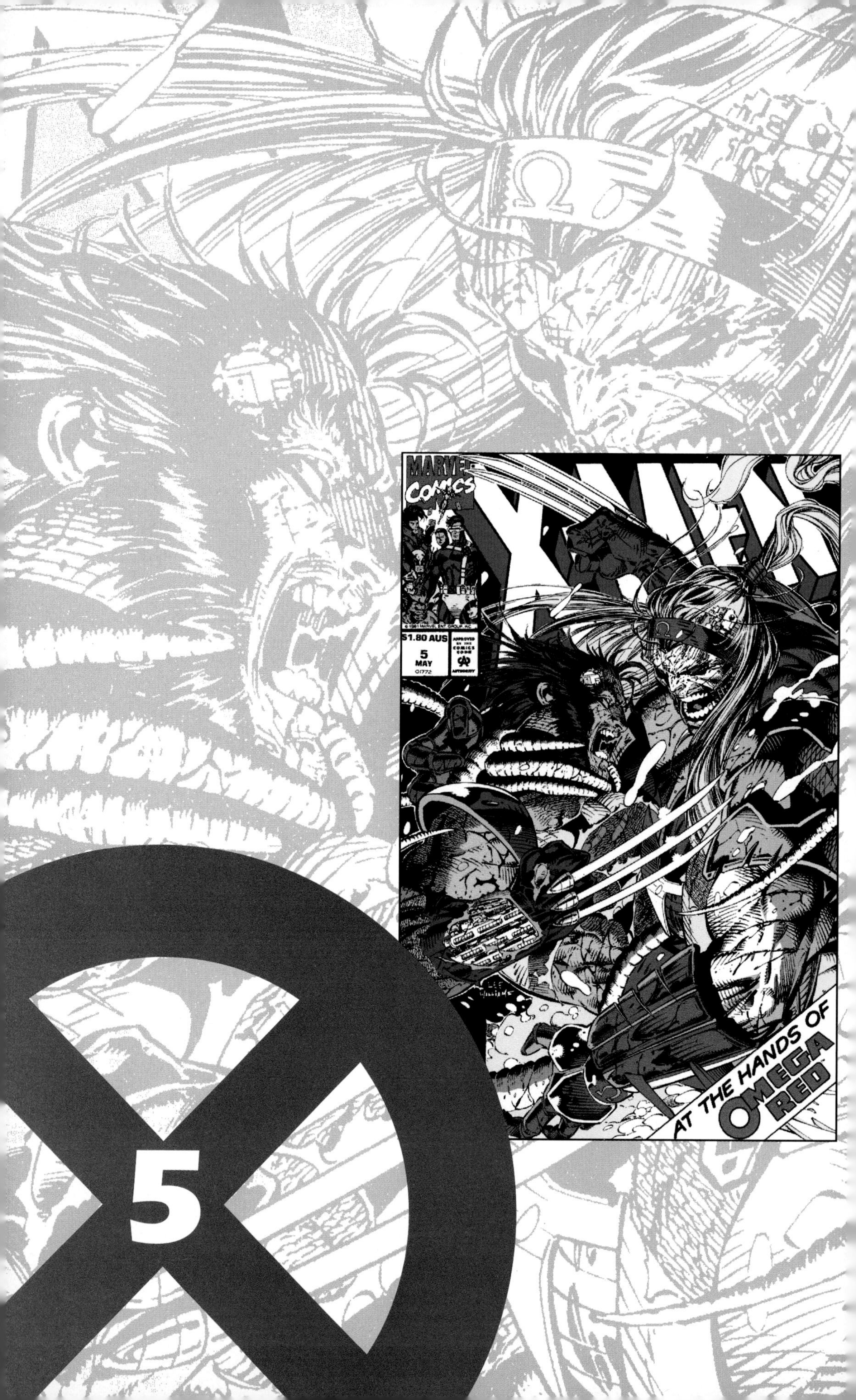
MARVEL COMICS
$1.80 AUS
5
MAY
APPROVED BY THE COMICS CODE AUTHORITY
AT THE HANDS OF
OMEGA RED
5

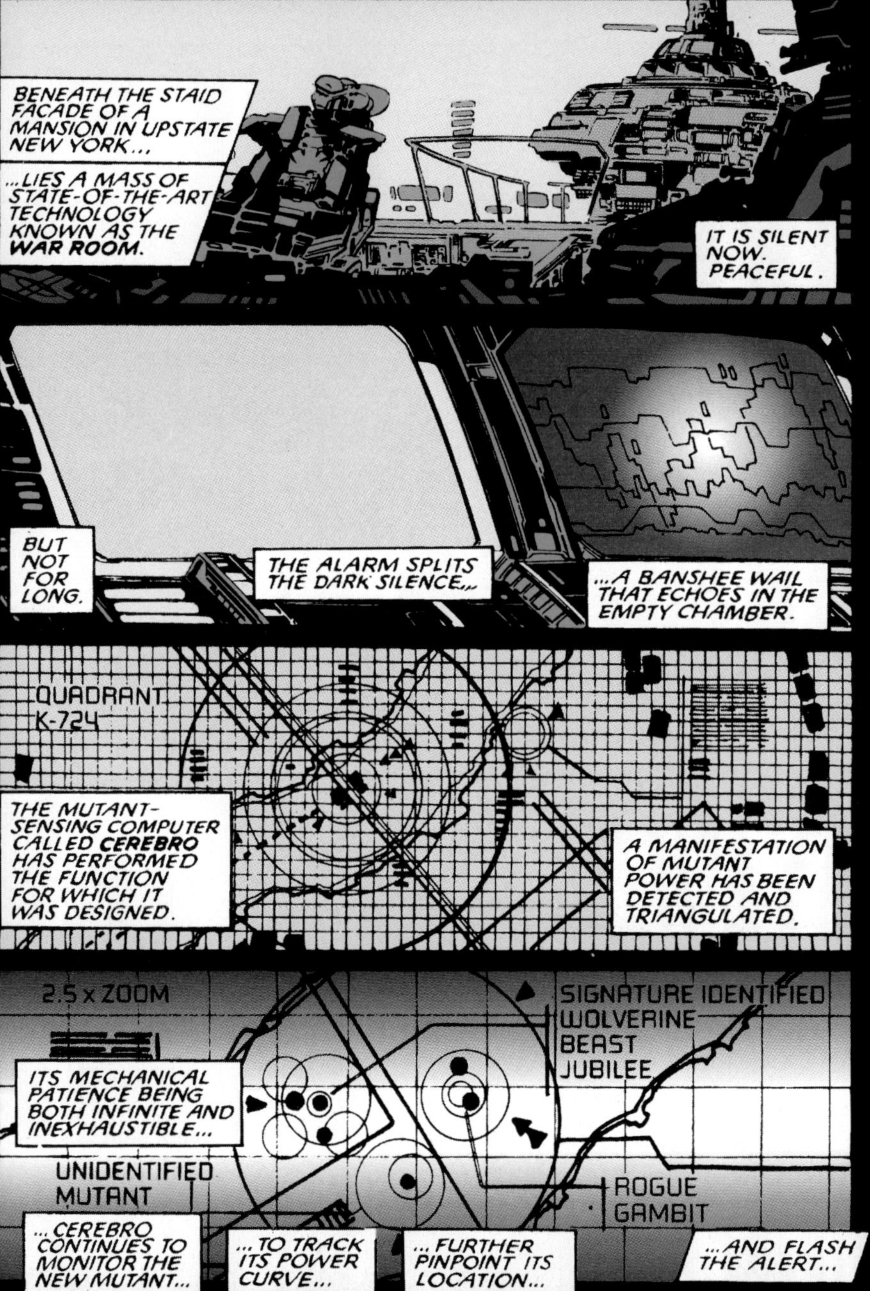
BENEATH THE STAID FACADE OF A MANSION IN UPSTATE NEW YORK...
...LIES A MASS OF STATE-OF-THE-ART TECHNOLOGY KNOWN AS THE **WAR ROOM**.
IT IS SILENT NOW. PEACEFUL.
BUT NOT FOR LONG.
THE ALARM SPLITS THE DARK SILENCE...
...A BANSHEE WAIL THAT ECHOES IN THE EMPTY CHAMBER.
QUADRANT K-724
THE MUTANT-SENSING COMPUTER CALLED **CEREBRO** HAS PERFORMED THE FUNCTION FOR WHICH IT WAS DESIGNED.
A MANIFESTATION OF MUTANT POWER HAS BEEN DETECTED AND TRIANGULATED.
2.5 x ZOOM
SIGNATURE IDENTIFIED
WOLVERINE
BEAST
JUBILEE
ITS MECHANICAL PATIENCE BEING BOTH INFINITE AND INEXHAUSTIBLE...
UNIDENTIFIED MUTANT
ROGUE
GAMBIT
...CEREBRO CONTINUES TO MONITOR THE NEW MUTANT...
...TO TRACK ITS POWER CURVE...
...FURTHER PINPOINT ITS LOCATION...
...AND FLASH THE ALERT...

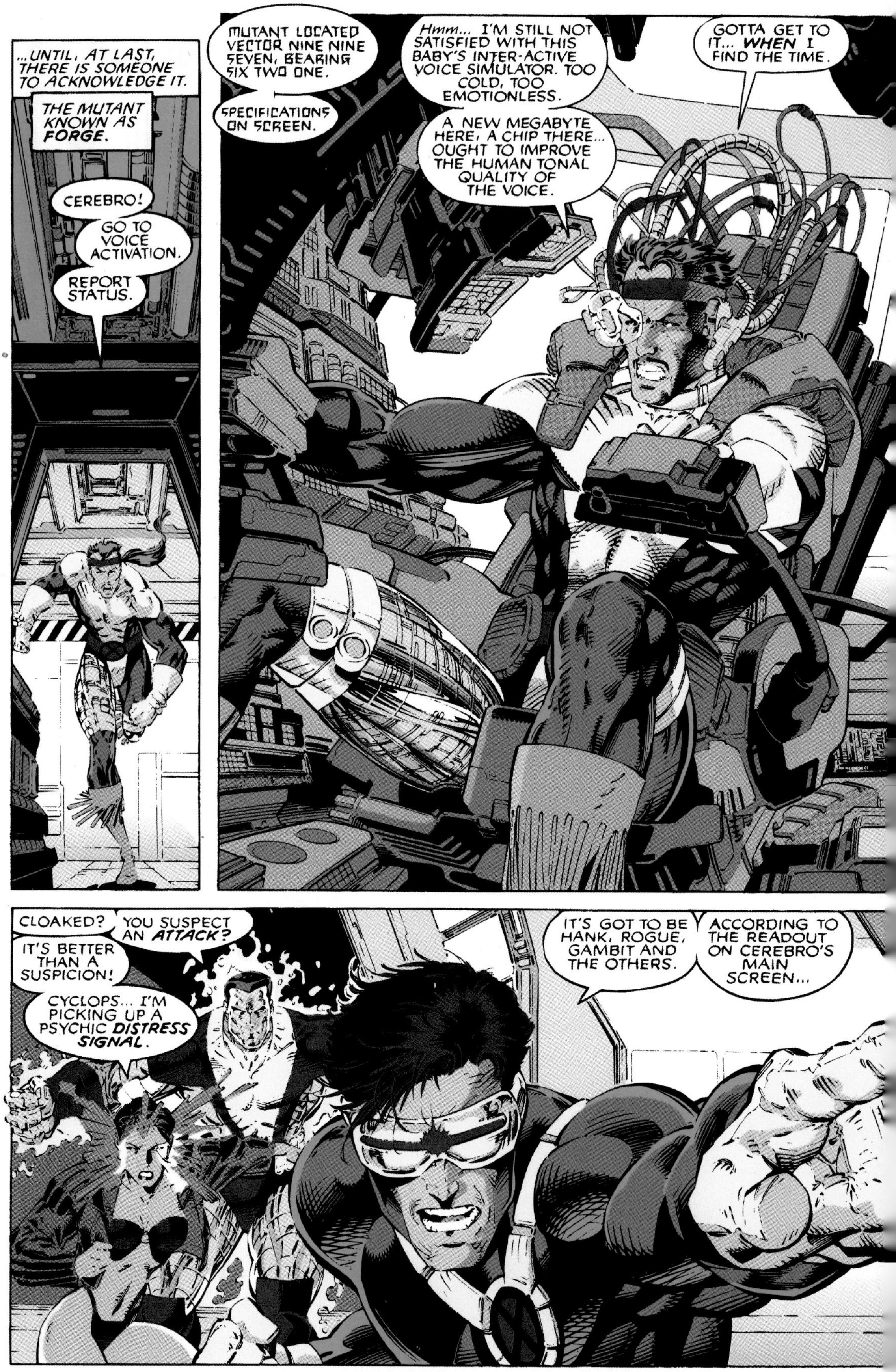
...UNTIL, AT LAST, THERE IS SOMEONE TO ACKNOWLEDGE IT.
THE MUTANT KNOWN AS FORGE.
CEREBRO!
GO TO VOICE ACTIVATION.
REPORT STATUS.
MUTANT LOCATED VECTOR NINE NINE SEVEN, BEARING SIX TWO ONE.
SPECIFICATIONS ON SCREEN.
Hmm... I'M STILL NOT SATISFIED WITH THIS BABY'S INTER-ACTIVE VOICE SIMULATOR. TOO COLD, TOO EMOTIONLESS.
A NEW MEGABYTE HERE, A CHIP THERE... OUGHT TO IMPROVE THE HUMAN TONAL QUALITY OF THE VOICE.
GOTTA GET TO IT... WHEN I FIND THE TIME.
CLOAKED?
YOU SUSPECT AN ATTACK?
IT'S BETTER THAN A SUSPICION!
CYCLOPS... I'M PICKING UP A PSYCHIC DISTRESS SIGNAL.
IT'S GOT TO BE HANK, ROGUE, GAMBIT AND THE OTHERS.
ACCORDING TO THE READOUT ON CEREBRO'S MAIN SCREEN...

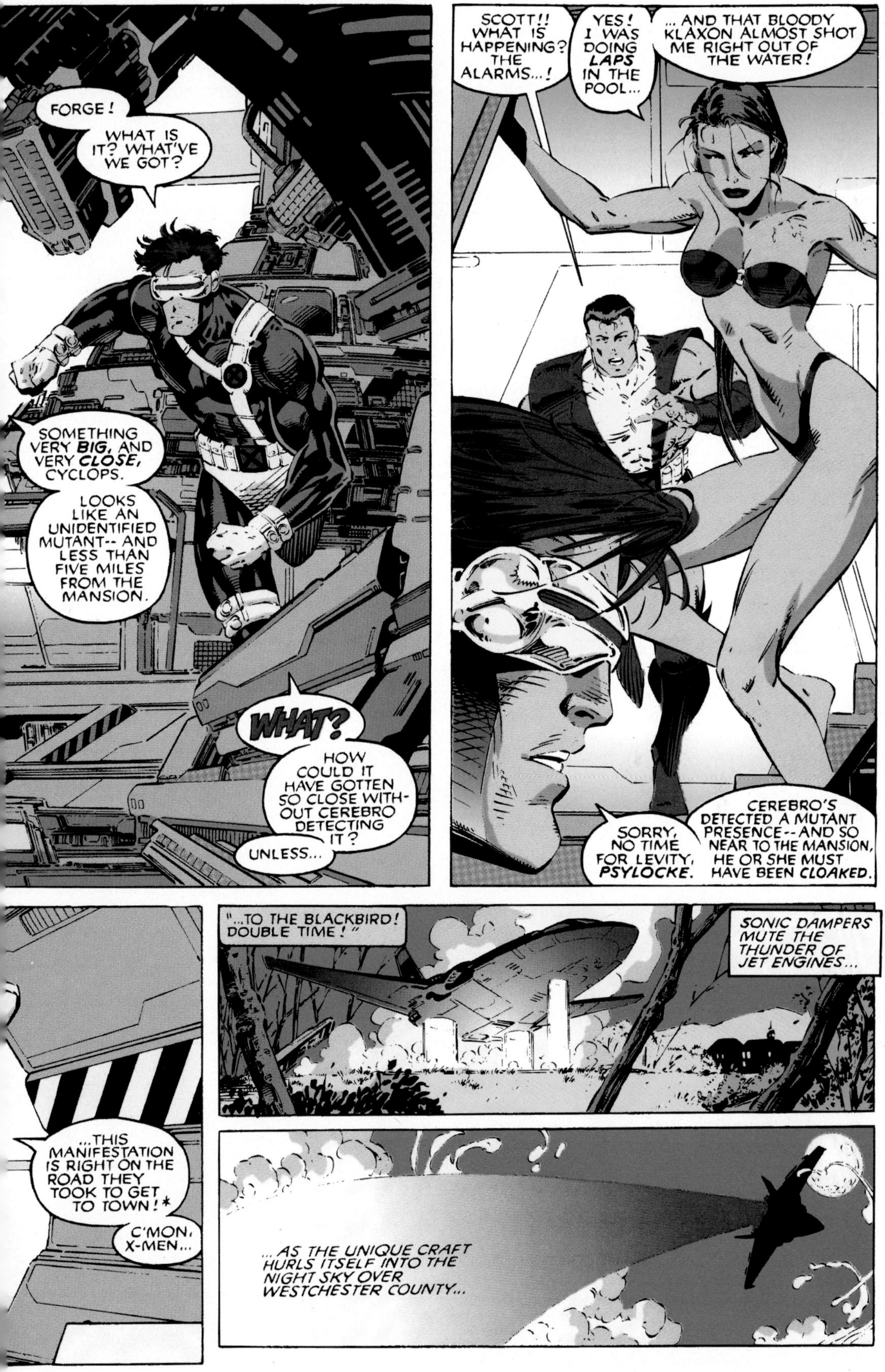
FORGE!
WHAT IS IT? WHAT'VE WE GOT?
SOMETHING VERY BIG, AND VERY CLOSE, CYCLOPS.
LOOKS LIKE AN UNIDENTIFIED MUTANT-- AND LESS THAN FIVE MILES FROM THE MANSION.
WHAT?
HOW COULD IT HAVE GOTTEN SO CLOSE WITH-OUT CEREBRO DETECTING IT?
UNLESS...
SCOTT!! WHAT IS HAPPENING? THE ALARMS...!
YES! I WAS DOING LAPS IN THE POOL...
...AND THAT BLOODY KLAXON ALMOST SHOT ME RIGHT OUT OF THE WATER!
SORRY, NO TIME FOR LEVITY, PSYLOCKE.
CEREBRO'S DETECTED A MUTANT PRESENCE--AND SO NEAR TO THE MANSION, HE OR SHE MUST HAVE BEEN CLOAKED.
...THIS MANIFESTATION IS RIGHT ON THE ROAD THEY TOOK TO GET TO TOWN!*
C'MON, X-MEN...
"...TO THE BLACKBIRD! DOUBLE TIME!"
SONIC DAMPERS MUTE THE THUNDER OF JET ENGINES...
...AS THE UNIQUE CRAFT HURLS ITSELF INTO THE NIGHT SKY OVER WESTCHESTER COUNTY...

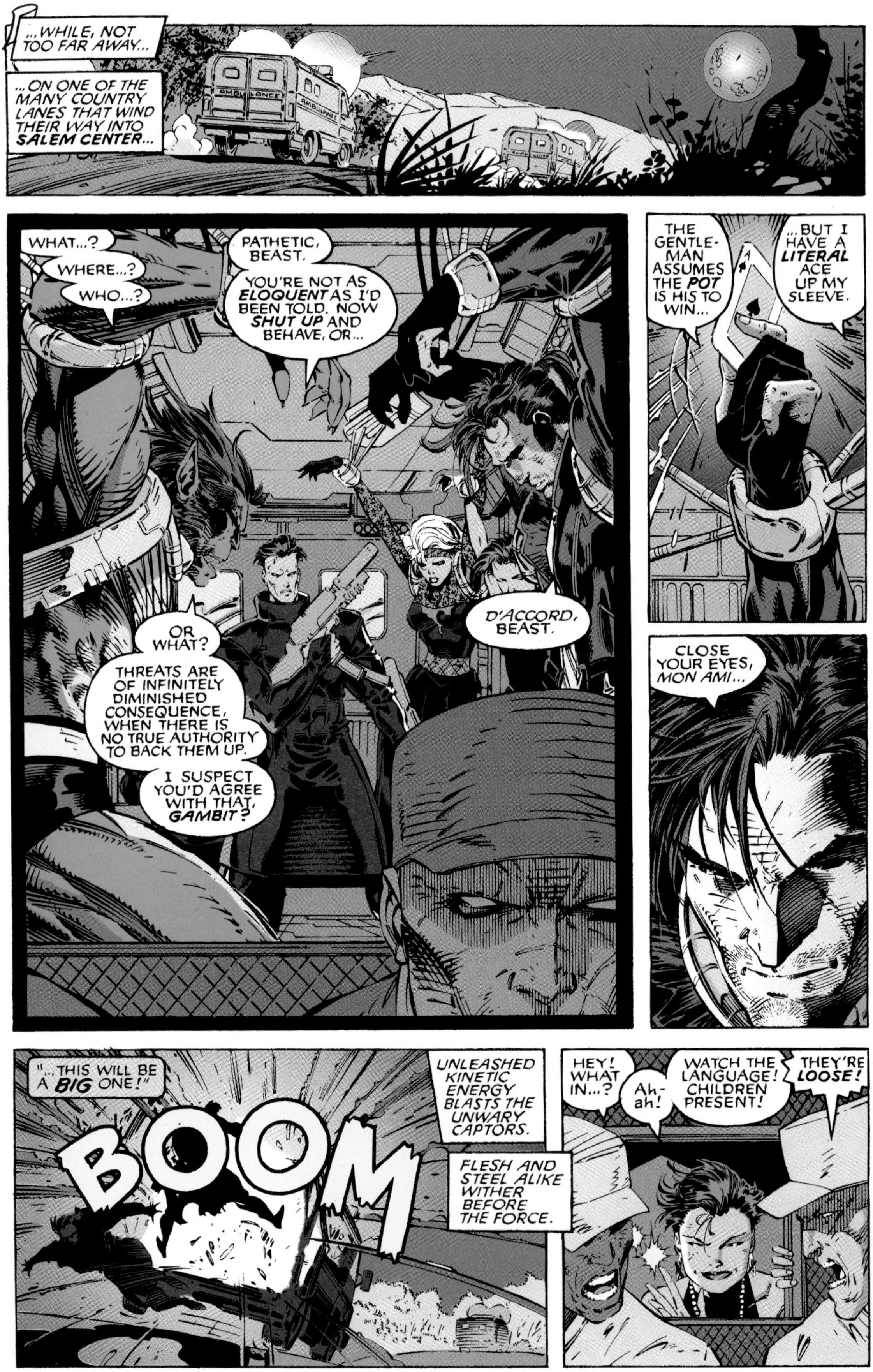
...WHILE, NOT TOO FAR AWAY...
...ON ONE OF THE MANY COUNTRY LANES THAT WIND THEIR WAY INTO SALEM CENTER...
AMBULANCE
WHAT...?
WHERE...?
WHO...?
PATHETIC, BEAST.
YOU'RE NOT AS ELOQUENT AS I'D BEEN TOLD. NOW SHUT UP AND BEHAVE, OR...
OR WHAT?
THREATS ARE OF INFINITELY DIMINISHED CONSEQUENCE, WHEN THERE IS NO TRUE AUTHORITY TO BACK THEM UP.
I SUSPECT YOU'D AGREE WITH THAT, GAMBIT?
D'ACCORD, BEAST.
THE GENTLE-MAN ASSUMES THE POT IS HIS TO WIN...
...BUT I HAVE A LITERAL ACE UP MY SLEEVE.
CLOSE YOUR EYES, MON AMI...
"...THIS WILL BE A BIG ONE!"
BOOM
UNLEASHED KINETIC ENERGY BLASTS THE UNWARY CAPTORS.
FLESH AND STEEL ALIKE WITHER BEFORE THE FORCE.
HEY! WHAT IN...?
Ah-ah!
WATCH THE LANGUAGE! CHILDREN PRESENT!
THEY'RE LOOSE!

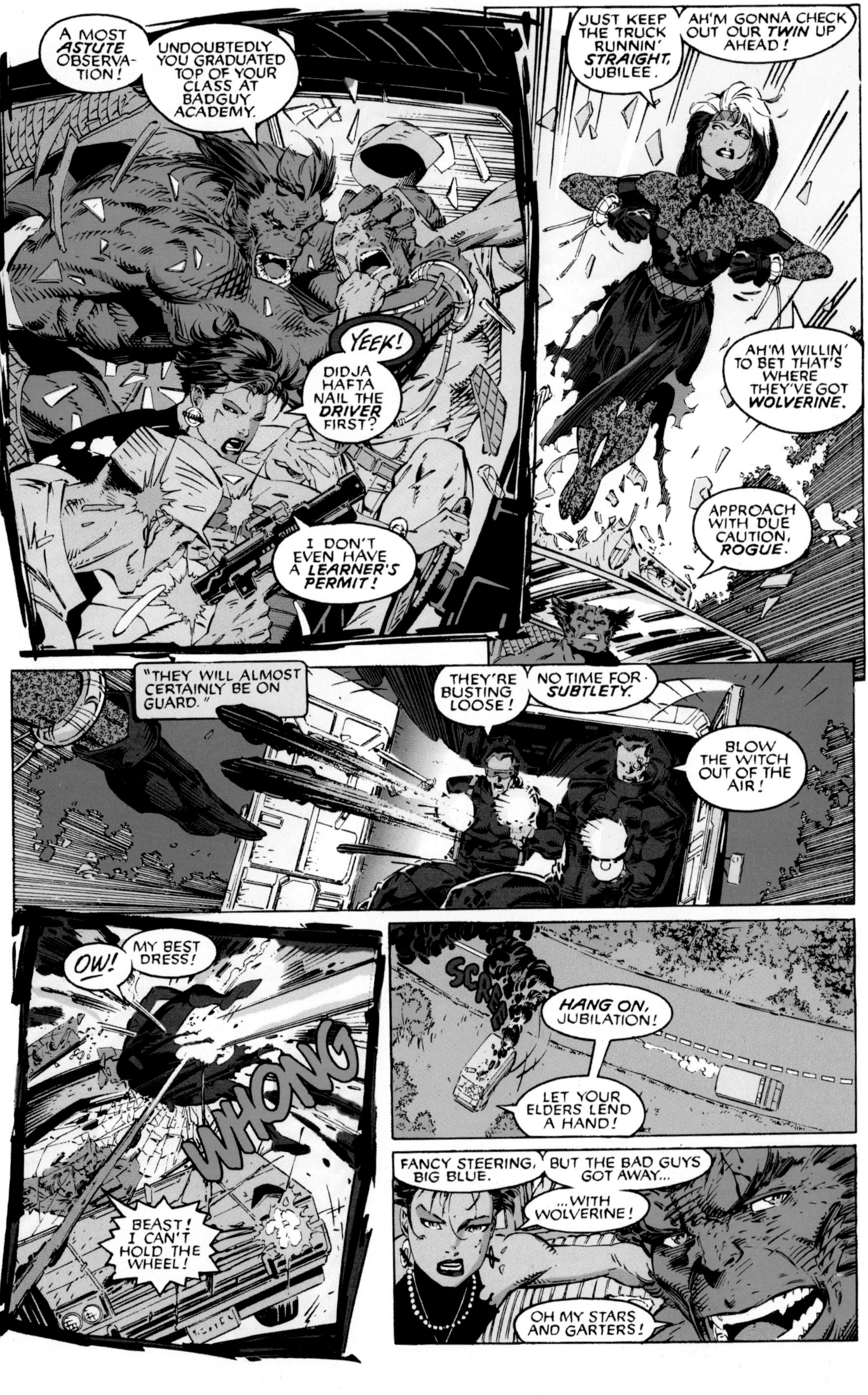
A MOST ASTUTE OBSERVATION!
UNDOUBTEDLY YOU GRADUATED TOP OF YOUR CLASS AT BADGUY ACADEMY.
YEEK!
DIDJA HAFTA NAIL THE DRIVER FIRST?
I DON'T EVEN HAVE A LEARNER'S PERMIT!
JUST KEEP THE TRUCK RUNNIN' STRAIGHT, JUBILEE.
AH'M GONNA CHECK OUT OUR TWIN UP AHEAD!
AH'M WILLIN' TO BET THAT'S WHERE THEY'VE GOT WOLVERINE.
APPROACH WITH DUE CAUTION, ROGUE.
"THEY WILL ALMOST CERTAINLY BE ON GUARD."
THEY'RE BUSTING LOOSE!
NO TIME FOR SUBTLETY.
BLOW THE WITCH OUT OF THE AIR!
OW!
MY BEST DRESS!
WHONG
BEAST! I CAN'T HOLD THE WHEEL!
SCREE
HANG ON, JUBILATION!
LET YOUR ELDERS LEND A HAND!
FANCY STEERING, BIG BLUE.
BUT THE BAD GUYS GOT AWAY...
...WITH WOLVERINE!
OH MY STARS AND GARTERS!

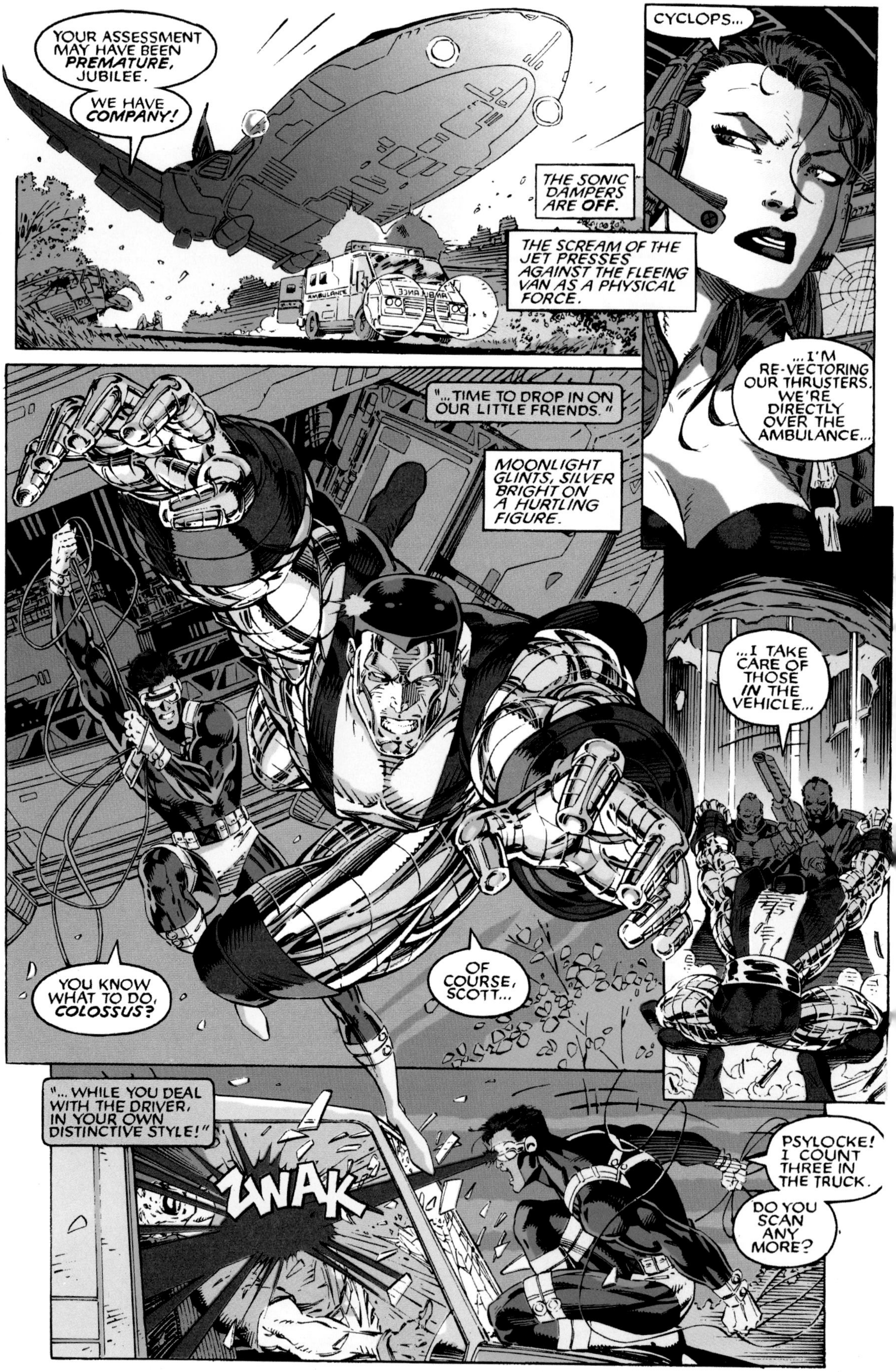
YOUR ASSESSMENT MAY HAVE BEEN **PREMATURE,** JUBILEE.
WE HAVE **COMPANY!**
THE SONIC DAMPERS ARE **OFF.**
THE SCREAM OF THE JET PRESSES AGAINST THE FLEEING VAN AS A PHYSICAL FORCE.
AMBULANCE
CYCLOPS...
...I'M RE-VECTORING OUR THRUSTERS. WE'RE DIRECTLY OVER THE AMBULANCE...
"...TIME TO DROP IN ON OUR LITTLE FRIENDS."
MOONLIGHT GLINTS, SILVER BRIGHT ON A HURTLING FIGURE.
YOU KNOW WHAT TO DO, **COLOSSUS?**
OF COURSE, SCOTT...
...I TAKE CARE OF THOSE **IN** THE VEHICLE...
"...WHILE YOU DEAL WITH THE DRIVER, IN YOUR OWN DISTINCTIVE STYLE!"
ZWAK
PSYLOCKE! I COUNT THREE IN THE TRUCK.
DO YOU SCAN ANY MORE?

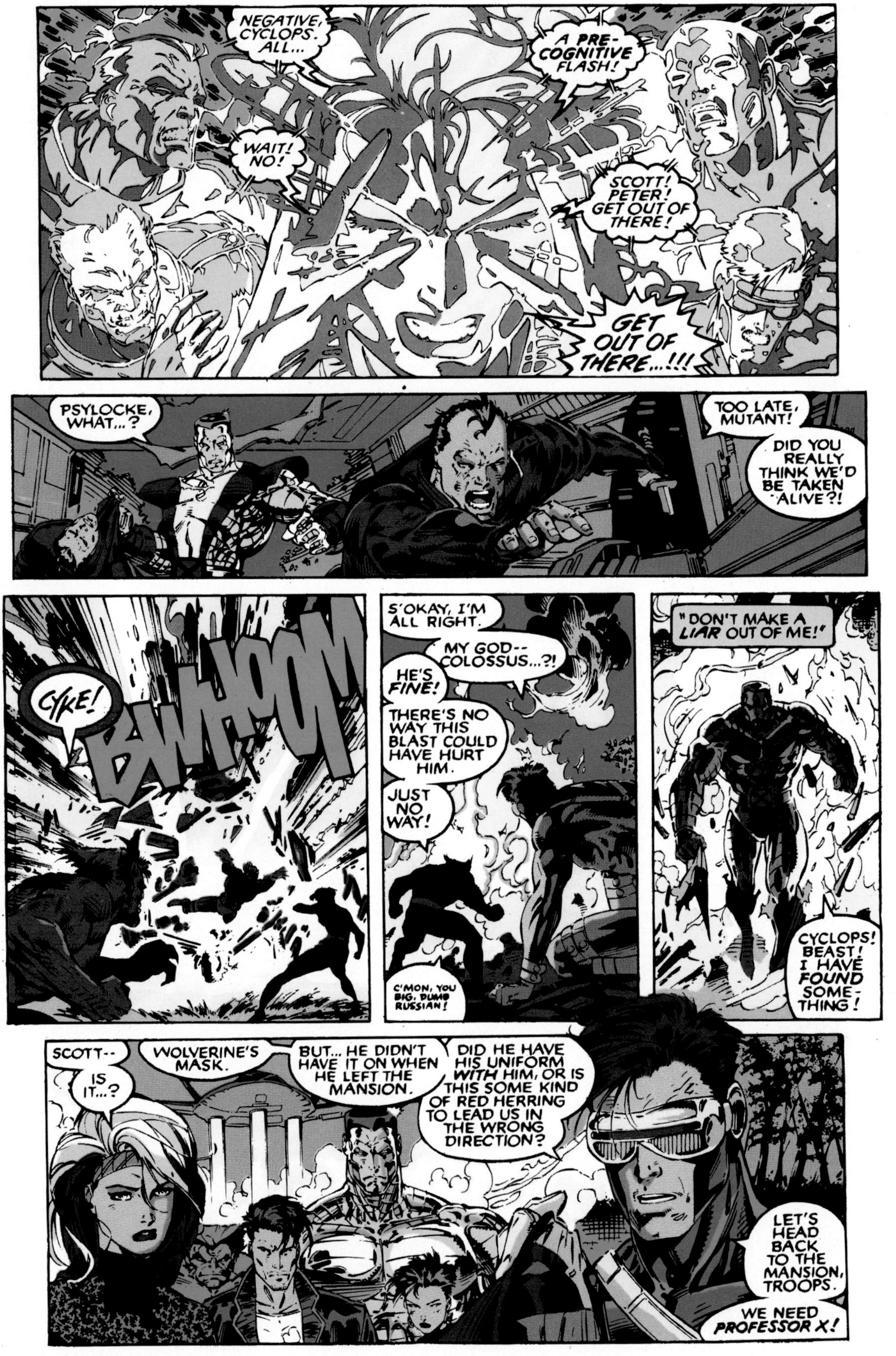
NEGATIVE, CYCLOPS. ALL...
A PRE-COGNITIVE FLASH!
WAIT! NO!
SCOTT! PETER! GET OUT OF THERE!
GET OUT OF THERE...!!!
PSYLOCKE, WHAT...?
TOO LATE, MUTANT!
DID YOU REALLY THINK WE'D BE TAKEN ALIVE?!
CYKE!
BWHOOM
S'OKAY, I'M ALL RIGHT.
MY GOD-- COLOSSUS...?!
HE'S FINE!
THERE'S NO WAY THIS BLAST COULD HAVE HURT HIM.
JUST NO WAY!
C'MON, YOU BIG, DUMB RUSSIAN!
"DON'T MAKE A LIAR OUT OF ME!"
CYCLOPS! BEAST! I HAVE FOUND SOME-THING!
SCOTT--
IS IT...?
WOLVERINE'S MASK.
BUT... HE DIDN'T HAVE IT ON WHEN HE LEFT THE MANSION.
DID HE HAVE HIS UNIFORM WITH HIM, OR IS THIS SOME KIND OF RED HERRING TO LEAD US IN THE WRONG DIRECTION?
LET'S HEAD BACK TO THE MANSION, TROOPS.
WE NEED PROFESSOR X!

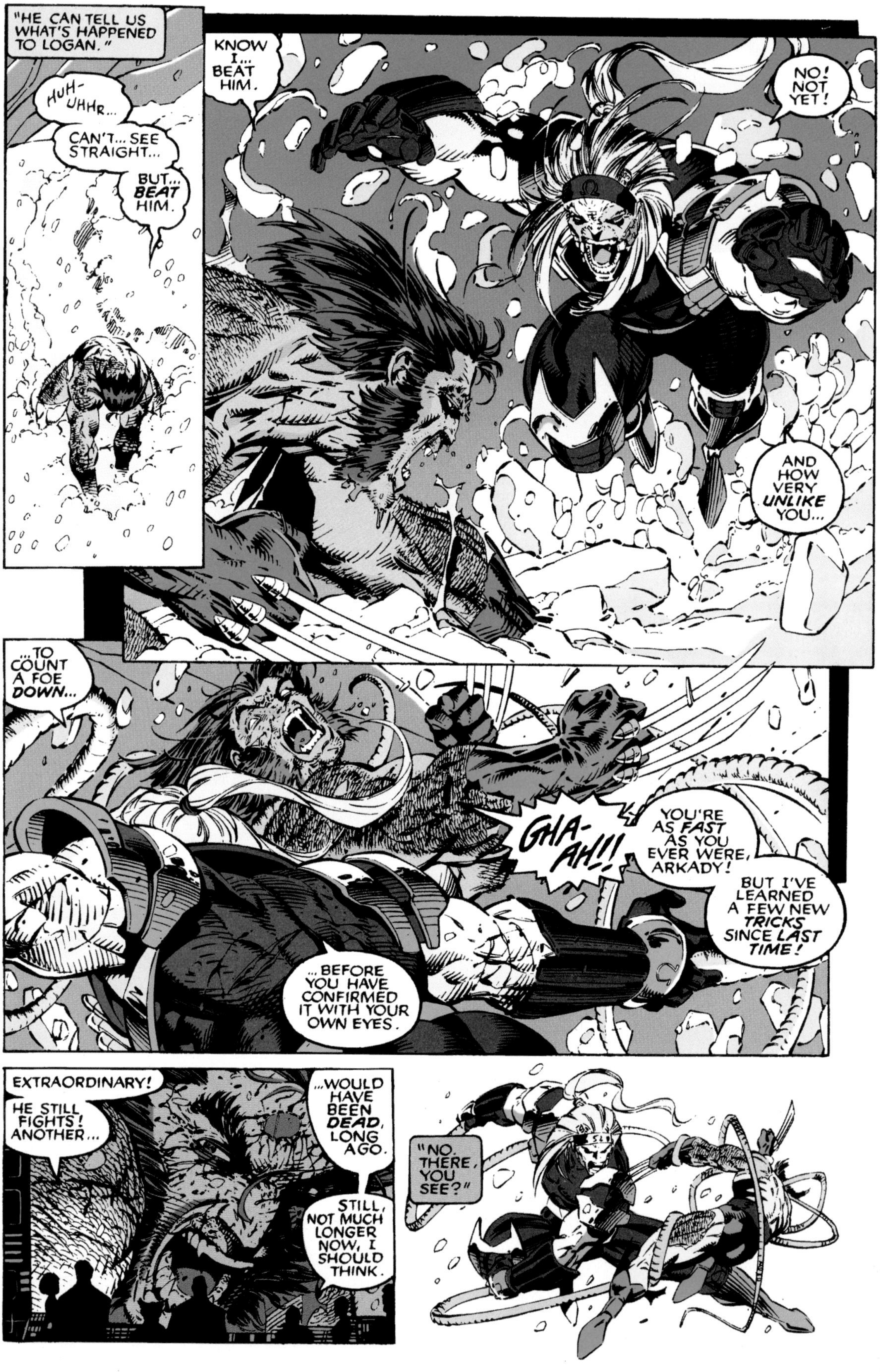
"HE CAN TELL US WHAT'S HAPPENED TO LOGAN."
HUH-UHHR...
CAN'T... SEE STRAIGHT...
BUT... BEAT HIM.
KNOW I... BEAT HIM.
NO! NOT YET!
AND HOW VERY UNLIKE YOU...
...TO COUNT A FOE DOWN...
...BEFORE YOU HAVE CONFIRMED IT WITH YOUR OWN EYES.
GHA-AH!!
YOU'RE AS FAST AS YOU EVER WERE, ARKADY!
BUT I'VE LEARNED A FEW NEW TRICKS SINCE LAST TIME!
EXTRAORDINARY!
HE STILL FIGHTS! ANOTHER...
...WOULD HAVE BEEN DEAD, LONG AGO.
STILL, NOT MUCH LONGER NOW, I SHOULD THINK.
"NO. THERE, YOU SEE?"

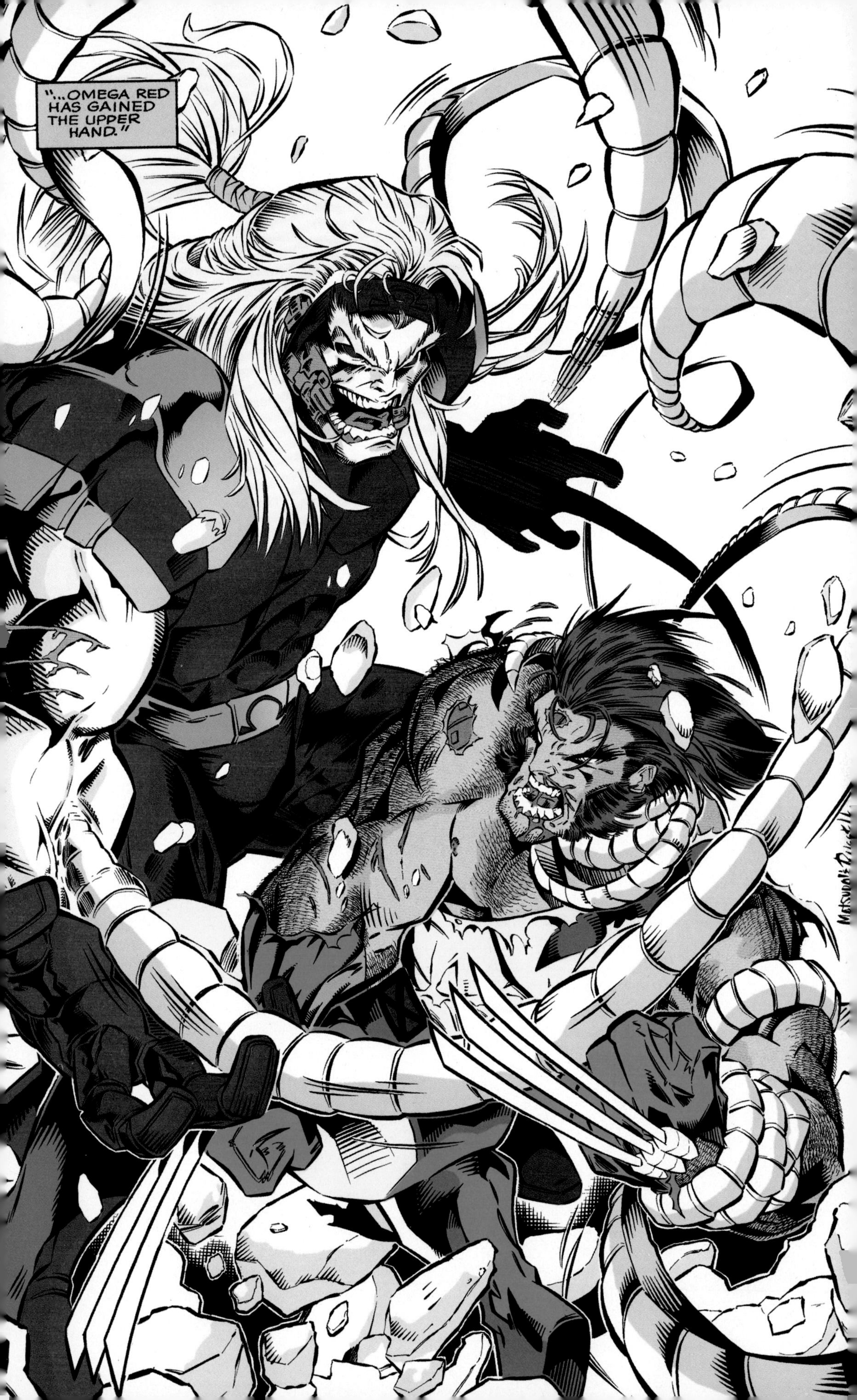
"...OMEGA RED HAS GAINED THE UPPER HAND."

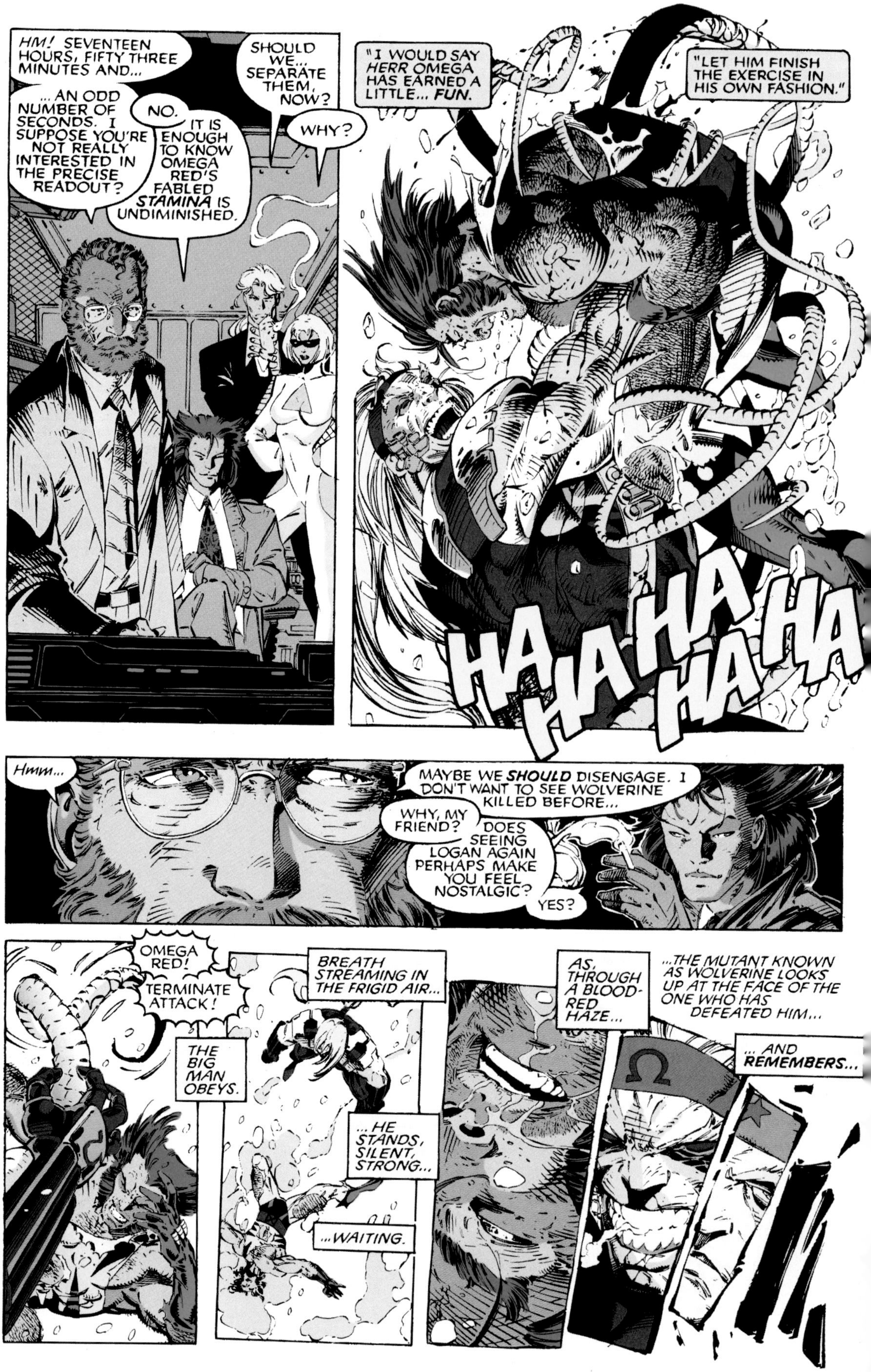
HM! SEVENTEEN HOURS, FIFTY THREE MINUTES AND...
... AN ODD NUMBER OF SECONDS. I SUPPOSE YOU'RE NOT REALLY INTERESTED IN THE PRECISE READOUT?
NO.
IT IS ENOUGH TO KNOW OMEGA RED'S FABLED STAMINA IS UNDIMINISHED.
SHOULD WE... SEPARATE THEM, NOW?
WHY?
"I WOULD SAY HERR OMEGA HAS EARNED A LITTLE... FUN.
"LET HIM FINISH THE EXERCISE IN HIS OWN FASHION."
HA HA HA HA HA HA HA
Hmm...
MAYBE WE SHOULD DISENGAGE. I DON'T WANT TO SEE WOLVERINE KILLED BEFORE...
WHY, MY FRIEND?
DOES SEEING LOGAN AGAIN PERHAPS MAKE YOU FEEL NOSTALGIC?
YES?
OMEGA RED!
TERMINATE ATTACK!
THE BIG MAN OBEYS.
BREATH STREAMING IN THE FRIGID AIR...
...HE STANDS, SILENT, STRONG...
...WAITING.
AS, THROUGH A BLOOD-RED HAZE...
...THE MUTANT KNOWN AS WOLVERINE LOOKS UP AT THE FACE OF THE ONE WHO HAS DEFEATED HIM...
... AND REMEMBERS...

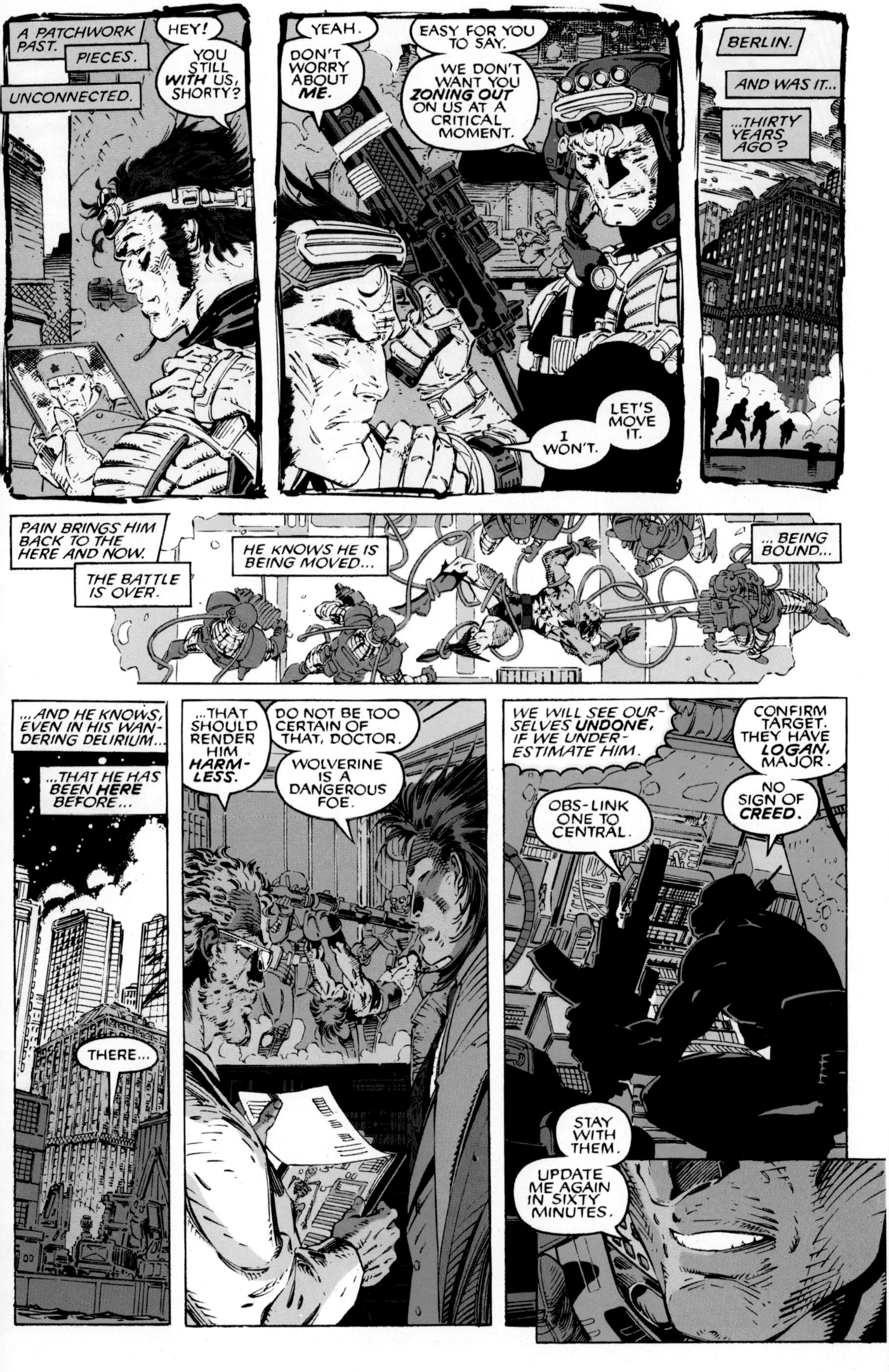
A PATCHWORK PAST.
PIECES.
UNCONNECTED.
HEY!
YOU STILL WITH US, SHORTY?
YEAH.
DON'T WORRY ABOUT ME.
EASY FOR YOU TO SAY.
WE DON'T WANT YOU ZONING OUT ON US AT A CRITICAL MOMENT.
I WON'T.
LET'S MOVE IT.
BERLIN.
AND WAS IT...
...THIRTY YEARS AGO?
PAIN BRINGS HIM BACK TO THE HERE AND NOW.
THE BATTLE IS OVER.
HE KNOWS HE IS BEING MOVED...
...BEING BOUND...
...AND HE KNOWS, EVEN IN HIS WANDERING DELIRIUM...
...THAT HE HAS BEEN HERE BEFORE...
THERE...
...THAT SHOULD RENDER HIM HARMLESS.
DO NOT BE TOO CERTAIN OF THAT, DOCTOR.
WOLVERINE IS A DANGEROUS FOE.
WE WILL SEE OURSELVES UNDONE, IF WE UNDERESTIMATE HIM.
OBS-LINK ONE TO CENTRAL.
CONFIRM TARGET. THEY HAVE LOGAN, MAJOR.
NO SIGN OF CREED.
STAY WITH THEM.
UPDATE ME AGAIN IN SIXTY MINUTES.

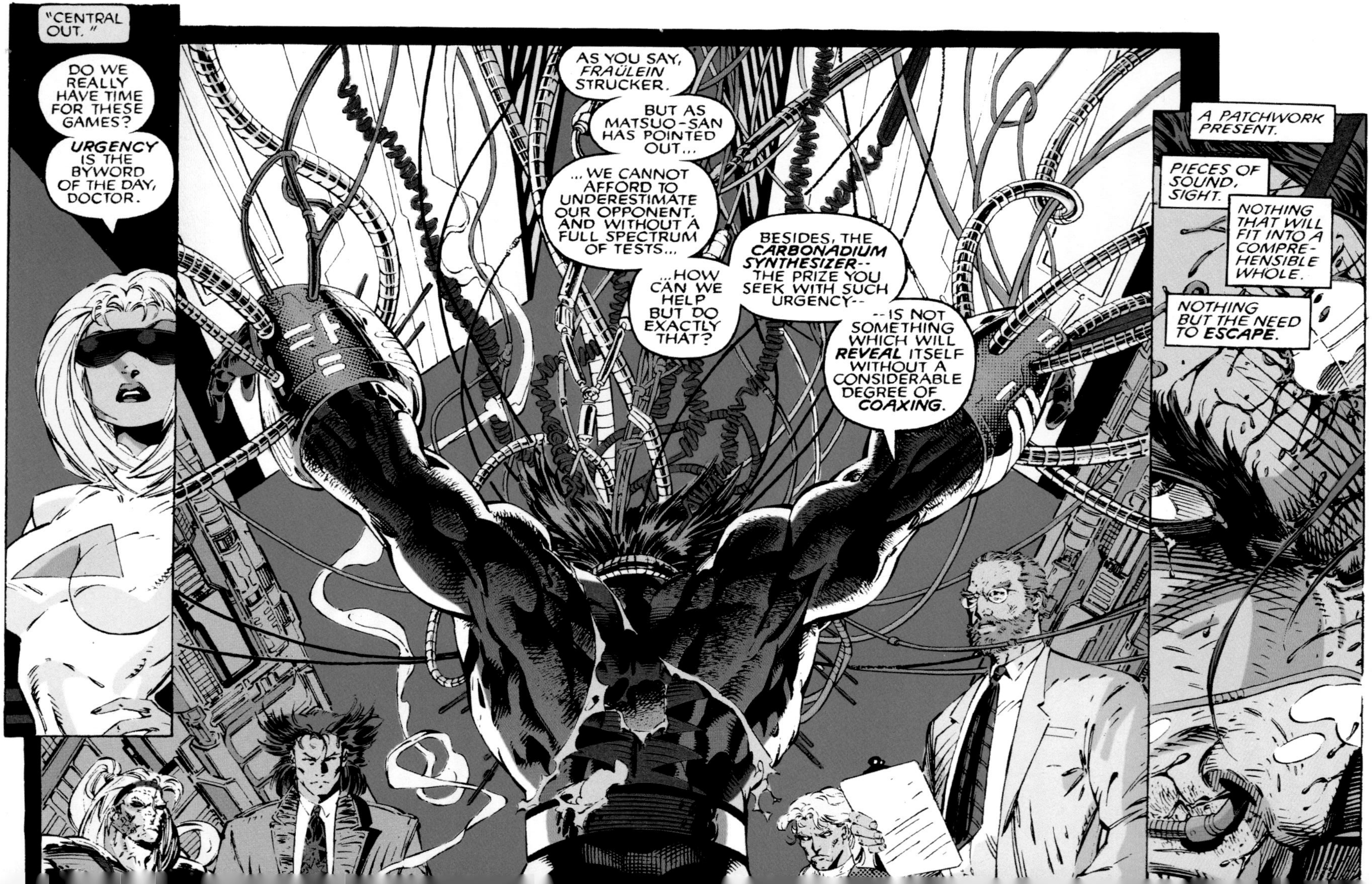
"CENTRAL OUT."
DO WE REALLY HAVE TIME FOR THESE GAMES?
URGENCY IS THE BYWORD OF THE DAY, DOCTOR.
AS YOU SAY, FRAÜLEIN STRUCKER.
BUT AS MATSUO-SAN HAS POINTED OUT...
...WE CANNOT AFFORD TO UNDERESTIMATE OUR OPPONENT, AND WITHOUT A FULL SPECTRUM OF TESTS...
...HOW CAN WE HELP BUT DO EXACTLY THAT?
BESIDES, THE CARBONADIUM SYNTHESIZER-- THE PRIZE YOU SEEK WITH SUCH URGENCY--
--IS NOT SOMETHING WHICH WILL REVEAL ITSELF WITHOUT A CONSIDERABLE DEGREE OF COAXING.
A PATCHWORK PRESENT.
PIECES OF SOUND, SIGHT.
NOTHING THAT WILL FIT INTO A COMPRE-HENSIBLE WHOLE.
NOTHING BUT THE NEED TO ESCAPE.

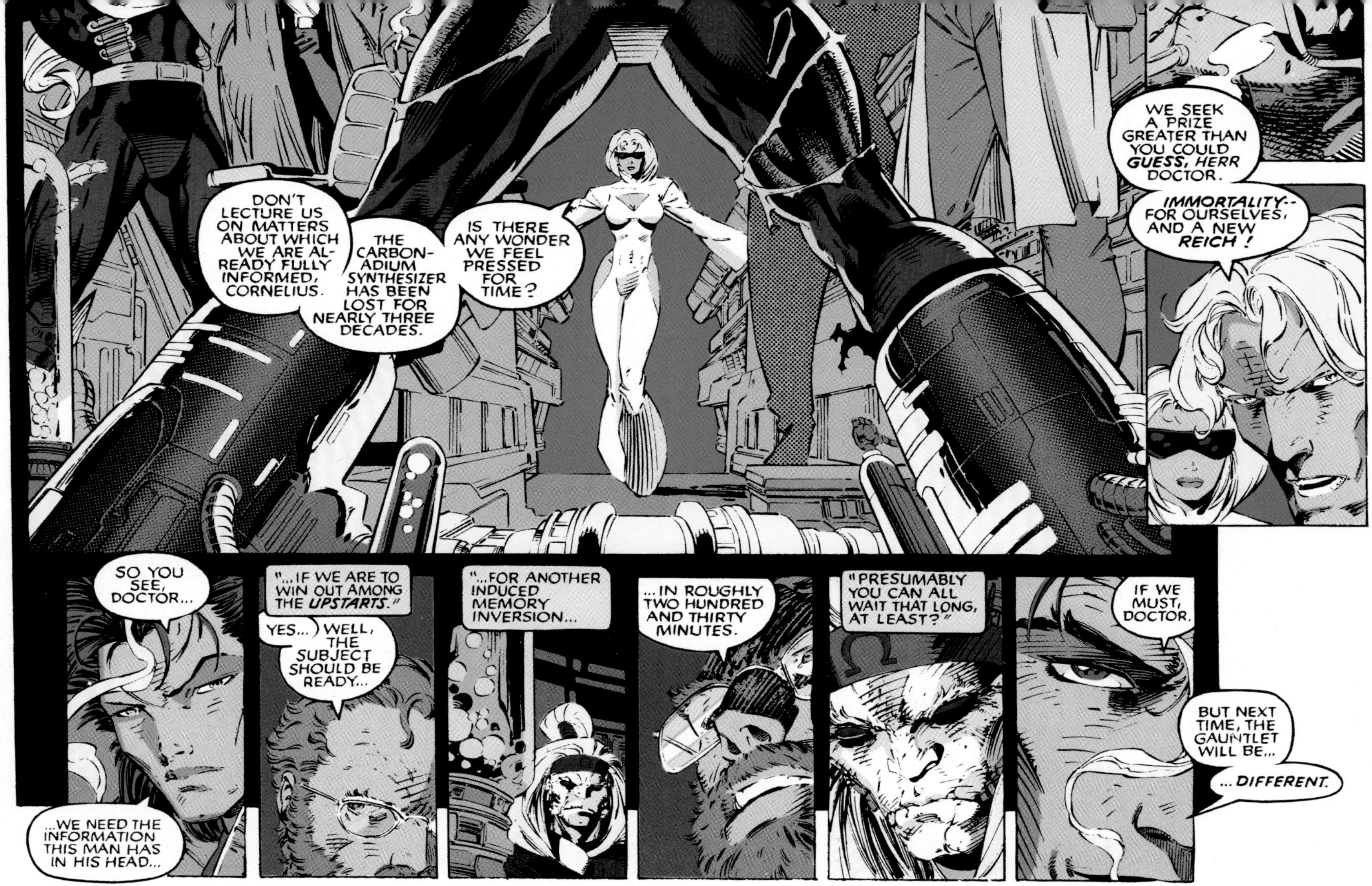
DON'T LECTURE US ON MATTERS ABOUT WHICH WE ARE AL-READY FULLY INFORMED, CORNELIUS.
THE CARBON-ADIUM SYNTHESIZER HAS BEEN LOST FOR NEARLY THREE DECADES.
IS THERE ANY WONDER WE FEEL PRESSED FOR TIME?
WE SEEK A PRIZE GREATER THAN YOU COULD GUESS, HERR DOCTOR.
IMMORTALITY-- FOR OURSELVES, AND A NEW REICH!
SO YOU SEE, DOCTOR...
...WE NEED THE INFORMATION THIS MAN HAS IN HIS HEAD...
"...IF WE ARE TO WIN OUT AMONG THE UPSTARTS."
YES...) WELL, THE SUBJECT SHOULD BE READY...
"...FOR ANOTHER INDUCED MEMORY INVERSION...
...IN ROUGHLY TWO HUNDRED AND THIRTY MINUTES.
"PRESUMABLY YOU CAN ALL WAIT THAT LONG, AT LEAST?"
IF WE MUST, DOCTOR.
BUT NEXT TIME, THE GAUNTLET WILL BE...
...DIFFERENT.

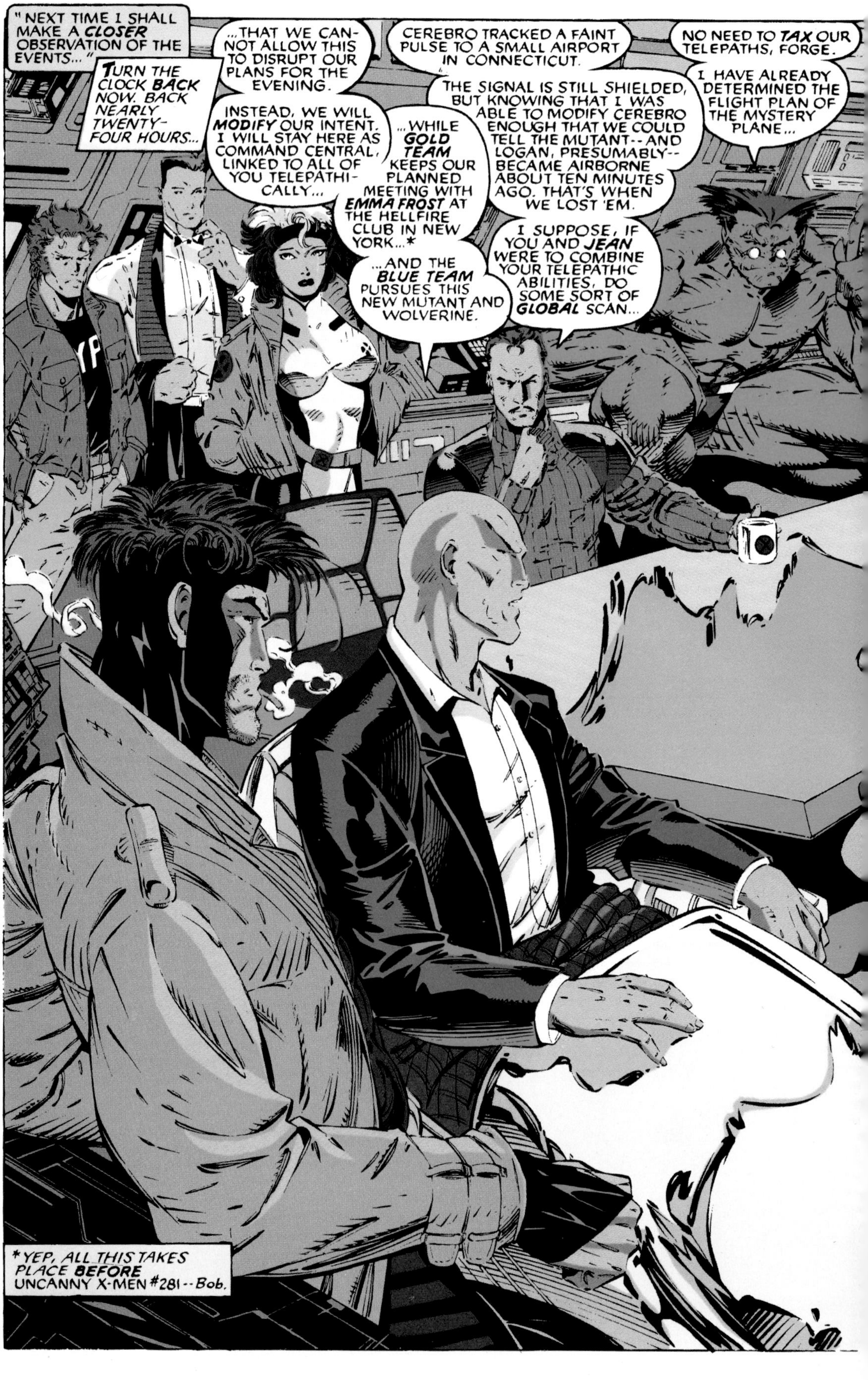
"NEXT TIME I SHALL MAKE A CLOSER OBSERVATION OF THE EVENTS..."
TURN THE CLOCK BACK NOW. BACK NEARLY TWENTY-FOUR HOURS...
...THAT WE CANNOT ALLOW THIS TO DISRUPT OUR PLANS FOR THE EVENING.
INSTEAD, WE WILL MODIFY OUR INTENT. I WILL STAY HERE AS COMMAND CENTRAL, LINKED TO ALL OF YOU TELEPATHICALLY...
...WHILE GOLD TEAM KEEPS OUR PLANNED MEETING WITH EMMA FROST AT THE HELLFIRE CLUB IN NEW YORK...*
...AND THE BLUE TEAM PURSUES THIS NEW MUTANT AND WOLVERINE.
CEREBRO TRACKED A FAINT PULSE TO A SMALL AIRPORT IN CONNECTICUT.
THE SIGNAL IS STILL SHIELDED, BUT KNOWING THAT I WAS ABLE TO MODIFY CEREBRO ENOUGH THAT WE COULD TELL THE MUTANT-- AND LOGAN, PRESUMABLY-- BECAME AIRBORNE ABOUT TEN MINUTES AGO. THAT'S WHEN WE LOST 'EM.
I SUPPOSE, IF YOU AND JEAN WERE TO COMBINE YOUR TELEPATHIC ABILITIES, DO SOME SORT OF GLOBAL SCAN...
NO NEED TO TAX OUR TELEPATHS, FORGE.
I HAVE ALREADY DETERMINED THE FLIGHT PLAN OF THE MYSTERY PLANE...
*YEP, ALL THIS TAKES PLACE BEFORE UNCANNY X-MEN #281--Bob.

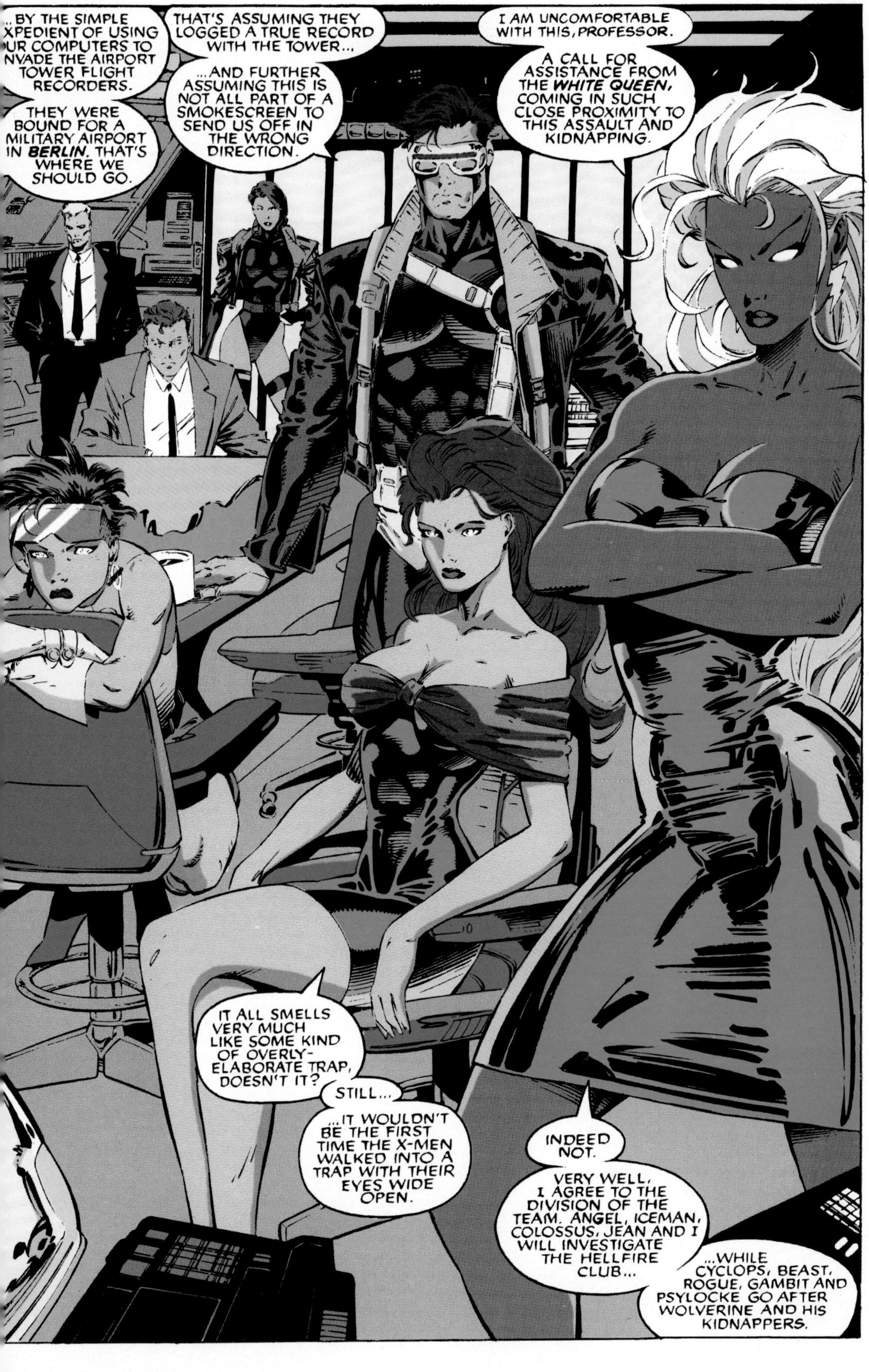
..BY THE SIMPLE XPEDIENT OF USING UR COMPUTERS TO NVADE THE AIRPORT TOWER FLIGHT RECORDERS.
THEY WERE BOUND FOR A MILITARY AIRPORT IN BERLIN. THAT'S WHERE WE SHOULD GO.
THAT'S ASSUMING THEY LOGGED A TRUE RECORD WITH THE TOWER...
...AND FURTHER ASSUMING THIS IS NOT ALL PART OF A SMOKESCREEN TO SEND US OFF IN THE WRONG DIRECTION.
I AM UNCOMFORTABLE WITH THIS, PROFESSOR.
A CALL FOR ASSISTANCE FROM THE WHITE QUEEN, COMING IN SUCH CLOSE PROXIMITY TO THIS ASSAULT AND KIDNAPPING.
IT ALL SMELLS VERY MUCH LIKE SOME KIND OF OVERLY-ELABORATE TRAP, DOESN'T IT?
STILL...
...IT WOULDN'T BE THE FIRST TIME THE X-MEN WALKED INTO A TRAP WITH THEIR EYES WIDE OPEN.
INDEED NOT.
VERY WELL, I AGREE TO THE DIVISION OF THE TEAM. ANGEL, ICEMAN, COLOSSUS, JEAN AND I WILL INVESTIGATE THE HELLFIRE CLUB...
...WHILE CYCLOPS, BEAST, ROGUE, GAMBIT AND PSYLOCKE GO AFTER WOLVERINE AND HIS KIDNAPPERS.

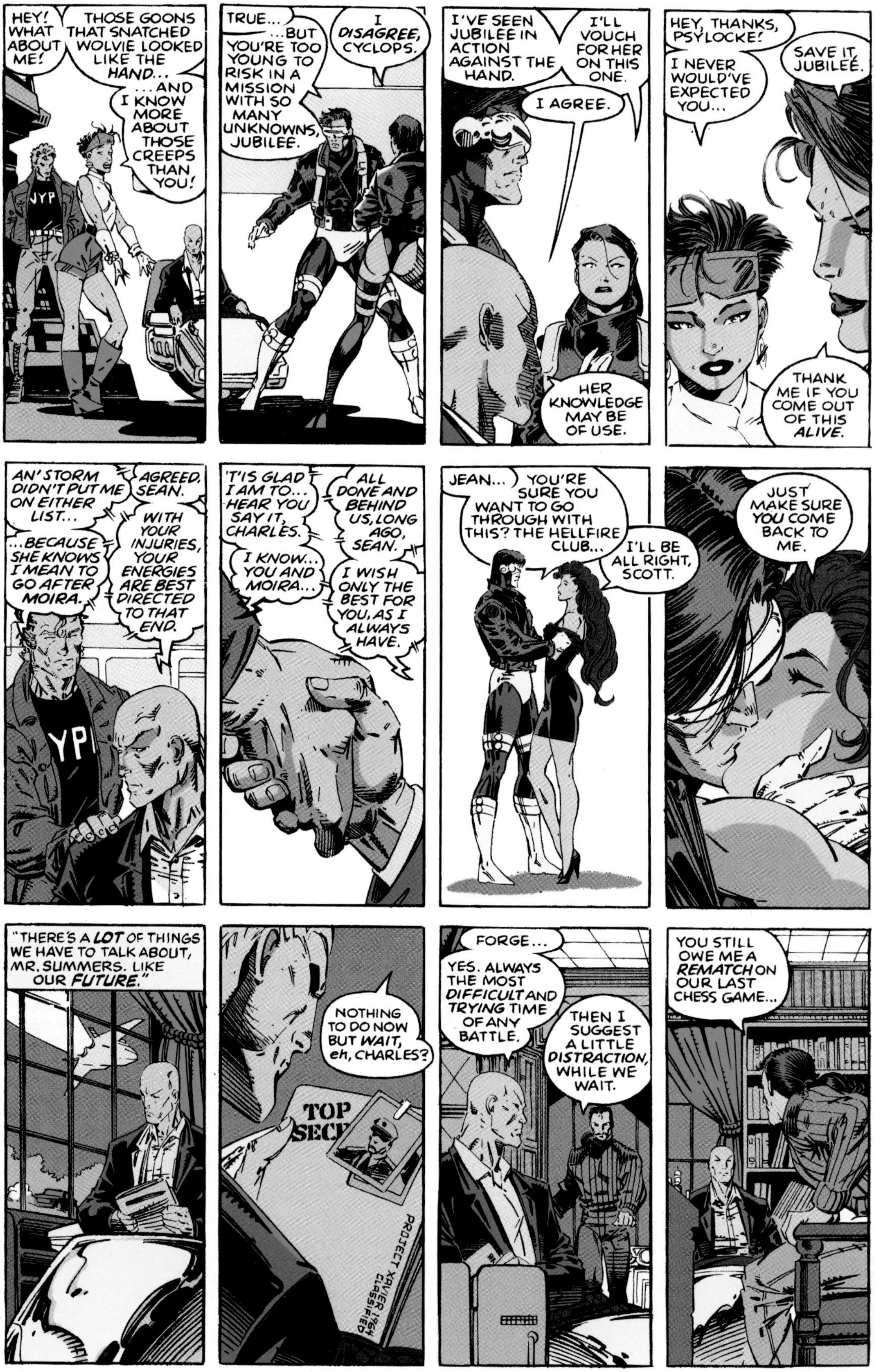
HEY! WHAT ABOUT ME!
THOSE GOONS THAT SNATCHED WOLVIE LOOKED LIKE THE HAND...
...AND I KNOW MORE ABOUT THOSE CREEPS THAN YOU!
JYP
TRUE... ...BUT YOU'RE TOO YOUNG TO RISK IN A MISSION WITH SO MANY UNKNOWNS, JUBILEE.
I DISAGREE, CYCLOPS.
I'VE SEEN JUBILEE IN ACTION AGAINST THE HAND.
I'LL VOUCH FOR HER ON THIS ONE.
I AGREE.
HER KNOWLEDGE MAY BE OF USE.
HEY, THANKS, PSYLOCKE!
I NEVER WOULD'VE EXPECTED YOU...
SAVE IT, JUBILEE.
THANK ME IF YOU COME OUT OF THIS ALIVE.
AN' STORM DIDN'T PUT ME ON EITHER LIST...
...BECAUSE SHE KNOWS I MEAN TO GO AFTER MOIRA.
AGREED, SEAN.
WITH YOUR INJURIES, YOUR ENERGIES ARE BEST DIRECTED TO THAT END.
'T'IS GLAD I AM TO... HEAR YOU SAY IT, CHARLES.
ALL DONE AND BEHIND US, LONG AGO, SEAN.
I KNOW... YOU AND MOIRA...
I WISH ONLY THE BEST FOR YOU, AS I ALWAYS HAVE.
JEAN...
YOU'RE SURE YOU WANT TO GO THROUGH WITH THIS? THE HELLFIRE CLUB...
I'LL BE ALL RIGHT, SCOTT.
JUST MAKE SURE YOU COME BACK TO ME.
"THERE'S A LOT OF THINGS WE HAVE TO TALK ABOUT, MR. SUMMERS. LIKE OUR FUTURE."
NOTHING TO DO NOW BUT WAIT, eh, CHARLES?
TOP SECR
PROJECT XAVIER 1964 CLASSIFIED
FORGE...
YES. ALWAYS THE MOST DIFFICULT AND TRYING TIME OF ANY BATTLE.
THEN I SUGGEST A LITTLE DISTRACTION, WHILE WE WAIT.
YOU STILL OWE ME A REMATCH ON OUR LAST CHESS GAME...

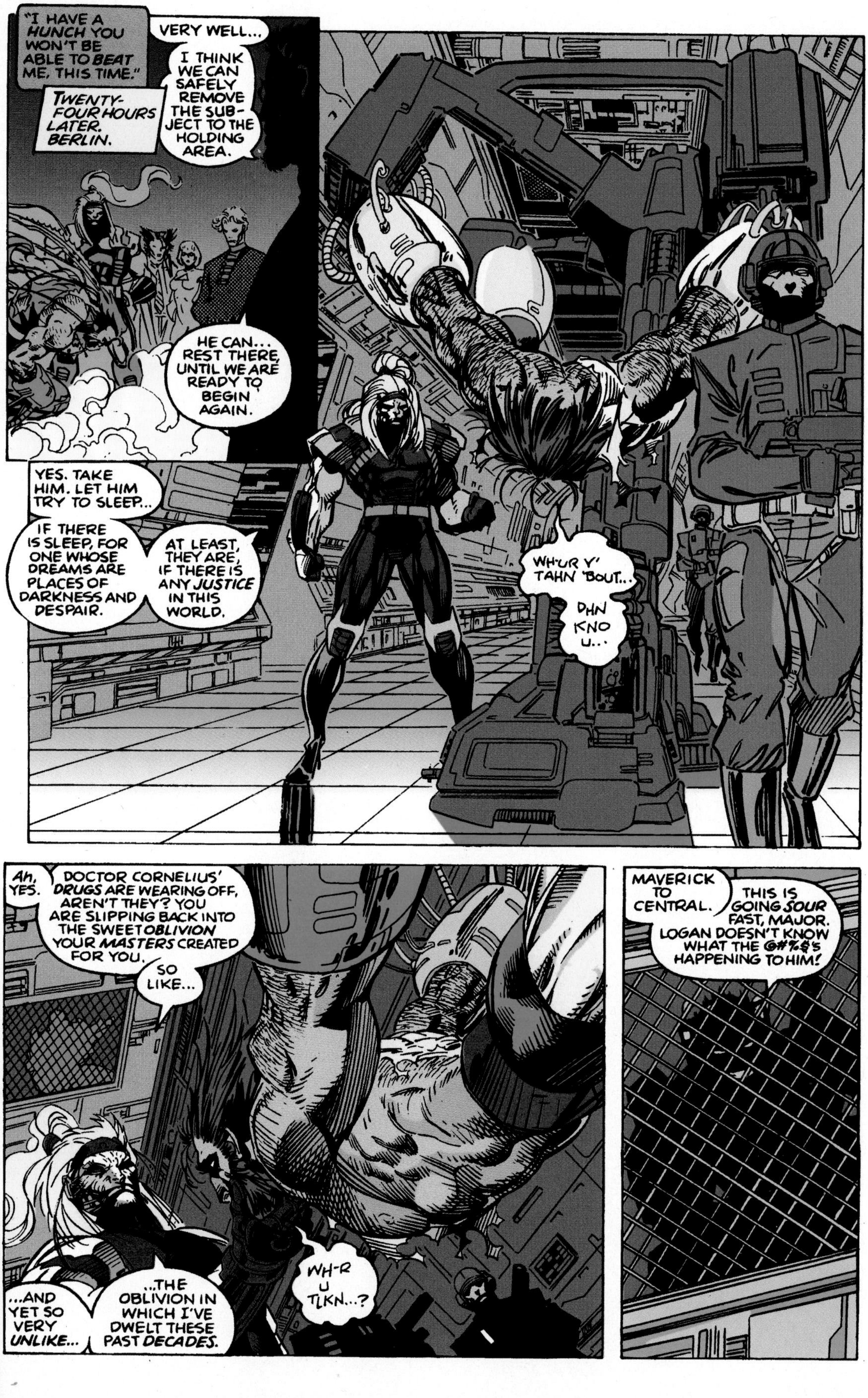
"I HAVE A *HUNCH* YOU WON'T BE ABLE TO *BEAT* ME, THIS TIME."
TWENTY-FOUR HOURS LATER. BERLIN.
VERY WELL...
I THINK WE CAN SAFELY REMOVE THE SUBJECT TO THE HOLDING AREA.
HE CAN... REST THERE, UNTIL WE ARE READY TO BEGIN AGAIN.
YES. TAKE HIM. LET HIM TRY TO SLEEP...
IF THERE IS SLEEP, FOR ONE WHOSE DREAMS ARE PLACES OF DARKNESS AND DESPAIR.
AT LEAST, THEY ARE, IF THERE IS ANY *JUSTICE* IN THIS WORLD.
WH'UR Y' TAHN 'BOUT...
DHN KNO U...
Ah, YES.
DOCTOR CORNELIUS' *DRUGS* ARE WEARING OFF, AREN'T THEY? YOU ARE SLIPPING BACK INTO THE SWEET *OBLIVION* YOUR *MASTERS* CREATED FOR YOU.
SO LIKE...
...AND YET SO VERY *UNLIKE*...
...THE OBLIVION IN WHICH I'VE DWELT THESE PAST *DECADES*.
WH-R U TLKN...?
MAVERICK TO CENTRAL.
THIS IS GOING *SOUR* FAST, MAJOR. LOGAN DOESN'T KNOW WHAT THE @#%$'S HAPPENING TO HIM!

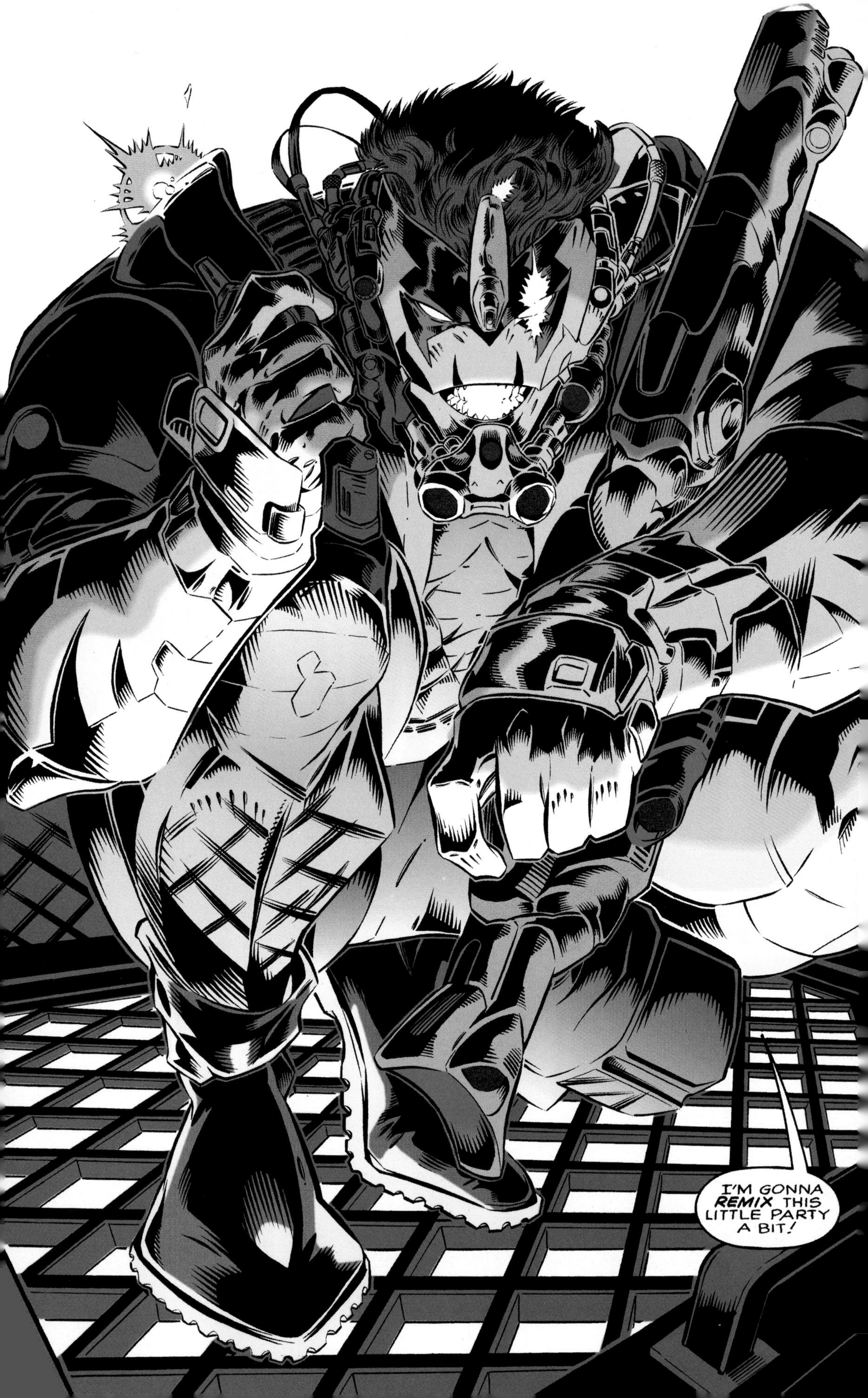
I'M GONNA REMIX THIS LITTLE PARTY A BIT!

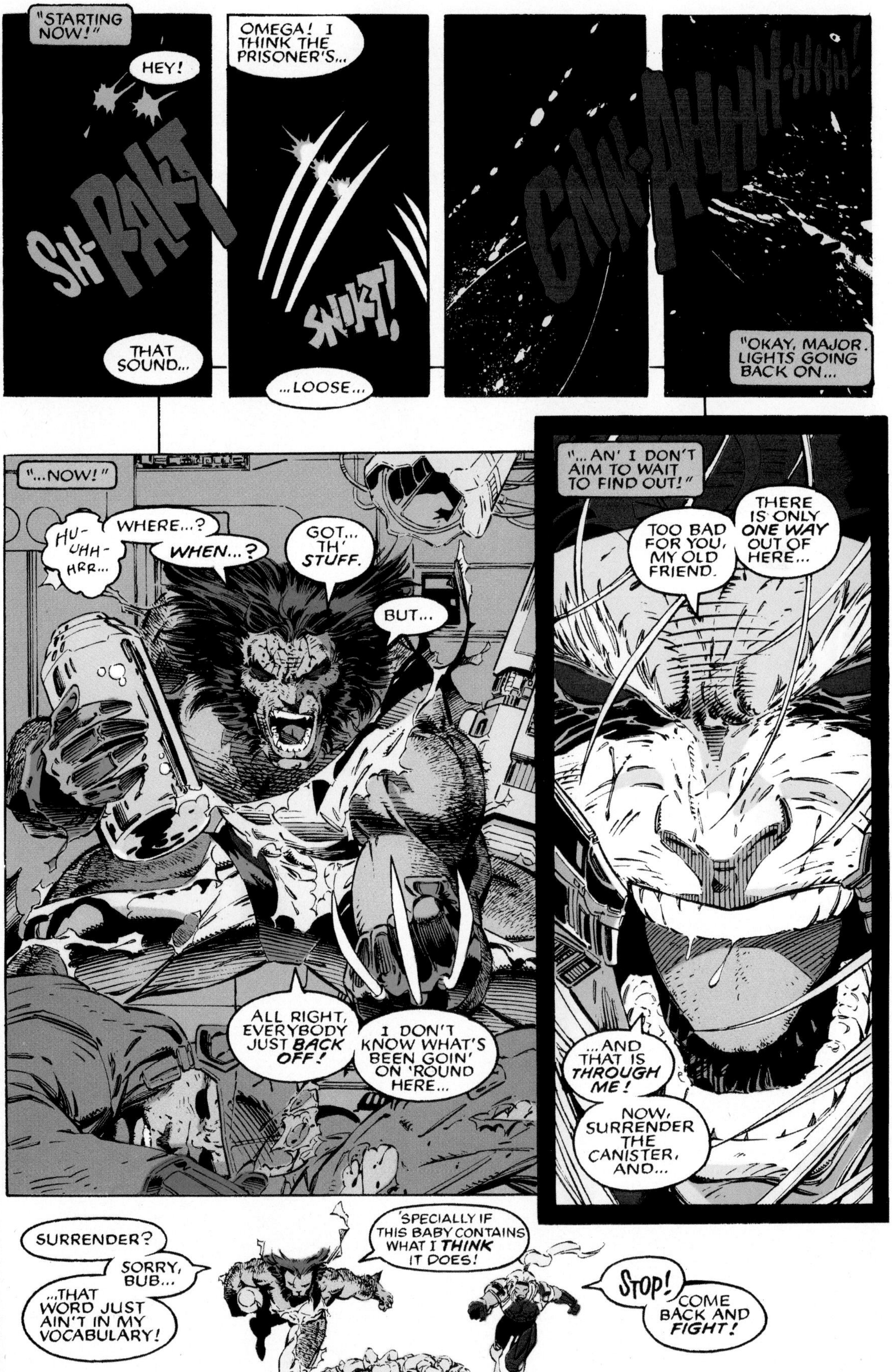
"STARTING NOW!"
HEY!
SH-RAKT
THAT SOUND...
OMEGA! I THINK THE PRISONER'S...
SNIKT!
...LOOSE...
GNN-AHHH-HHH!
"OKAY, MAJOR. LIGHTS GOING BACK ON...
"...NOW!"
HU-UHH-HRR...
WHERE...? WHEN...?
GOT... TH' STUFF.
BUT...
ALL RIGHT, EVERYBODY JUST BACK OFF!
I DON'T KNOW WHAT'S BEEN GOIN' ON 'ROUND HERE...
"...AN' I DON'T AIM TO WAIT TO FIND OUT!"
TOO BAD FOR YOU, MY OLD FRIEND.
THERE IS ONLY ONE WAY OUT OF HERE...
...AND THAT IS THROUGH ME!
NOW, SURRENDER THE CANISTER, AND...
SURRENDER?
SORRY, BUB...
...THAT WORD JUST AIN'T IN MY VOCABULARY!
'SPECIALLY IF THIS BABY CONTAINS WHAT I THINK IT DOES!
STOP!
COME BACK AND FIGHT!

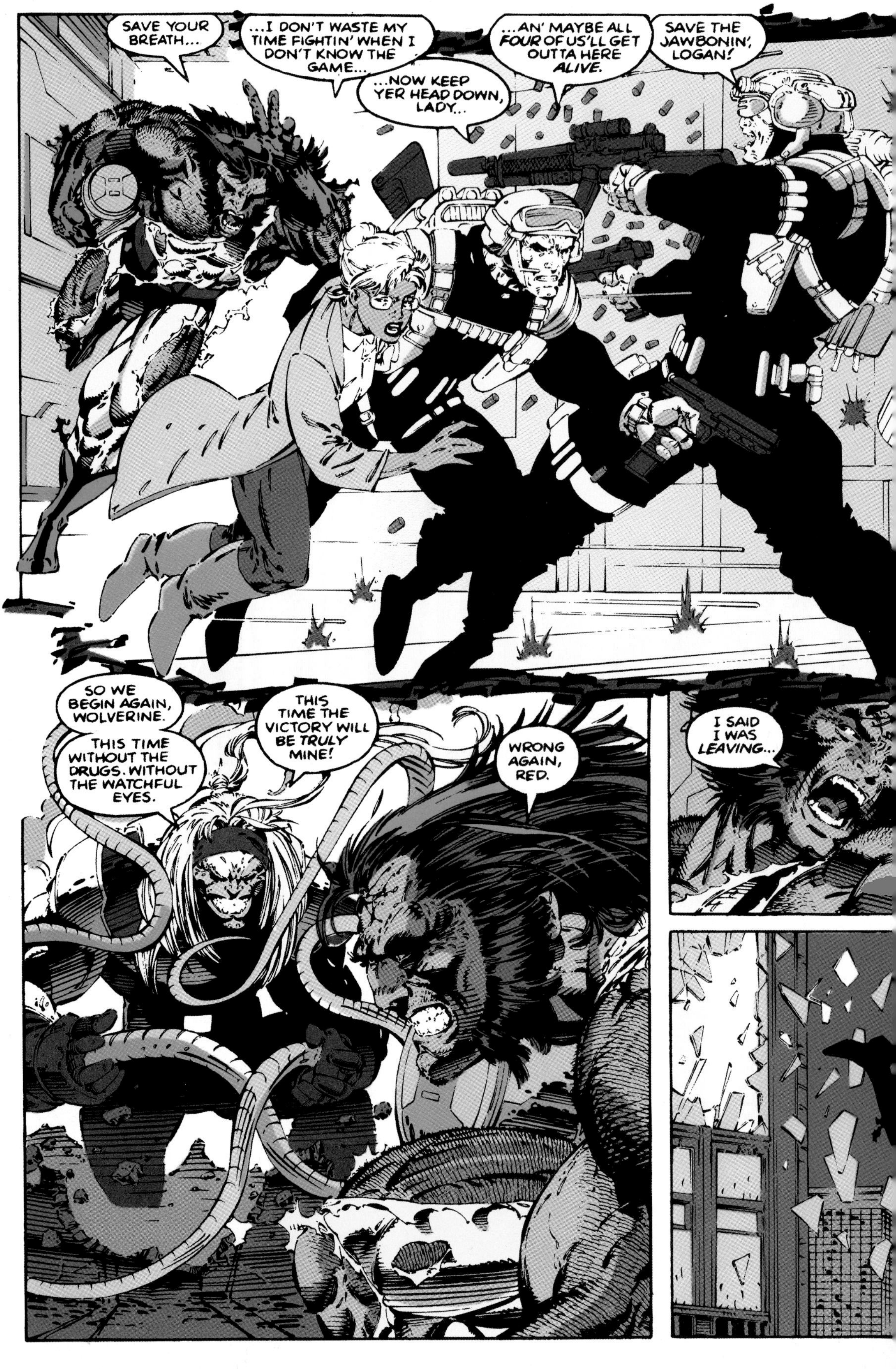
SAVE YOUR BREATH...
...I DON'T WASTE MY TIME FIGHTIN' WHEN I DON'T KNOW THE GAME...
...NOW KEEP YER HEAD DOWN, LADY...
...AN' MAYBE ALL FOUR OF US'LL GET OUTTA HERE ALIVE.
SAVE THE JAWBONIN', LOGAN!
SO WE BEGIN AGAIN, WOLVERINE.
THIS TIME WITHOUT THE DRUGS. WITHOUT THE WATCHFUL EYES.
THIS TIME THE VICTORY WILL BE TRULY MINE!
WRONG AGAIN, RED.
I SAID I WAS LEAVING...

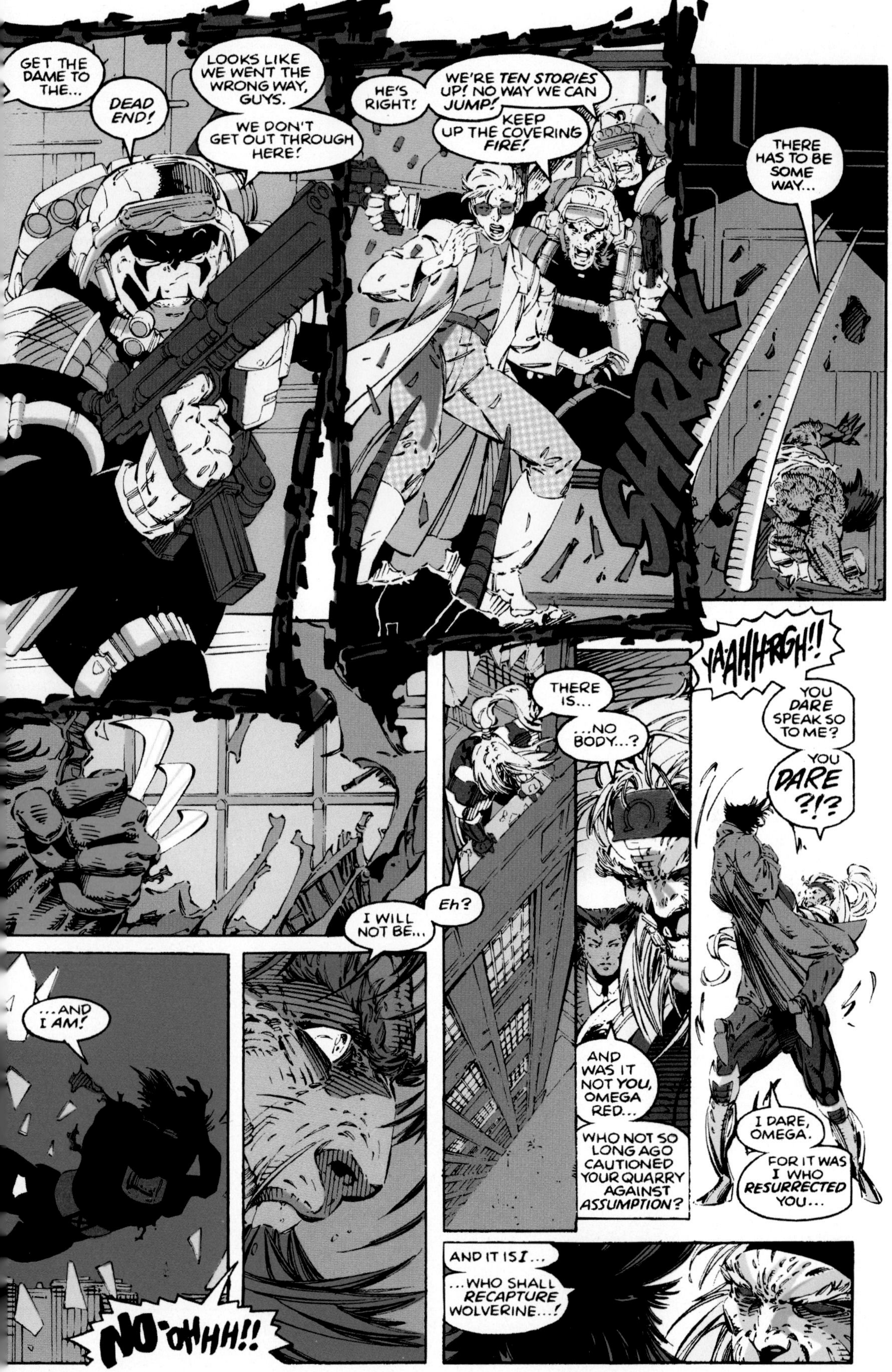
GET THE DAME TO THE...
DEAD END!
LOOKS LIKE WE WENT THE WRONG WAY, GUYS.
WE DON'T GET OUT THROUGH HERE!
HE'S RIGHT!
WE'RE TEN STORIES UP! NO WAY WE CAN JUMP!
KEEP UP THE COVERING FIRE!
THERE HAS TO BE SOME WAY...
SHRAK
YA-AHHRGH!!
THERE IS...
...NO BODY...?
YOU DARE SPEAK SO TO ME?
YOU DARE ?!?
Eh?
I WILL NOT BE...
...AND I AM!
AND WAS IT NOT YOU, OMEGA RED...
WHO NOT SO LONG AGO CAUTIONED YOUR QUARRY AGAINST ASSUMPTION?
I DARE, OMEGA.
FOR IT WAS I WHO RESURRECTED YOU...
AND IT IS I...
...WHO SHALL RECAPTURE WOLVERINE...!
NO-OHHH!!

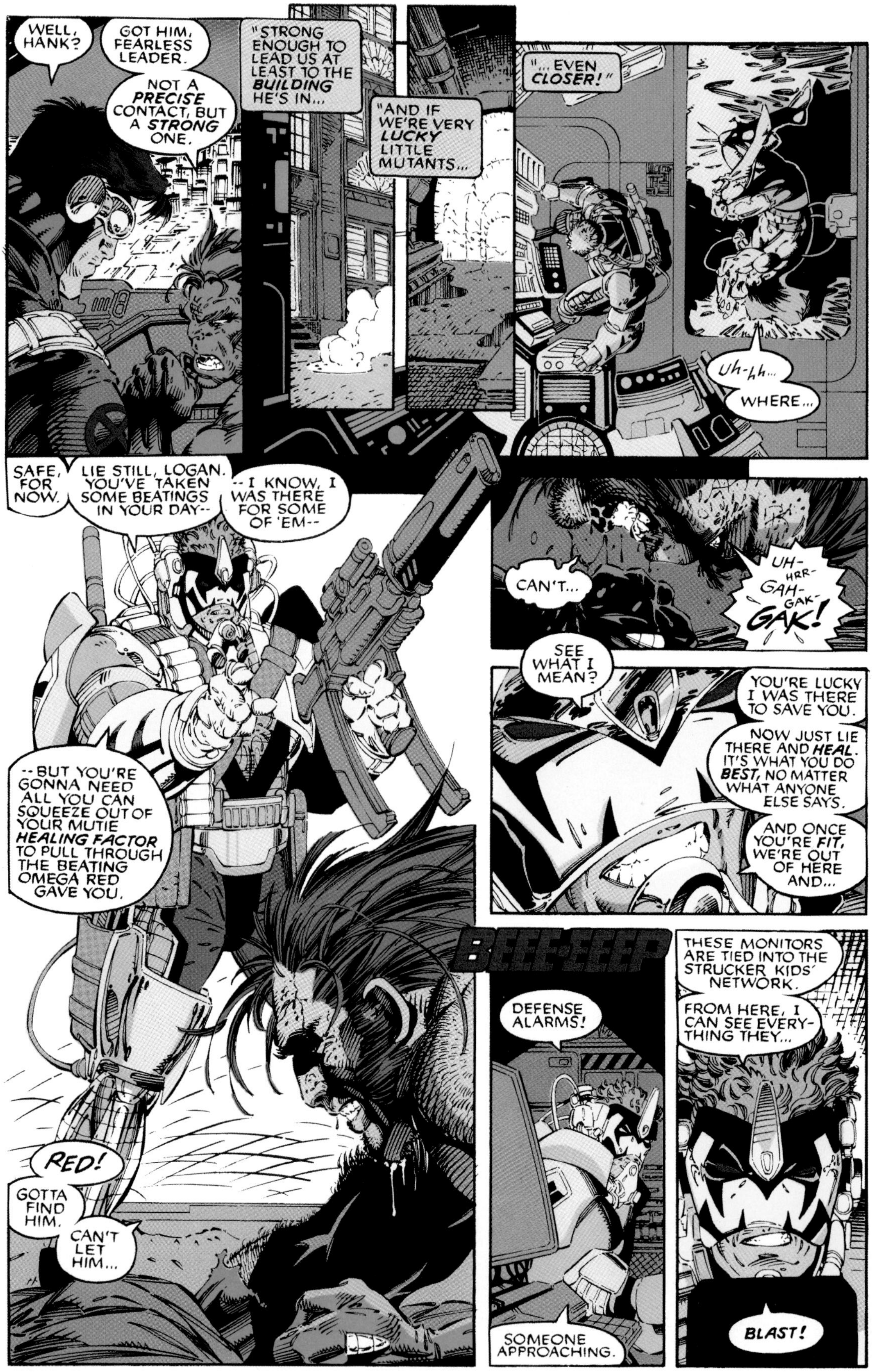
WELL, HANK?
GOT HIM, FEARLESS LEADER.
NOT A PRECISE CONTACT, BUT A STRONG ONE.
"STRONG ENOUGH TO LEAD US AT LEAST TO THE BUILDING HE'S IN...
"AND IF WE'RE VERY LUCKY LITTLE MUTANTS...
"... EVEN CLOSER!"
Uh-hh...
WHERE...
SAFE, FOR NOW.
LIE STILL, LOGAN. YOU'VE TAKEN SOME BEATINGS IN YOUR DAY--
--I KNOW, I WAS THERE FOR SOME OF 'EM--
--BUT YOU'RE GONNA NEED ALL YOU CAN SQUEEZE OUT OF YOUR MUTIE HEALING FACTOR TO PULL THROUGH THE BEATING OMEGA RED GAVE YOU.
RED!
GOTTA FIND HIM.
CAN'T LET HIM...
CAN'T...
UH-HRR-GAH-GAK-GAK!
SEE WHAT I MEAN?
YOU'RE LUCKY I WAS THERE TO SAVE YOU.
NOW JUST LIE THERE AND HEAL. IT'S WHAT YOU DO BEST, NO MATTER WHAT ANYONE ELSE SAYS.
AND ONCE YOU'RE FIT, WE'RE OUT OF HERE AND...
BEEE-EEEP
DEFENSE ALARMS!
SOMEONE APPROACHING.
THESE MONITORS ARE TIED INTO THE STRUCKER KIDS' NETWORK.
FROM HERE, I CAN SEE EVERYTHING THEY...
BLAST!

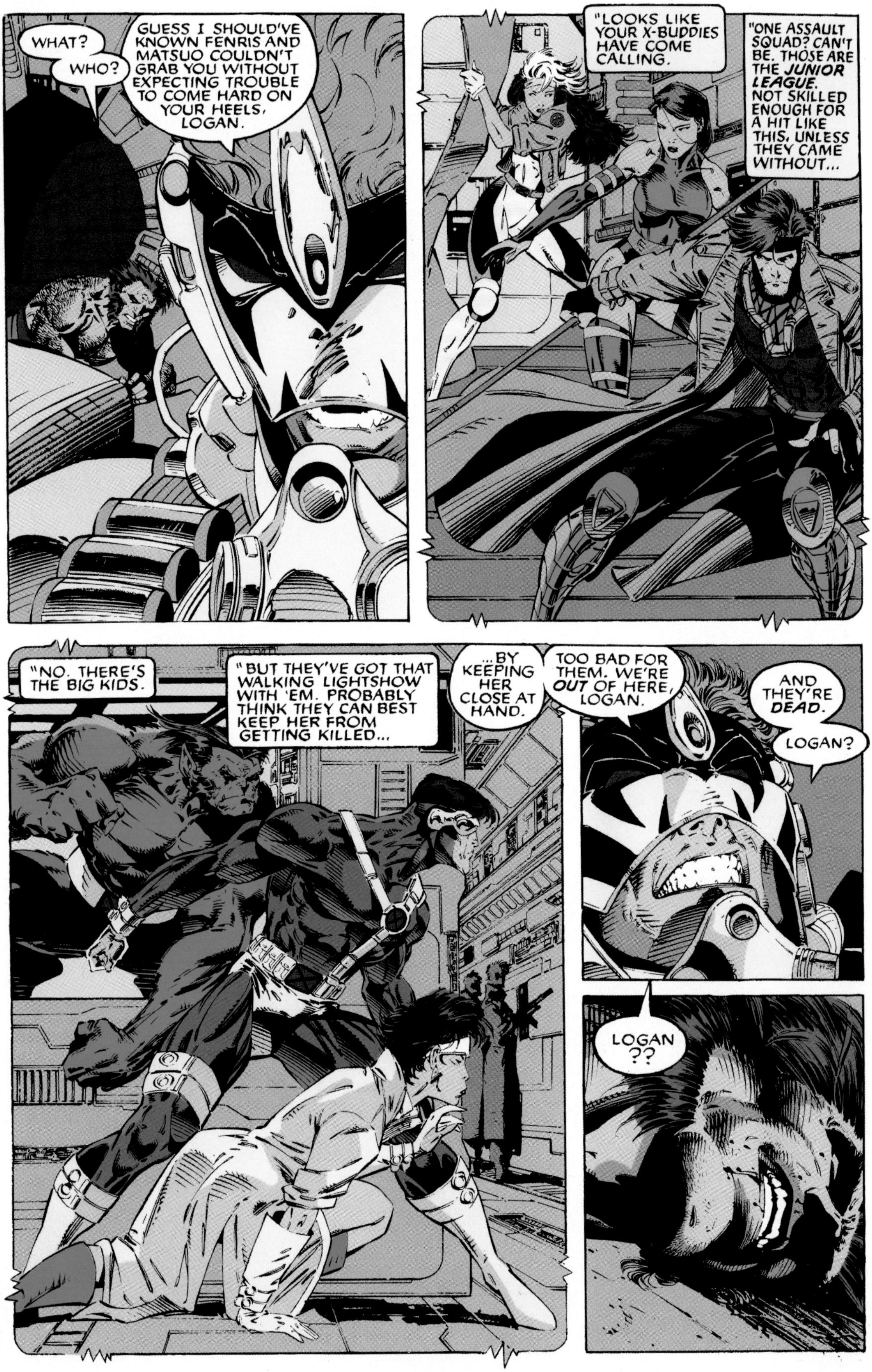
WHAT?
WHO?
GUESS I SHOULD'VE KNOWN FENRIS AND MATSUO COULDN'T GRAB YOU WITHOUT EXPECTING TROUBLE TO COME HARD ON YOUR HEELS, LOGAN.
"LOOKS LIKE YOUR X-BUDDIES HAVE COME CALLING.
"ONE ASSAULT SQUAD? CAN'T BE. THOSE ARE THE *JUNIOR LEAGUE*. NOT SKILLED ENOUGH FOR A HIT LIKE THIS, UNLESS THEY CAME WITHOUT...
"NO. THERE'S THE BIG KIDS.
"BUT THEY'VE GOT THAT WALKING LIGHTSHOW WITH 'EM. PROBABLY THINK THEY CAN BEST KEEP HER FROM GETTING KILLED...
...BY KEEPING HER CLOSE AT HAND.
TOO BAD FOR THEM. WE'RE *OUT* OF HERE, LOGAN.
AND THEY'RE *DEAD*.
LOGAN?
LOGAN ??

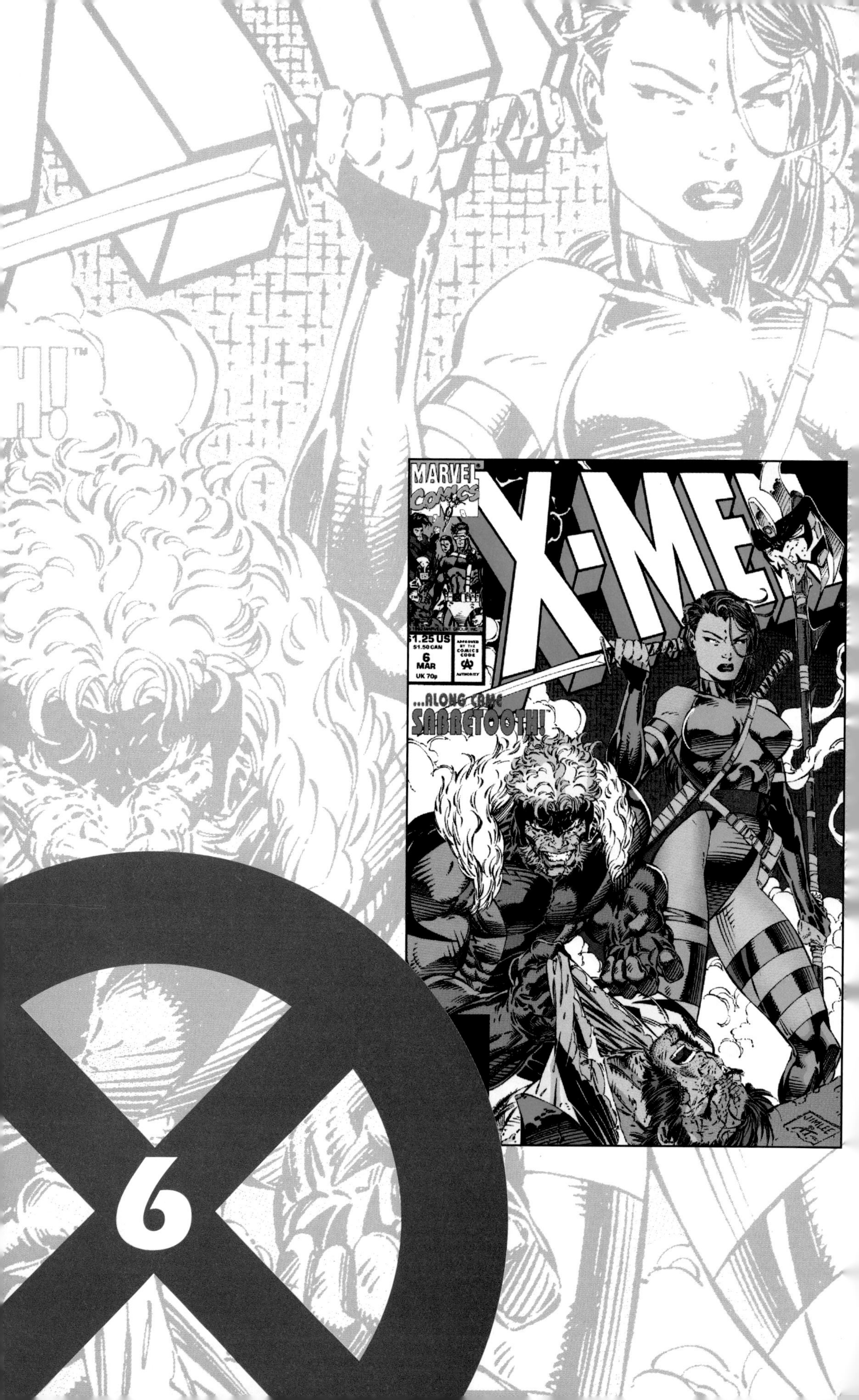
MARVEL COMICS
X-MEN
$1.25 US
$1.50 CAN
6
MAR
UK 70p
APPROVED BY THE COMICS CODE AUTHORITY
...ALONG CAME SABRETOOTH!
6

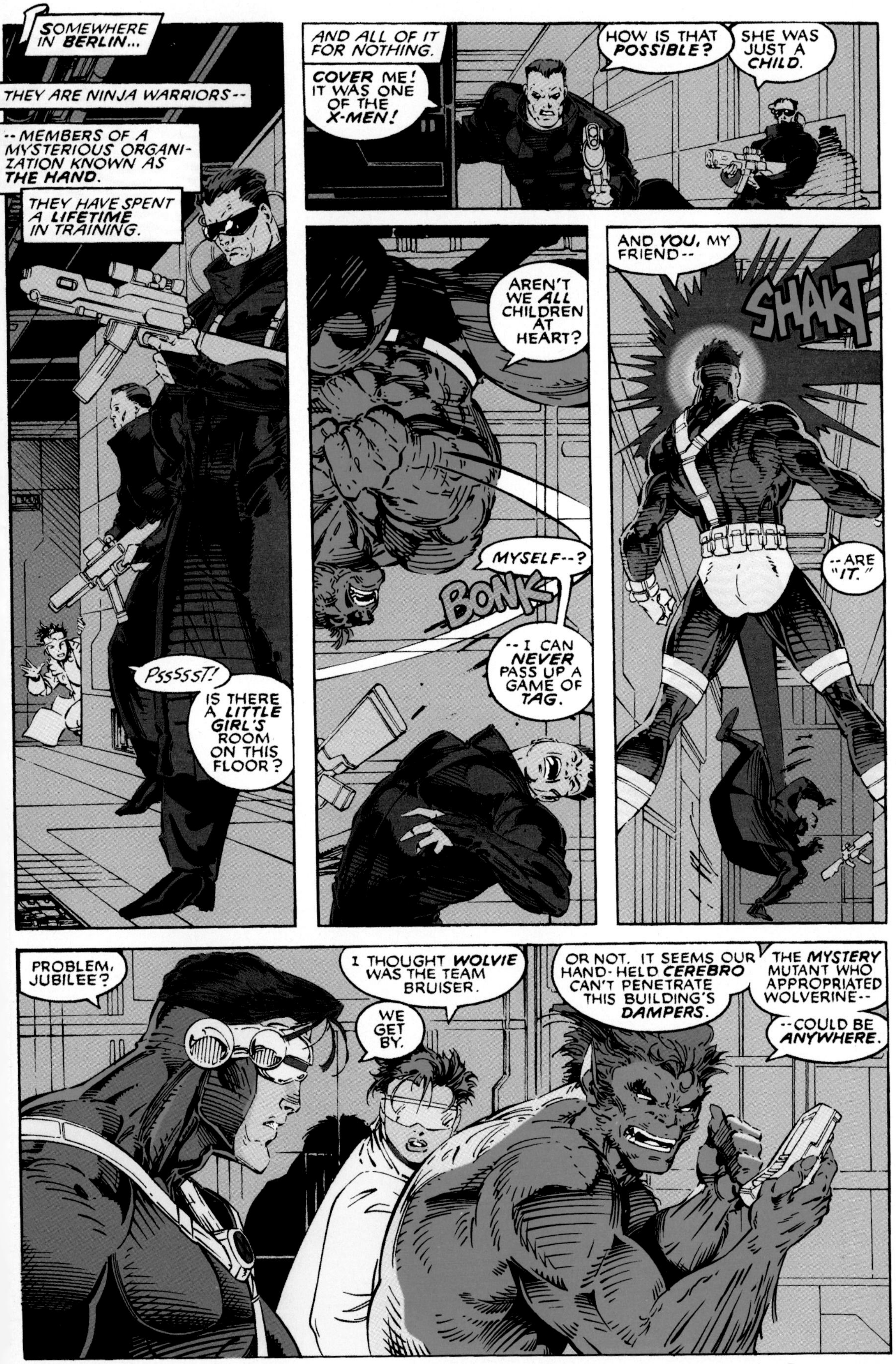

SOMEWHERE IN BERLIN...
THEY ARE NINJA WARRIORS--
--MEMBERS OF A MYSTERIOUS ORGANIZATION KNOWN AS THE HAND.
THEY HAVE SPENT A LIFETIME IN TRAINING.
PSSSSST!
IS THERE A LITTLE GIRL'S ROOM ON THIS FLOOR?
AND ALL OF IT FOR NOTHING.
COVER ME! IT WAS ONE OF THE X-MEN!
HOW IS THAT POSSIBLE?
SHE WAS JUST A CHILD.
AREN'T WE ALL CHILDREN AT HEART?
MYSELF--?
BONK
--I CAN NEVER PASS UP A GAME OF TAG.
AND YOU, MY FRIEND--
SHAKT
--ARE "IT."
PROBLEM, JUBILEE?
I THOUGHT WOLVIE WAS THE TEAM BRUISER.
WE GET BY.
OR NOT. IT SEEMS OUR HAND-HELD CEREBRO CAN'T PENETRATE THIS BUILDING'S DAMPERS.
THE MYSTERY MUTANT WHO APPROPRIATED WOLVERINE--
--COULD BE ANYWHERE.

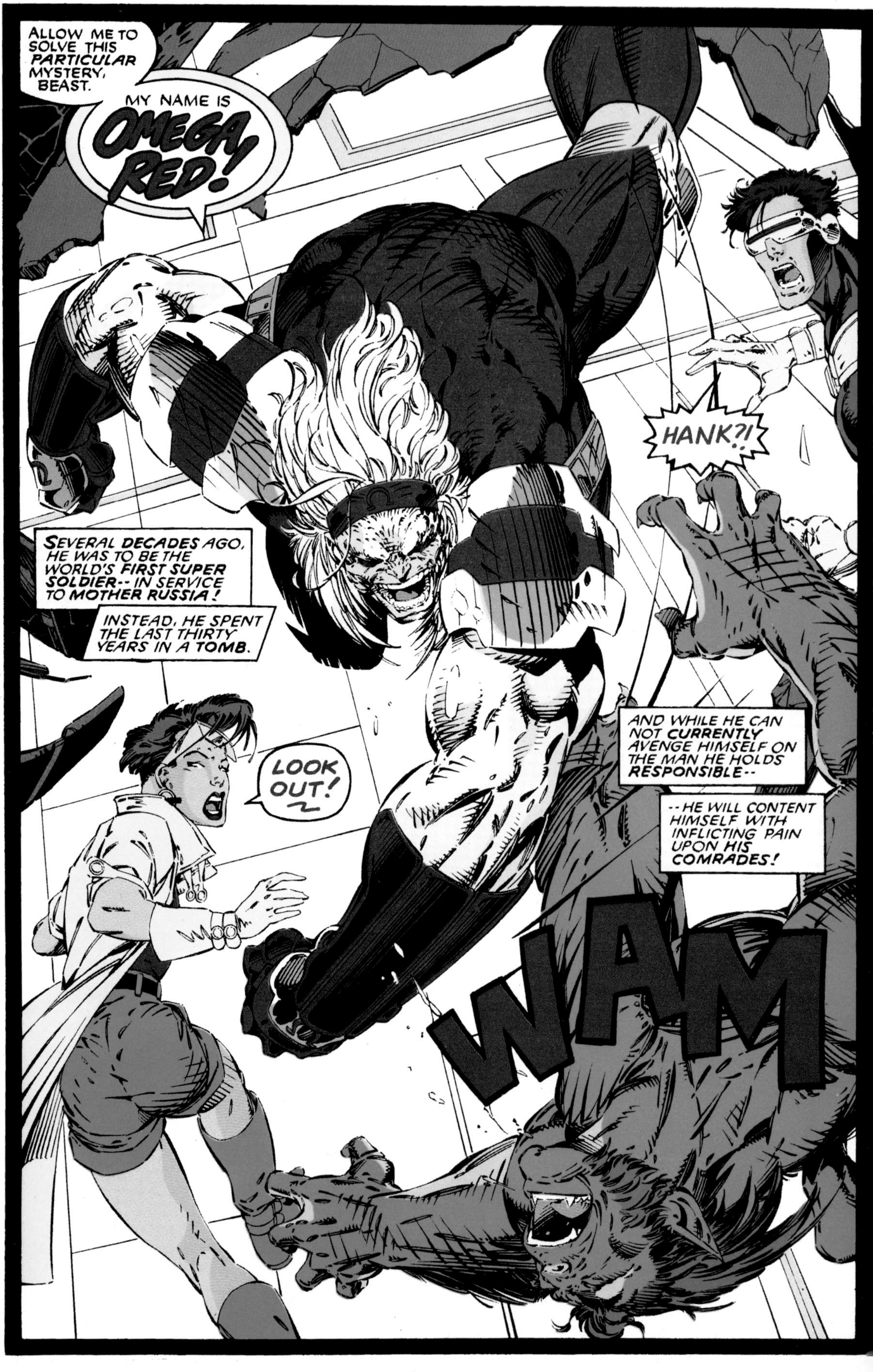
ALLOW ME TO SOLVE THIS PARTICULAR MYSTERY, BEAST.
MY NAME IS OMEGA RED!
HANK?!
SEVERAL DECADES AGO, HE WAS TO BE THE WORLD'S FIRST SUPER SOLDIER-- IN SERVICE TO MOTHER RUSSIA!
INSTEAD, HE SPENT THE LAST THIRTY YEARS IN A TOMB.
LOOK OUT!
AND WHILE HE CAN NOT CURRENTLY AVENGE HIMSELF ON THE MAN HE HOLDS RESPONSIBLE--
--HE WILL CONTENT HIMSELF WITH INFLICTING PAIN UPON HIS COMRADES!
WAM

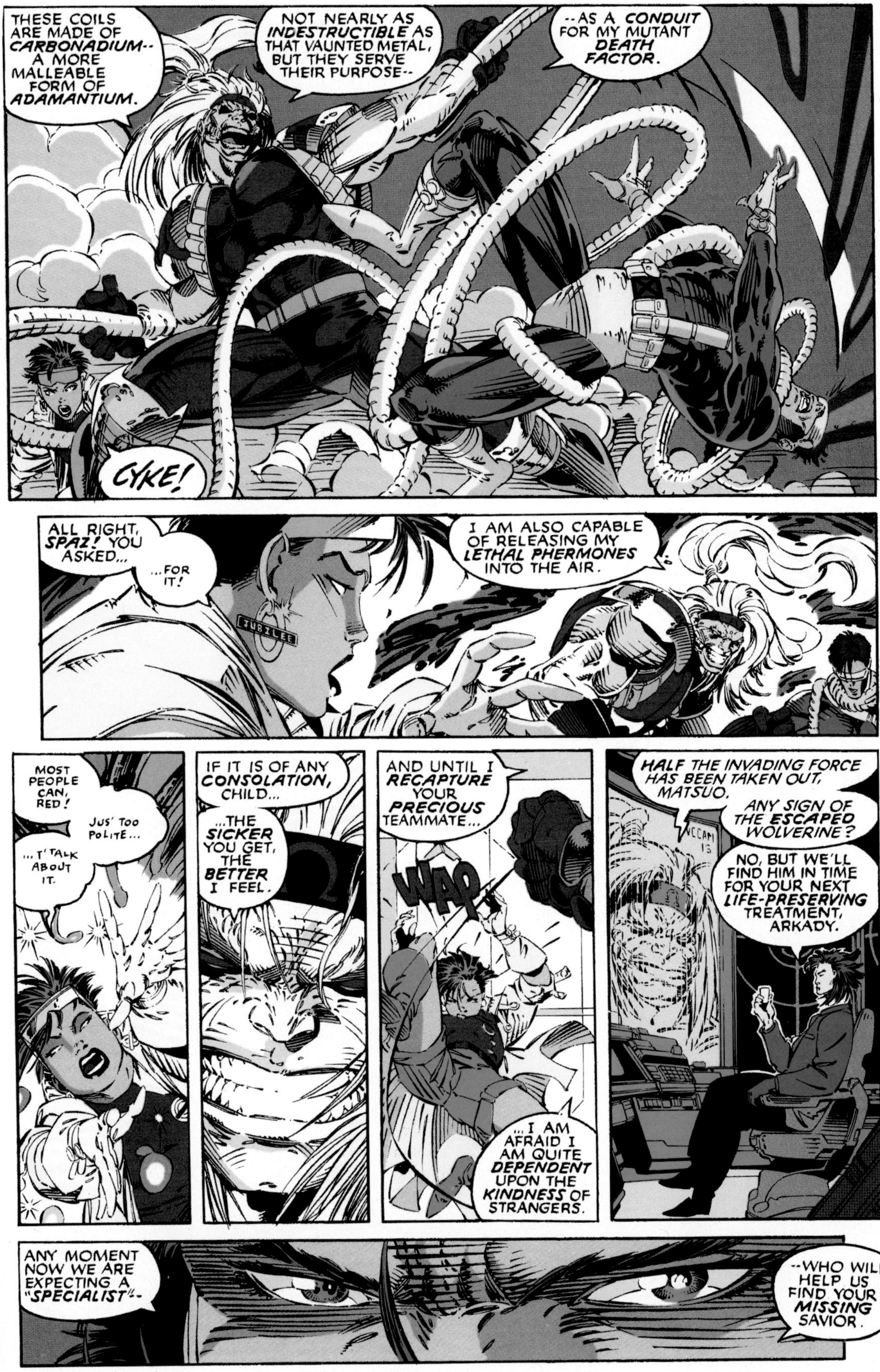

THESE COILS ARE MADE OF CARBONADIUM-- A MORE MALLEABLE FORM OF ADAMANTIUM.
NOT NEARLY AS INDESTRUCTIBLE AS THAT VAUNTED METAL, BUT THEY SERVE THEIR PURPOSE--
--AS A CONDUIT FOR MY MUTANT DEATH FACTOR.
CYKE!
ALL RIGHT, SPAZ! YOU ASKED...
...FOR IT!
JUBILEE
I AM ALSO CAPABLE OF RELEASING MY LETHAL PHERMONES INTO THE AIR.
MOST PEOPLE CAN, RED!
JUS' TOO POLITE...
...T' TALK ABOUT IT.
IF IT IS OF ANY CONSOLATION, CHILD...
...THE SICKER YOU GET, THE BETTER I FEEL.
AND UNTIL I RECAPTURE YOUR PRECIOUS TEAMMATE...
WAP
...I AM AFRAID I AM QUITE DEPENDENT UPON THE KINDNESS OF STRANGERS.
HALF THE INVADING FORCE HAS BEEN TAKEN OUT, MATSUO.
ANY SIGN OF THE ESCAPED WOLVERINE?
NO, BUT WE'LL FIND HIM IN TIME FOR YOUR NEXT LIFE-PRESERVING TREATMENT, ARKADY.
ANY MOMENT NOW WE ARE EXPECTING A "SPECIALIST"--
--WHO WILL HELP US FIND YOUR MISSING SAVIOR.

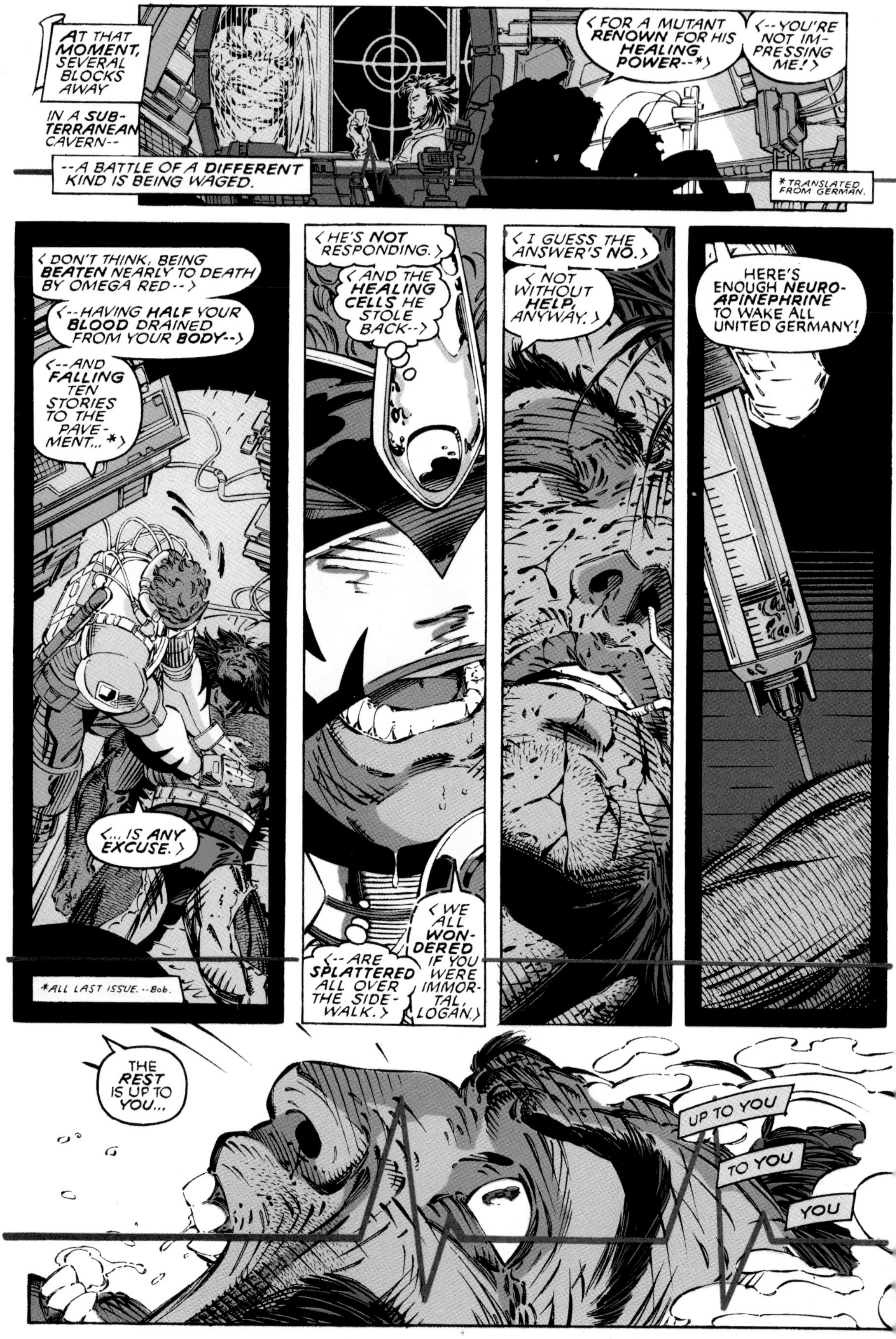
AT THAT MOMENT, SEVERAL BLOCKS AWAY
IN A SUBTERRANEAN CAVERN--
--A BATTLE OF A DIFFERENT KIND IS BEING WAGED.
‹FOR A MUTANT RENOWN FOR HIS HEALING POWER--*›
‹--YOU'RE NOT IMPRESSING ME!›
*TRANSLATED FROM GERMAN.
‹DON'T THINK, BEING BEATEN NEARLY TO DEATH BY OMEGA RED--›
‹--HAVING HALF YOUR BLOOD DRAINED FROM YOUR BODY--›
‹--AND FALLING TEN STORIES TO THE PAVEMENT...*›
‹...IS ANY EXCUSE.›
*ALL LAST ISSUE. --Bob.
‹HE'S NOT RESPONDING.›
‹AND THE HEALING CELLS HE STOLE BACK--›
‹--ARE SPLATTERED ALL OVER THE SIDEWALK.›
‹WE ALL WONDERED IF YOU WERE IMMORTAL, LOGAN.›
‹I GUESS THE ANSWER'S NO.›
‹NOT WITHOUT HELP, ANYWAY.›
HERE'S ENOUGH NEURO-APINEPHRINE TO WAKE ALL UNITED GERMANY!
THE REST IS UP TO YOU...
UP TO YOU
TO YOU
YOU

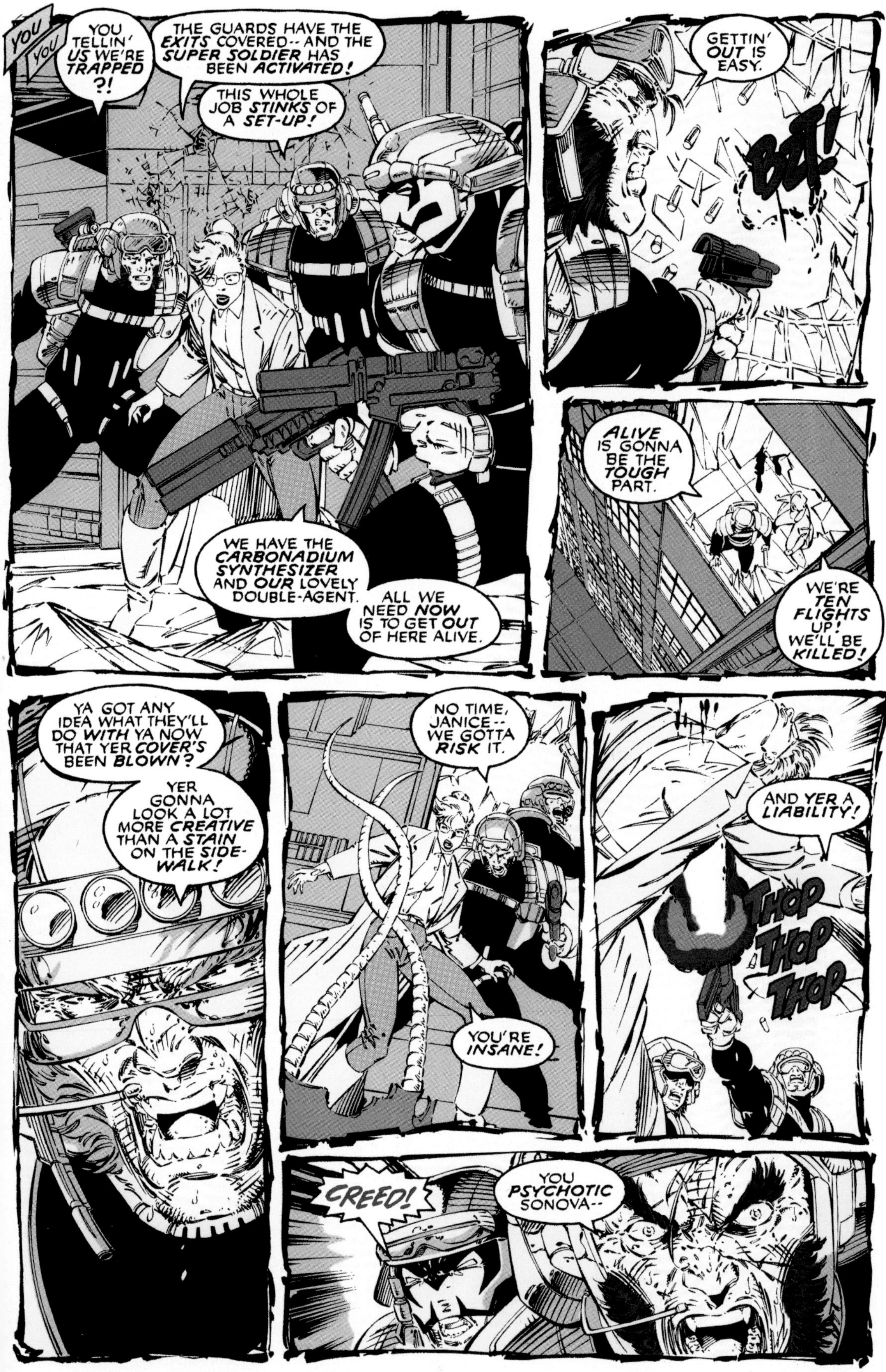
YOU
YOU
YOU TELLIN' US WE'RE TRAPPED ?!
THE GUARDS HAVE THE EXITS COVERED-- AND THE SUPER SOLDIER HAS BEEN ACTIVATED!
THIS WHOLE JOB STINKS OF A SET-UP!
WE HAVE THE CARBONADIUM SYNTHESIZER AND OUR LOVELY DOUBLE-AGENT.
ALL WE NEED NOW IS TO GET OUT OF HERE ALIVE.
GETTIN' OUT IS EASY.
BZT!
ALIVE IS GONNA BE THE TOUGH PART.
WE'RE TEN FLIGHTS UP! WE'LL BE KILLED!
YA GOT ANY IDEA WHAT THEY'LL DO WITH YA NOW THAT YER COVER'S BEEN BLOWN?
YER GONNA LOOK A LOT MORE CREATIVE THAN A STAIN ON THE SIDE-WALK!
NO TIME, JANICE-- WE GOTTA RISK IT.
YOU'RE INSANE!
AND YER A LIABILITY!
THOP THOP THOP
CREED!
YOU PSYCHOTIC SONOVA--

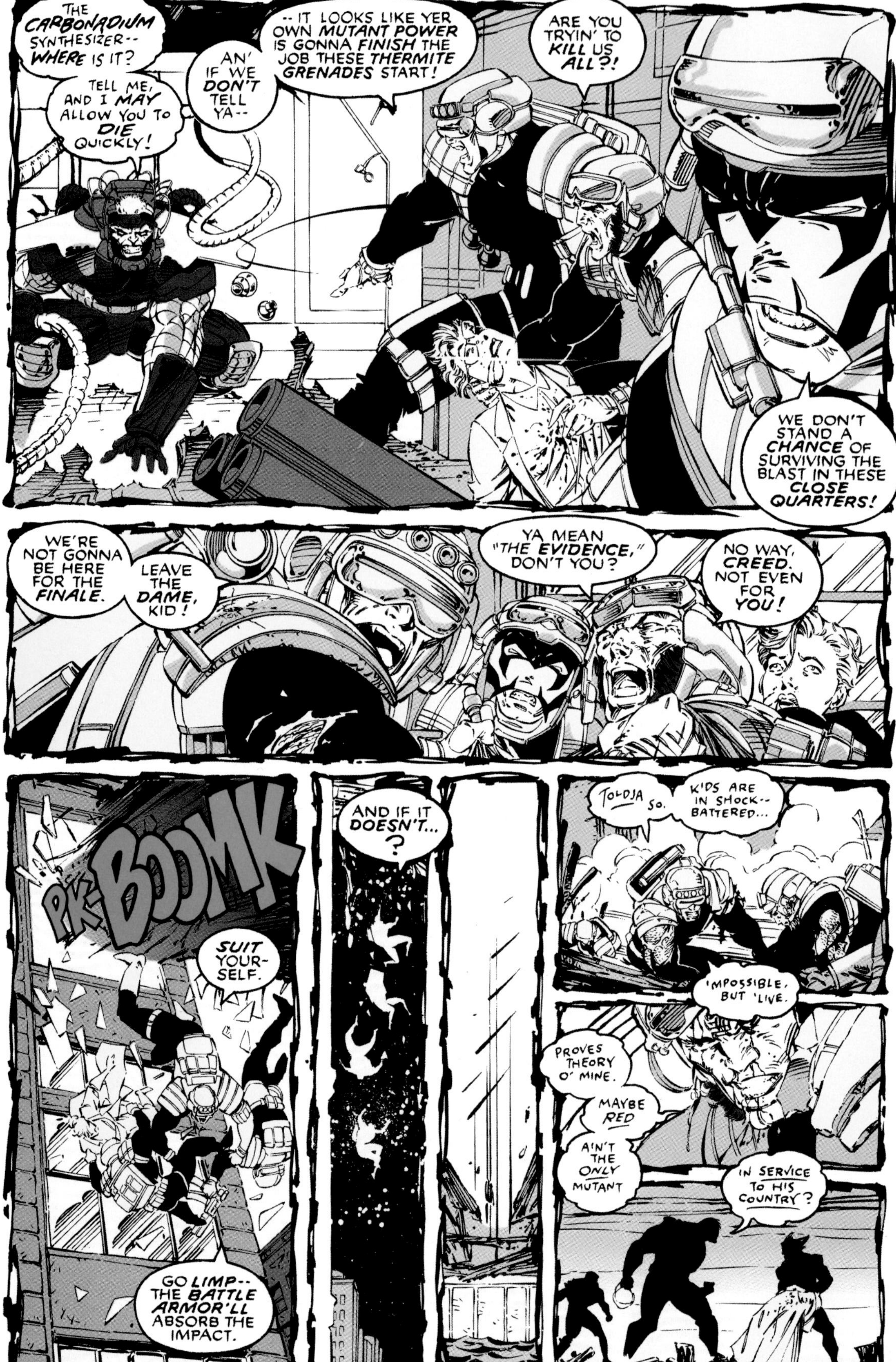

THE CARBONADIUM SYNTHESIZER-- WHERE IS IT?
TELL ME, AND I MAY ALLOW YOU TO DIE QUICKLY!
AN' IF WE DON'T TELL YA--
--IT LOOKS LIKE YER OWN MUTANT POWER IS GONNA FINISH THE JOB THESE THERMITE GRENADES START!
ARE YOU TRYIN' TO KILL US ALL?!
WE DON'T STAND A CHANCE OF SURVIVING THE BLAST IN THESE CLOSE QUARTERS!
WE'RE NOT GONNA BE HERE FOR THE FINALE.
LEAVE THE DAME, KID!
YA MEAN "THE EVIDENCE," DON'T YOU?
NO WAY, CREED. NOT EVEN FOR YOU!
PK-BOOMK
SUIT YOURSELF.
GO LIMP-- THE BATTLE ARMOR'LL ABSORB THE IMPACT.
AND IF IT DOESN'T...?
TOLDJA SO.
KIDS ARE IN SHOCK-- BATTERED...
IMPOSSIBLE, BUT 'LIVE.
PROVES THEORY O' MINE.
MAYBE RED
AIN'T THE ONLY MUTANT
IN SERVICE TO HIS COUNTRY?

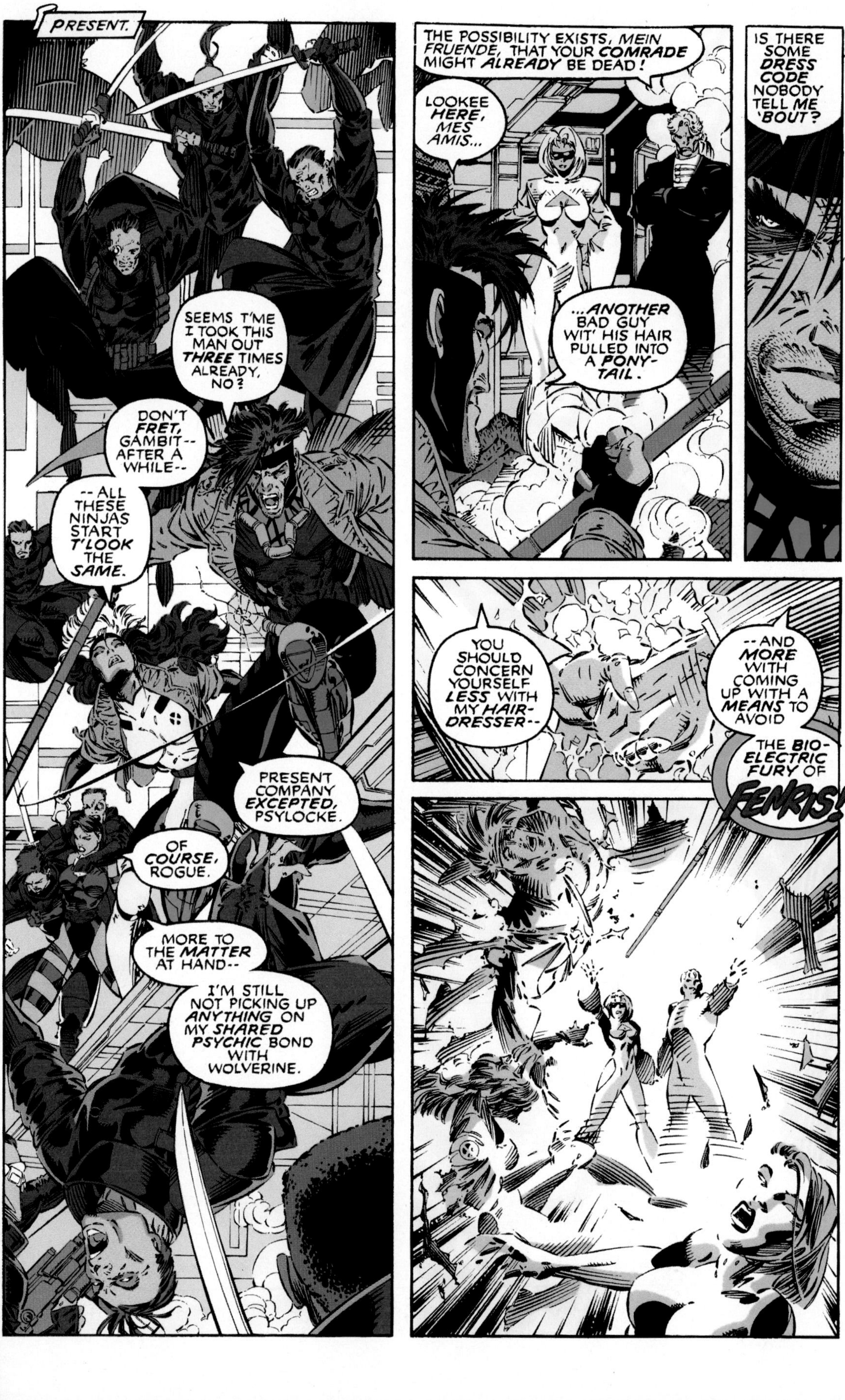
PRESENT.
SEEMS T'ME I TOOK THIS MAN OUT THREE TIMES ALREADY, NO?
DON'T FRET, GAMBIT-- AFTER A WHILE--
--ALL THESE NINJAS START T'LOOK THE SAME.
PRESENT COMPANY EXCEPTED, PSYLOCKE.
OF COURSE, ROGUE.
MORE TO THE MATTER AT HAND--
I'M STILL NOT PICKING UP ANYTHING ON MY SHARED PSYCHIC BOND WITH WOLVERINE.
THE POSSIBILITY EXISTS, MEIN FRUENDE, THAT YOUR COMRADE MIGHT ALREADY BE DEAD!
LOOKEE HERE, MES AMIS...
...ANOTHER BAD GUY WIT' HIS HAIR PULLED INTO A PONY-TAIL.
IS THERE SOME DRESS CODE NOBODY TELL ME 'BOUT?
YOU SHOULD CONCERN YOURSELF LESS WITH MY HAIR-DRESSER--
--AND MORE WITH COMING UP WITH A MEANS TO AVOID
THE BIO-ELECTRIC FURY OF
FENRIS!

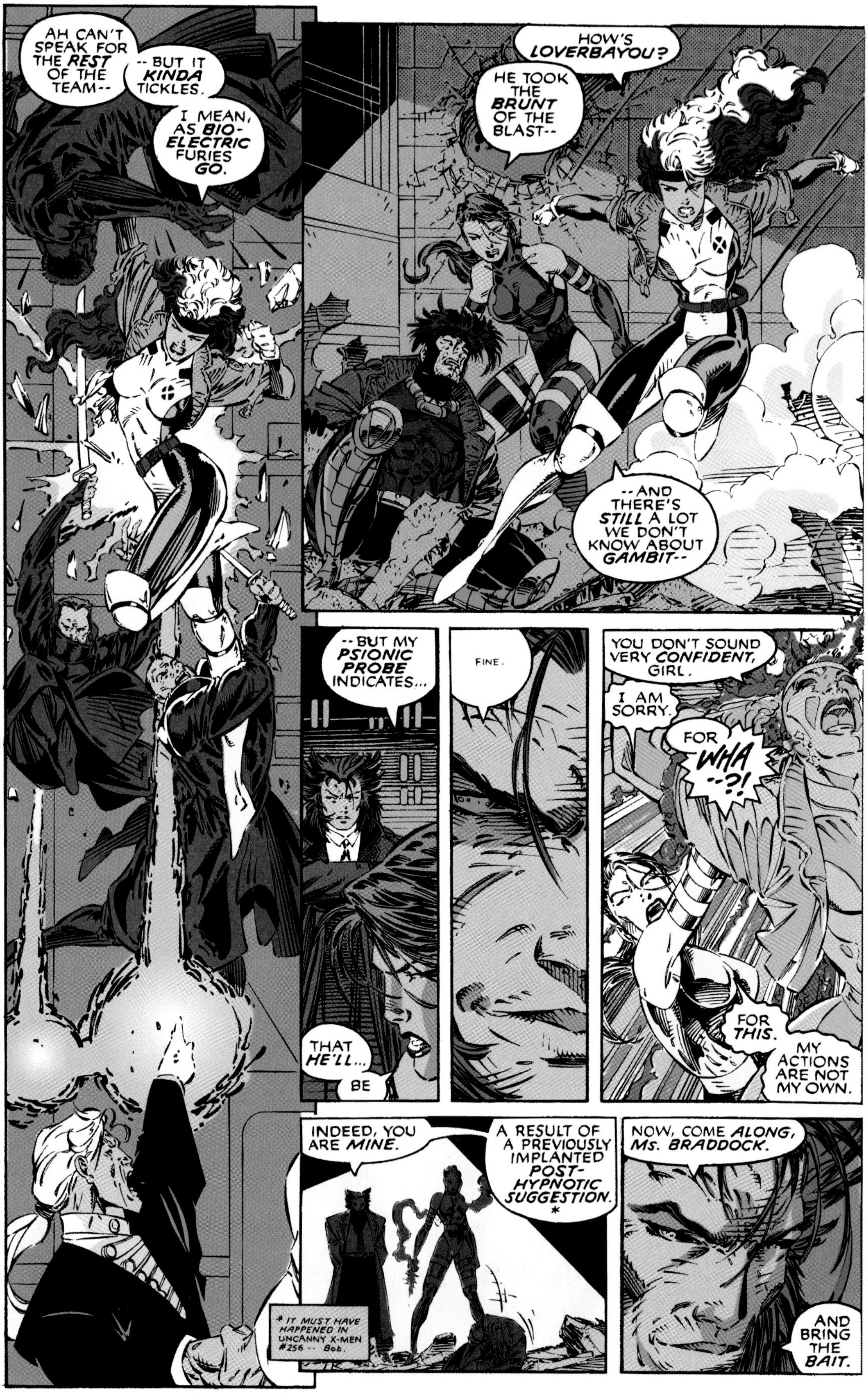

AH CAN'T SPEAK FOR THE REST OF THE TEAM--
-- BUT IT KINDA TICKLES.
I MEAN, AS BIO-ELECTRIC FURIES GO.
HOW'S LOVERBAYOU?
HE TOOK THE BRUNT OF THE BLAST--
--AND THERE'S STILL A LOT WE DON'T KNOW ABOUT GAMBIT--
--BUT MY PSIONIC PROBE INDICATES...
THAT HE'LL...
BE
FINE.
YOU DON'T SOUND VERY CONFIDENT, GIRL.
I AM SORRY.
FOR WHA--?!
FOR THIS.
MY ACTIONS ARE NOT MY OWN.
INDEED, YOU ARE MINE.
A RESULT OF A PREVIOUSLY IMPLANTED POST-HYPNOTIC SUGGESTION. *
* IT MUST HAVE HAPPENED IN UNCANNY X-MEN #256 -- Bob.
NOW, COME ALONG, MS. BRADDOCK.
AND BRING THE BAIT.

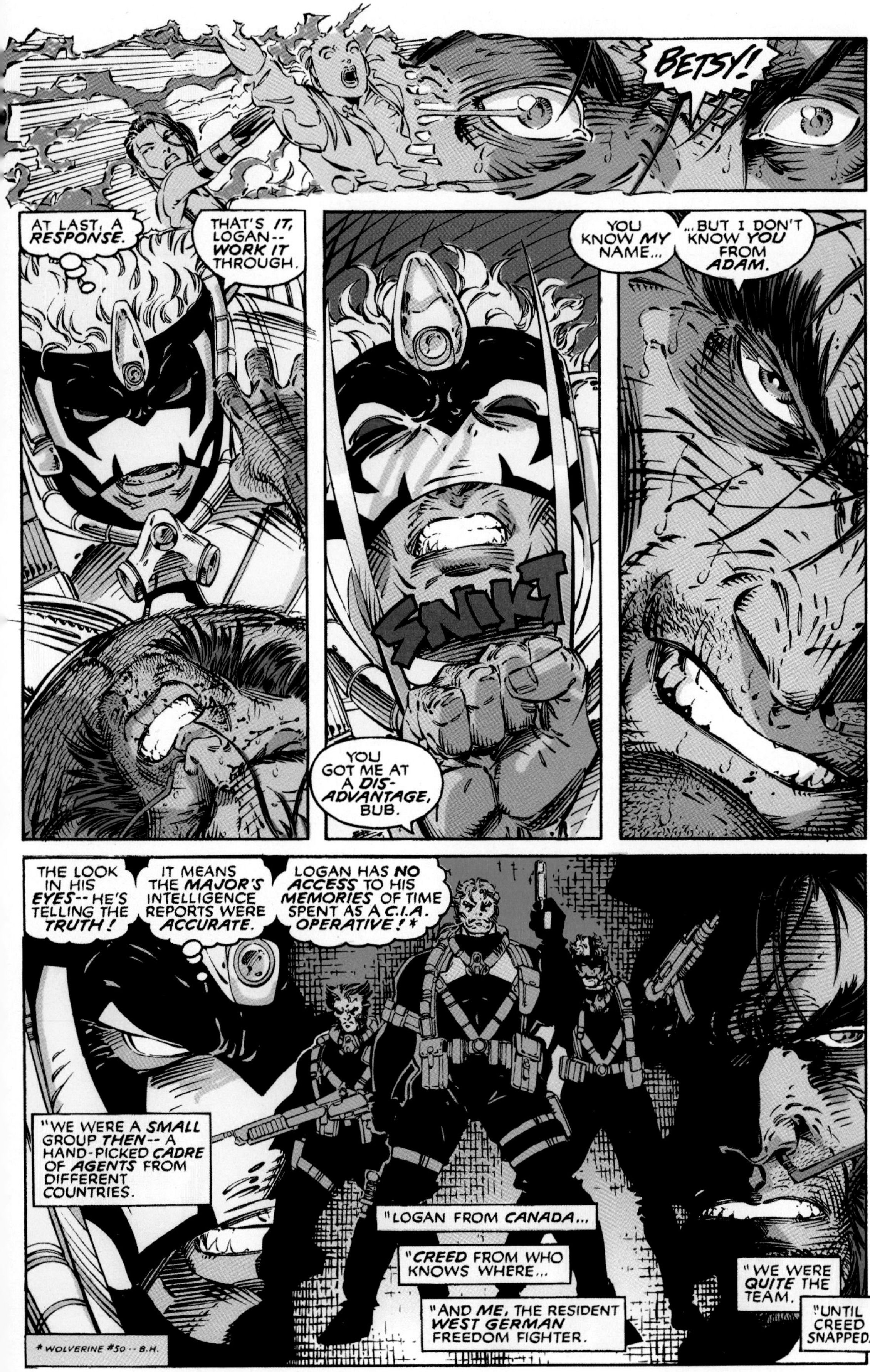
BETSY!
AT LAST, A RESPONSE.
THAT'S IT, LOGAN-- WORK IT THROUGH.
SNIKT
YOU GOT ME AT A DIS-ADVANTAGE, BUB.
YOU KNOW MY NAME...
...BUT I DON'T KNOW YOU FROM ADAM.
THE LOOK IN HIS EYES-- HE'S TELLING THE TRUTH!
IT MEANS THE MAJOR'S INTELLIGENCE REPORTS WERE ACCURATE.
LOGAN HAS NO ACCESS TO HIS MEMORIES OF TIME SPENT AS A C.I.A. OPERATIVE! *
"WE WERE A SMALL GROUP THEN-- A HAND-PICKED CADRE OF AGENTS FROM DIFFERENT COUNTRIES.
"LOGAN FROM CANADA...
"CREED FROM WHO KNOWS WHERE...
"AND ME, THE RESIDENT WEST GERMAN FREEDOM FIGHTER.
"WE WERE QUITE THE TEAM.
"UNTIL CREED SNAPPED...
* WOLVERINE #50 -- B.H.

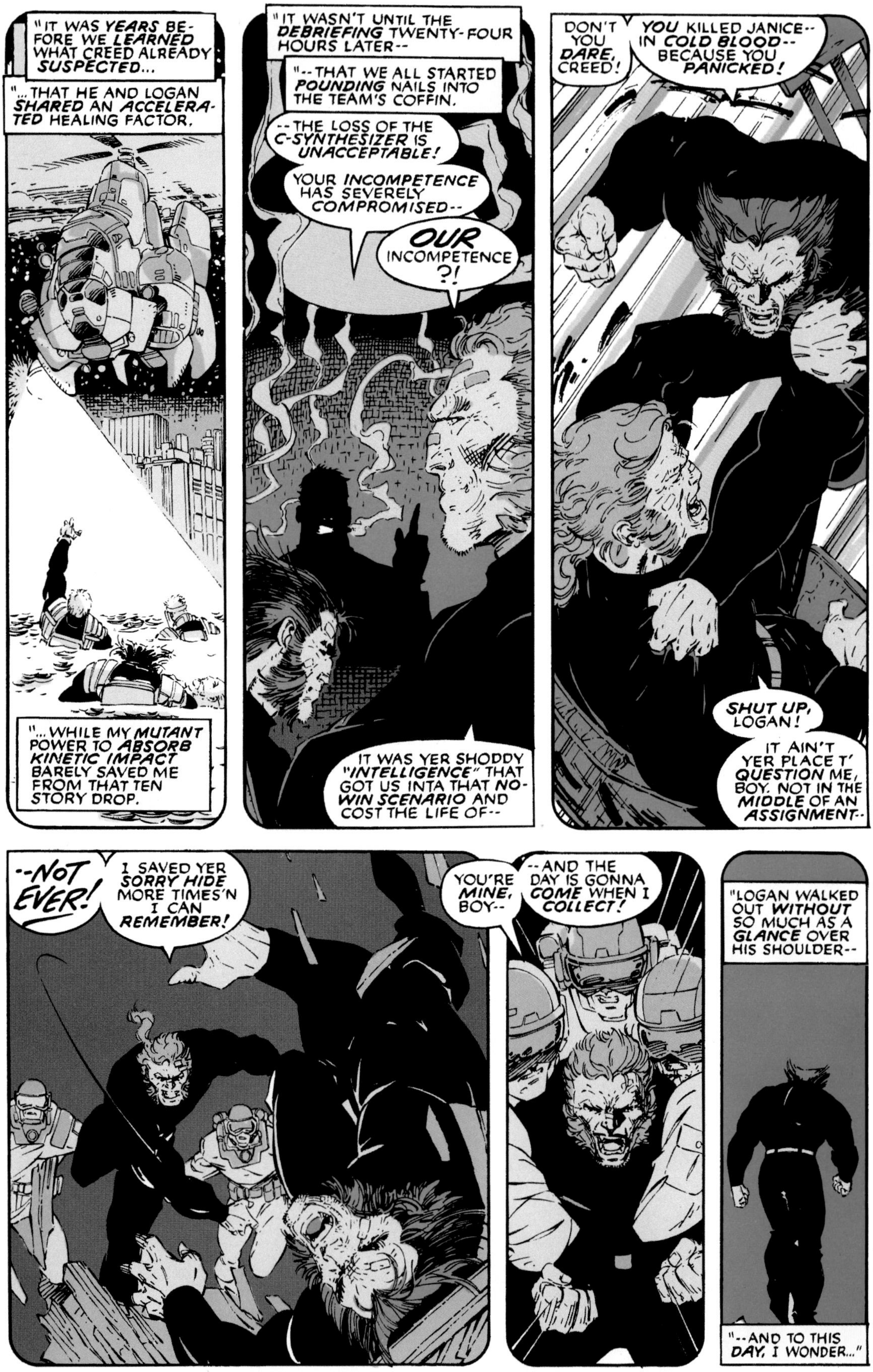
"IT WAS YEARS BEFORE WE LEARNED WHAT CREED ALREADY SUSPECTED...
"...THAT HE AND LOGAN SHARED AN ACCELERATED HEALING FACTOR,
"...WHILE MY MUTANT POWER TO ABSORB KINETIC IMPACT BARELY SAVED ME FROM THAT TEN STORY DROP.
"IT WASN'T UNTIL THE DEBRIEFING TWENTY-FOUR HOURS LATER--
"--THAT WE ALL STARTED POUNDING NAILS INTO THE TEAM'S COFFIN.
--THE LOSS OF THE C-SYNTHESIZER IS UNACCEPTABLE!
YOUR INCOMPETENCE HAS SEVERELY COMPROMISED--
OUR INCOMPETENCE ?!
IT WAS YER SHODDY "INTELLIGENCE" THAT GOT US INTA THAT NO-WIN SCENARIO AND COST THE LIFE OF--
DON'T YOU DARE, CREED!
YOU KILLED JANICE--IN COLD BLOOD--BECAUSE YOU PANICKED!
SHUT UP, LOGAN!
IT AIN'T YER PLACE T' QUESTION ME, BOY. NOT IN THE MIDDLE OF AN ASSIGNMENT--
--NOT EVER!
I SAVED YER SORRY HIDE MORE TIMES'N I CAN REMEMBER!
YOU'RE MINE, BOY--
--AND THE DAY IS GONNA COME WHEN I COLLECT!
"LOGAN WALKED OUT WITHOUT SO MUCH AS A GLANCE OVER HIS SHOULDER--
"--AND TO THIS DAY, I WONDER..."

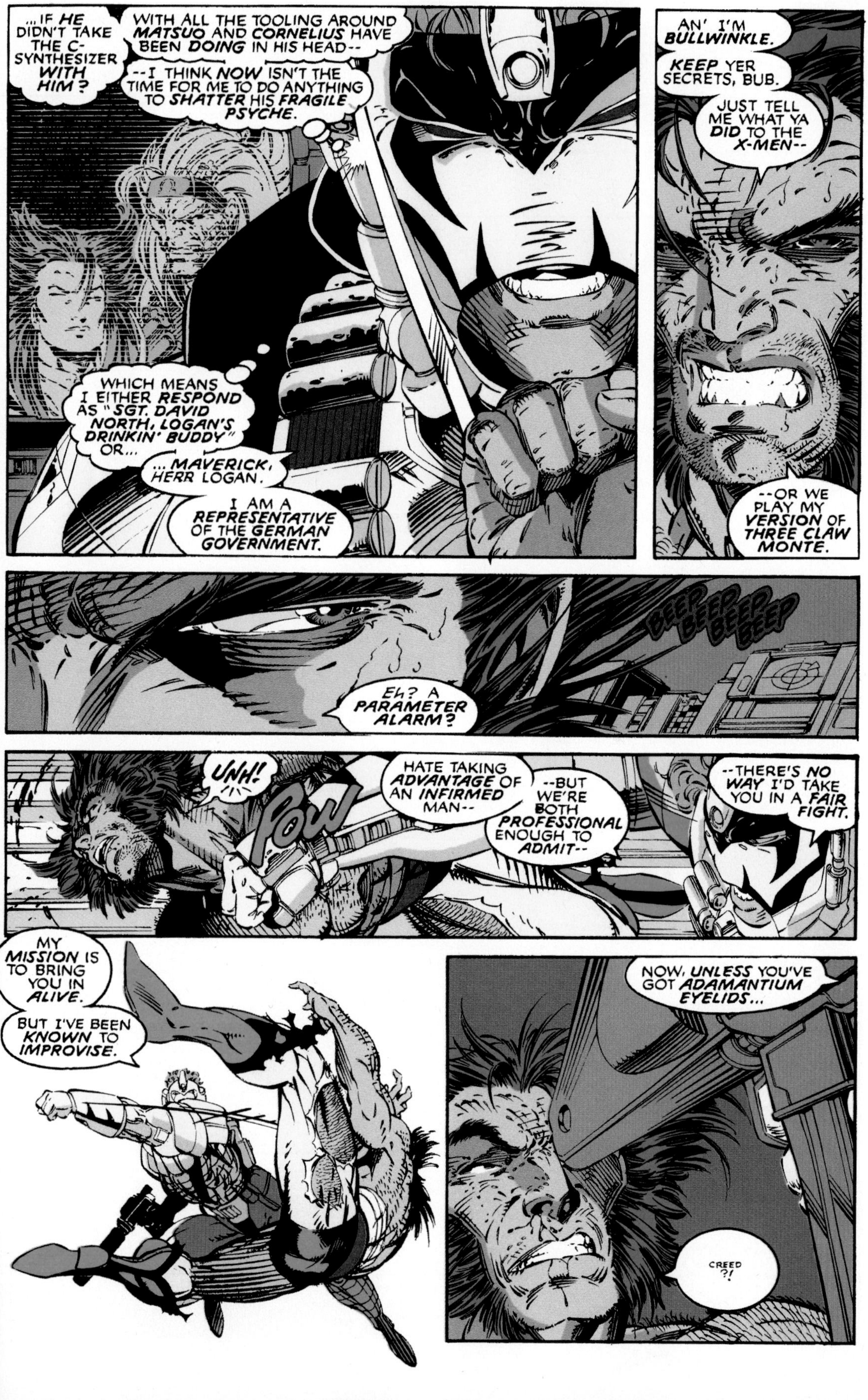
...IF HE DIDN'T TAKE THE C-SYNTHESIZER WITH HIM?
WITH ALL THE TOOLING AROUND MATSUO AND CORNELIUS HAVE BEEN DOING IN HIS HEAD--
--I THINK NOW ISN'T THE TIME FOR ME TO DO ANYTHING TO SHATTER HIS FRAGILE PSYCHE.
WHICH MEANS I EITHER RESPOND AS "SGT. DAVID NORTH, LOGAN'S DRINKIN' BUDDY" OR...
...MAVERICK, HERR LOGAN.
I AM A REPRESENTATIVE OF THE GERMAN GOVERNMENT.
AN' I'M BULLWINKLE.
KEEP YER SECRETS, BUB.
JUST TELL ME WHAT YA DID TO THE X-MEN--
--OR WE PLAY MY VERSION OF THREE CLAW MONTE.
BEEP BEEP BEEP BEEP
EH? A PARAMETER ALARM?
UNH!
POW
HATE TAKING ADVANTAGE OF AN INFIRMED MAN--
--BUT WE'RE BOTH PROFESSIONAL ENOUGH TO ADMIT--
--THERE'S NO WAY I'D TAKE YOU IN A FAIR FIGHT.
MY MISSION IS TO BRING YOU IN ALIVE.
BUT I'VE BEEN KNOWN TO IMPROVISE.
NOW, UNLESS YOU'VE GOT ADAMANTIUM EYELIDS...
CREED ?!

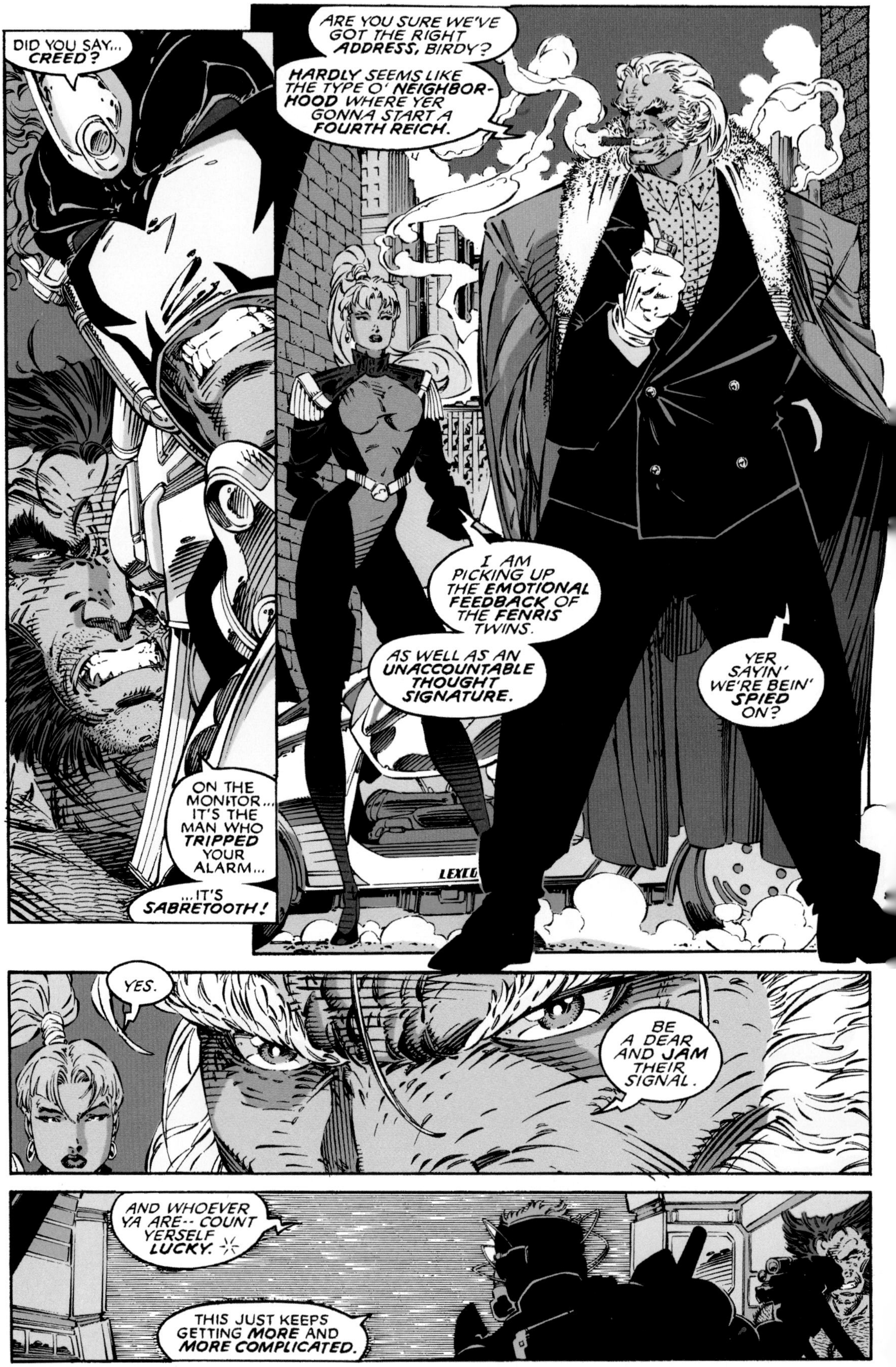
DID YOU SAY... CREED?
ARE YOU SURE WE'VE GOT THE RIGHT ADDRESS, BIRDY?
HARDLY SEEMS LIKE THE TYPE O' NEIGHBOR-HOOD WHERE YER GONNA START A FOURTH REICH.
I AM PICKING UP THE EMOTIONAL FEEDBACK OF THE FENRIS TWINS.
AS WELL AS AN UNACCOUNTABLE THOUGHT SIGNATURE.
YER SAYIN' WE'RE BEIN' SPIED ON?
ON THE MONITOR... IT'S THE MAN WHO TRIPPED YOUR ALARM...
...IT'S SABRETOOTH!
YES.
BE A DEAR AND JAM THEIR SIGNAL.
AND WHOEVER YA ARE-- COUNT YERSELF LUCKY.
THIS JUST KEEPS GETTING MORE AND MORE COMPLICATED.

QUITE THE *TEA PARTY* YA GOT HERE, *MATSUO.*

YA STARTIN' A *COLLECTION* O' X-MEN--

--OR JUST HOLDIN' A *MUTANT CLEARANCE SALE?*

IF YOU HIRED THIS GUY FOR HIS *SENSE OF HUMOR*-- IT MIGHT NOT BE TOO LATE TO GET YOUR *DEPOSIT* BACK.

BE A DEAR AND *HANG UP* THE COAT.

NOT IN *THIS* LIFE-TIME.

PSYLOCKE ONLY RESPONDS TO *MY* COMMANDS, SABRETOOTH-- AND THEN ONLY *GRUDGINGLY.*

I TRUST YOU'LL BE MORE *ACCOMODATING...*

...IN YOUR *SEARCH* FOR *WOLVERINE?*

WE BELIEVE HE HAS *ACCESS* TO A PARTICULAR *DEVICE* WHICH WILL AID OUR *RUSSIAN ALLY.*

S'FUNNY THING ABOUT YER *RED BUDDY--*

--SOMETHIN' VAGUELY *FAMILIAR.*

IT'LL *COME* TO ME.

Sniff SEE? I *NEVER FORGET* A *SCENT.*

A LONG WAYS FROM THE *BIG EASY*, REMY.

AND SINCE WHEN YOU *WORKIN'* THE *SIDE* OF THE *ANGELS?*

OR DID I JUST *BLOW* YER *LATEST SCAM?*

JE M'EXCUSE, M'SIEU TOOTH--

PIWT

--BUT, SECOND-HAND *SMOKE* IS THE *LEADIN'* CAUSE OF *LUNG CANCER.*

SLCCCT!

YUM. *SPICIER* THAN I *REMEMBER.*

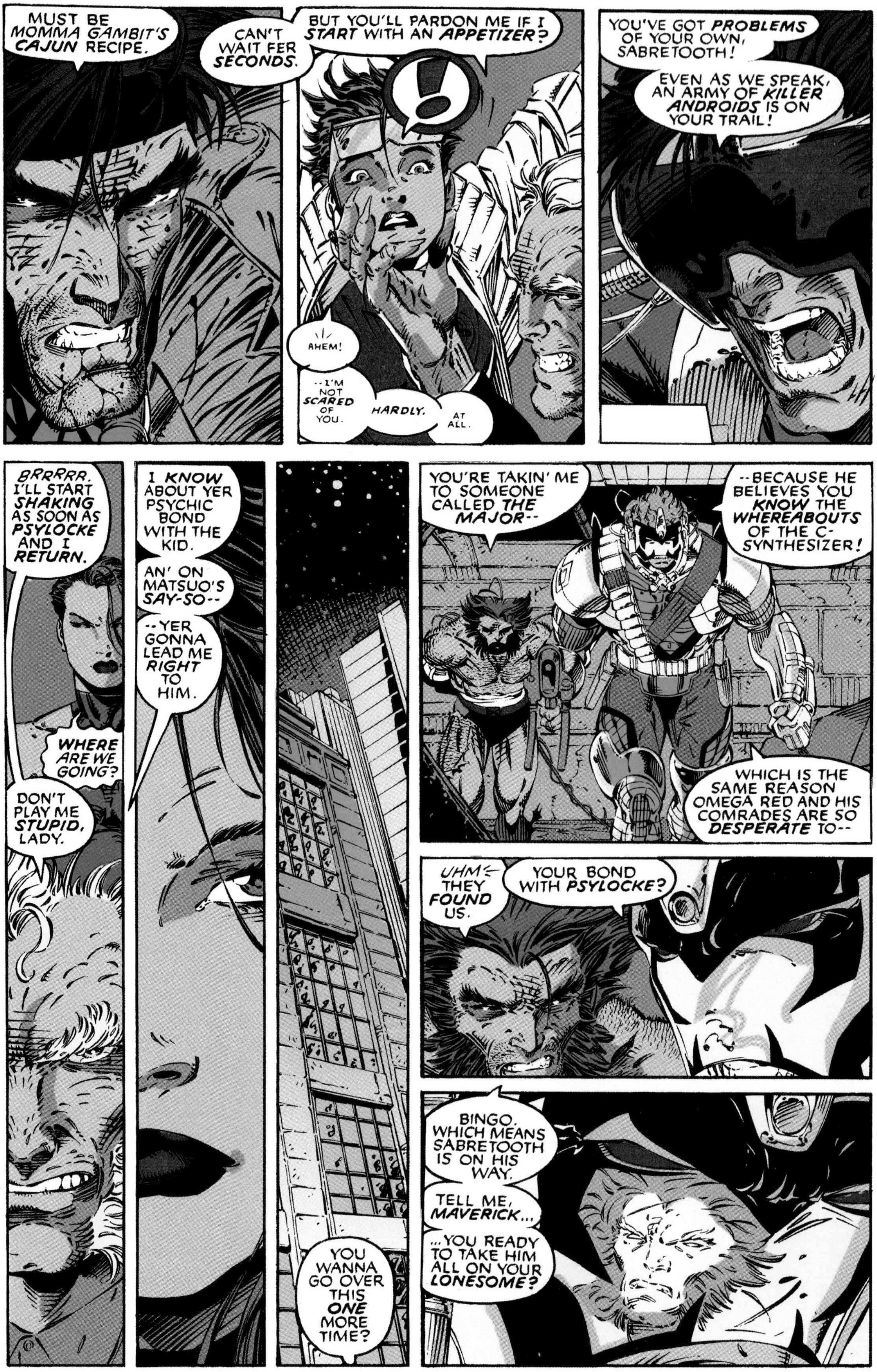

MUST BE MOMMA GAMBIT'S CAJUN RECIPE.
CAN'T WAIT FER SECONDS.
BUT YOU'LL PARDON ME IF I START WITH AN APPETIZER?
!
AHEM!
--I'M NOT SCARED OF YOU.
HARDLY.
AT ALL.
YOU'VE GOT PROBLEMS OF YOUR OWN, SABRETOOTH!
EVEN AS WE SPEAK, AN ARMY OF KILLER ANDROIDS IS ON YOUR TRAIL!
BRRRRR. I'LL START SHAKING AS SOON AS PSYLOCKE AND I RETURN.
WHERE ARE WE GOING?
DON'T PLAY ME STUPID, LADY.
I KNOW ABOUT YER PSYCHIC BOND WITH THE KID.
AN' ON MATSUO'S SAY-SO--
--YER GONNA LEAD ME RIGHT TO HIM.
YOU WANNA GO OVER THIS ONE MORE TIME?
YOU'RE TAKIN' ME TO SOMEONE CALLED THE MAJOR--
--BECAUSE HE BELIEVES YOU KNOW THE WHEREABOUTS OF THE C-SYNTHESIZER!
WHICH IS THE SAME REASON OMEGA RED AND HIS COMRADES ARE SO DESPERATE TO--
UHM-- THEY FOUND US.
YOUR BOND WITH PSYLOCKE?
BINGO. WHICH MEANS SABRETOOTH IS ON HIS WAY.
TELL ME, MAVERICK...
...YOU READY TO TAKE HIM ALL ON YOUR LONESOME?

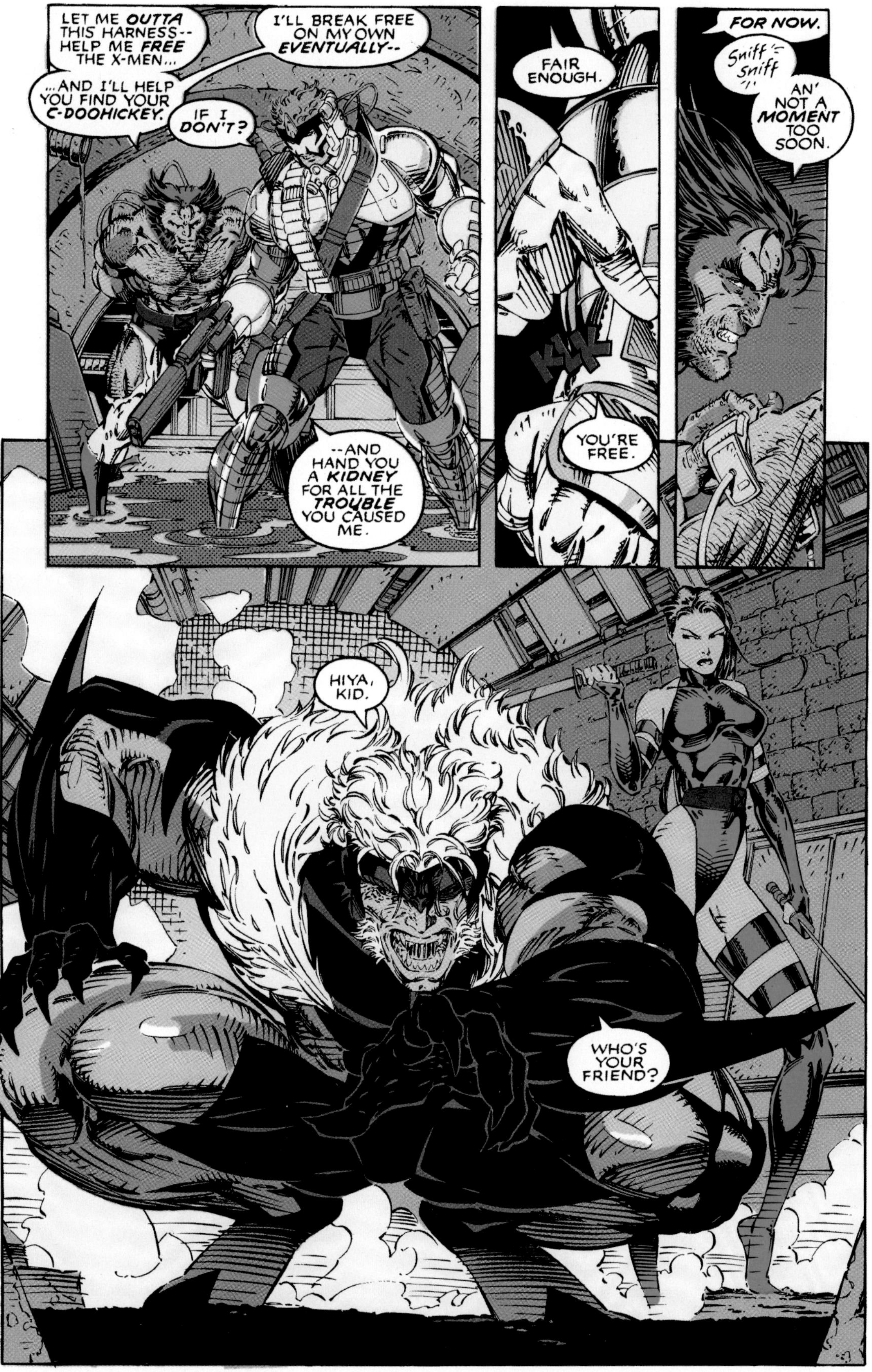
LET ME OUTTA THIS HARNESS-- HELP ME FREE THE X-MEN...
...AND I'LL HELP YOU FIND YOUR C-DOOHICKEY.
I'LL BREAK FREE ON MY OWN EVENTUALLY--
IF I DON'T?
--AND HAND YOU A KIDNEY FOR ALL THE TROUBLE YOU CAUSED ME.
FAIR ENOUGH.
KLIK
YOU'RE FREE.
FOR NOW.
Sniff sniff
AN' NOT A MOMENT TOO SOON.
HIYA, KID.
WHO'S YOUR FRIEND?

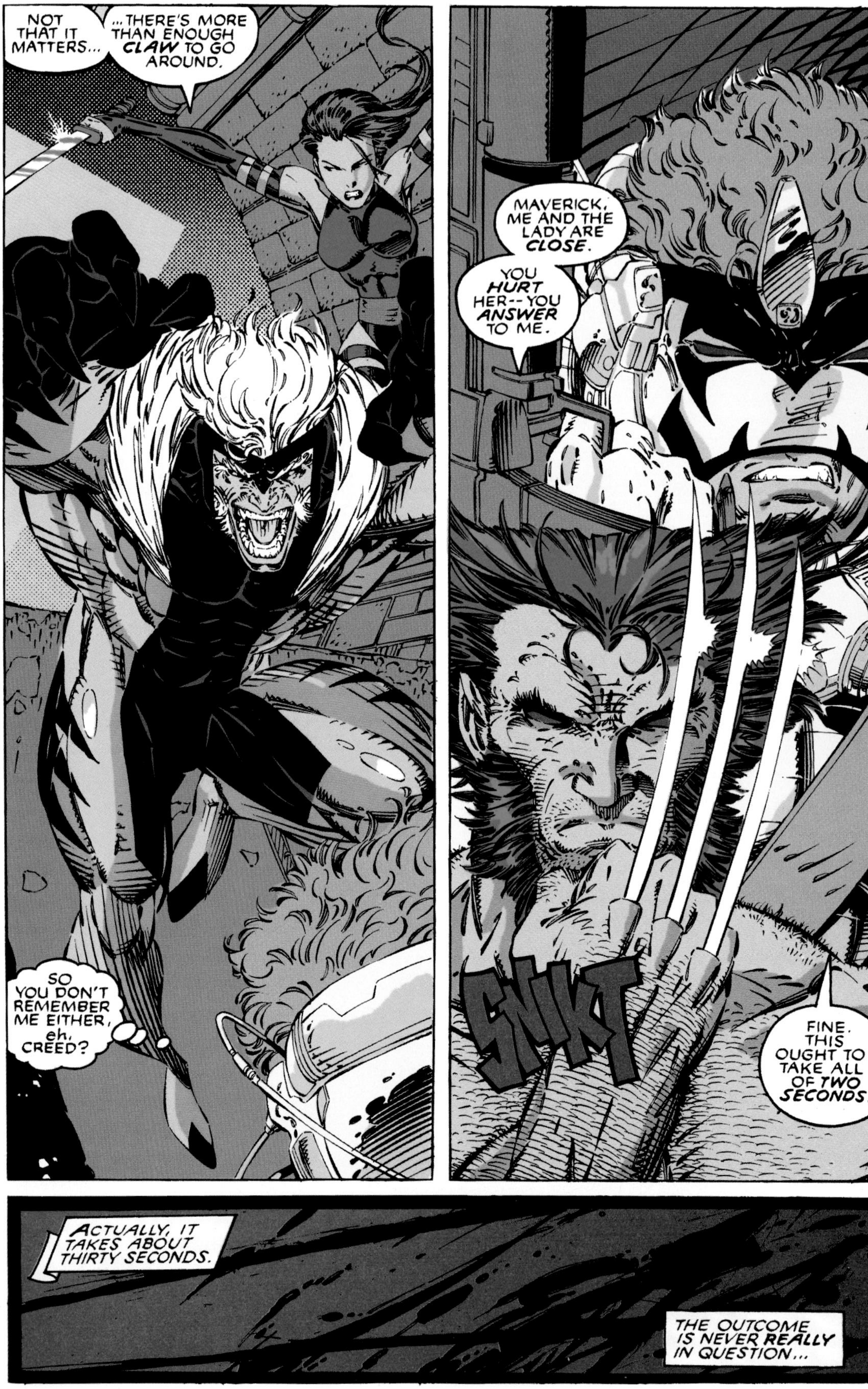
NOT THAT IT MATTERS...
...THERE'S MORE THAN ENOUGH CLAW TO GO AROUND.
SO YOU DON'T REMEMBER ME EITHER, eh, CREED?
MAVERICK, ME AND THE LADY ARE CLOSE.
YOU HURT HER--YOU ANSWER TO ME.
SNIKT
FINE. THIS OUGHT TO TAKE ALL OF TWO SECONDS.
ACTUALLY, IT TAKES ABOUT THIRTY SECONDS.
THE OUTCOME IS NEVER REALLY IN QUESTION...

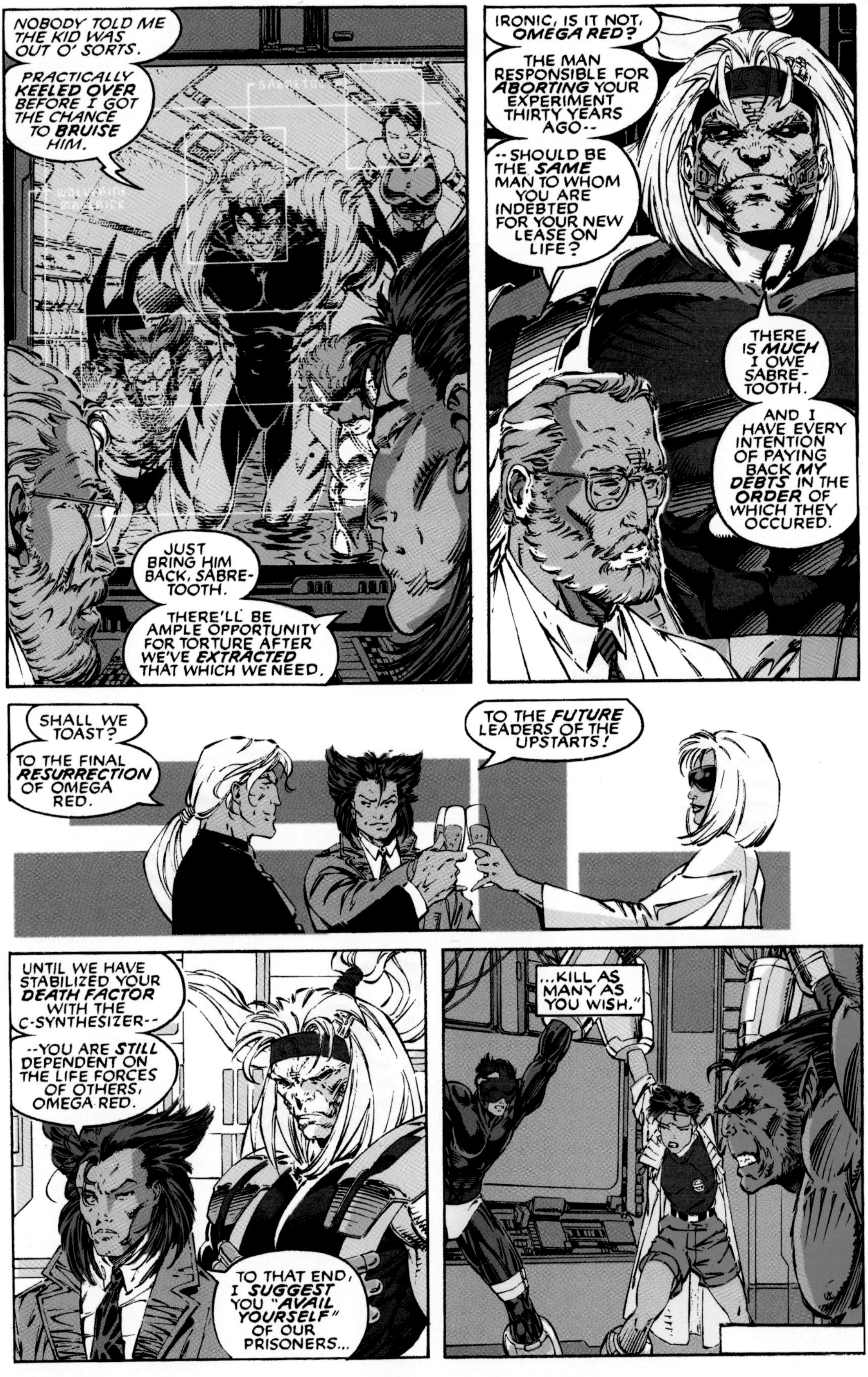
NOBODY TOLD ME THE KID WAS OUT O' SORTS.
PRACTICALLY KEELED OVER BEFORE I GOT THE CHANCE TO BRUISE HIM.
JUST BRING HIM BACK, SABRE-TOOTH.
THERE'LL BE AMPLE OPPORTUNITY FOR TORTURE AFTER WE'VE EXTRACTED THAT WHICH WE NEED.
IRONIC, IS IT NOT, OMEGA RED?
THE MAN RESPONSIBLE FOR ABORTING YOUR EXPERIMENT THIRTY YEARS AGO--
--SHOULD BE THE SAME MAN TO WHOM YOU ARE INDEBTED FOR YOUR NEW LEASE ON LIFE?
THERE IS MUCH I OWE SABRE-TOOTH.
AND I HAVE EVERY INTENTION OF PAYING BACK MY DEBTS IN THE ORDER OF WHICH THEY OCCURED.
SHALL WE TOAST?
TO THE FINAL RESURRECTION OF OMEGA RED.
TO THE FUTURE LEADERS OF THE UPSTARTS!
UNTIL WE HAVE STABILIZED YOUR DEATH FACTOR WITH THE C-SYNTHESIZER--
--YOU ARE STILL DEPENDENT ON THE LIFE FORCES OF OTHERS, OMEGA RED.
TO THAT END, I SUGGEST YOU "AVAIL YOURSELF" OF OUR PRISONERS...
...KILL AS MANY AS YOU WISH."

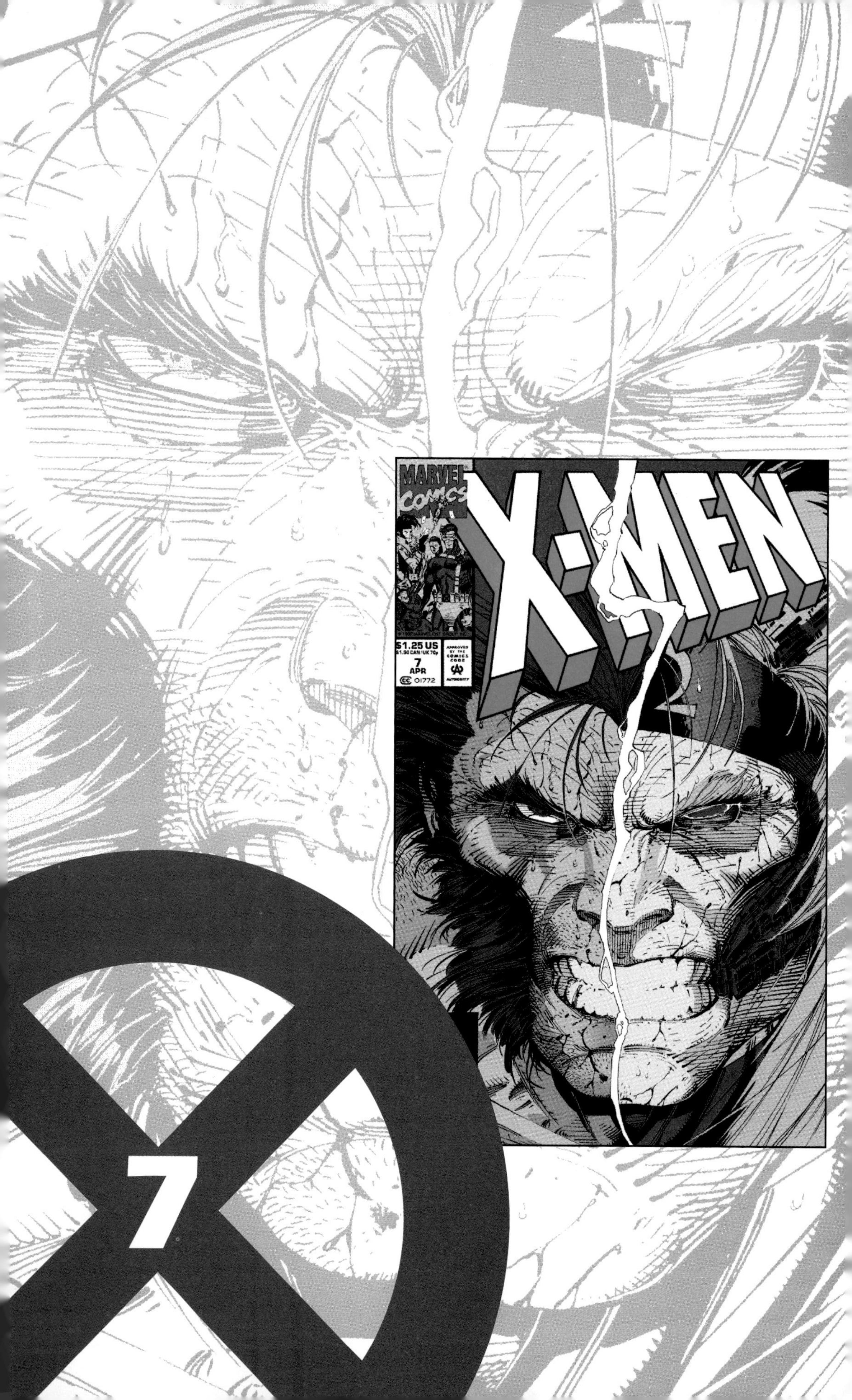
MARVEL COMICS
X-MEN
$1.25 US
7
APR
01772
APPROVED BY THE COMICS CODE AUTHORITY
7

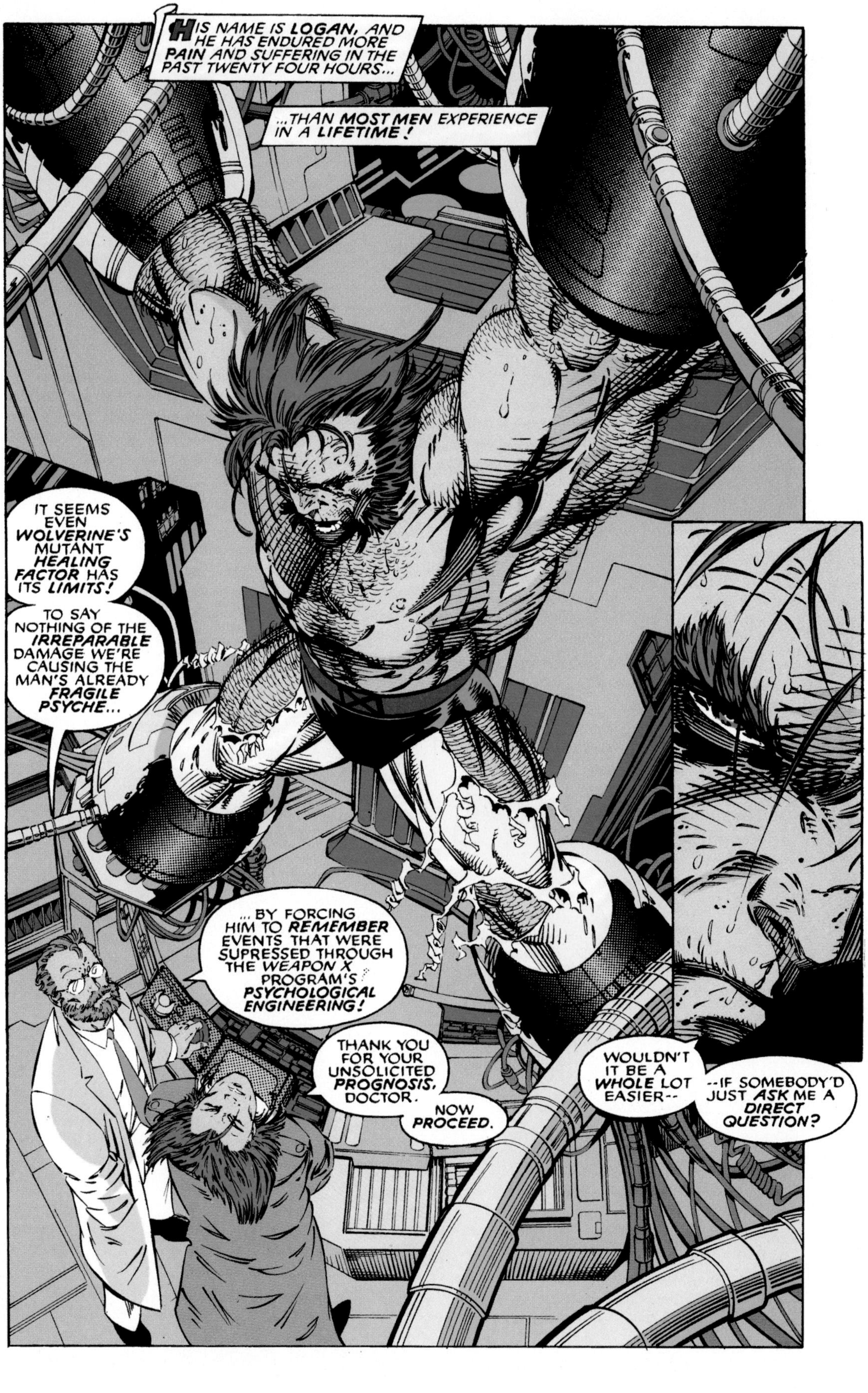
HIS NAME IS LOGAN, AND HE HAS ENDURED MORE PAIN AND SUFFERING IN THE PAST TWENTY FOUR HOURS...
...THAN MOST MEN EXPERIENCE IN A LIFETIME!
IT SEEMS EVEN WOLVERINE'S MUTANT HEALING FACTOR HAS ITS LIMITS!
TO SAY NOTHING OF THE IRREPARABLE DAMAGE WE'RE CAUSING THE MAN'S ALREADY FRAGILE PSYCHE...
...BY FORCING HIM TO REMEMBER EVENTS THAT WERE SUPRESSED THROUGH THE WEAPON X PROGRAM'S PSYCHOLOGICAL ENGINEERING!
THANK YOU FOR YOUR UNSOLICITED PROGNOSIS, DOCTOR.
NOW PROCEED.
WOULDN'T IT BE A WHOLE LOT EASIER--
--IF SOMEBODY'D JUST ASK ME A DIRECT QUESTION?

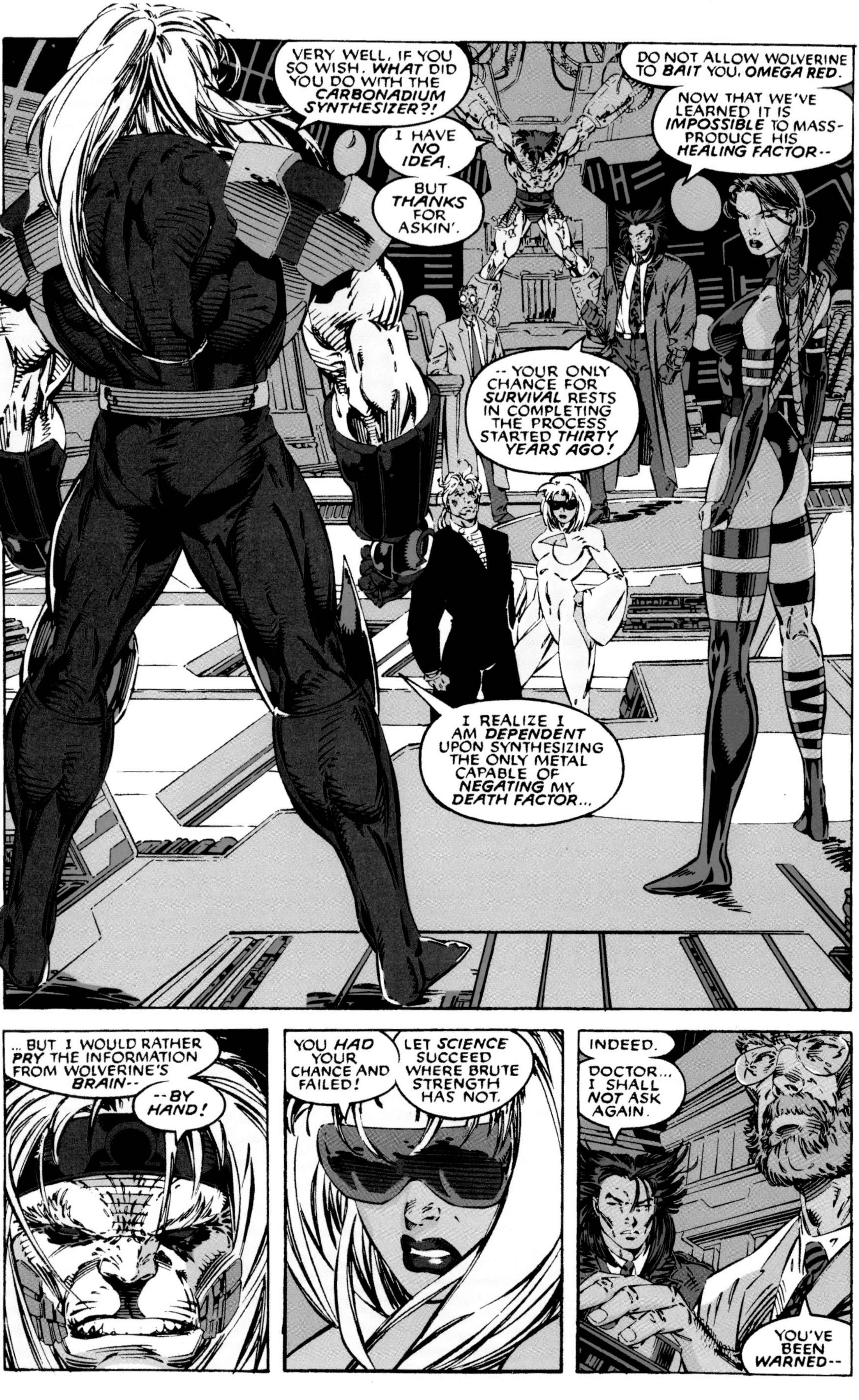

VERY WELL, IF YOU SO WISH. WHAT DID YOU DO WITH THE CARBONADIUM SYNTHESIZER?!
I HAVE NO IDEA.
BUT THANKS FOR ASKIN'.
DO NOT ALLOW WOLVERINE TO BAIT YOU, OMEGA RED.
NOW THAT WE'VE LEARNED IT IS IMPOSSIBLE TO MASS-PRODUCE HIS HEALING FACTOR--
-- YOUR ONLY CHANCE FOR SURVIVAL RESTS IN COMPLETING THE PROCESS STARTED THIRTY YEARS AGO!
I REALIZE I AM DEPENDENT UPON SYNTHESIZING THE ONLY METAL CAPABLE OF NEGATING MY DEATH FACTOR...
... BUT I WOULD RATHER PRY THE INFORMATION FROM WOLVERINE'S BRAIN--
--BY HAND!
YOU HAD YOUR CHANCE AND FAILED!
LET SCIENCE SUCCEED WHERE BRUTE STRENGTH HAS NOT.
INDEED.
DOCTOR... I SHALL NOT ASK AGAIN.
YOU'VE BEEN WARNED--

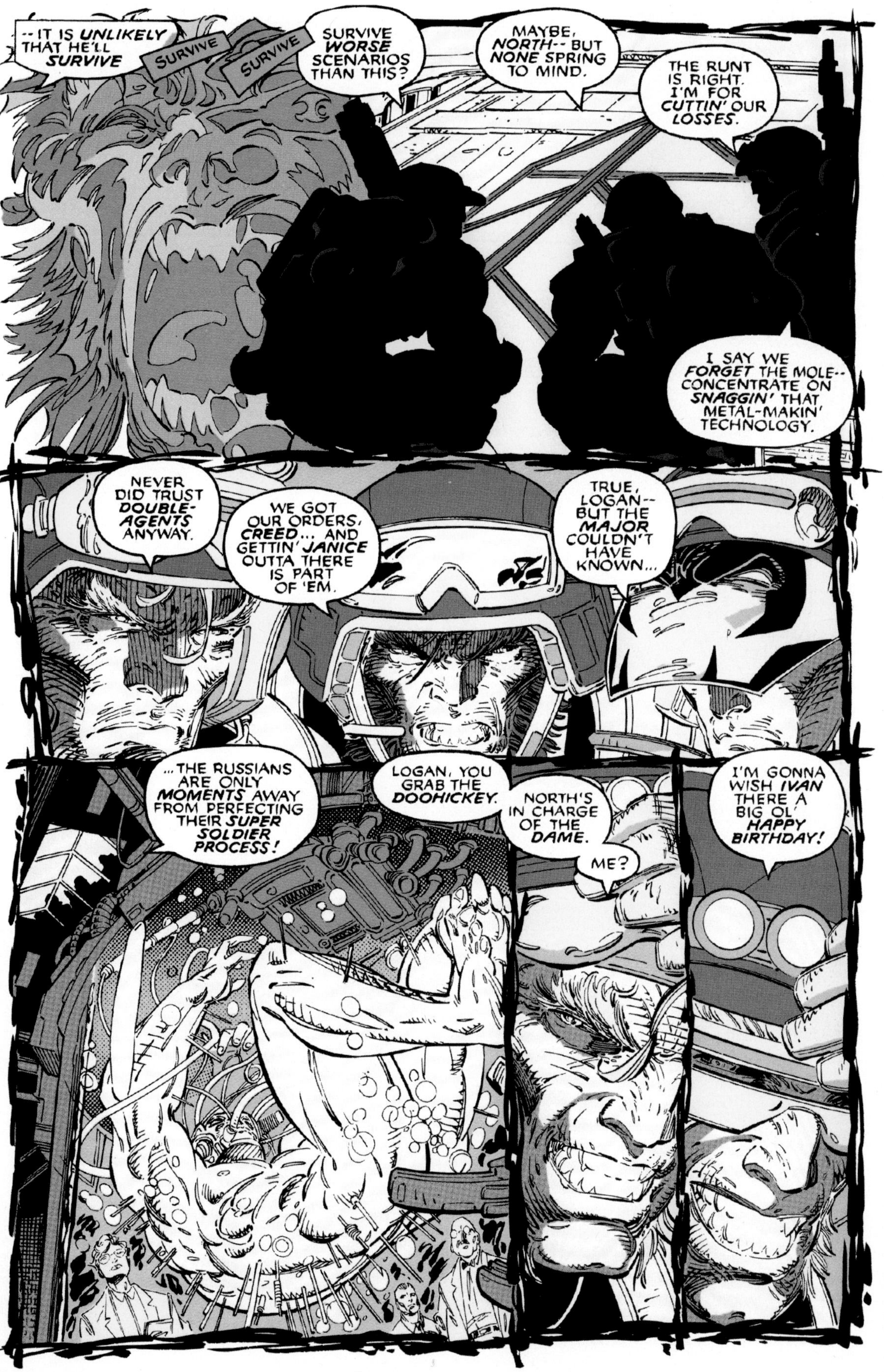
-- IT IS UNLIKELY THAT HE'LL SURVIVE
SURVIVE
SURVIVE
SURVIVE WORSE SCENARIOS THAN THIS?
MAYBE, NORTH-- BUT NONE SPRING TO MIND.
THE RUNT IS RIGHT. I'M FOR CUTTIN' OUR LOSSES.
I SAY WE FORGET THE MOLE-- CONCENTRATE ON SNAGGIN' THAT METAL-MAKIN' TECHNOLOGY.
NEVER DID TRUST DOUBLE-AGENTS ANYWAY.
WE GOT OUR ORDERS, CREED... AND GETTIN' JANICE OUTTA THERE IS PART OF 'EM.
TRUE, LOGAN-- BUT THE MAJOR COULDN'T HAVE KNOWN...
...THE RUSSIANS ARE ONLY MOMENTS AWAY FROM PERFECTING THEIR SUPER SOLDIER PROCESS!
LOGAN, YOU GRAB THE DOOHICKEY.
NORTH'S IN CHARGE OF THE DAME.
ME?
I'M GONNA WISH IVAN THERE A BIG OL' HAPPY BIRTHDAY!

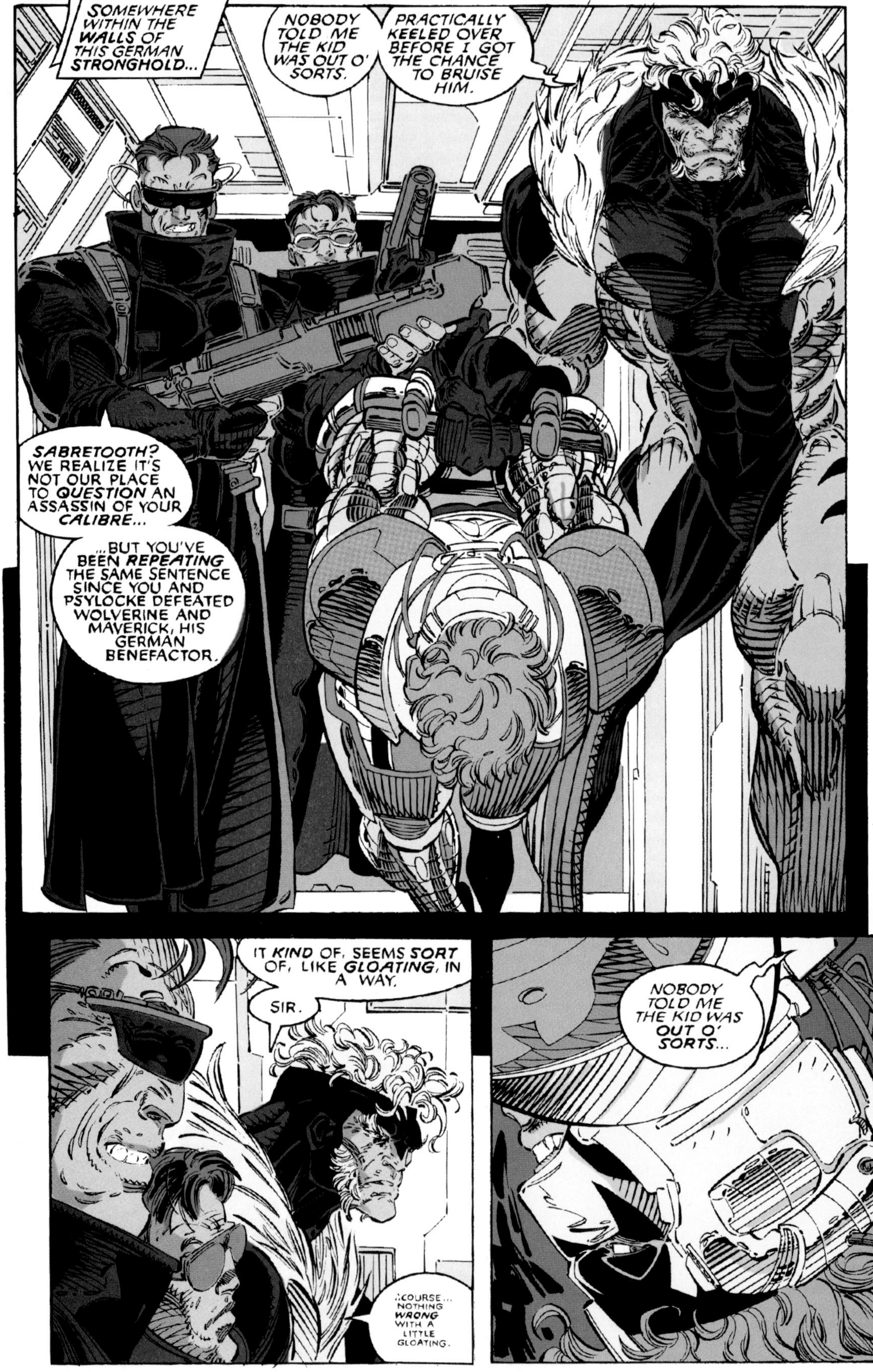
SOMEWHERE WITHIN THE WALLS OF THIS GERMAN STRONGHOLD...
NOBODY TOLD ME THE KID WAS OUT O' SORTS.
PRACTICALLY KEELED OVER BEFORE I GOT THE CHANCE TO BRUISE HIM.
SABRETOOTH? WE REALIZE IT'S NOT OUR PLACE TO QUESTION AN ASSASSIN OF YOUR CALIBRE...
...BUT YOU'VE BEEN REPEATING THE SAME SENTENCE SINCE YOU AND PSYLOCKE DEFEATED WOLVERINE AND MAVERICK, HIS GERMAN BENEFACTOR.
IT KIND OF, SEEMS SORT OF, LIKE GLOATING, IN A WAY.
SIR.
..COURSE... NOTHING WRONG WITH A LITTLE GLOATING.
NOBODY TOLD ME THE KID WAS OUT O' SORTS...

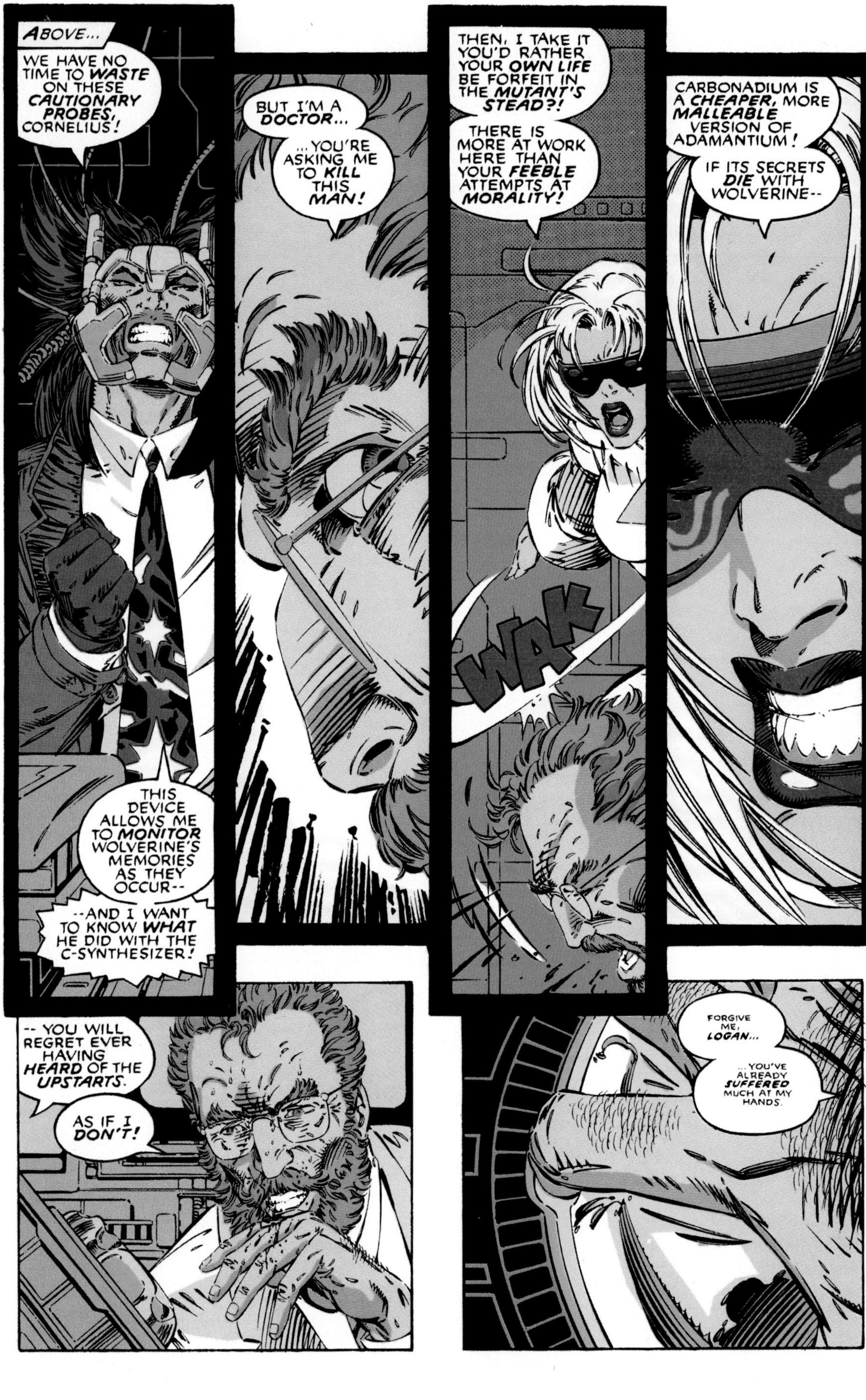
ABOVE...
WE HAVE NO TIME TO WASTE ON THESE CAUTIONARY PROBES, CORNELIUS!
THIS DEVICE ALLOWS ME TO MONITOR WOLVERINE'S MEMORIES AS THEY OCCUR--
--AND I WANT TO KNOW WHAT HE DID WITH THE C-SYNTHESIZER!
BUT I'M A DOCTOR...
...YOU'RE ASKING ME TO KILL THIS MAN!
THEN, I TAKE IT YOU'D RATHER YOUR OWN LIFE BE FORFEIT IN THE MUTANT'S STEAD?!
THERE IS MORE AT WORK HERE THAN YOUR FEEBLE ATTEMPTS AT MORALITY!
WAK
CARBONADIUM IS A CHEAPER, MORE MALLEABLE VERSION OF ADAMANTIUM!
IF ITS SECRETS DIE WITH WOLVERINE--
-- YOU WILL REGRET EVER HAVING HEARD OF THE UPSTARTS.
AS IF I DON'T!
FORGIVE ME, LOGAN...
...YOU'VE ALREADY SUFFERED MUCH AT MY HANDS.

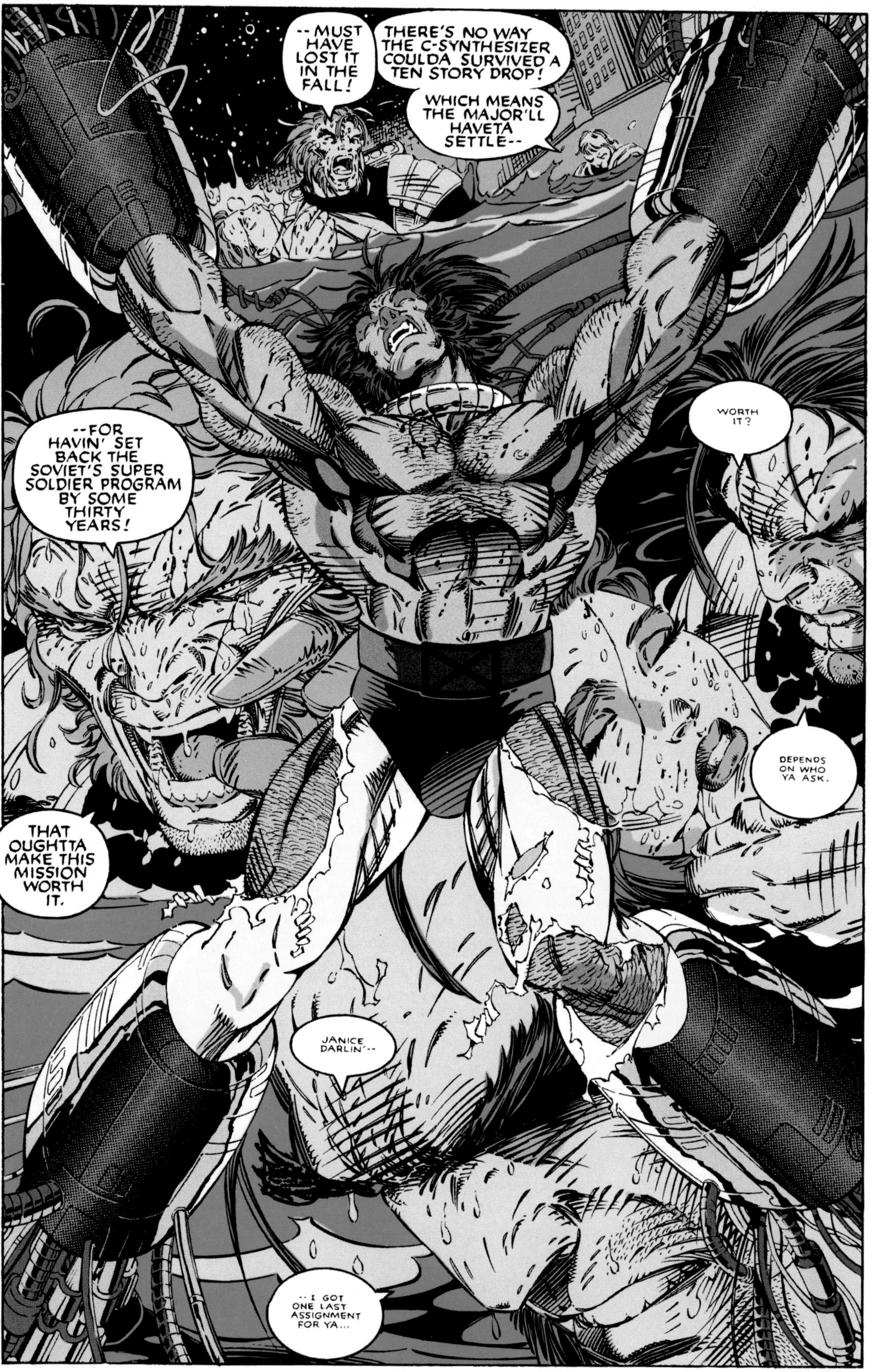
--MUST HAVE LOST IT IN THE FALL!
THERE'S NO WAY THE C-SYNTHESIZER COULDA SURVIVED A TEN STORY DROP!
WHICH MEANS THE MAJOR'LL HAVETA SETTLE--
--FOR HAVIN' SET BACK THE SOVIET'S SUPER SOLDIER PROGRAM BY SOME THIRTY YEARS!
THAT OUGHTTA MAKE THIS MISSION WORTH IT.
WORTH IT?
DEPENDS ON WHO YA ASK.
JANICE, DARLIN'--
--I GOT ONE LAST ASSIGNMENT FOR YA...

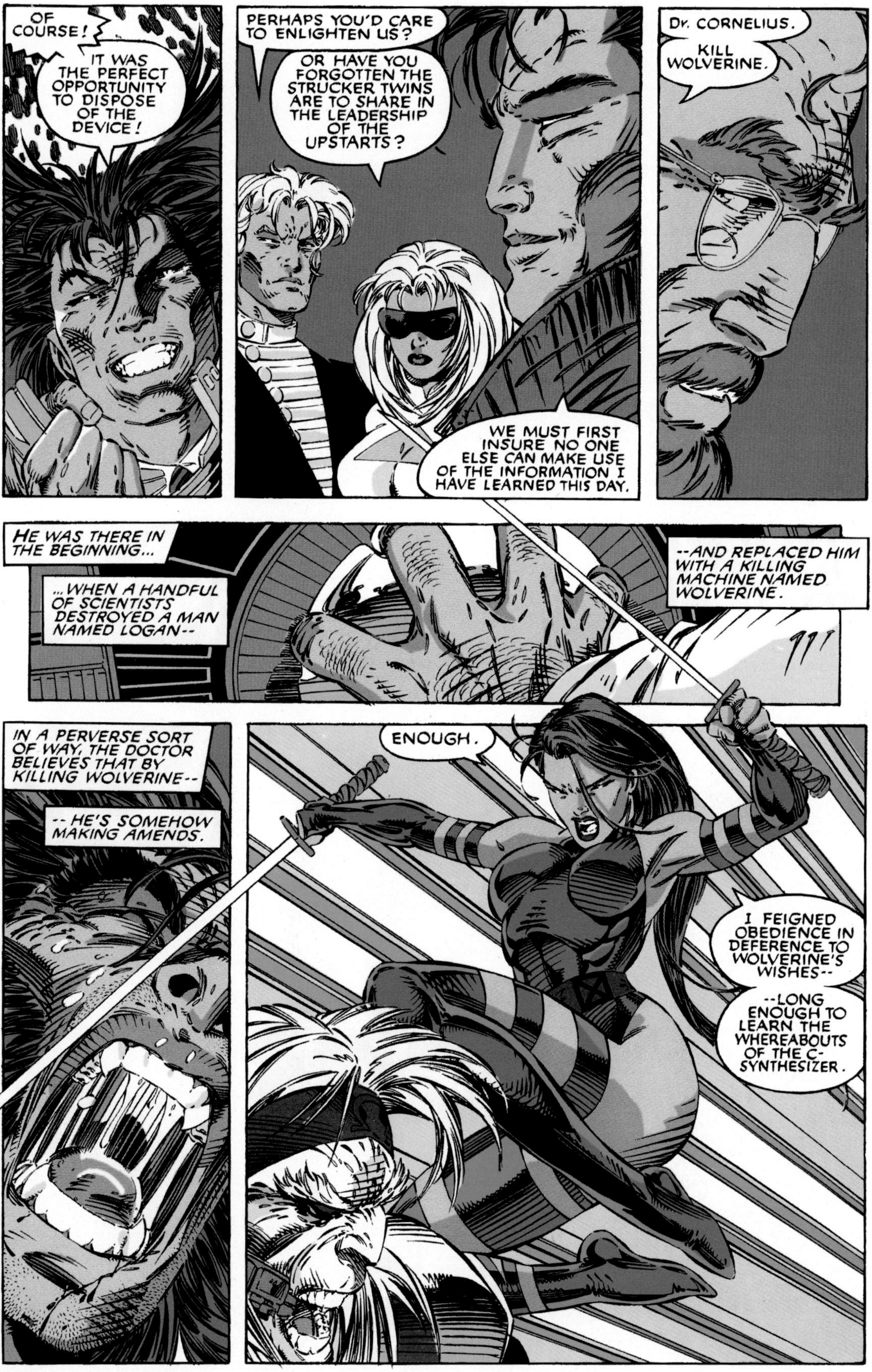
OF COURSE!
IT WAS THE PERFECT OPPORTUNITY TO DISPOSE OF THE DEVICE!
PERHAPS YOU'D CARE TO ENLIGHTEN US?
OR HAVE YOU FORGOTTEN THE STRUCKER TWINS ARE TO SHARE IN THE LEADERSHIP OF THE UPSTARTS?
WE MUST FIRST INSURE NO ONE ELSE CAN MAKE USE OF THE INFORMATION I HAVE LEARNED THIS DAY.
Dr. CORNELIUS.
KILL WOLVERINE.
HE WAS THERE IN THE BEGINNING...
...WHEN A HANDFUL OF SCIENTISTS DESTROYED A MAN NAMED LOGAN--
--AND REPLACED HIM WITH A KILLING MACHINE NAMED WOLVERINE.
IN A PERVERSE SORT OF WAY, THE DOCTOR BELIEVES THAT BY KILLING WOLVERINE--
--HE'S SOMEHOW MAKING AMENDS.
ENOUGH.
I FEIGNED OBEDIENCE IN DEFERENCE TO WOLVERINE'S WISHES--
--LONG ENOUGH TO LEARN THE WHEREABOUTS OF THE C-SYNTHESIZER.

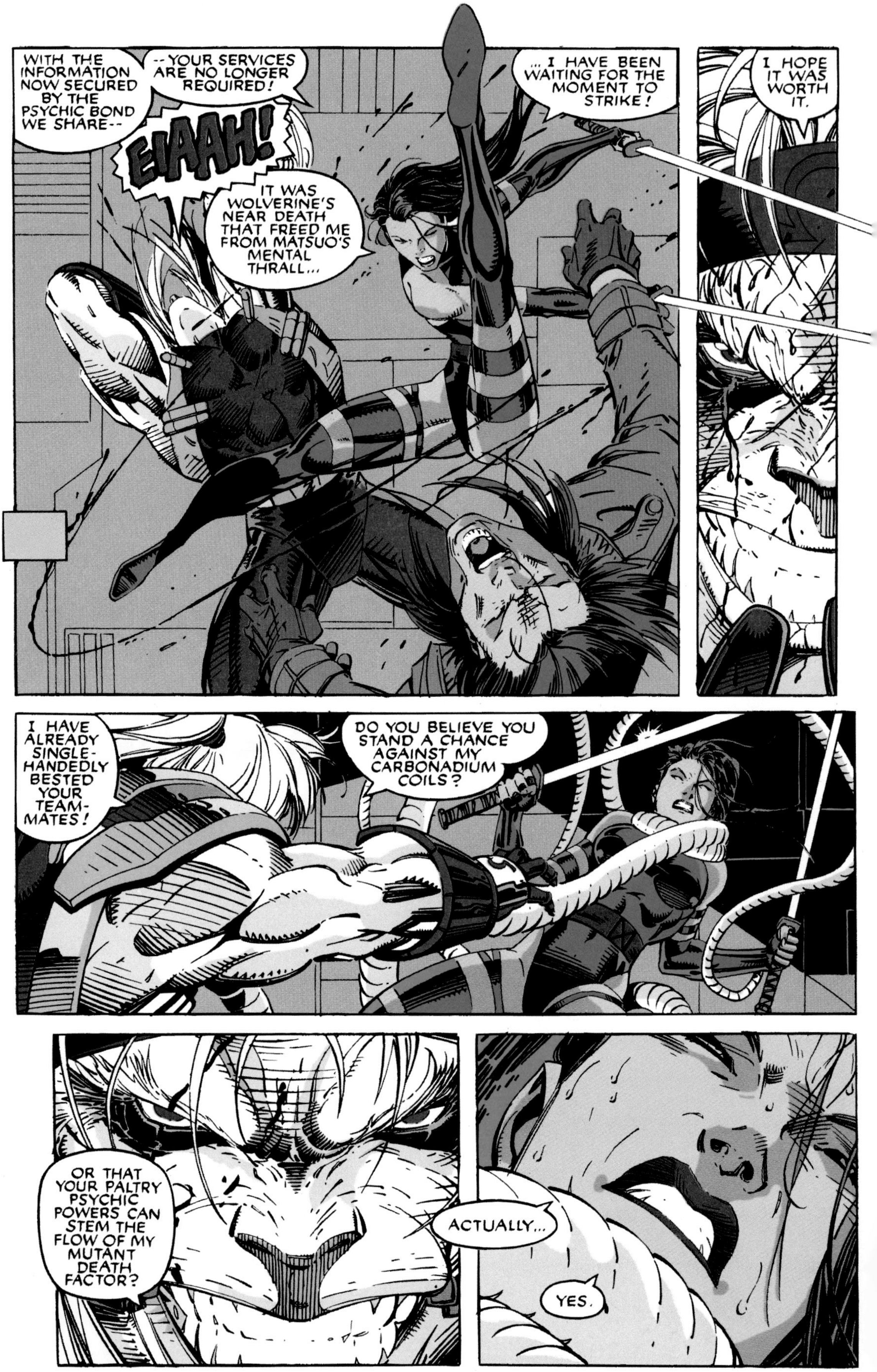
WITH THE INFORMATION NOW SECURED BY THE PSYCHIC BOND WE SHARE--
--YOUR SERVICES ARE NO LONGER REQUIRED!
EIAAH!
IT WAS WOLVERINE'S NEAR DEATH THAT FREED ME FROM MATSUO'S MENTAL THRALL...
...I HAVE BEEN WAITING FOR THE MOMENT TO STRIKE!
I HOPE IT WAS WORTH IT.
I HAVE ALREADY SINGLE-HANDEDLY BESTED YOUR TEAM-MATES!
DO YOU BELIEVE YOU STAND A CHANCE AGAINST MY CARBONADIUM COILS?
OR THAT YOUR PALTRY PSYCHIC POWERS CAN STEM THE FLOW OF MY MUTANT DEATH FACTOR?
ACTUALLY...
YES.

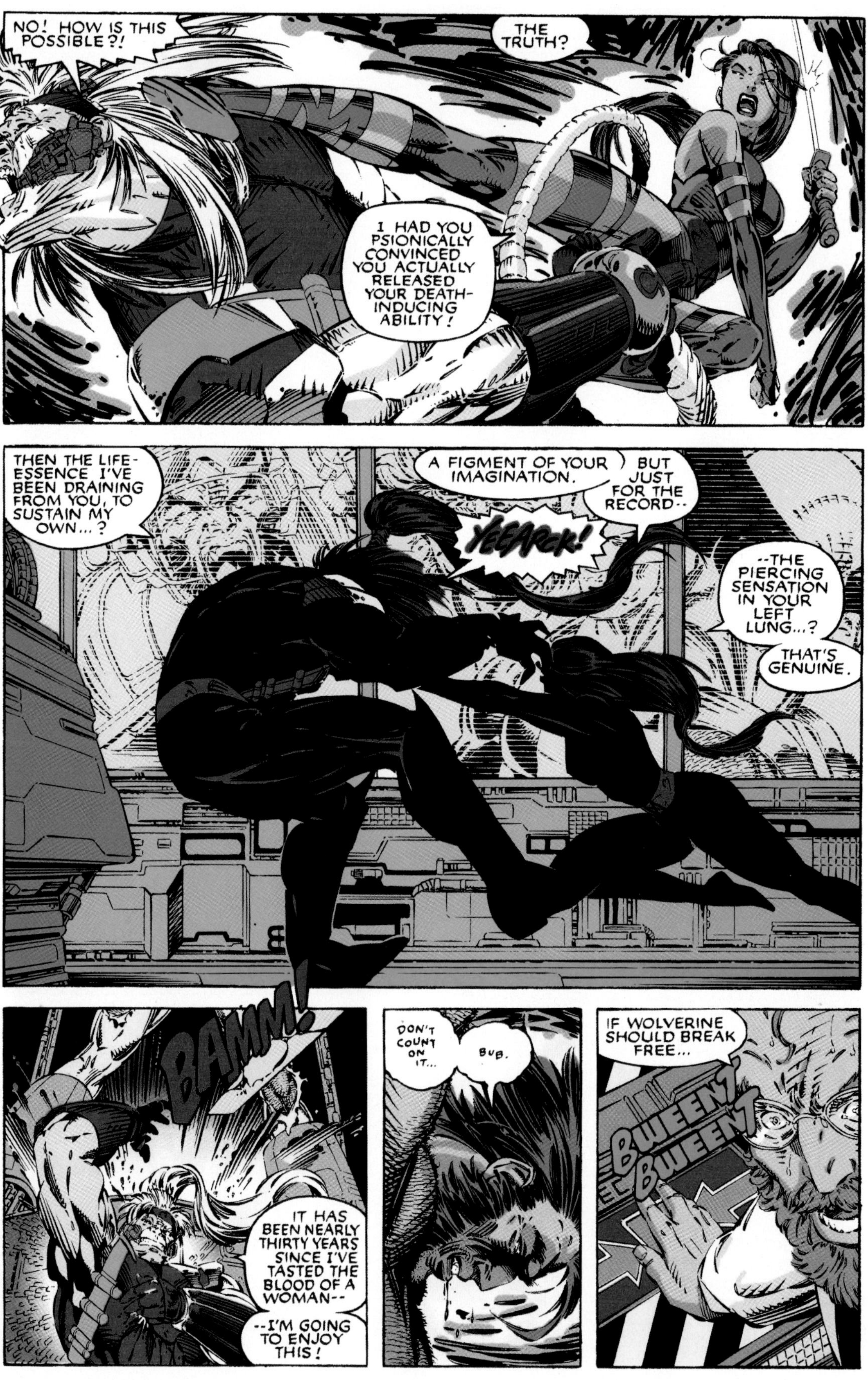
NO! HOW IS THIS POSSIBLE?!
THE TRUTH?
I HAD YOU PSIONICALLY CONVINCED YOU ACTUALLY RELEASED YOUR DEATH-INDUCING ABILITY!
THEN THE LIFE-ESSENCE I'VE BEEN DRAINING FROM YOU, TO SUSTAIN MY OWN...?
A FIGMENT OF YOUR IMAGINATION.
BUT JUST FOR THE RECORD--
YEEARCK!
--THE PIERCING SENSATION IN YOUR LEFT LUNG...?
THAT'S GENUINE.
BAMM!
IT HAS BEEN NEARLY THIRTY YEARS SINCE I'VE TASTED THE BLOOD OF A WOMAN--
--I'M GOING TO ENJOY THIS!
DON'T COUNT ON IT...
BUB.
IF WOLVERINE SHOULD BREAK FREE...
BWEENT BWEENT

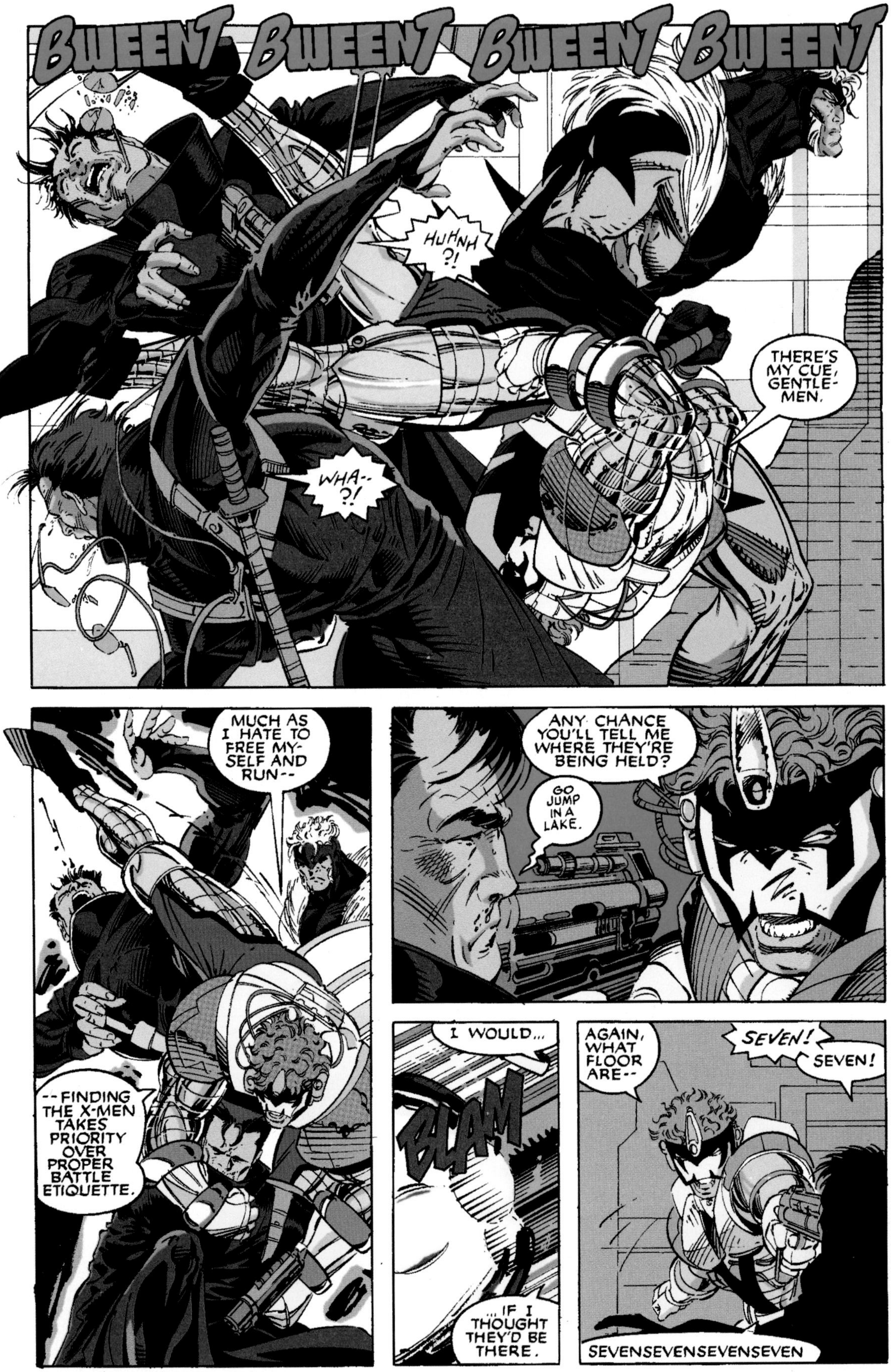
BWEENT BWEENT BWEENT BWEENT
HUHNH ?!
THERE'S MY CUE, GENTLE-MEN.
WHA-- ?!
MUCH AS I HATE TO FREE MY-SELF AND RUN--
--FINDING THE X-MEN TAKES PRIORITY OVER PROPER BATTLE ETIQUETTE.
ANY CHANCE YOU'LL TELL ME WHERE THEY'RE BEING HELD?
GO JUMP IN A LAKE.
I WOULD...
BLAM
...IF I THOUGHT THEY'D BE THERE.
AGAIN, WHAT FLOOR ARE--
SEVEN!
SEVEN!
SEVENSEVENSEVENSEVEN

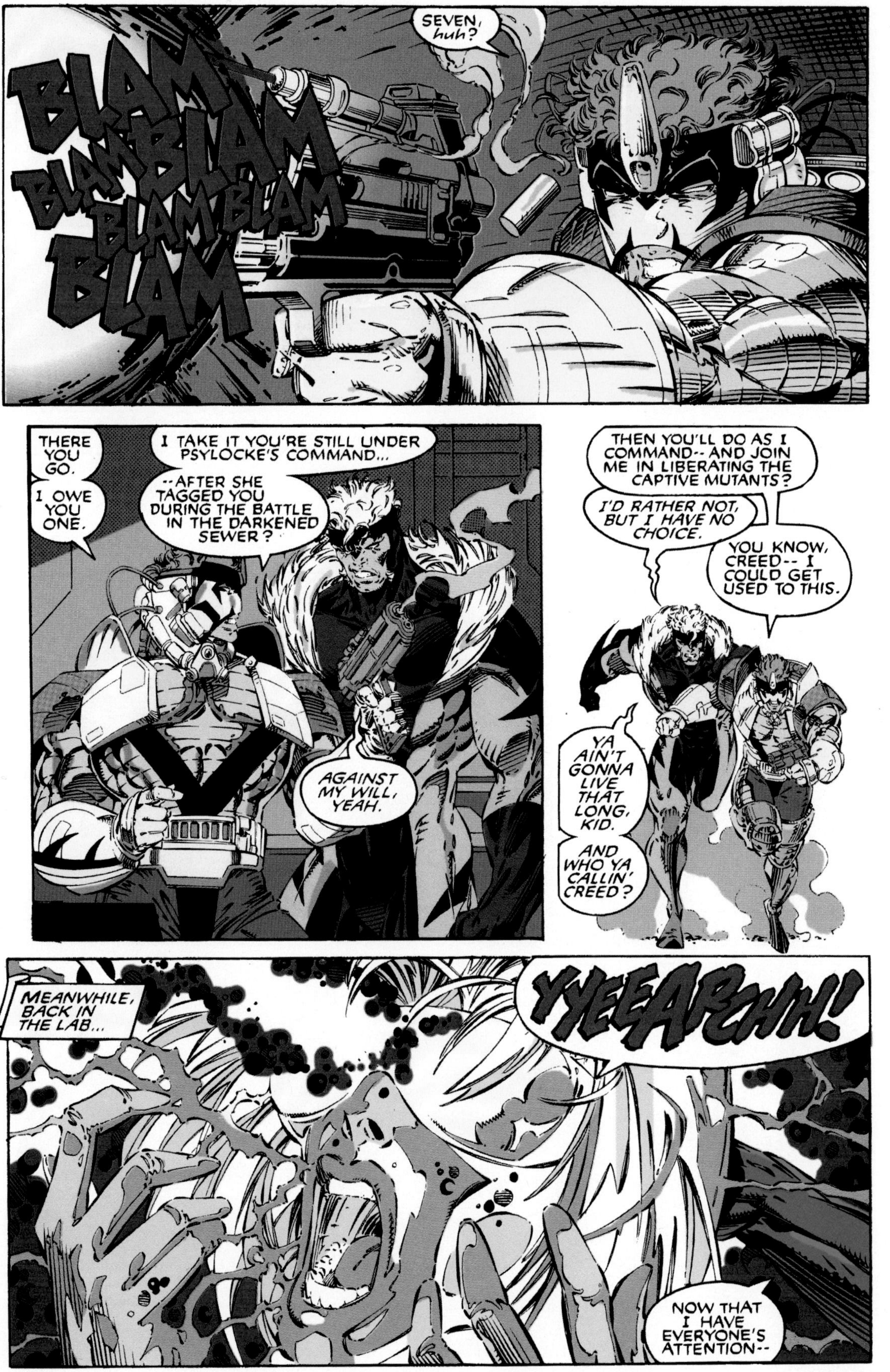
SEVEN, *huh?*
BLAM BLAM BLAM BLAM BLAM BLAM BLAM
THERE YOU GO.
I OWE YOU ONE.
I TAKE IT YOU'RE STILL UNDER PSYLOCKE'S COMMAND...
--AFTER SHE TAGGED YOU DURING THE BATTLE IN THE DARKENED SEWER?
AGAINST MY WILL, YEAH.
THEN YOU'LL DO AS I COMMAND-- AND JOIN ME IN LIBERATING THE CAPTIVE MUTANTS?
I'D RATHER NOT, BUT I HAVE NO CHOICE.
YOU KNOW, CREED-- I COULD GET USED TO THIS.
YA AIN'T GONNA LIVE THAT LONG, KID.
AND WHO YA CALLIN' CREED?
MEANWHILE, BACK IN THE LAB...
YYEEAARCHH!
NOW THAT I HAVE EVERYONE'S ATTENTION--

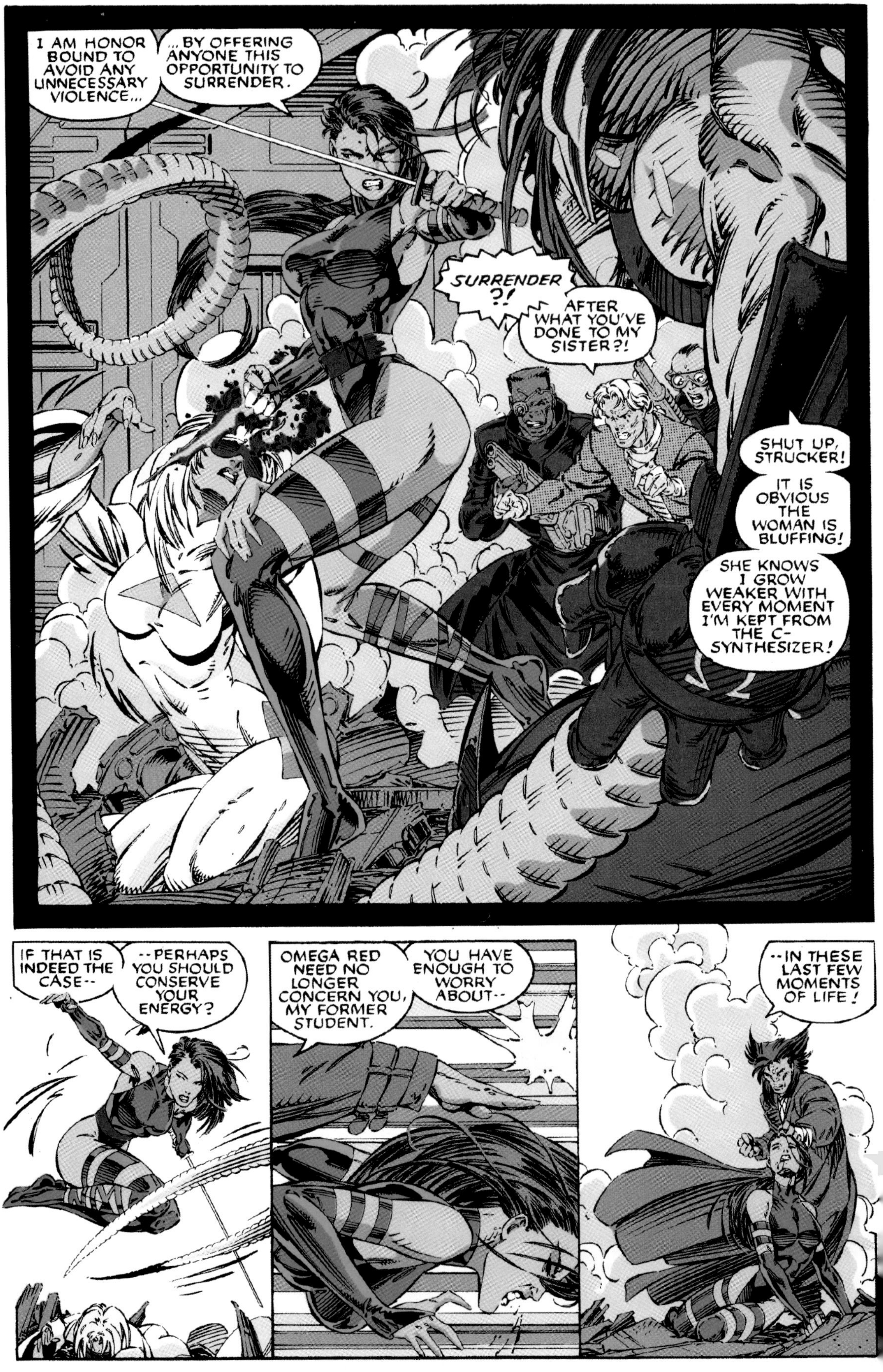
I AM HONOR BOUND TO AVOID ANY UNNECESSARY VIOLENCE...
...BY OFFERING ANYONE THIS OPPORTUNITY TO SURRENDER.
SURRENDER ?!
AFTER WHAT YOU'VE DONE TO MY SISTER?!
SHUT UP, STRUCKER!
IT IS OBVIOUS THE WOMAN IS BLUFFING!
SHE KNOWS I GROW WEAKER WITH EVERY MOMENT I'M KEPT FROM THE C-SYNTHESIZER!
IF THAT IS INDEED THE CASE--
--PERHAPS YOU SHOULD CONSERVE YOUR ENERGY?
OMEGA RED NEED NO LONGER CONCERN YOU, MY FORMER STUDENT.
YOU HAVE ENOUGH TO WORRY ABOUT--
--IN THESE LAST FEW MOMENTS OF LIFE!

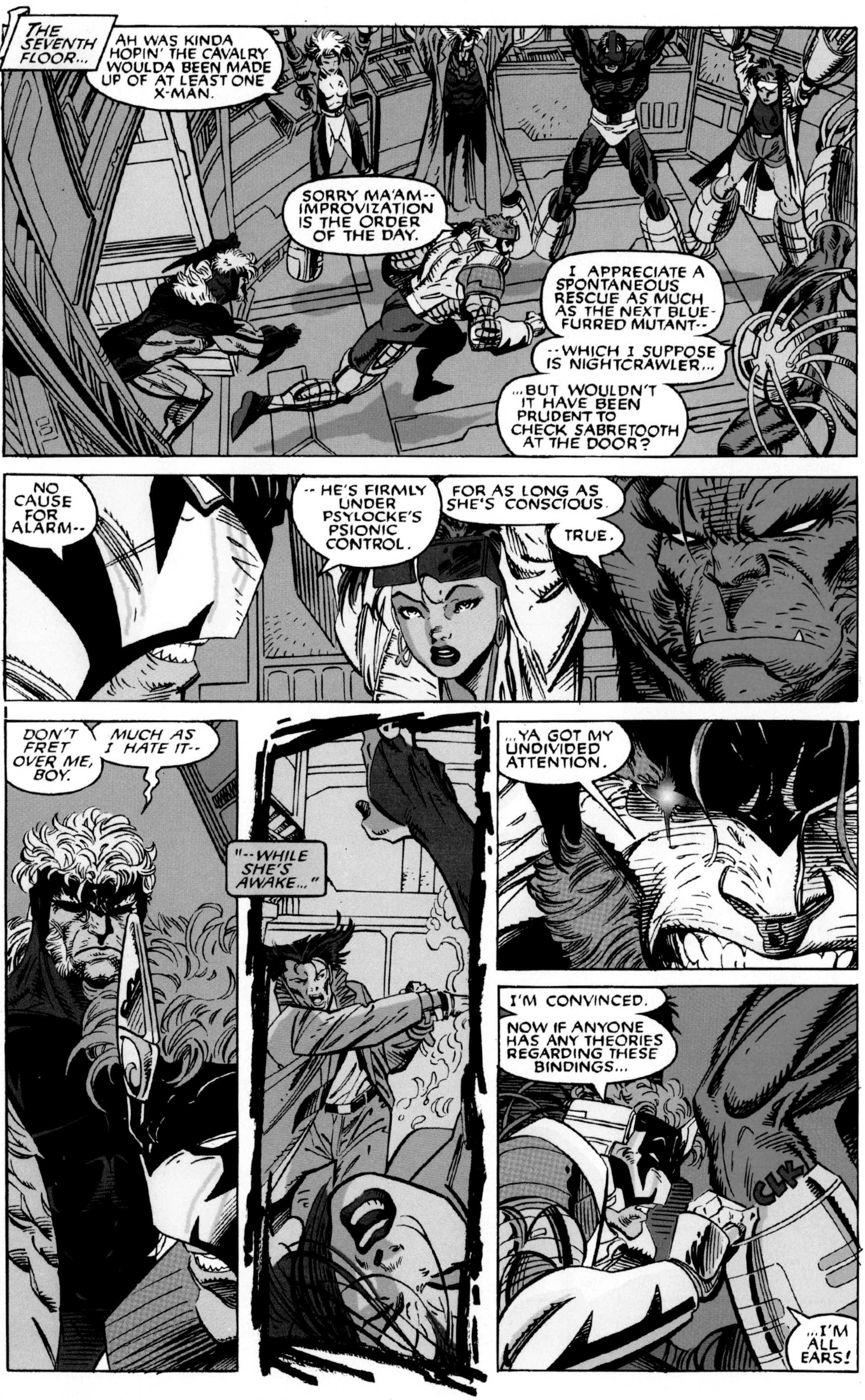
THE SEVENTH FLOOR...
AH WAS KINDA HOPIN' THE CAVALRY WOULDA BEEN MADE UP OF AT LEAST ONE X-MAN.
SORRY MA'AM-- IMPROVIZATION IS THE ORDER OF THE DAY.
I APPRECIATE A SPONTANEOUS RESCUE AS MUCH AS THE NEXT BLUE-FURRED MUTANT--
--WHICH I SUPPOSE IS NIGHTCRAWLER...
...BUT WOULDN'T IT HAVE BEEN PRUDENT TO CHECK SABRETOOTH AT THE DOOR?
NO CAUSE FOR ALARM--
--HE'S FIRMLY UNDER PSYLOCKE'S PSIONIC CONTROL.
FOR AS LONG AS SHE'S CONSCIOUS.
TRUE.
DON'T FRET OVER ME, BOY.
MUCH AS I HATE IT--
"--WHILE SHE'S AWAKE..."
...YA GOT MY UNDIVIDED ATTENTION.
I'M CONVINCED.
NOW IF ANYONE HAS ANY THEORIES REGARDING THESE BINDINGS...
CLIK
...I'M ALL EARS!

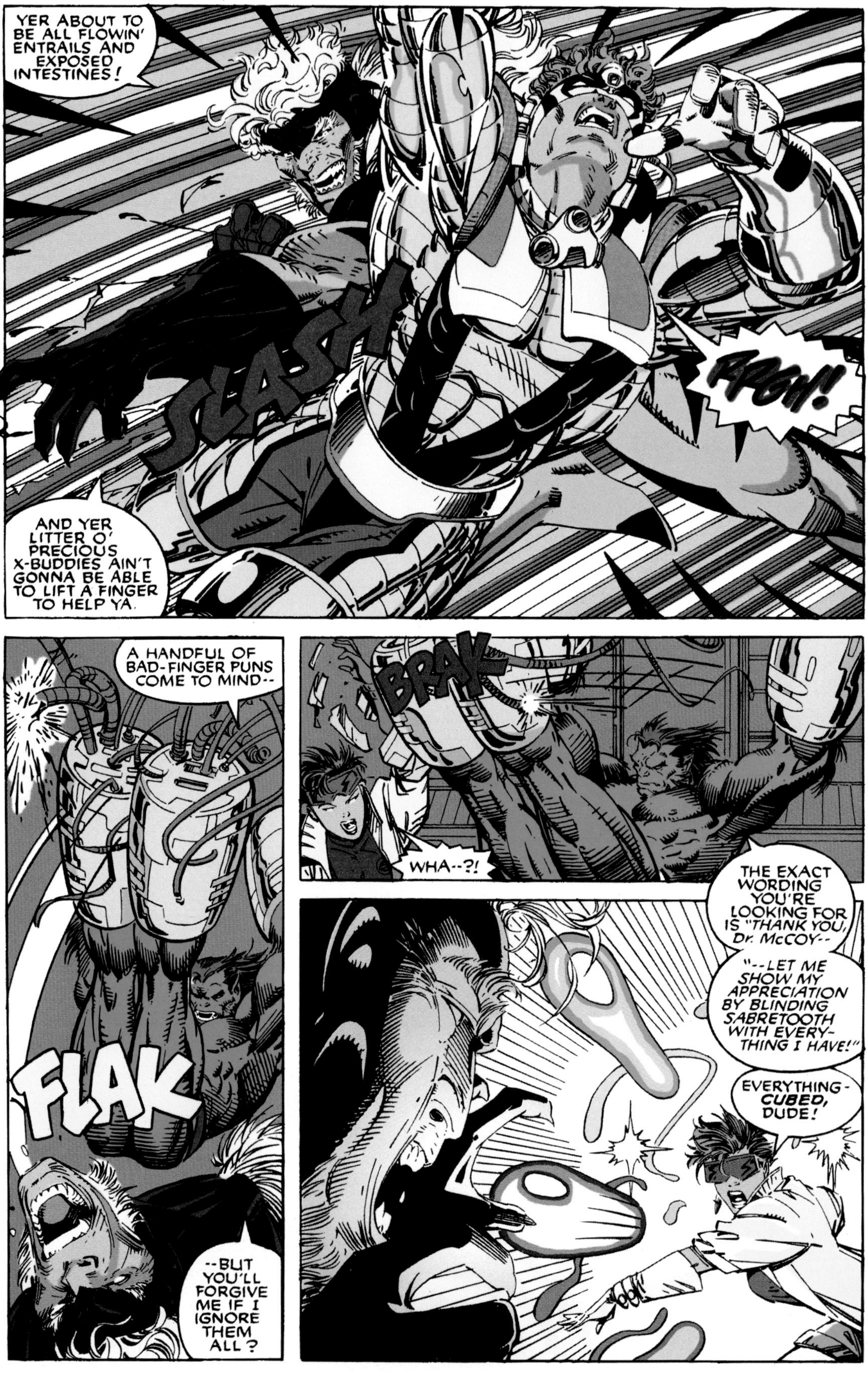
YER ABOUT TO BE ALL FLOWIN' ENTRAILS AND EXPOSED INTESTINES!
SLASH
RRGH!!
AND YER LITTER O' PRECIOUS X-BUDDIES AIN'T GONNA BE ABLE TO LIFT A FINGER TO HELP YA.
A HANDFUL OF BAD-FINGER PUNS COME TO MIND--
FLAK
--BUT YOU'LL FORGIVE ME IF I IGNORE THEM ALL?
BRAK
WHA--?!
THE EXACT WORDING YOU'RE LOOKING FOR IS "THANK YOU, Dr. McCOY--
"--LET ME SHOW MY APPRECIATION BY BLINDING SABRETOOTH WITH EVERY-THING I HAVE!"
EVERYTHING-CUBED, DUDE!

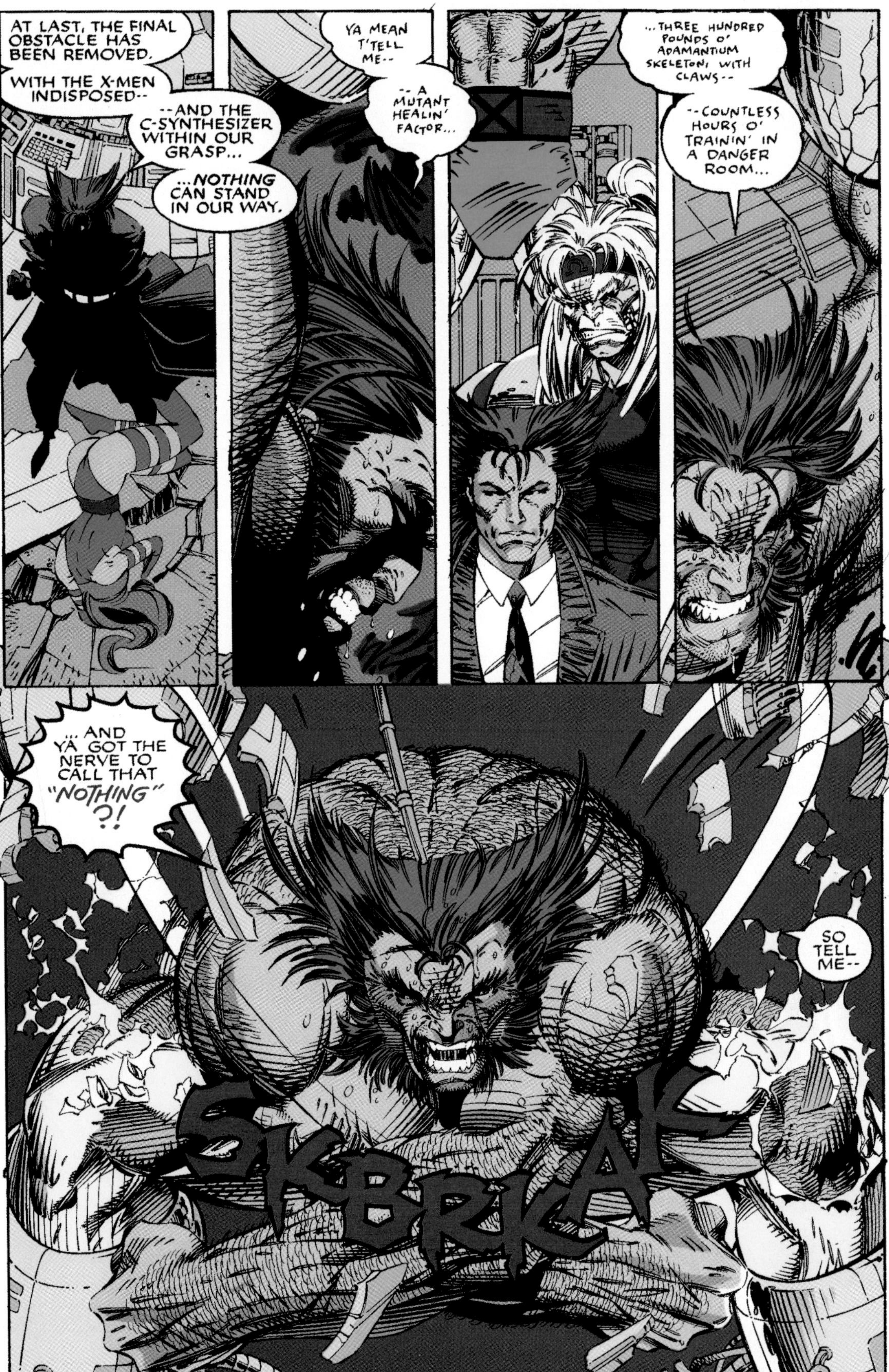
AT LAST, THE FINAL OBSTACLE HAS BEEN REMOVED.
WITH THE X-MEN INDISPOSED--
--AND THE C-SYNTHESIZER WITHIN OUR GRASP...
...NOTHING CAN STAND IN OUR WAY.
YA MEAN T'TELL ME--
--A MUTANT HEALIN' FACTOR...
...THREE HUNDRED POUNDS O' ADAMANTIUM SKELETON, WITH CLAWS--
--COUNTLESS HOURS O' TRAININ' IN A DANGER ROOM...
...AND YA GOT THE NERVE TO CALL THAT "NOTHING" ?!
SKBRKAK
SO TELL ME--

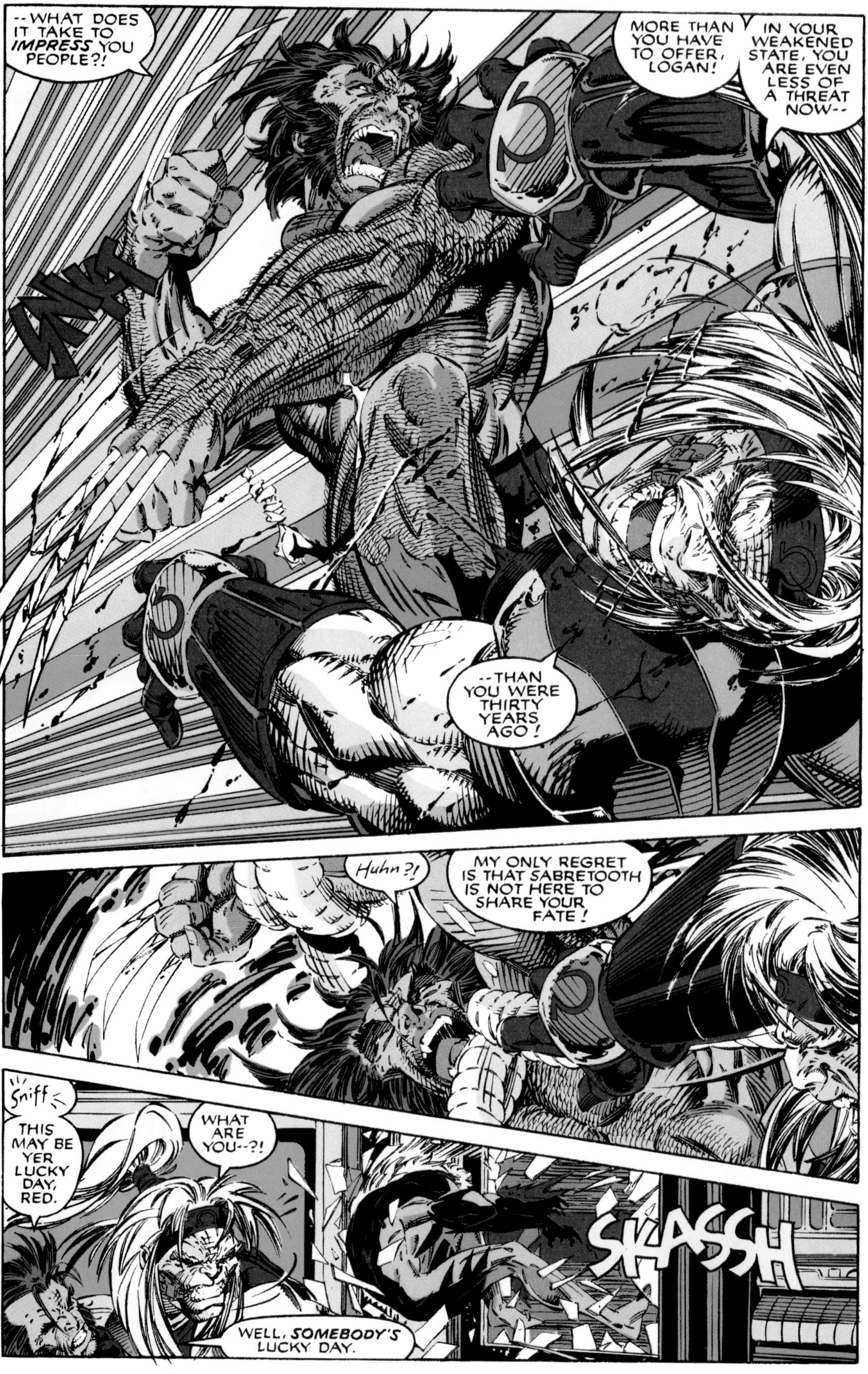
--WHAT DOES IT TAKE TO IMPRESS YOU PEOPLE?!
MORE THAN YOU HAVE TO OFFER, LOGAN!
IN YOUR WEAKENED STATE, YOU ARE EVEN LESS OF A THREAT NOW--
--THAN YOU WERE THIRTY YEARS AGO!
Huhn?!
MY ONLY REGRET IS THAT SABRETOOTH IS NOT HERE TO SHARE YOUR FATE!
Sniff
THIS MAY BE YER LUCKY DAY, RED.
WHAT ARE YOU--?!
SKASSH
WELL, SOMEBODY'S LUCKY DAY.

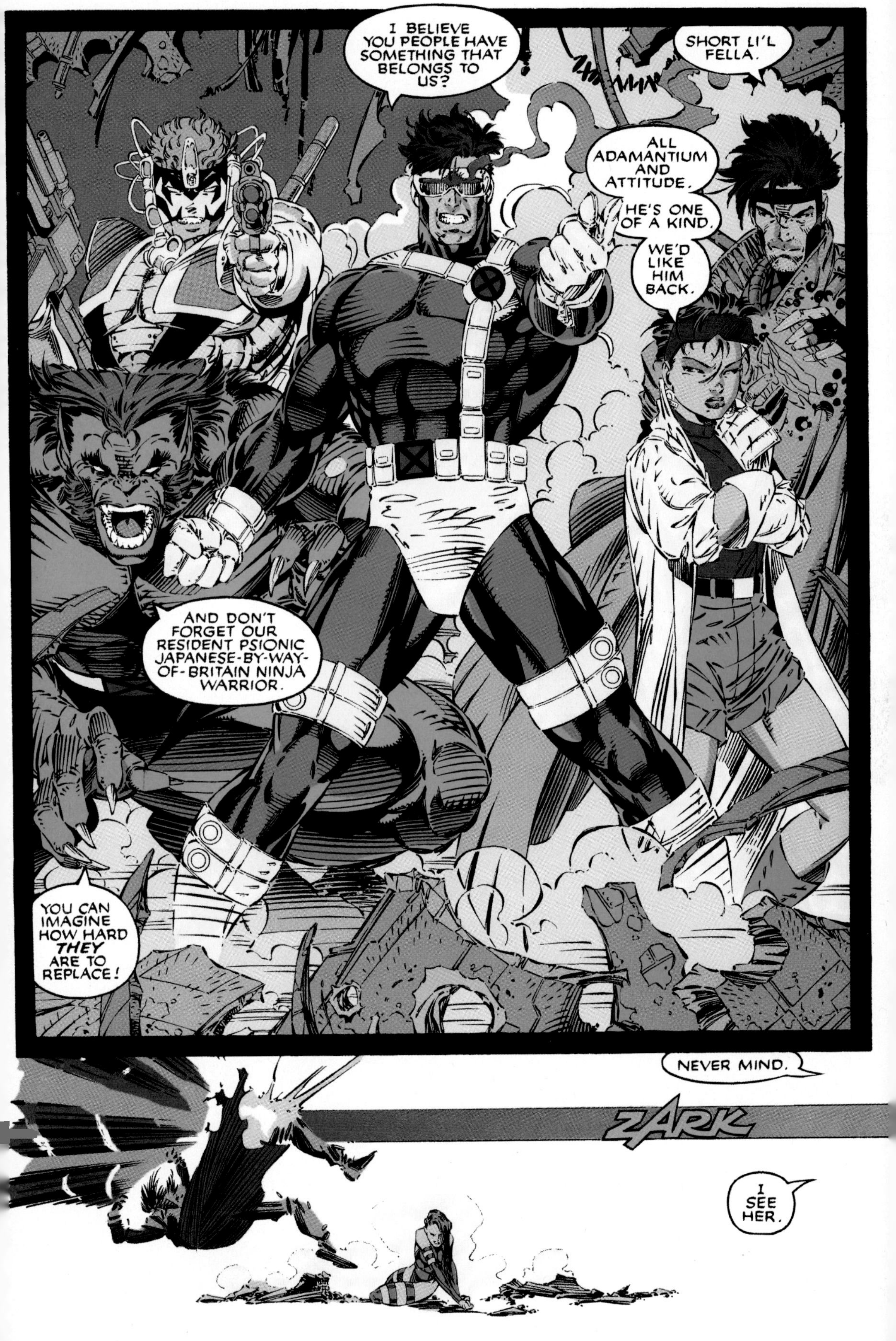
I BELIEVE YOU PEOPLE HAVE SOMETHING THAT BELONGS TO US?
SHORT LI'L FELLA.
ALL ADAMANTIUM AND ATTITUDE.
HE'S ONE OF A KIND.
WE'D LIKE HIM BACK.
AND DON'T FORGET OUR RESIDENT PSIONIC JAPANESE-BY-WAY-OF-BRITAIN NINJA WARRIOR.
YOU CAN IMAGINE HOW HARD THEY ARE TO REPLACE!
NEVER MIND.
ZARK
I SEE HER.

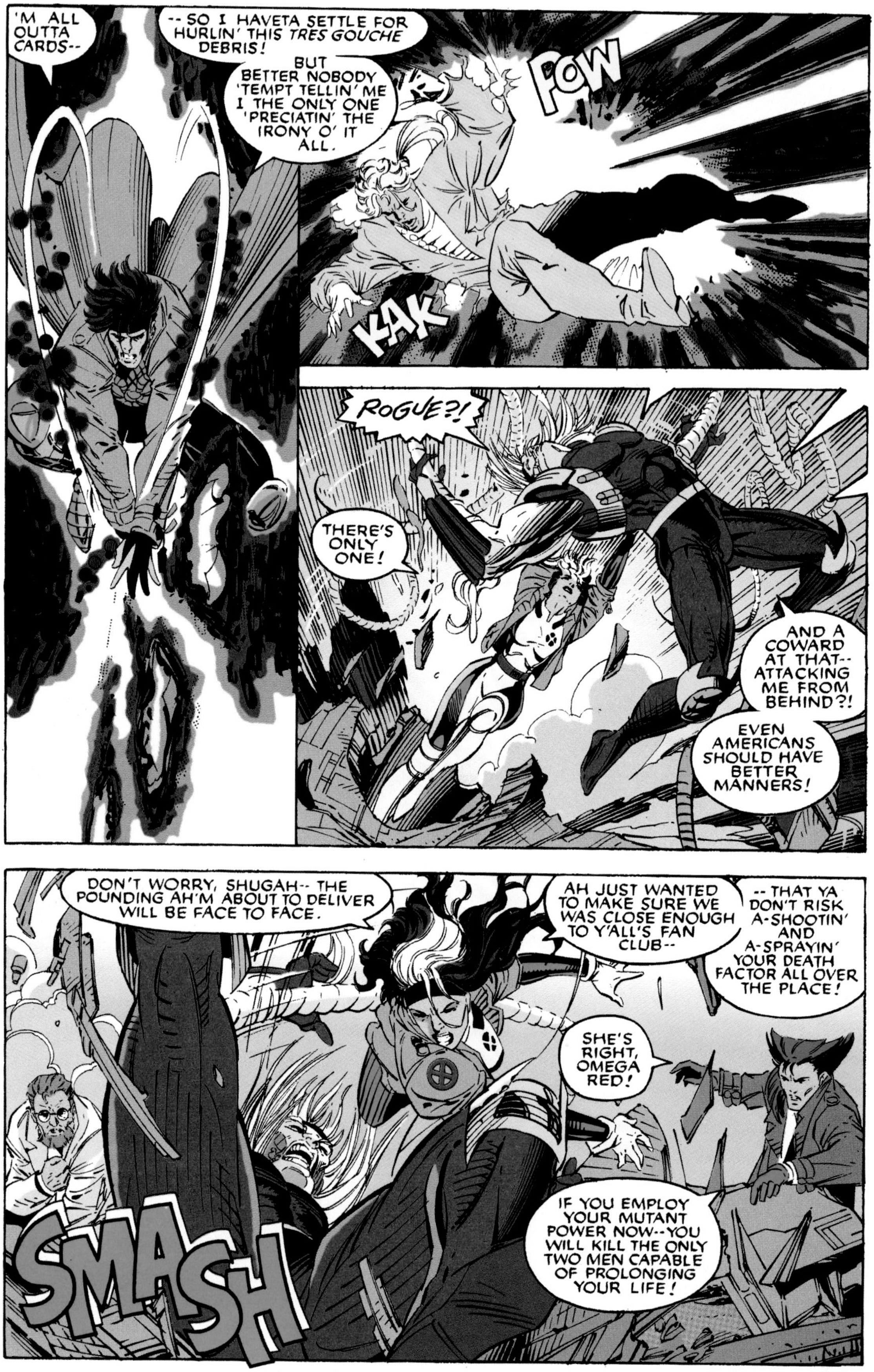
'M ALL OUTTA CARDS--
-- SO I HAVETA SETTLE FOR HURLIN' THIS TRES GOUCHE DEBRIS!
BUT BETTER NOBODY 'TEMPT TELLIN' ME I THE ONLY ONE 'PRECIATIN' THE IRONY O' IT ALL.
POW
KAK
ROGUE?!
THERE'S ONLY ONE!
AND A COWARD AT THAT-- ATTACKING ME FROM BEHIND?!
EVEN AMERICANS SHOULD HAVE BETTER MANNERS!
DON'T WORRY, SHUGAH-- THE POUNDING AH'M ABOUT TO DELIVER WILL BE FACE TO FACE.
AH JUST WANTED TO MAKE SURE WE WAS CLOSE ENOUGH TO Y'ALL'S FAN CLUB--
-- THAT YA DON'T RISK A-SHOOTIN' AND A-SPRAYIN' YOUR DEATH FACTOR ALL OVER THE PLACE!
SHE'S RIGHT, OMEGA RED!
IF YOU EMPLOY YOUR MUTANT POWER NOW--YOU WILL KILL THE ONLY TWO MEN CAPABLE OF PROLONGING YOUR LIFE!
SMASH

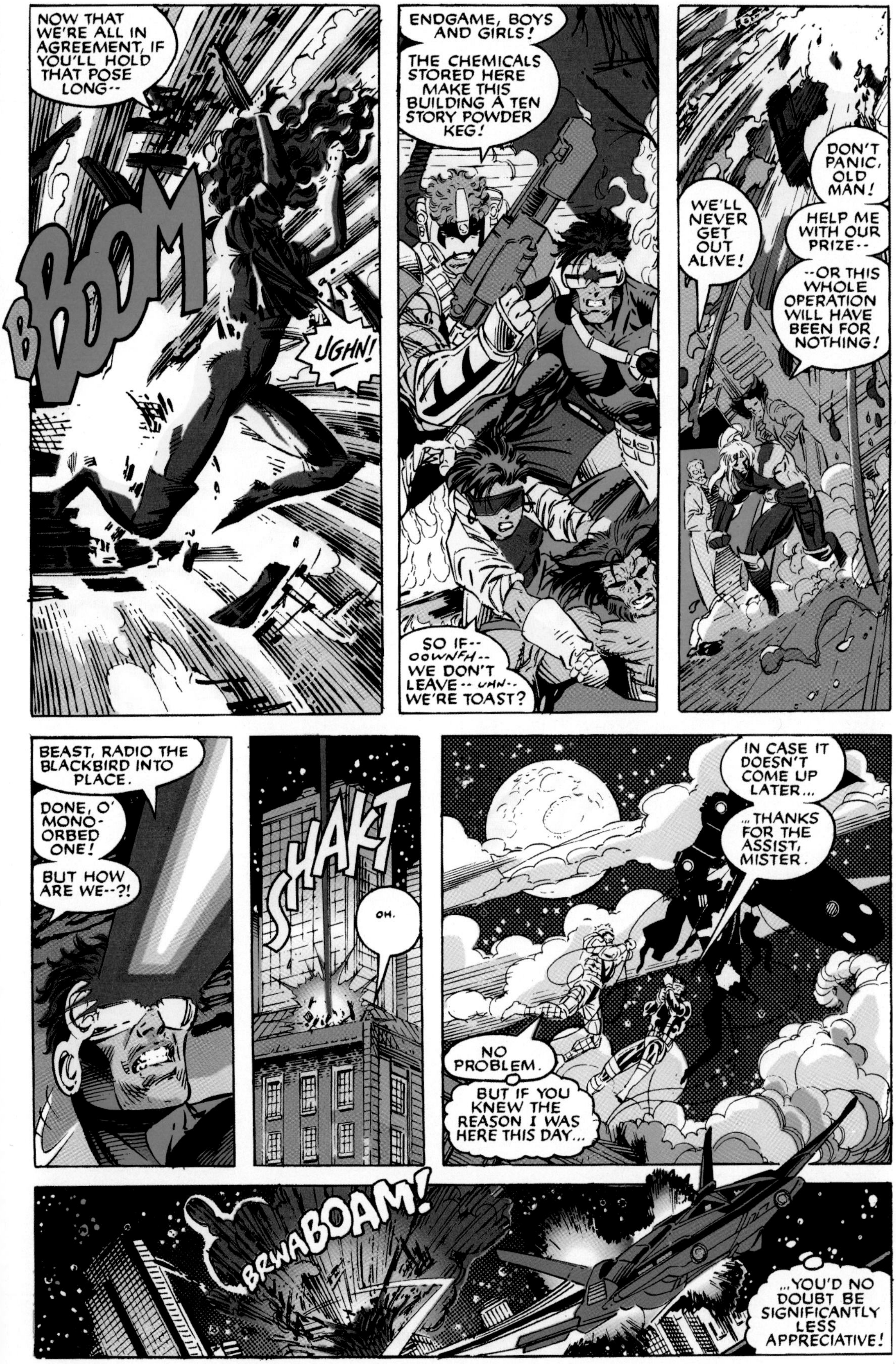
NOW THAT WE'RE ALL IN AGREEMENT, IF YOU'LL HOLD THAT POSE LONG--
BBOOM
UGHN!
ENDGAME, BOYS AND GIRLS!
THE CHEMICALS STORED HERE MAKE THIS BUILDING A TEN STORY POWDER KEG!
SO IF-- OOWNFH-- WE DON'T LEAVE-- UHN-- WE'RE TOAST?
WE'LL NEVER GET OUT ALIVE!
DON'T PANIC, OLD MAN!
HELP ME WITH OUR PRIZE--
--OR THIS WHOLE OPERATION WILL HAVE BEEN FOR NOTHING!
BEAST, RADIO THE BLACKBIRD INTO PLACE.
DONE, O' MONO-ORBED ONE!
BUT HOW ARE WE--?!
SHAKT
OH.
IN CASE IT DOESN'T COME UP LATER...
...THANKS FOR THE ASSIST, MISTER.
NO PROBLEM.
BUT IF YOU KNEW THE REASON I WAS HERE THIS DAY...
BRWABOAM!
...YOU'D NO DOUBT BE SIGNIFICANTLY LESS APPRECIATIVE!

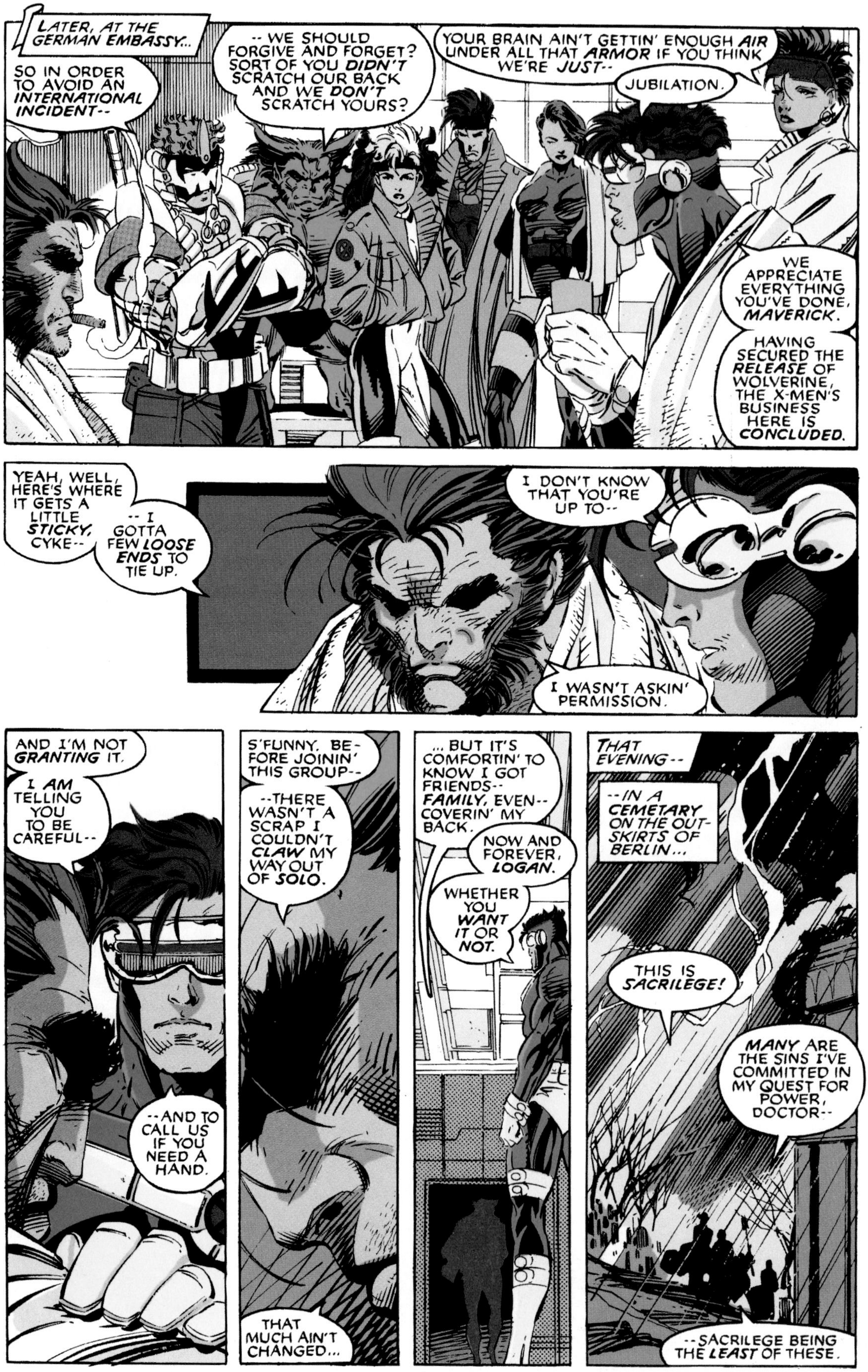
LATER, AT THE GERMAN EMBASSY...
SO IN ORDER TO AVOID AN INTERNATIONAL INCIDENT--
-- WE SHOULD FORGIVE AND FORGET? SORT OF YOU DIDN'T SCRATCH OUR BACK AND WE DON'T SCRATCH YOURS?
YOUR BRAIN AIN'T GETTIN' ENOUGH AIR UNDER ALL THAT ARMOR IF YOU THINK WE'RE JUST--
JUBILATION.
WE APPRECIATE EVERYTHING YOU'VE DONE, MAVERICK.
HAVING SECURED THE RELEASE OF WOLVERINE, THE X-MEN'S BUSINESS HERE IS CONCLUDED.
YEAH, WELL, HERE'S WHERE IT GETS A LITTLE STICKY, CYKE--
-- I GOTTA FEW LOOSE ENDS TO TIE UP.
I DON'T KNOW THAT YOU'RE UP TO--
I WASN'T ASKIN' PERMISSION.
AND I'M NOT GRANTING IT.
I AM TELLING YOU TO BE CAREFUL--
--AND TO CALL US IF YOU NEED A HAND.
S'FUNNY. BEFORE JOININ' THIS GROUP--
--THERE WASN'T A SCRAP I COULDN'T CLAW MY WAY OUT OF SOLO.
THAT MUCH AIN'T CHANGED...
... BUT IT'S COMFORTIN' TO KNOW I GOT FRIENDS-- FAMILY, EVEN-- COVERIN' MY BACK.
NOW AND FOREVER, LOGAN.
WHETHER YOU WANT IT OR NOT.
THAT EVENING--
--IN A CEMETARY ON THE OUTSKIRTS OF BERLIN...
THIS IS SACRILEGE!
MANY ARE THE SINS I'VE COMMITTED IN MY QUEST FOR POWER, DOCTOR--
--SACRILEGE BEING THE LEAST OF THESE.

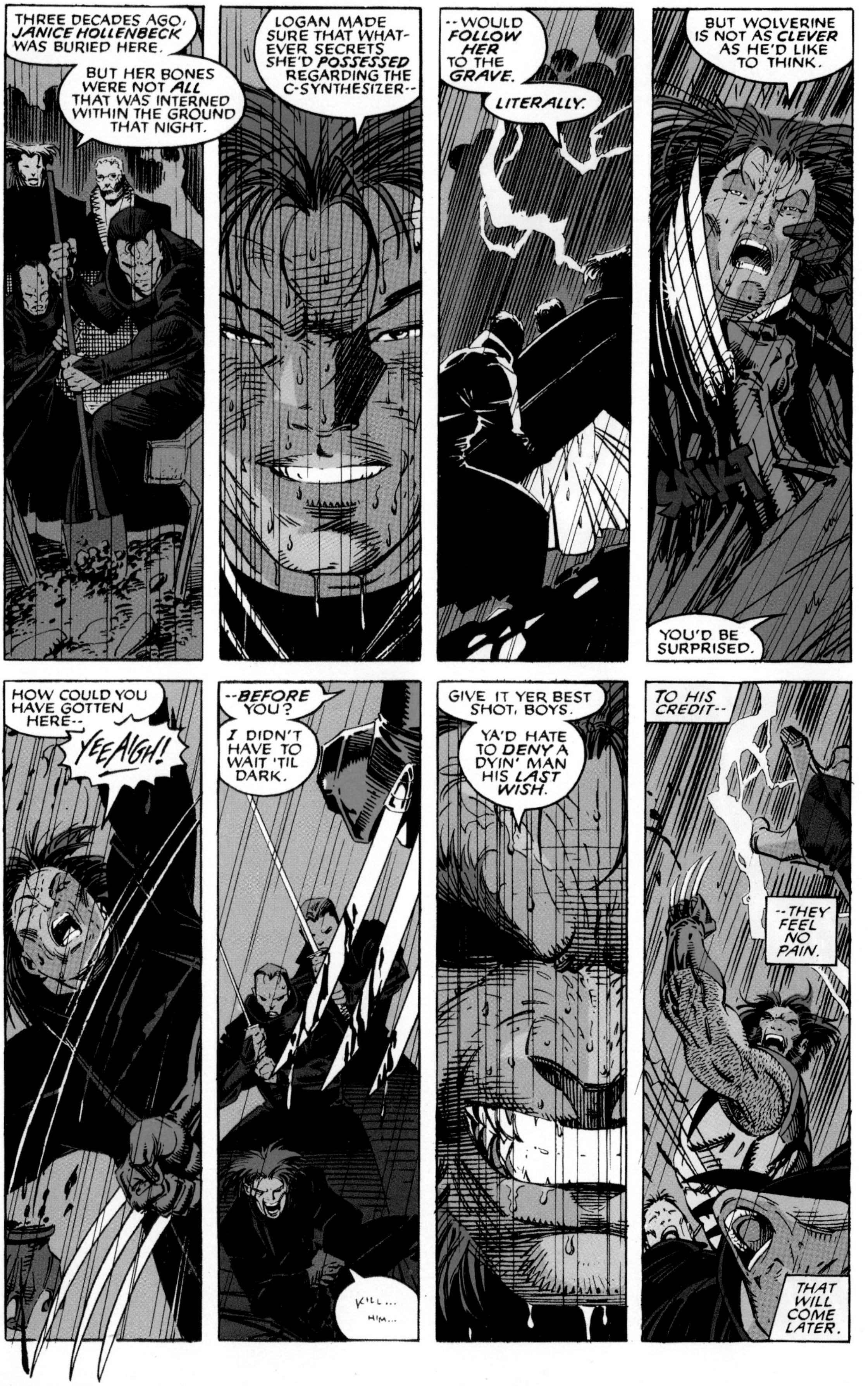
THREE DECADES AGO, JANICE HOLLENBECK WAS BURIED HERE.
BUT HER BONES WERE NOT ALL THAT WAS INTERNED WITHIN THE GROUND THAT NIGHT.
LOGAN MADE SURE THAT WHATEVER SECRETS SHE'D POSSESSED REGARDING THE C-SYNTHESIZER--
--WOULD FOLLOW HER TO THE GRAVE.
LITERALLY.
BUT WOLVERINE IS NOT AS CLEVER AS HE'D LIKE TO THINK.
YOU'D BE SURPRISED.
HOW COULD YOU HAVE GOTTEN HERE--
YEEAIGH!
--BEFORE YOU?
I DIDN'T HAVE TO WAIT 'TIL DARK.
KILL... HIM...
GIVE IT YER BEST SHOT, BOYS.
YA'D HATE TO DENY A DYIN' MAN HIS LAST WISH.
TO HIS CREDIT--
--THEY FEEL NO PAIN.
THAT WILL COME LATER.

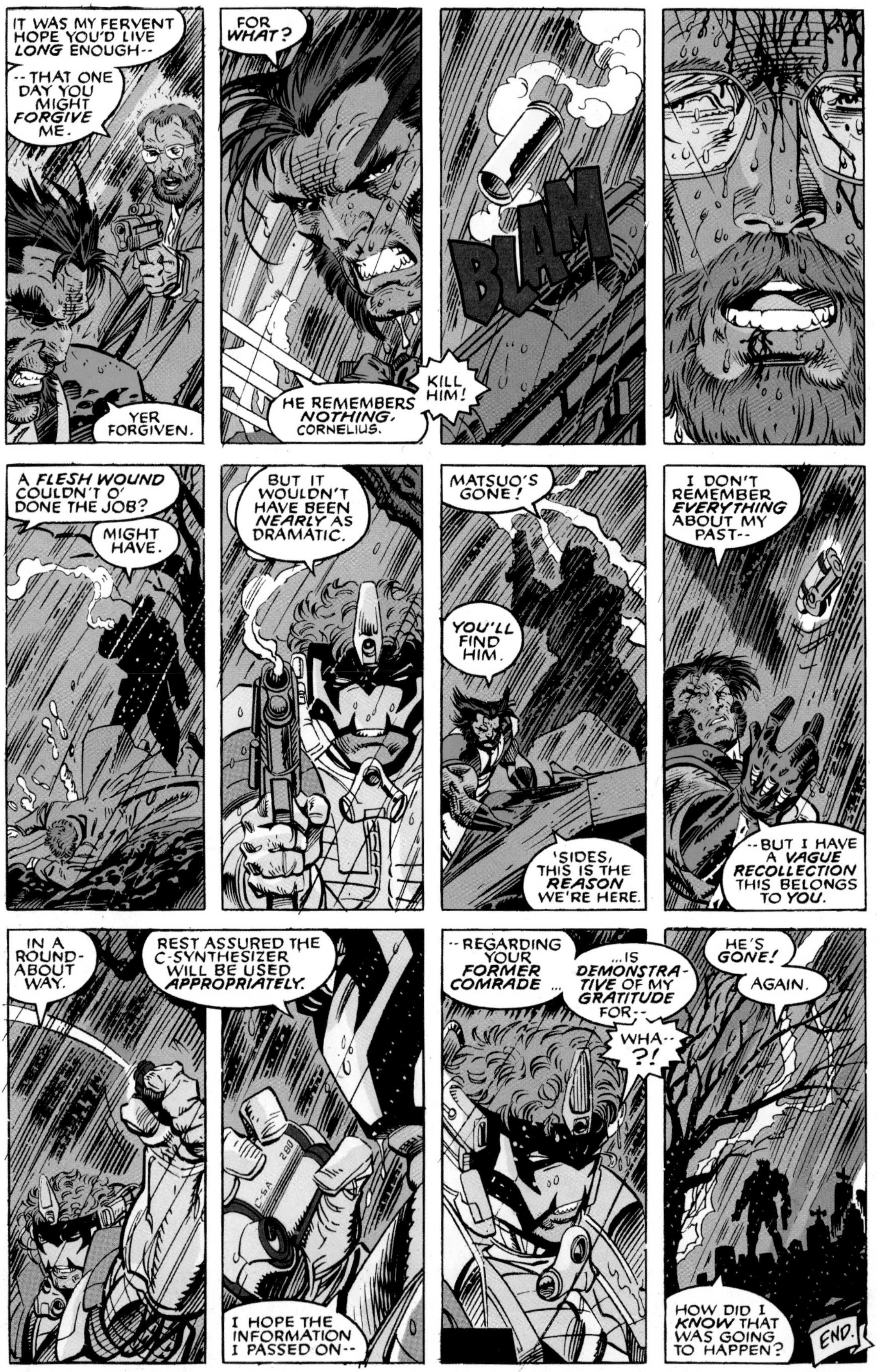
IT WAS MY FERVENT HOPE YOU'D LIVE LONG ENOUGH--
--THAT ONE DAY YOU MIGHT FORGIVE ME.
YER FORGIVEN.
FOR WHAT?
HE REMEMBERS NOTHING, CORNELIUS.
KILL HIM!
BLAM
A FLESH WOUND COULDN'T O' DONE THE JOB?
MIGHT HAVE.
BUT IT WOULDN'T HAVE BEEN NEARLY AS DRAMATIC.
MATSUO'S GONE!
YOU'LL FIND HIM.
'SIDES, THIS IS THE REASON WE'RE HERE.
I DON'T REMEMBER EVERYTHING ABOUT MY PAST--
--BUT I HAVE A VAGUE RECOLLECTION THIS BELONGS TO YOU.
IN A ROUND-ABOUT WAY.
REST ASSURED THE C-SYNTHESIZER WILL BE USED APPROPRIATELY.
I HOPE THE INFORMATION I PASSED ON--
--REGARDING YOUR FORMER COMRADE...
...IS DEMONSTRATIVE OF MY GRATITUDE FOR--
WHA--?!
HE'S GONE!
AGAIN.
HOW DID I KNOW THAT WAS GOING TO HAPPEN?
END.